80E 10.00

Social
Science
Research
Handbook

About the Authors

Raymond G. McInnis is Head Reference Librarian, with the rank of Associate Professor, at Western Washington State College. He received his B.A. degree from the University of British Columbia and his M.L.S. degree from the University of Washington. He is a member of the American Association of University Professors and the American Library Association.

James W. Scott is Associate Professor, Department of Geography, Western Washington State College. He received his B.A. and M.A. degrees from Cambridge University and his Ph.D. degree from Indiana University. He has taught in various private schools in England, Argentina, and Canada and has been Visiting Lecturer at Queens University, Kingston, Ontario (1964) and the University of Manitoba (1968).

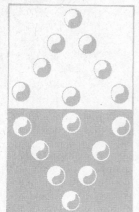

Social
Science
Research
Handbook

Raymond G. McInnis

James W. Scott

BARNES & NOBLE BOOKS

A DIVISION OF HARPER & ROW, PUBLISHERS

New York, Evanston, San Francisco, London

To Karen, Michael, and Erin; and to Netteke

First BARNES & NOBLE BOOKS edition published 1975

LIBRARY OF CONGRESS CATALOG CARD NUMBER: 73–21854

STANDARD BOOK NUMBER: 06–460140–4

Contents

Preface

Many people have helped in the production of this book, but we wish to express our gratitude to the following for the various ways in which they assisted us: Dr. R. L. DeLorme (American Studies), Dr. Barry Gough (Canadian and European Studies), Fred Jamison (Anthropology), Dr. Edward Kaplan (Asian Studies), Dr. John MacGregor (Sociology), Dr. Michael Mischaikow (Economics), Dr. Robert Monahan (Geography), Dr. F. Stanley Moore (Geography), Dr. Ingeborg Paulus (Sociology), Dr. Harry Ritter (Eastern European and Russian Studies), and Dr. Louis Truschel (African Studies); Mary Hoppe, Jean Rottman, and Connie Clements of Western's Library; Jane Clark and others in Western's Bureau of Faculty Research; and Nancy Cone and Libby Siegel at Barnes and Noble. Finally, we express particular appreciation to Karen McInnis for her able assistance and criticism, but most of all, for her understanding.

Introduction

Perhaps the most important quality a researcher can possess when seeking facts, sifting data, and drawing conclusions is an inquiring attitude. It soon becomes evident, however, that the desire to undertake effective research in any discipline must be accompanied by a knowledge of research materials and procedures. Highly motivated students, particularly, soon become frustrated when their attempts at independent study are thwarted by a lack of knowledge of research procedures, which too often is a neglected aspect of a college education.

Purpose of This Book. Researchers with little prior knowledge of a subject must develop certain habits of thought and action in order to determine which sources of the many that may be available to them are most appropriate to consult for required information. The following questions describe typical situations in which researchers must determine what types of sources must be consulted: 1) Lacking a table giving complete titles of periodicals in a bibliography where citations are abbreviated, are there logical sources to consult? 2) Is it necessary to examine journal articles or books to determine quickly the essence of their contents? 3) Assuming that five years ago several studies were published by authorities on a topic of concern, is it possible to determine if any studies have been published since on the same topic? The answer to all of these questions is, of course, yes; all that is required is the conviction that others have encountered similar problems in the past, resulting, more than likely, in a method to alleviate the problem. The 1,500-odd selected reference works described in this book are proof that the expressed needs of social scientists have resulted in the production of many reference sources. Therefore, research strategy (i.e., procedures for obtaining information) should include knowledge of the types and functions of reference works, along with some understanding of the principles on which they are usually organized.

The aim of this book is to provide students and others doing research in the social sciences with an integrated and analytical guide to sources of information available in most academic libraries. No attempt has been made to list all materials in any particular subject. A single section that attempted this might well consist of many more items than are contained in this entire handbook. The experience of the authors in dealing with academic research— particularly that relating to undergraduate studies—indicates that it is most beneficial for students to be directed to a select number of the more important and widely used books in a particular subject. By making use of the bibliographies, dictionaries, encyclopedias, and handbooks described here, student researchers should be able to track down quickly and efficiently the best sources for solutions to their problems of research, which might range from the identification of terms to the compiling of a bibliography for a thesis or dissertation. Each item included in this handbook is accompanied by an evaluative description which points out its strengths and its limitations; in some instances a comparison with other similar or related works on the same subject is provided.

Arrangement. The book is in two sections: the first consists of parts on disciplines embraced by the social sciences; the second consists of parts on each of the major areas of the world. Materials within parts are arranged in a uniform format. Each part, except the first, contains two sections. The first section comprises reference books and related materials on a particular subject arranged by type, such as dictionaries, bibliographies, handbooks, atlases, and so forth. The second section contains references to works on specialized subfields of the discipline or geographical area. (For example, subfields of anthropology are social and cultural anthropology and linguistics.) Parts on area studies are similarly arranged. Once the arrangement of the parts is understood, it becomes an easy matter for the student to go to the section of the relevant part, even if he is not familiar with the subject.

Bibliographical System. One of our chief concerns about bibliographies designed to assist researchers in the social sciences has been the treatment given large, general reference works that provide information relating to a wide range of subjects. When such items are mentioned only once in a large bibliography, inexperienced researchers are inclined to overlook them, particularly if these items have been listed in a general, introductory chapter and if research is focused on a specialized subsection of a subject. In other words, because of unfamiliarity with research materials, inexperienced researchers do not make use of many of the most obvious sources of information available to them. The authors believe that this difficulty can be overcome if such works are cited wherever appropriate. For this purpose, it will be necessary to repeat such items as the *International Encyclopedia of Social Sciences* (A.1.e:2) or the *London Bibliography of the Social Sciences* (A.1.b:5) in almost every part of this book, since each of these contains information pertinent to all the disciplines considered here, as well as information on each of the major areas. However, repeating the full bibliographical citation every time an entry is listed is too space-consuming. To overcome this problem, the authors have devised a system which provides only a brief bibliographical citation for each item in the text. At its first appearance, a number is assigned, together with the imprint date or, for periodicals, the date of the first issue. Full bibliographical citations are provided in the final section of the book, where each item is listed in the same order as its first appearance in the text; by turning to this section, students can obtain all the bibliographical information needed for finding the book in a college library. Except for a few commercial series requiring different treatment, works are listed according to North American library standards. In general, the most detailed description of a work occurs at its first mention; where a brief description is made of an item before its detailed description, readers are referred to the main description. For example, in the parentheses following the first item above, the *International Encyclopedia of Social Sciences,* A stands for the part, 1 the section of the part, and e the subsection of the part where the reference first appears; the number after the colon, 2, refers to the order in which the work is mentioned in the part.

Interrelationships of Sources. Having undertaken research in any discipline, one soon learns that secondary sources (i.e., published studies) are linked in a network of interdependent relationships: that is, each research study on a given topic is supported by, and adds to, the knowledge set forth in earlier studies of that topic. Citation indexes have been developed on the basis of such explicit interdependent relationships among secondary sources. These indexes can function effectively as intermediary devices, particularly as bibliographies, by the substitution of the name of the author of a research study for the subject of his study. [See the *Social Sciences Citation Index* (A.1.b:6) for an extensive description of the principles and uses of citation indexes.]

Primary sources, raw statistical data, and such unpublished materials as questionnaires, surveys, official documents, and diaries, are also an integral part of the research network. This network of primary and secondary sources is connected by explicit links, which refer directly from one source to another.

All reference works function as intermediary devices or sources, providing various kinds of information and various amounts of detail about the knowledge contained in primary and secondary sources for a given subject or topic. Reference works and other intermediary sources are related to each other by either explicit links or implicit links, which must be supplied by the researcher because direct reference from one intermediary source to another is lacking. The functions or uses of some reference works—dictionaries, handbooks, yearbooks, bibliographies, and encyclopedias —are well known. But their potential is not often fully exploited; many other reference works are, unfortunately, not known at all. The phrase *multiple functions* is intended to suggest that most reference works have several uses and several different kinds of information, often implied neither in their titles nor (more significantly) by their traditional functions. Thus, while dictionaries are generally considered only as sources of definitions, Gould (A.1.e:4), Hultkrantz (B.1.d:2), Mitchell (H.1.d:1), Keller (H.2.d:15), and the *McGraw-Hill Dictionary of Modern Economics* (D.1.d:1), to name a few examples, contain both definitions and bibliographical citations. Similarly, while handbooks are commonly thought to contain only factual data, Faris (H.1.b:4), Smigel (H.2.d:5), and Christensen (H.2.a:4), for example, provide large bibliographies as well. Likewise, scholarly journals are not merely sources of articles, book reviews, and notices; many, such as the *Middle East Journal* (J.1.b:21), *Social Science Information* (B.1.f:5), and the *Journal of Economic Literature* (D.1.b:9), regularly contain bibliographies. Acquiring self-sufficiency and facility in research requires careful examination of the annotations for all works described in part A, along with those given for a particular discipline and perhaps also a geographical area. Take special note of the possible combined uses that can be made of several titles. Do not be limited by explicit links; implicit links provide the opportunity to make joint use of almost all intermediary sources. One of the most useful combinations in sociology, for example, is the *SSCI* (A.1.b:6), *Sociological Abstracts* (H.1.b:1), and Gould (A.1.e:4).[1]

Taking advantage of explicit or implicit relationships requires familiarity with all the common types of reference works. Brief definitions of each type are provided in a glossary at the end of this introduction.

Research Strategy. Readers may wonder why so many items are recommended. Editors and compilers work from different points of view and use different criteria, with the result that bibliographies and other sources may have a wide range of differences. Often it is necessary to consult numerous bibliographies or other works, such as dictionaries or handbooks, in order to find needed information. Of course, not every title is owned by all academic libraries. Research strategy is determined by the forms of publications and the comprehensiveness of the literature in a particular field.

The essential ideas to keep in mind are that disciplines in the social sciences are closely interrelated and that area studies consist largely of particular aspects of studies in various disciplines. Further, there is currently a powerful stimulus for area studies to be interdisciplinary, a factor which makes more important the use of many different sources of information. For example, students should recognize and appreciate the implicit link between the sentence in an article in the *International Encyclopedia of the Social Sciences* (A.1.e:2), which analyzes and compares anthropological and sociological phenomena in Africa, and a large body of published articles and books listed in the bibliographies in section 2 of the African Studies part. The following graphic representation of research strategy illustrates the principles outlined above.

DISCIPLINARY STUDIES   AREA STUDIES

General works on the social sciences cited in part A		General works in area studies cited in part I
Works covering a particular discipline, as indicated in the first sections of parts A–H	TOPIC	General works on a specific area, as indicated in the first sections of parts I–Q
Works on subfields of a discipline, as indicated in the second sections of parts A–H		Works on a specific discipline treating a particular area, as indicated in the second sections of parts I–Q

The following example from the literature of economics demonstrates the importance of a determined systematic search through general and specialized bibliographies, as well as a familiarity with the special features of various reference works in a particular area. After encountering an obscure reference to a bibliography on the historiography of economic thought on page 59 of Maltby (D.1. b:2), the authors attempted to obtain the article in order to determine its usefulness. Maltby had neglected to indicate the author of the article; thus a search through bibliographies of economics, such as the AEA's *Index of Economic Journals* (D.1.b:10), the

International Bibliography of Economics (D.1.b:12), or the *Journal of Economic Literature* (D.1.b:9) would probably be a tedious and perhaps futile job. Knowing the special features of the *International Bibliography of Historical Sciences* (F.1.b:4)—first, that it regularly includes a chapter on modern economic and social history (noted in F.1.b., with a reference from D.2.a); and second, that at the head of each division or subdivision of each category (noted with an asterisk [*]) bibliographies covering the particular topic are indicated—we consulted it. In volume 33 of the *International Bibliography of Historical Sciences* we encountered the reference to Oreste Popescu's "On the Historiography of Economic Thought: A Bibliographical Survey" (D.2.b:1), which appeared in the *Journal of World History* in 1964. (It is true the citation in Maltby is not quite the same as the one in the *International Bibliography of Historical Sciences,* but careful researchers would have noticed that the article title, date, and page numbers of the journal were identical, thus marking the end of the search.)

Use of Library.   Using a library is not so formidable a task as it appears; in fact, most students find it easy. Students will find, too, that college reference librarians are generally easy to approach and sympathetic to their needs. Students should locate the reference section of the library and identify themselves, along with their interests, to the reference librarians. In the reference department they should ask about other sources, such as documents collections and pamphlet files. Next, they should discover how periodicals and other serial publications are treated in their college library. In some libraries periodicals are fully cataloged and are arranged on the same shelves as the books; in others, periodicals are not cataloged, but arranged on separate shelves in alphabetical order.

Attention, of course, should also be directed to the card catalog, since it is one of the most important intermediary sources in the library. Books held by academic libraries are listed in the card catalog by author, title, and general subject. Cards are arranged alphabetically in a "word-by-word" or "letter-by-letter" sequence. Also, the Library of Congress's *Subject Headings* and supplementary volumes listing in a dictionary format many of the library's subject headings and suggested cross references are available in most libraries. The dictionary-style format of the Library of Congress's *Subject Headings* volumes is an efficient device for determining appropriate subject headings to consult when access to the card catalog by subject is required. A brief description of the card catalog and the procedures for finding books in a library are usually found on one of several handouts describing aspects of library service available in a library's reference department.

Since much of the material listed in the bibliographies in this volume may be held by college libraries in some form of micro-print, students should familiarize themselves with the methods used to organize such items by their college library. Sometimes materials on microfilm, microfiche, or other types of microprint are listed in the card catalog in the same manner as books. More often, however, microprint materials are not listed individually in the card catalog. In these cases, students should inquire of the reference librarian about the existence of certain items in their college library.

Glossary of Terms
Used in This Handbook

Almanac: This term is used in a number of contexts. It was originally an annual publication giving certain predictive information, such as weather forecasts, farming prospects, and so forth; *Old Moore's Almanac* is an example. Now the term is used mainly to denote an annual publication giving miscellaneous information on recent and current events, for example the *Reader's Digest Almanac.*

Atlas: A collection of small-scale maps which present in graphic form miscellaneous material on particular countries and regions. The use of conventional signs, zip-a-tone patterns, and a range of colors and shades makes it possible for a large amount of information to be seen at a glance.

Bibliographies: In its simplest form a bibliography is little more than a listing of books and related materials, either on a particular subject or on a broad range of subjects. Most often, information provided for each item included in a bibliography consists of author's name, title, place of publication, publisher, and imprint date for books; and author's name, title, periodical name, volume, number, date of issue, and inclusive pages for articles. An *annotated bibliography* provides, in addition to this information, a brief analysis of the contents of a work. Another type of bibliography, usually limited to material from a certain type of source, is known as an *index.* For example, the best-known index, the *Reader's Guide to Periodical Literature,* is an author-subject index to about 180 popular magazines. *Abstracts* are another type of bibliography and, like indexes, are sometimes limited to one type of source; most often, however, abstracts include books as well as articles. The purpose of an abstract bibliography is to provide brief statements or summaries of the contents of published research articles either in periodicals or in books. These abstracts save valuable time because one can often determine from them whether or not a particular research paper would likely be useful without seeking out the actual article, which is a more time-consuming and often an expensive activity. Keyword-in-context indexes, popularly known as *KWIC indexes,* are appearing in greater numbers. The KWIC index is an attempt to produce, with the assistance of data-processing techniques, a large bibliography on a particular subject. Punched cards are used, and the "key words" in the titles of articles and books are put in alphabetical order, resulting in a sort of subject arrangement of the titles. A *retrospective bibliography* is one which lists books from an early period to a certain specified date. A *selected bibliography,* on the other hand, lists only recommended books, and a *classified bibliography* is one arranged according to subject or geographical region.

Biographical Dictionaries and Directories: A biographical dictionary is a collection of articles on selected individuals of particular nations (e.g., *Dictionary of National Biography* [U.K.]) or within a special field. A biographical directory is a compilation of brief information on individuals and/or institutions, usually of a particular profession or discipline. In general, information for directories is obtained by the mailing of questionnaires requesting information such as profession, education, and publications. *Who's Who in America* is a good example.

Dictionary: Essentially a word list which briefly gives the meaning of particular words and which may also include etymological and historical information, in addition to specific examples of usage. Foreign-language dictionaries, such as Velázquez's *English-Spanish, Spanish-English Dictionary,* give equivalent words in the other language. Special dictionaries dealing only with words and phrases used in a limited field or discipline are common, for example, the *Penguin Dictionary of Biology* and W. G. Moore's *Dictionary of Geography.*

Encyclopedia: A compilation of articles on miscellaneous subjects usually arranged alphabetically, for example, the *Encyclopaedia Britannica,* but also by subject, as in the *Oxford Junior Encyclopedia.* More specialized encyclopedias exist for many disciplines, such as the *Encyclopedia of World History.* In general, articles in encyclopedias are larger than those in dictionaries.

Gazetteer: A special dictionary which lists (usually in alphabetical order) geographical names and places, cites exact locations, and gives a variety of other information—geographical, historical, and political. An example is the *Times Index Gazetteer of the World.*

Glossary: A list of definitions of terms and phrases used in a particular field or discipline, for example, *A Glossary of Geographical Terms,* Sir Dudley Stamp, editor.

Handbooks and Yearbooks: Often reference works are published that do not fit neatly into the categories librarians have created. Hence it is necessary to provide a miscellaneous section where everything left over is placed. In order to make this volume as useful as possible, the authors have created the section "Handbooks and Yearbooks." Here we have placed the indefinable items that cannot be ignored but which do not fit appropriately in any other section. Besides yearbooks of activities of various disciplines and areas, readers will find compendia of facts of geographical areas and collections of data on various subjects related to a certain subject or area such as the American Field Staff Reports (I.1.e:14) and the U. S. Army Area Handbooks (I.1.e:12).

Reviews of Research: Provide authoritative appraisals of the advancement of research in a given field. They also function, however, as bibliographies, as sources of definitions of concepts, and as a means of identifying key people. For example, in sociology, Faris (H.1.b:4), March (H.2.a:9), Lindzey (H.1.d:3), Smigel (H.2.d:5) and Christensen (H.2.a:4) serve all of these functions. The *Social Sciences Citation Index* (A.1.b:6) provides a key to locating reviews of research in scholarly journals.

Yearbooks: See Handbooks and Yearbooks.

Part A

Social Sciences:
General Works

Works Covering the Social Sciences in General, Arranged by Type

A.1.a Atlases

Atlases constitute a unique class of reference literature. Maps, diagrams, and photographs are employed to present geographical and other information by graphic means, such as colors and shadings. Conventional signs, a key to which is usually provided on the map itself, provide additional information. Relief is shown in a variety of ways, most often in atlases by means of layer tinting or coloring. Fractional and linear scales are usually given.

There are many different types of atlases. The largest class is that of general geography, which may be subdivided into world, macro-regional (continental, oceanic, and so on), national, and micro-regional groups. Special atlases are devoted to historical events and botanical and other scientific distributions.

World Atlases. Among the many general world atlases, three are widely recognized as the most authoritative. The *Times Atlas of the World* (1971) (1), published by the *Times* of London, appeared first in sheets issued between 1920 and 1922. The mid-century edition, prepared under the direction of the renowned

1

cartographer John Bartholomew, was published in five volumes
between 1955 and 1960. The individual volumes are: 1. *World,
Australia, East Asia;* 2. *Southwest Asia and Russia;* 3. *Northern
Europe;* 4. *Southern Europe and Africa;* and 5. *The Americas.* A
one-volume comprehensive edition appeared in 1967, and a second edition in 1971. The maps, mainly physical but showing political boundaries, are among the most legible in any atlas, and
the format and arrangement are aesthetically pleasing. All important regions of the world are shown on a scale of one to five million or larger. Nearly 200,000 place names are included in the
combined indexes of the midcentury edition and the comprehensive edition.

The *Atlante Internazionale* (1968) (2) of the Touring Club
Italiano of Milan is one of the most beautiful and detailed of world
atlases, with more than 170 plates. The maps are generally on a
smaller scale than those of the *Times Atlas.* An extensive index
of about 200,000 place names is provided in an accompanying
volume.

The World Atlas (1967) (3), published in English by Glavnoe
upravlenie geodezii i kartografii of the Soviet Union (and often referred to as the *Soviet World Atlas*) is also excellent. The maps,
like those of the *Times Atlas* and the *Atlante Internazionale,* are
physical-political maps, with special emphasis on the USSR. Many
are double-page spreads; a few have a third, fold-out page. Unfortunately, there is no place-name index.

Among other general world atlases that can be recommended
as informative and reliable are the following: the *Oxford Atlas*
(1966) (4); the *McGraw-Hill International Atlas* (1964) (5),
which is based on *Der grosser Bertelsmann Weltatlas* (1964),
published by the Cartographical Institute, Bertelsmann Verlag,
Germany; Bartholomew's *Advanced Atlas of Modern Geography*
(1964) (6); Hammond's *Medallion World Atlas* (1969) (7); the
National Geographic Atlas of the World (1970) (8); and the two
most widely used atlases in American colleges and universities,
Goode's World Atlas (1970) (9); and the *Aldine University Atlas*
(1969) (10).

Bibliographies of Maps and Atlases.   An invaluable guide to the
whole subject of maps and atlases is C. B. Muriel Lock's *Modern
Maps and Atlases* (1969) (11). It has highly informative chapters on the techniques of modern cartography, international maps
and atlases, national maps and atlases, thematic maps and atlases,
and map librarianship. Among lists of maps and atlases are *A List
of Geographical Atlases in the Library of Congress* (1909–) (12),
in six volumes to date, citing more than 10,000 atlases received

by the Library; the British Museum's *Catalog of Printed Maps* (1884–) (13), in fifteen volumes, listing all maps, atlases, globes, and other cartographic materials in the map room and in other major collections of the Museum; and the American Geographical Society's *Index to Maps in Books and Periodicals* (1967) (14), in ten volumes.

A.1.b Bibliographies

Bibliographies of Bibliographies.   The largest, most familiar general bibliography of bibliographies is Besterman's five-volume *World Bibliography of Bibliographies* (1965) (1). It lists 117,000 bibliographies covering all subjects, periods, and languages and giving the number of items in each bibliography. (Bibliographies published as sections of books or in periodicals are not included.) It is arranged alphabetically by subject and has an author index. The *Bibliographic Index* (1938–) (2) is another general bibliography of bibliographies. It is published semiannually, cumulating annually and into volumes covering a number of years. Arrangement is by subject. International in scope, it includes bibliographies published as books, those appearing at the ends of monographs, and those included in about 1,500 periodicals. It is especially valuable for minor topics. A work with a new approach is Gray's *Serial Bibliographies in the Humanities and Social Sciences* (1969) (3). This provides information on over 1,400 selected periodicals (or serials) which regularly or irregularly publish bibliographies. Gray's work is particularly useful where information on the latest published research is needed, although it also includes references to defunct bibliographies. It is arranged according to the Dewey decimal classification system, with title and subject indexes. A code indicates the language, scope, and other general features (such as book-review citations) of each periodical. Max Arnim's *Internationale Personalbibliographie* (1944–1952), (1944–1963) (4) is a three-volume index to bibliographies of approximately 90,000 individuals from 1800 through 1959. It is useful for determining sources of little-known bibliographies appearing in biographical dictionaries, periodical articles, and books. The first volume of the second edition eliminated some names for political reasons; hence the first edition should also be consulted.

Reference and General Bibliographies.   The *London Bibliography of the Social Sciences* (1931–) (5) is the most extensive subject bibliography in the social sciences. It consists of eighteen volumes and lists about one million books and documents in all major languages. An irritating feature of volumes up to the fifth

supplement is the greatly abbreviated bibliographical data. In the
sixth supplement, photographic reproduction of cards from library
card catalogs has eliminated the need to abbreviate information,
but has also resulted in the elimination of cross-references, a useful
feature of earlier volumes. All supplements have a table of subject
headings and subdivisions, as well as a list of subject headings
arranged under broader topics, such as education and finance.
Volumes 1–6 and 15–21 have as main headings under the section
"Geography, History, and Topography" a list of individual countries and localities. Author indexes exist only for volumes 1–6.

Issued three times a year, the *Social Sciences Citation Index*
(1973–) (6) promises to add a dramatic, innovative dimension
to research procedures in the social sciences. Based on the prin-
ciple that the names of people can be substituted for the subjects
with which they are associated, the *SSCI* enables the reader to
advance from earlier research to more recent studies on the same
subject. Anthropology, archaeology, area studies, community
health, demography, economics, educational research, ethnic group
studies, geography, sociology, statistics, and urban planning and
development are among the subjects covered. *SSCI* consists of
three separate but related indexes—the *Source Index,* the *Citation
Index,* and the *Permuterm Subject Index*. Of the three, the *Citation Index* is the largest and most useful, but for a clear understanding it is better to describe the *Source Index* first. Articles that
appear in 1,000-odd periodicals are arranged in it alphabetically
by author. Along with names, information given includes the article title; the abbreviated title of the periodical; the volume, date,
and page of the issue; and the number of footnote references. In
the *Citation Index,* also arranged alphabetically by author, are
articles cited by authors in the *Source Index*. Below each entry
are names and brief bibliographical data from the *Source Index*.
Because authors appearing in the *Source Index* ordinarily cite numerous studies, the *Citation Index* is several times larger than the
Source Index. (About 80,000 citations are predicted for 1973.)
The *Permuterm Subject Index* is useful when researchers do not
know a specific author on a topic for which they require information. In general, the *SSCI* will be useful for tracing the trends and
developments resulting from the publication of particular research
studies. The authors' experience with the *Science Citation Index*
(1967–) suggests, however, that many other uses are possible.[1]

The title *Encyclopedia of Business Information Sources* (1970)
(7) fails to imply the extensive range of subjects and geographical
areas covered in this bibliography. Volume 1 is arranged alphabetically, with over 2,000 entries ranging from abbreviations to
zoology, but with an emphasis on economics. Volume 2 is ar-

ranged by geographic areas, including continents, countries, states, provinces, and cities, as well as multinational sources, again with emphasis on economics. In general, materials are arranged under the following headings: encyclopedias and dictionaries, handbooks and manuals, bibliographies, abstract services and indexes, trade associations and professional societies, periodicals, directories, biographical sources, statistics sources, price sources, almanacs and yearbooks, financial ratios, other sources, and general works. The bibliography suffers from the lack of annotation, but each item gives the place of publication, the address of the sponsoring organization, and the subscription prices. Only English-language materials are cited.

The *ABS Guide* (1965–) (8) is a selective bibliography of recent books and articles in the social sciences. About 400 international social science journals are searched regularly. The main volume has over 6,600 items; supplements with about 1,000 items each were published in 1966, 1967, 1968, 1969, and 1970. These volumes are updated in the "New Studies" section in the monthly issues of *American Behavioral Scientist*. Items are arranged alphabetically by author, and each is briefly annotated. This bibliography, produced with the aid of data-processing techniques, features a large, multifaceted index, which provides more leads than other bibliographies to the contents of books and articles, though its truncated terms are often confusing.

The next four works provide information on a broad range of materials, each from its own point of view. In Hoselitz's *Reader's Guide to the Social Sciences* (1970) (9), bibliographical essays by specialists cover the following disciplines: geography, political science, economics, sociology, and anthropology. Directions and features of recent research in each discipline are noted. A more comprehensive, although now dated work, is White's *Sources of Information in the Social Sciences* (1964) (10),[2] which treats the social sciences in general, history, economics and business, sociology, anthropology, psychology, education, and political science. Chapters consist of two main sections: (1) a bibliographic essay which reviews a substantial number of monographs and other types of published research on various aspects of the discipline and (2) an annotated list of reference works, such as guides to the literature, handbooks, and encyclopedias. The work is well indexed by author and title. Although criticized for its lack of emphasis on statistical sources, it remains one of the best starting points for serious research. Lewis's *Literature of the Social Sciences* (1960) (11) and the second volume of Walford's *Guide to Reference Material* (1968–70) (12) (subtitled "Social and Historical Sciences, Philosophy, and Religion") are British works and reflect a British approach. Lewis's bibliography resembles White's *Sources of Information in the Social Sciences,* though there is more emphasis upon statistical sources.

In Walford, the term *reference* is broadly interpreted. This is a generally reliable, critical bibliography to which specialists on various systematic and area studies have contributed. It is exceptional for its inclusion of little-known items for regions throughout the world. The U.S. counterpart of Walford is Winchell's *Guide to Reference Books* (1967–) (13), with supplements appearing every two years. Organization is similar to Walford, with sections on systematic and area studies of the social sciences. Winchell has well-annotated but uncritical descriptions for each reference work cited and an excellent index. Walford's index is more difficult to use, because it omits title entries and gives unusual treatments to subject entries. Although compiled for geographical research by a well-known geographer, Harris's *Bibliographies and Reference Works for Research in Geography* (forthcoming) (14) has such a broad range of material that it is useful in most branches of the social sciences.

Perhaps the least-known work in this category, but the one with the widest coverage in the social sciences, is the Public Affairs Information Service *Bulletin* (1913–) (15) (hereafter usually referred to as *PAIS*). This subject index has maintained an extremely high standard of coverage, although limited to the English language and selective in scope. It includes books, parts of books, pamphlets, articles from about 1,000 periodicals, a few newspapers (e.g., the *Wall Street Journal*), reports of private and public agencies, and government publications, all relating to worldwide economic and social conditions, public administrations, and international relations. It is issued in weekly supplements, with biannual cumulations and a final annual volume. An author index for the 1965–69 period, published in 1971 by Pierian Press, further increases its usefulness. The Public Affairs Information Service *Foreign Language Index* (1971–) (16) is a selective subject list of the latest books, pamphlets, government publications, reports of public and private agencies, and periodical articles, relating to economic and social conditions, public administration, and international relations, published in French, German, Italian, Portuguese, or Spanish throughout the world. It contains the same subjects as the PAIS *Bulletin* (15), and the brief annotations accompanying most citations are in English.

Periodical indexes are useful sources of material for research, but students are urged to note the characteristics of each of the most popular indexes. Along with the *London Bibliography of Social Sciences* (A.1.b:5), a valuable source to consult for historical and current information is the *Social Sciences and Humanities Index* (1907–) (17). Formerly known as the *International Index,* it appears in quarterly supplements, with annual and two-to-four-year cumulations. It covers about 200 Canadian, British, and American scholarly periodicals, with entries arranged by subject and author in one alphabetical list.

Sociology, economics, history, archaeology, and related subjects are indexed in the *British Humanities Index* (1915–) (18). Issued quarterly with annual cumulations, it includes an index to authors. About 300 periodicals are searched regularly. From 1915 to 1961, it was known as the *Subject Index to Periodicals.* The most extensive and one of the oldest indexes, covering all fields of knowledge, the *Internationale Bibliographie der Zeitschriftenliteratur* [International bibliography of periodical literature] (1897–1963, 1963–1964–) (19) appeared in two sections until 1963 (volumes 26–29, for 1944–48, have not yet been published). Section A is an index to over 3,600 German-language periodicals and 45 newspapers. Section B is an index to over 3,200 periodicals in languages other than German. Popularly known as *IBZ,* it is arranged alphabetically by broad subjects (in German), indicating for each citation the title in its original language, the author's name, and reference to the periodical by number, page, and sometimes volume. Each volume has an author index (in section A since 1925), and a numbered list of periodicals indexed is given at the beginning of each volume. In 1963–64, sections A and B merged into a combined series (*Kombierte Folge*), becoming a subject index to world periodical literature. The subject headings are in German, with cross-references from English and French forms. The arrangement is similar to the old sections A and B, with coverage increased to 6,600 periodicals.

The periodicals indexed in the *Readers' Guide* (1900–) (20) are of a more popular nature than those in the *Social Sciences and Humanities Index* (17). However, the *Readers' Guide* is extremely important because the articles it indexes comprise a reflection of and commentary on the social, economic, and cultural aspects of the contemporary world. For example, interested readers might look under the subject heading "Democracy" to trace the misgivings some Americans had about representative government earlier in the century, or under "Spock, Benjamin" to find out why he is a hero to some people and a villain to others. The *Readers' Guide* and the *Social Sciences and Humanities Index* both index articles by author as well as subject. According to Winchell (A.1.b:13), *Poole's Index to Periodical Literature* (1802–1907) (21) is "the pioneer index and, though now discontinued, still an important index to American and English periodicals since it covers the long-

est period (105 years) and indexes about 590,000 articles in 12,-
241 volumes of 479 American and English periodicals." Unfortunately, access to authors has been limited because it is arranged
by subject. C. Edward Wall has edited an *Author Index* (1971)
to *Poole's Index to Periodical Literature.*

Although primarily known as a directory of current periodicals
(with over 16,000 titles from 118 countries listed in the second
volume, *Arts, Humanities, Business, and Social Sciences,* of the
twelfth edition), Ulrich's *International Periodicals Directory*
(1932–) (22) indicates where periodicals are indexed, as well as
noting selected indexes and abstracting services on a broad range
of subjects. *Indexed Periodicals* (1970–) (23) promises to be a
guide to 165 years of periodicals, indicating where they are indexed, inclusive dates, and irregularities of indexing. Volume 1
lists all periodicals indexed since 1802 by *Poole's Index* (21), the
H. W. Wilson services (except *Bibliographic Index*), *Catholic
Periodicals Index,* and other widely used services. The chief use
of *Indexed Periodicals* will be as an aid in finding articles previously elusive principally because another source has given an
incorrect citation.

The bibliographies discussed above are selected from among the
most prominent in the social sciences. The list is not comprehensive, of course; many more-specialized works will be introduced
later. In most research, bibliographical information is obtained
through the specialized bibliographies and related works. Occasionally, however, these do not provide the required information,
and it is necessary to look elsewhere. Some difficulties associated
with bibliographical activity, either general or specialized, can be
overcome by using the sources discussed below. It should be emphasized, however, that these are only briefly described, the idea
being to give a general idea of their scope and organization. It is
recommended that a reference librarian be consulted for further
assistance in using them. Extensive discussions of the various
systems are to be found in Winchell (A.1.b:13) and Walford
(A.1.b:12).

Large national bibliographies are useful to verify authors' names,
titles of books, and information on date and place of publication.
In the United States the national bibliographies are the Library
of Congress's *Catalog* (1942–46) (24) and related sets, such as
the Library of Congress's *Author Catalog* (1948–52) (25), the
National Union Catalog (1953–) (26), and the not yet completed *National Union Catalog of Pre-1956 Imprints* (1968–)
(27). Each of these large, multivolume sets lists by author books
published in the United States or acquired by U.S. libraries, providing the same information as that found in library card catalogs.

Indeed, most libraries buy or reproduce Library of Congress catalog cards. Since these bibliographies are arranged only by author, it is necessary to consult other, related types of bibliographies if the only information available on a book is its subject or title. The Library of Congress's *Books: Subjects* (1955–) (28), a subject arrangement of books cataloged by the Library of Congress since 1950, is a large, multivolume set. Its subject headings are those established by the Library of Congress and are the same as those in card catalogs of academic libraries. An almost indispensable aid for verifying details about books, especially if only the title is known, is the *Cumulative Book Index* (1898–) (29). Popularly referred to as *CBI,* this large set lists books in the English language by author, title, and subject (all in one alphabetical arrangement). Another set of book catalogs useful for verifying details about books is the *Publishers' Trade List Annual* (1873–) (30) and its companion volumes, *Books in Print* (1948–) (31) and *Subject Guide to Books in Print* (1957–) (32). This set is designed to publicize to libraries and bookstores the availability and prices of books in the United States. *Publishers' Trade List Annual,* popularly known as *PTLA,* is an annual publication currently consisting of the catalogs of 1,900 publishers, arranged alphabetically by publisher and uniformly bound in a multivolume set. An alphabetically arranged list of the publishers included appears on colored pages at the beginning of the first volume. Also in this colored-page section is an alphabetical arrangement of the trade lists of small publishers. *Books in Print,* in a two-volume set, is an author and title index to *PTLA* containing an estimated 275,000 titles. The *Subject Guide to Books in Print* is a companion to *Books in Print,* listing approximately 210,000 books under some 37,000 Library of Congress subject headings.

Another useful catalog of books is *Paperbound Books in Print* (1955–) (33), issued monthly, with three cumulations per year. Currently this volume lists about 100,000 books, arranged by author, title, and broad subject categories.

A.1.c   Book-Review Citations

Searching for the locations of book reviews can be frustrating, but it need not be. Frustration usually results from not knowing what various reference works are designed to do and what they are not designed to do. One mistake often made in searches for book reviews (particularly with paperback reprints) is using the wrong imprint (publishing) date. Book reviews appear shortly after a book is originally published; a paperback reprint is seldom reviewed. An account of a book's publishing history often appears on the back of a book's title page. The earliest year listed is usu-

ally the most significant and is the date to use in beginning a
search for reviews.

The *Book Review Digest* (1906–) (1) is a good example of a
reference work about which there is a great deal of misinforma-
tion, although it is the best-known work in its field. It is a digest
and index of selected book reviews in about 75 general English
and American periodicals, such as the *New York Times Book Review,* the *Saturday Review,* and the *Times Literary Supplement.*
A few specialized periodicals, such as the *American Historical
Review* and *Annals of the American Academy of Political and
Social Science,* are also included. In order to appear in the *Book
Review Digest,* a book must be published in the United States;
paperbacks are excluded. A nonfiction work must have at least
two reviews, and fiction must have at least four reviews in the
periodicals regularly searched within eighteen months after publication. At least one review must be from a periodical published
in the United States. Reviews are arranged alphabetically by author of the book reviewed, and there is a subject and title index.
Cumulated subject and title indexes for the previous five-year period appear in the annual volumes for 1921, 1926, 1931, 1936,
1941, 1946, 1951, 1956, and 1961; a separate volume was published with a cumulated subject and title index for 1962–66. Each
book reviewed has a brief descriptive note; quotations, giving
sources, from selected reviews; and references, without quotation,
to other reviews.

Much more useful to social scientists are the *Book Review Index* (1965–) (2), the *Mental Health Book Review Index* (1956–)
(3), the *Social Science Book Review Index* (1971–) (4), the
Index to Book Reviews in the Humanities (1960–) (5), and the
recently revived *Internationale Bibliographie der Rezensionen wissenschaftlicher Literatur* (1900–43, 1971–) (6). In the *Book Review Index,* references to all reviews appearing in over 200 English-language periodicals are arranged alphabetically by author
of the book reviewed. There is no title or subject index. This publication was issued bimonthly, with three cumulations a year and
annual cumulations, but after 1968 publication was suspended
until 1972. Retrospective volumes for 1969, 1970, and 1971 are
projected. The *Mental Health Book Review Index* includes references to signed book reviews when three or more references are
found in about 275 English-language periodicals in the fields of
the behavioral sciences and mental health (psychology, psychiatry,
psychoanalysis, social work, criminology, and education). The
work is listed again if at least three additional references are ac-
cumulated. Within each issue, books are arranged alphabetically
by author and in a serial numerical order continuing from issue

to issue (except when a title is repeated from an earlier issue, in which case it bears its original serial number, indicating the issue of its first appearance). The *Mental Health Book Review Index* was published semiannually through 1959 and has been an annual since 1960. There is a cumulative author-title index for 1956–67. The annual *Index to Book Reviews in the Humanities* covers art, architecture, biography, drama, dance, folklore, history, language, literature, music, philosophy, travel, and adventure. About 700 English-language periodicals are searched; arrangement is by author of the book reviewed, with no subject or title index. Periodicals in which reviews appear are identified by code numbers, with periodicals listed numerically at the beginning of each volume. Reviews are indexed as they appear, making it necessary to refer to several volumes to find all review citations. Although not examined by the authors, the *Book Review Index to Social Science Periodicals* (4) is described as an annual index designed to supplement the *Index to Book Reviews in the Humanities*. According to the publisher, "it will cover several hundred journals in the areas of history, sociology, education, political science, anthropology, economics, geography, and related subjects."

The *Internationale Bibliographie der Rezensionen wissenschaftlicher Literatur* [International bibliography of book reviews of scholarly literature] offers worldwide coverage of book reviews of scholarly literature. Over 1,000 periodicals are presently included, but this number is to be increased. It is arranged in three lists: a subject index in German with cross-references from English and French equivalents, an alphabetical index of reviewed authors, and an alphabetical index of reviewing authors. Periodicals are identified by number. Under the heading "Book Reviews" in the *New York Times Index* (A.1.g:2), all books reviewed in the *Times* are listed by author, in the case of single-author works, and by title for collaborations, anthologies, and other multiauthor works. Gray's *Guide to Book Review Citations* (1969) (7) and *Serial Bibliographies in the Humanities and Social Sciences* (A.1.b:3) are useful for finding periodicals and books that refer to book reviews. *A Guide to Book Review Citations* is an annotated list of continuing series and separately published works of sources, such as book-review indexes, periodical indexes, serial bibliographies, and monographic bibliographies. It has author, title, and subject indexes. Item numbers are provided in the indexes. Gray's *Serial Bibliographies in the Humanities and Social Sciences* includes references to book-review citations in serial bibliographies. Book reviews are also quickly found by using the *SSCI* (A.1.b:6); a "B" symbol in a citation indicates a review.

A.l.d   Biographical Dictionaries and Directories

Biographical information presents special problems to researchers in the social sciences, since almost always it requires consulting special sources. When researchers encounter difficulty in obtaining biographical information, the quickest, simplest solution is to consult a reference librarian. At the same time, there are several types of biographical reference titles with which it is convenient to be familiar. Four biographical dictionaries widely used for information on prominent people (living and deceased) throughout the world are *Chambers's Biographical Dictionary* (1968) (1), the three-volume *New Century Cyclopedia of Names* (1954) (2), *Webster's Biographical Dictionary* (1963) (3), and *Lippincott's Pronouncing Biographical Dictionary* (1930) (4).

Chambers's includes recommended biographies among the information provided in its approximately 15,000 brief articles. The *New Century* has over 100,000 entries; it includes geographical places; historical events; mythological, biblical, and literary characters; and biographical articles, predominantly from the English-speaking world. *Lippincott's Pronouncing Biographical Dictionary* has fewer entries but covers all nations and periods up to the date of publication. About one-third of the approximately 40,000 articles in *Webster's Biographical Dictionary* are on people still living, with attention directed mostly to the English-speaking world. About 40 percent of the 75,000 articles in the single-volume *Columbia Encyclopedia* (A.1.e:7) are biographical. Like *Chambers's,* the *Columbia Encyclopedia* includes references to recommended biographies.

Webster's Dictionary of Proper Names (1970) (5) is useful as a companion or updating of the *New Century*. It gives definitions or explanations of over 11,000 selected names, acronyms and abbreviations, phrases, and related words. Words in small capitals in definitions indicate cross-references to other entries.

The *International Who's Who* (1935–) (6) currently provides directory information on over 16,000 prominent individuals from every part of the world. It is especially useful for information about persons from countries without national biographical directories, and also for the major publications of many of the individuals cited. *Who's Who in the World* (1971–) (7) is a new directory issued by the firm which publishes the Who's Who in Amerca series. Brief, reliable information is provided on leading world figures from many different fields.

The *McGraw-Hill Encyclopedia of World Biography* (1972) (8) is a twelve-volume work with 5,000 entries on famous men and women "of all times, all countries, and all vocations." Each article is written by an authority. The final volume is an index.

Slocum's *Biographical Dictionaries and Related Works* (1967) (9) and its *Supplement* (1972) provide a classified listing of some 8,200 briefly annotated titles, with author, subject, and title indexes. It is extremely valuable for its coverage of regional and national biographical (as well as universal and vocational) dictionaries and directories.

The *Biography Index* (1937–) (10), Arnim (A.1.b:4), and Hyamson's *Dictionary of Universal Biography* (1951) (11) are the best known of a special type of biographical index featuring references to biographical information in other sources. The *Biography Index* has quarterly issues, and annual and larger cumulations. The editors regularly survey 1,500 periodicals listed in the publisher's other indexes, as well as other works of collective biography, such as *New York Times* obituaries of prominent people. Existence of bibliographies and portraits is indicated, and full bibliographical details are provided for each item. Hyamson indexes biographical articles in a selected number of prominent encyclopedias and related works in European languages. This work is very strong on figures of the nineteenth century and earlier. Arnim's focus is more bibliographical, but often the sources also contain biographical information. Included in all three works are birth and death dates and profession. Recently the *New York Times* intiated two biographical services worth noting. The *New York Times Obituaries Index, 1858–1968* (1970) (12) contains obituary notices on prominent people for over a century. It refers to biographical information listed under "Deaths" in the *New York Times Index*. (Occasionally deaths are noted in the main part of the *New York Times Index,* and not in the "Deaths" section.) The *New York Times Biographical Edition* (1970–) (13) contains profiles of newsworthy figures reprinted from the newspaper. It is arranged alphabetically in loose-leaf format and provides easier, quicker access to information than microfilm does. *Current Biography* (1940–) (14) attempts to provide extensive biographical information on about 350 to 400 prominent people each year. Most of its information is obtained from popular sources such as *Newsweek* and the *New York Times*. It is issued monthly with annual cumulations. Each volume has a cumulative index for the decade.

A regular feature of *PAIS* (A.1.b:15) is a subject listing of the biographical and institutional directories. About 1,000 of these are indexed in each annual volume. For additional sources of brief biographical articles in general and specialized encyclopedias, see section A.1.e.

Excellent sources of information on American scholars are the social and behavioral sciences volumes of *American Men and Women of Science* (1906–) (15). Currently this continuing series provides information on the education, experience, and publications of approximately 30,000 social scientists in the United States and Canada. Later volumes refer to information in earlier volumes.

A.I.e   Encyclopedias and Dictionaries

The two most prominent multivolume encyclopedias in the social sciences are the 15-volume *Encyclopedia of the Social Sciences* (1930–35) (1) and the 17-volume *International Encyclopedia of the Social Sciences* (1968) (2). The editorial policy on the later work was to complement rather than supersede the original. The two together represent excellent sources for information on a wide range of subjects within and related to the disciplines of the social sciences.

The aim of the *Encyclopedia of the Social Sciences* was to present a synopsis of the progress that had been made in the social sciences, to provide a repository of facts and principles useful to researchers in the subjects, and to create a body of authoritative knowledge to assist in promoting social progress and development. The *Encyclopedia of the Social Sciences* includes articles on major topics in politics, economics, law, anthropology, sociology, penology, and social work, with some attention to peripheral subjects such as ethics, education, philosophy, psychology, and geography. In addition, there are some 4,000 biographies of deceased persons whose work has been significant in these fields. Articles are of varying lengths, signed by their authors, and arranged alphabetically. Cross-references to related articles are provided, and the final volume has a comprehensive index and a classification of the articles in subject and biography groups. Most articles have a brief bibliography.

Their experience in assembling the original encyclopedia prompted the editors of the *International Encyclopedia of the Social Sciences* to make some changes in scope and format, but this work has a marked resemblance to the original. There are extensive articles on the concepts, theories, and methods of anthropology, economics, geography, history, law, political science, psychology, sociology, and statistics. By consulting the entry on each discipline, one can find cross-references to major topical and biographical articles related to it. The emphasis is on analytical and comparative aspects of topics, with historical and descriptive material used to illustrate concepts and theories. Throughout the new encyclopedia, articles appear on many analytical levels, of which the editors have noted fourteen. Topics of articles include features of social processes such as acculturation, cooperation, and socialization; social and individual pathologies such as crime, poverty, blindness, and drug addiction; economic processes and institutions; political doctrines and forms of government; forms of settlement and of social life; and methods of empirical research and of presenting research results. Statistics are treated as an important auxiliary discipline. The *International Encyclopedia of the Social Sciences* has only 600 biographies, compared with over 4,000 in the earlier work, but the articles are longer and emphasize individuals not included in the first work, including prominent social scientists still living, but born before 1890. Biographical articles are cross-referenced to related articles. The bibliographies for each article consist of works cited in the text, suggestions for further reading, sources for data, and related journals. Contributors come from 30 countries; 60 of them contributed to the original work. See section F.1.d for a comparison of the encyclopedias of the social sciences, the *New Larned History* (F.1.d:3), and the eleventh edition of the *Encyclopaedia Britannica* (F.1.d:5).

Two single-volume works worth consulting are Zadrozny's *Dictionary of Social Science* (1959) (3) and Gould's *Dictionary of the Social Sciences* (1964) (4). The first consists of brief definitions of several thousand terms, primarily in sociology, political science, and economics. Gould defines about one-fourth as many terms as Zadrozny, but his treatment of the terms is more intensive. There are more than 1,000 terms from anthropology and economics, but political-science and sociological terms predominate; they are extensively defined by some 270 noted U.S. and British social scientists. With a few exceptions, entries are arranged as follows: *A,* the generally accepted meaning of the term; *B,* its historical background or a more extensive explanation. *C, D, E,* and so on, are used where "controversies and divergencies of meaning have been explored and an attempt made to place them in their perspective." Many definitions are illustrated with quotes from authorities. A similar treatment of definitions is used by Hultkrantz (B.1.d:2) for anthropology, by Mitchell (H.1.d:1) for sociology, and to a lesser extent by the *McGraw-Hill Dictionary of Economics* (D.1.d:1).

General encyclopedias such as the *Encyclopaedia Britannica* (5) and the *Encyclopedia Americana* (6) (both of which have a continuous-revision policy), and the single-volume *Columbia Encyclopedia* (1963) (7) should not be overlooked. Often these can be used to obtain preliminary information on a major topic, the definition of a term, or the details of an event. All three feature brief bibliographies at the ends of most articles, and are also a source of biographical information, especially the *Columbia Encyclopedia*. Generally, the *Britannica* is considered to have a more scholarly approach than the *Americana*. Surprisingly, the single-volume *Columbia Encyclopedia* has 75,000 articles, most of which include a brief list of the most prominent books on a particular topic. A majority of the articles focus on biographical, geographical, or historical material. In addition to these general encyclopedias, several more-specialized, multivolume encyclopedias often have information needed in the social sciences. The *Encyclopedia of Philosophy* (1967) (8) features long articles on major philosophical issues and philosophers throughout the world. Each article is written by a specialist and contains a surprisingly large bibliography. The *Encyclopedia of Religion and Ethics* (1908–26) (9), the Schaff-Herzog *New Encyclopedia of Religion* (1908–14) (10), the *New Catholic Encyclopedia* (1967) (11), and the *Encyclopedia Judaica* (1972) (12) are other good specialized encyclopedias. The first two are older Protestant works which do not reflect contemporary Protestant attitudes. The *New Catholic Encyclopedia* has a broader, more secular approach than was formerly true of Catholic encyclopedias. The 16-volume *Encyclopedia Judaica* represents an attempt to set forth and interpret the progress of study, discoveries, scientific perspectives, and new areas that concern Jewish studies, from the earliest archaeological records to current statistics. In particular, the encyclopedia gives special attention to "the rise of 'racial' anti-Semitism and the Holocaust" associated with World War II and to the development of the Zionist movement. There are over 8,000 illustrations, including colored and black-and-white photographs, maps, charts, and diagrams. The work is especially useful for research on Europe and the Middle East. All these encyclopedias feature brief bibliographies. It should be noted that many more religious or denominational encyclopedias and dictionaries are available. Consult the sections on religious encyclopedias in Walford (A.1.b:12) or Winchell (A.1.b:13).

Two useful, specialized dictionaries are the *Code Names Dictionary* (1963) (13) and the *Acronyms and Initialisms Dictionary* (1970) (14). The publisher issues occasional supplements to the latter. With over 80,000 entries, it is a key to abbreviations and acronyms used throughout the world. A companion, *Reverse Acronyms and Initialisms Dictionary* (1972) (15) contains acronyms arranged alphabetically by name of organization or by term. The *Code Names Dictionary* is a key to a large number of code names and slang terms.

A.1.f Handbooks and Yearbooks

For the meaning of *handbooks* and *yearbooks* as they are used here, see the Glossary of Terms on p. xix. In Part A only one work fits the criteria for handbooks, the two-volume *Encyclopedia of Business Information Sources* (A.1.b:7). It covers a much broader spectrum of subjects than its title suggests, and is appropriate here because it refers to sources of information normally found in handbooks. The arrangement is alphabetical by subject, with cross-references to related subjects. Among yearbooks, the oldest and one of the most useful is the *Annual Register* (A.1.g:4). Two general encyclopedias, the *Britannica* (A.1.e:5) and the *Americana* (A.1.e:6), publish yearbooks, comprising for the most part an updating of material in the encyclopedia volumes. Users of the present volume will obtain more satisfactory results by consulting the specialized handbooks and yearbooks devoted to a particular subject or area.

There are five well-known almanacs useful for general information. Of these, only *Whitaker's Almanack* (1869–) (1) is issued outside the United States. Whitaker's is published in Great Britain and has proportionately more information on British and European affairs. The four almanacs published in the United States are the *World Almanac* (1868–) (2), the *Information Please Almanac* (1947–) (3), the *Reader's Digest Almanac* (1966–) (4), and the *New York Times Almanac* (1970–) (5). The material in almanacs consists of statistics, reviews of events of the world, and a large body of miscellaneous information. Some reference librarians claim that 75 percent of the information required to fill the needs of library users can be obtained from almanacs. It should be understood, however, that the information, though reliable, is frustratingly brief.

A.1.g   Newspapers and News Digests

Obtaining information on past events is sometimes baffling to researchers, especially undergraduate students. In general, newspapers and news digests are the best sources. However, academic libraries of small and medium-sized universities usually have limited files of newspapers, and since newspapers generally are not indexed, searching for specific accounts of events is difficult. There are some exceptions. Although representing a large investment, the *New York Times* (1851–) (1) daily newspaper and the *New York Times Index* (1851–) (2) are held by many academic libraries. The newspaper section is usually on microfilm, but the *Index* has been published almost completely in hardbound volumes. The newspaper, acknowledged as one of the world's greatest, along with the *Index,* represents one of the most important sources of information on world events since the middle of the nineteenth century. It also includes texts of important speeches

and documents. Besides being a detailed subject index to the
Times, with references to the date, page, and column of articles,
the *Index* provides brief synopses of news events (sometimes making it unnecessary to use the actual article). Older than the *New
York Times,* but not so widely available in U.S. academic libraries,
is the *Times* (1785–) (3) of London. Like the *New York Times,*
this newspaper has been almost completely indexed. The British
Annual Register (1758–) (4) is the oldest and one of the most
useful reviews of events. In each volume the events of the previous
year are reviewed by specialists. Summaries of important speeches
and texts of documents are often included. Information in recent
volumes is arranged in the following manner: United Kingdom,
the Commonwealth, international organizations, nations of the
world outside the Commonwealth, religion, science, law, arts and
literature, economics, and index of names and subjects.

The best-known news digest is *Keesing's Contemporary Archives* (1931–) (5). This British publication has airmailed weekly
issues, and weekly, biweekly, quarterly, annual, and biennial indexes. It features condensed reports on important events and developments throughout the world, listing newspapers and other
publications used as sources at the end of each article. (This feature makes *Keesing's* a rough index to a considerable number of
prominent world newspapers.) *Keesing's* also includes texts or
summaries of important speeches and documents, statistics and
charts, maps, and obituaries. Annually since 1959, approximately
4,000 entries appear in the index of names. *Facts on File* (1941–)
(6) is another news-digest service that attempts world coverage.
Although not so ambitious as *Keesing's* in the amount and type
of material provided, it is useful for verifying dates and events,
and as a brief summary of news. *Facts on File* provides a fuller
coverage of U.S. events and sometimes includes texts of important
speeches and documents. In addition to these works, there are
news digests (noted below) devoted to regions such as Africa and
Asia.

A.1.h Statistics Sources

As well as the *Encyclopedia of Business Information Sources*
(A.1.b:7), the expanded third edition of Wasserman's *Statistics
Sources* (1971) (1) should be consulted. As indicated in its sub-
title, "A Subject Guide to Data on Industrial, Business, Social,
Educational, Financial, and Other Topics for the United States and
Selected Foreign Countries," its format is similar to the *Encyclo-
pedia of Business Information Sources,* but coverage is limited to
statistical data. Further indication of its scope is given in the pref-

ace. It is a "comprehensive and inclusive compilation of source data on foreign countries and statistics about them. Added to the citations on international activities and the identification of the principal statistical compilations for each of the countries of the world, the present edition provides very deep analysis of data governing all of the fields of concern in international affairs. Every subject covered in international statistical sources, notably the United Nations *Statistical Yearbook* [I.1.g:3], has been comprehensively indexed." The sources of statistical data are listed alphabetically under an estimated 12,000 subject headings. At the beginning of the volume is a useful annotated bibliography of the over 80 sources used. They are all in English and are arranged in the following categories: dictionaries of terms, bibliographies and guides, almanacs, U.S. government (monographs, annuals, and periodicals), annuals and yearbooks, and international sources. Many of the items included in *Statistics Sources* are discussed in the next section.[3]

A.1.i Government Publications

The publications of national governments and international agencies are a vast source of information for research in area studies as well as in the social sciences. In order to operate effectively, governments need information on population, economic activity, health and social conditions, and education. This information is gathered and published in such documents as statistical reports, censuses, and atlases. Altogether, the output is enormous, and librarians have a difficult task in arranging and indexing each document properly for fast retrieval. Many government documents are very well known, and they are treated in this volume as books or periodicals. Access to familiar documents such as the *U.S. Statistical Abstract* (O.1.g:2), the U.N. *Statistical Yearbook* (I.1. g:3), and the *Yearbook of International Organizations* (G.2.b:8) is generally not difficult because libraries treat them as books. Such documents are listed by agency, title, and subject in the card catalogs of libraries. Many publications of national and state governments and of international agencies such as the Organization of American States and UNESCO, however, are not listed in card catalogs. Obtaining these documents requires the assistance of a documents librarian.

In general, the listing of government documents in special bibliographies is well organized. Just as students should become familiar with the arrangement of the books and periodicals in the college library, so they should familiarize themselves with the library's documents collections. Find out what documents have been acquired: U.S. government publications? U.N.? OAS? Canadian? How extensive are the collections? Many libraries have purchased in microprint the output of U.S. government documents dating back to the eighteenth century. Many other countries are also publishing documents in microprint. Microprint collections, being complete or virtually complete, provide a scope almost unknown in libraries in the past. Only a small number of the largest libraries in the United States can boast of complete collections of original U.S. government documents. Today, all libraries that can afford it can obtain microprint documents collections. (Bibliographical listings of documents are described at appropriate places in this handbook, e.g., section 0.3 of the part on American studies.) For the most part, documents published by agencies of government bodies are listed in the many bibliographies described throughout this volume. These documents are usually obtained without difficulty; either they are listed in the library card catalog or they can be found by asking a documents librarian. *PAIS* (A.1.b:15) includes government publications. A useful annotated list of the most prominent handbooks and bibliographies associated with government publications is found in Winchell (A.1.b:13) and the second volume of Mason (G.2.c:2). C. L. and A. G. Vinge's *U.S. Government Publications for Teaching and Research in Geography* (1967) (1) identifies some 3,500 U.S. government publications issued since 1945 that are of value for research in geography and neighboring disciplines. Coverage is broader than the title implies; a considerable amount of material on such topics as air and water pollution, population problems, migration, poverty programs, and urban planning is included. U.S. Superintendent of Documents class numbers are provided for each item, and the volume is well indexed.

Sally Wynkoop's *Government Reference Books* (O.1.b:1) promises to be of lasting use. The following titles are examples of the range of items included: David Kasdon's *International Family Planning, 1966–1968: A Bibliography* (C.2.d:1), the U.S. Army's *USSR: Strategic Survey* (I.1.b:9), the Library of Congress's *Czechoslovakia: A Bibliographic Guide* (M.1.b:12), the U.S. National Institute of Mental Health's *Bibliography on the Urban Crisis,* Mary Lystad's *Social Aspects of Alienation,* and the U.S. Bureau of Indian Affairs' *Economic Development of American Indians and Eskimos, 1930–1967: A Bibliography.* A bibliography that indicates further the scope of the U.S. government's interests is Alexander Body's *Annotated Bibliography of Bibliographies of Selected Government Publications* (O.3:4).

Part B

Anthropology

Section 1

B.1.a   Atlases

R. R. Spencer and Elden Johnson's *Atlas of Anthropology* (1968) (1) is devoted to tribal, linguistic, and social groups, illustrated by maps. Arrangement is by cultural areas, language families, prehistory, and racial distributions. An alphabetical listing of about 500 tribal and ethnic groups, with map references, is included. The *Atlas narodov mira* (C.1.a:1) is useful for some types of anthropological research. Murdock's *Ethnographic Atlas* (B.1.e:1) is not really an atlas, but rather a coded arrangement of information from the Human Relations Area Files (I.3:1).

B.1.b   Bibliographies

Bibliographies of Bibliographies.   The most comprehensive bibliography of ethnographic bibliographies was compiled by Timothy O'Leary in *A Handbook of Method in Cultural Anthropology* (B.2.g:1). It notes over 370 items, in many languages and attempts to give a "fairly thorough" coverage of ethnographic and related bibliographies on continental, regional, and national levels, with a section at the end on subject treatments. Gaps are noted in the ethnographic bibliographies of Europe, the Middle East, and China. After a listing of general works, the book is divided into eight sections on Asia, South Asia, East Asia, the Soviet Union, Europe, Africa, the Americas, and the Pacific. In the chapter "Anthropology" in Downs and Jenkins's *Bibliography: Current State and Future Trends* (1967) (1), R. S. Beckham surveys 93 bibliographies—retrospective and current—concerned with anthropology, its subfields, and its geographical divisions. Excellent bibliographies of bibliographies for North and South America and Africa are noted in the appropriate area parts below. Besterman (A.1.b:1) and the *Bibliographic Index* (A.1.b:2) should be consulted for bibliographies in all fields of anthropology. Bibliographies are listed in the index of *International Bibliography of Social and Cultural Anthropology* (B.1.b:4) under the entry "Bibliography."

General Bibliographies.   Although anthropology is recognized as a distinct discipline, its borders overlap into such disciplines as biology, history, and sociology. Thus, bibliographies in these disciplines can often be consulted with profit. The *Author and Subject Catalog* (1963) (2) of Harvard University's Peabody Museum of Archaeology and Ethnology is the most important retrospective bibliography in anthropology. Its outstanding feature is the inclusion of journal articles. It dates back to 1866, when officials of Harvard's Peabody Museum began producing a catalog of cards having citations of books and articles in ethnology, archaeology, and physical anthropology. The catalog has a classified arrangement, including anthropological journals, proceedings, and reports of anthropological festschriften from societies and museums throughout the world. The author catalog contains approximately 300,000 items; the subject catalog approximately 315,000 items. It should be noted that some regional bibliographies (cited where appropriate) have been compiled using the Peabody Museum *Catalog*. In 1963 the G. K. Hall Publishing Company published both author and subject catalogs in 54 volumes. The set is expensive, and not many libraries have it. According to the *National Union Catalog* (A.1.b:26), twenty-two institutions have sets.

Annotated citations of important reference works in anthropology appear in Winchell (A.1.b:13) and Walford (A.1.b:12). White's *Sources of Information in the Social Sciences* (A.1.b:10), though somewhat dated, is one of the best attempts to provide a detailed description of the major reference works, monographs, and periodicals in anthropology and its subfields. Beckham's "Basic List of Books and Periodicals for College Libraries" (1963) (3), which is in Mandelbaum's *Resources for the Teaching of Anthropology,* has become a guide to purchases for academic libraries. It is a classified listing of 1,700 books and periodicals of recommended general surveys, case studies, and works on subfields of anthropology. There is an author index.

There are four regularly issued bibliographies in anthropology which together can be used to supplement the Peabody Museum *Catalog* (B.1.b:2). The largest is the *International Bibliography of Social and Cultural Anthropology* (1959–) (4). It contains annually about 5,000 citations for selected books and articles published throughout the world on ethnology, archaeology, linguistics, folklore, and applied anthropology, as well as related historical and geographical materials. Occasionally the existence of book reviews is noted. Reviews appearing after a book is cited are indicated by "Bibl." and the original volume and item number preceding the citation. Each volume has author and subject indexes. The *Anthropological Index to Current Periodicals* (1963–) (5) is one of the most comprehensive current indexes. In each issue, section 1 has general articles, while each of the five sections that follow is devoted to a geographical area. Each section has five categories: general, physical anthropology, archaeology, cultural anthropology and ethnography, and linguistics. There are no indexes. Citations with abstracts are divided into four major subdivisions—archaeology, ethnology, linguistics, and physical anthropology—in *Abstracts in Anthropology* (1970–) (6). There are about 200 entries for each issue, and over 30 periodicals are searched.

Anthropology is prominent in the *London Bibliography of the Social Sciences* (A.1.b:5), and the *Research Catalog* (E.1.b:4) of the American Geographical Society, though primarily dealing with geography, includes many items of anthropological and sociological interest. The *Social Sciences Citation Index* (A.1.b:6) promises to be an aid to certain aspects of research in anthropology.

Reviews of Research. The *Biennial Review of Anthropology* (1959–71) (7) was a series devoted to periodic reviews of published research in such fields as cultural change, social organization, language, and physical anthropology.[1] Each chapter surveyed about 100 books and articles. White (A.1.b:10) and Hoselitz's *Reader's Guide to the Social Sciences* (A.1.b:9) have critical assessments of recent research on anthropology. *Social Science Information* (B.1.f:5) regularly lists surveys of research in anthropology.

Case Studies.   In Spencer and Johnson's *Atlas for Anthropology* (B.1.a:1), pages 38 and 40 list 125 case studies of the "New World" and the "Old World." The editors characterize them as "classical ethnographic descriptions" and "shorter descriptive vignettes of various cultures." Lists of Holt, Rinehart & Winston's Case Studies in Cultural Anthropology series and John Wiley and Sons' Six Cultures series, are to be found in *PTLA* (A.1.b:30) in the catalogs of these publishers.

B.1.c   Biographical Dictionaries and Directories

Biographies of prominent anthropologists are included in the *Encyclopedia of Social Sciences* (A.1.e:1) and the *International Encyclopedia of the Social Sciences* (A.1.e:2). The fourth *International Directory of Anthropologists and Anthropological Institutions* (1967) (1) appeared in 1967. In June 1970, a revision of the biographical section was published. This is the only directory attempting to provide worldwide information. The Social and Behavioral Sciences volumes of *American Men and Women of Science* (A.1.d:15) lists many anthropologists. Although some searching is required, references to biographical articles on anthropologists appear in the general section of the *Anthropological Index to Current Periodicals* (B.1.b:5) and at the beginning of the *International Bibliography of Anthropology* (B.1.b:4).

B.1.d   Encyclopedias and Dictionaries

There is no multivolume encyclopedia devoted exclusively to anthropology, but it receives attention in the *Encyclopedia of the Social Sciences* (A.1.e:1) and the *International Encyclopedia of the Social Sciences* (A.1.e:2). Both works feature articles on cultural, economic, physical, political, social, and applied anthropology, as well as archaeology, ethnography, ethnology, kinship, linguistics, and race. *Anthropology Today: An Encyclopedic Inventory* (1953) (1), edited by A. L. Kroeber, presents a broad survey by 50 experts from all over the world. Each chapter covers a single geographical region, includes a detailed bibliography, and deals with contemporary methods and results of research in such subfields of anthropology as social structure, folklore, cultural history, and the biological basis of human behavior.

Volume 1 of the *International Dictionary of Regional European Ethnology and Folklore,* entitled *General Ethnological Concepts* (1960) (2) and edited by Ake Hultkrantz, deals with general concepts, schools, and methods in ethnology (and, to a certain extent, in folklore) in the fields of European regional ethnology, European general ethnology, and Anglo-American ethnology and anthropology. Except for tracing a chain of ideas in the context of a definition, no attempt is made to give the historical development of concepts. (Terms having obvious sociological connotations can be found in Gould's *Dictionary of the Social Sciences* [A.1.e:4] or Mitchell's *Dictionary of Sociology* [H.1.d:1].) Hultkrantz notes that "preference is given to the terms created by European regional ethnologists, and the space devoted to their definitions is relatively larger than that reserved for those of their American colleagues." The more functionally inclined British and American anthropology, particularly after 1945, has created a mass of new and often clearly delimited concepts. In this area, the contributions of the Anglo-Americans predominate, "as they are much more concerned with problems of definition." In general, after a short definition, each article has an account, with quotations, of how authorities have treated the term. Authorities are listed for each of the 400-odd definitions, and at the end there is a list of the approximately 500 works consulted. For example, the definition of *acculturation* consists of seven pages of text, including its etymology; French, Spanish, German, and Swedish equivalents; and a brief definition. The bulk of the article, however, comprises a discussion of the use of the term by 35 authorities. Other important terms are given similar treatment; thus the volume can function as a subject bibliography as well as a dictionary. Charles Winick's *Dictionary of Anthropology* (1956) (3) contains some 7,000 entries, including biographies. Coverage is not even, but definitions of special terms not found in general dictionaries are included. The *Encyclopedia of Religion and Ethics* (A.1.e:9) is an important source of information on many aspects of anthropology. (The words *religion* and *ethics* are used in their broadest sense by the editors of the encyclopedia.) The *New Catholic Encyclopedia* (A.1.e:11) and *Encyclopedia Judaica* (A.1.e:12) cover a wide range of secular as well as religious topics, usually from a nondogmatic point of view.

B.1.e   Handbooks and Yearbooks

The *Ethnographic Atlas* (1967) (1) presents ethnographic data in a codified format on 862 tribes and ethnic groups listed according to precise geographical location. The data was obtained from the Human Relations Area Files (I.3:1). Cultures are di-

vided into 412 culture areas or "clusters." Each culture is assigned an alphanumeric identification code and listed according to
cluster; coded tables, which make up most of the volume, indicate cultural features of the groups. Information includes population at the time of the survey, subsistence, type of family and
social structure, patterns of authority and politics, inheritance, linguistic affiliation, settlement and demographic pattern, and types
of games and houses. Another feature is the relationship of the
Atlas to the quarterly, *Ethnology* (1962–) (2). Included among
the information for each ethnic group in the *Atlas* are references
to the issues of *Ethnology* having pertinent bibliographies. In addition, issues of *Ethnology* often contain supplements to sections of
the *Ethnographic Atlas.*[2]

The *Outline of World Cultures* (1963) (3) is a guide to many
cultures, whereas the *Ethnographic Atlas* covers a limited number.
Both works use a combination of letters and numbers to identify
cultures. Unfortunately, the codes differ in the two volumes, making it difficult to move from one work to the other. There is, however, a useful "Concordance of the *Ethnographic Atlas* and the
Outline of World Cultures" (1969) (4), which has four approaches: the first lists societies alphabetically, the second is arranged according to the code used in the *Ethnographic Atlas,* the
third according to the code of the *Outline of World Cultures,* and
the fourth according to *Ethnographic Atlas* serial numbers. A +
symbol in the *Outline of World Cultures* code, indicates that material exists in the Human Relations Area Files on that culture.
The *Outline of Cultural Materials* (1967) (5) (designed to be used
jointly with Murdock's *Outline of World Cultures*) describes the
subject system on which the HRAF is based. All cultural and
background information on world cultures is divided into 79 major
divisions and 619 minor divisions. This work also contains a brief
history of the files, the theoretical basis of their organization, a
complete list of the categories that are used in marking or analyzing material, and definitions of these categories. The *HRAF Source
Bibliography* (1969–) (6) is a listing, with annual supplements,
of all books, articles, and manuscripts used as sources for material
appearing in the Human Relations Area Files. It is arranged by
culture group, and indexed by author and by area. A listing by
author of the books and articles deposited in the HRAF, a feature
not previously available, is one of its merits. Of greater significance
is the knowledge that all items in other languages deposited in
HRAF have been translated into English. (Over 50,000 pages of
translations from sixteen different languages are in HRAF.) Complete texts of all books and articles deposited in HRAF are in
category 116 for a given culture group; occasionally this means

finding a book or article that is not listed in your college library; however, many libraries list books deposited in HRAF in their card catalogs.

Textor's *Cross-Cultural Summary* (1967) (7), related to the *Ethnographic Atlas* (1), is a large computer-written volume containing information on those features of cultures which are common or overlap with others. Information is arranged dichotomously (e.g., "slavery present, slavery absent") and the work selectively utilizes thirty-eight sources of coded cross-cultural data for the 412 cultures in the *Ethnographic Atlas*. Numerous significant tests have been published between sets of many of the variables found in the book, which is difficult to use but important for the vast amount of information it contains.

B.I.f Methodological Works

The Royal Anthropological Institute's *Notes and Queries on Anthropology* (1951) (1) is a handbook of anthropological method, giving concise descriptions of the various factors and elements of the social life of non-Western peoples and including definitions of technical terms. There are four main sections: physical anthropology, social anthropology, material culture, and archaeology. Adams and Preiss's *Human Organization Research: Field Relations and Techniques* (1960) (2) is a collection of 32 papers and a bibliography devoted to aspects of research in applied anthropology. Among the topics are "Internal Research Group Relations" and "Researcher-Client Relations" in part 1 and "Categories of Data Analysis" and "Field Research Techniques" in part 2.

A discussion by J. W. Bennett and Gustav Thaiss of over 100 items in periodicals and books concerned with methods of research in anthropology appears in Glock's *Survey Research in the Social Sciences* (1967) (3) and in *A Handbook on Method in Cultural Anthropology* (B.2.g:1). Part 1 discusses literature on "Survey Research and Holistic Depiction," in which the purpose is to obtain information on single cultures. Part 2 discusses "Methods in Combination," with attention directed to literature on community, urbanization, applied anthropology, national character, multiethnic field research, and socialization. In part 3, marginal applications, analytic comparison, and systematic ethnography are examined. There is an author index. P. C. W. Gutkind annotates 348 works on anthropological field-work methods in *Anthropologists in the Field* (1967) (4). Among the titles in Holt, Rinehart & Winston's authoritative Studies in Anthropological Method series are Collier's *Visual Anthropology* (1967), Gudschinsky's *How to Learn an Unwritten Language* (1967), Henry and Saberwal's

Stress and Response in Fieldwork (1969), Hsu's *The Study of Literate Civilizations* (1969), Langness's *The Life History in Anthropological Science* (1965), Schusky's *Manual for Kinship Analysis* (1965), Spier's *Surveying and Mapping: A Manual of Simplified Techniques* (1970), and Williams's *Field Methods in the Study of Culture* (1967). Consult the firm's catalog in *PTLA* (A.1.b:30) for other volumes in the series. "Social Science Methodology: A Bibliography of Studies" is a biennial feature of *Social Science Information* (1962–) (5). Arranged in a detailed classification scheme, it lists consecutively, from issue to issue, articles and books in all languages. Among the main headings are general studies, basic orientations, observation—data collection, types of analysis, analytical tools, decisions analysis, and forecasting methods. Other regular bibliographical listings in *Social Science Information* are under the following headings: interdisciplinary relations in the social sciences, surveys of research in social science, studies concerning concepts in the social sciences, and the sociology of the social sciences (an international bibliography). The coverage is international; items are arranged according to detailed classification schemes; and there are some annotations.

Section 2

B.2.a   Archaeology

The most comprehensive bibliography of archaeology is the *COWA* [Council for Old World Archaeology] *Surveys and Bibliographies* (1957–) (1). Issues appear biennially for each of 22 areas and include reports on the archaeology of the area from paleolithic to recent times. Areas 1–8 cover Europe; 9–14, Africa; 15–20, Asia; and 21–22, the Pacific Islands and Australia. Each area report covers the previous two or three years of archaeological activity and includes an annotated bibliography of important books and articles, along with a survey of current work. Occasionally an article surveying a large number of recent archaeological studies appears in *Biennial Review of Anthropology* (B.1.b:7). (For example, Richard B. Woodbury surveyed 187 studies in New World archaeology in the 1961 volume.)

Cottrell's *Concise Encyclopedia of Archaeology* (1971) (2) contains brief articles on such topics as civilizations, cities, tombs, customs, discoveries, ancient languages, terms, methodology, and biographies. Although there are few references to Greece and Rome, coverage is worldwide, ranging from the antiquity of the Far East, Europe, and the Middle East to the pre-Columbian cultures of Latin America. The volume is illustrated and has a brief bibliography. A similar work, Bray and Trump's *American Heritage Guide to Archaeology* (1970) (3), is considered more technical, though entries are briefer. For archaeological methodology, see Heizer and Graham's *Guide to Field Methods in Archaeology* (1967) (4).

B.2.b Art

The *Encyclopedia of World Art* (1959–68) (1) is a multivolume work that includes long articles by scholars, large bibliographies, and excellent colored plates of art and related subjects of non-Western peoples. This is the only work in English providing such extensive coverage.

B.2.c Ethnomusicology

Using a narrative format, Nettl's *Reference Materials in Ethnomusicology* (1967) (1) directs attention to the problem of finding and evaluating information in ethnomusicology and attempts to show alternative ways of obtaining information where no research exists. Emphasis is on primitive cultures and advanced oriental cultures. The volume includes discussions of the following: surveys of ethnomusicology, primitive music, oriental music, folk music, and area surveys; techniques of research, such as collecting, archival matters, and transcribing; elements of music, such as melody, scale, rhythm, and structure; and instruments. In the final section special aspects of music such as origins, distribution and cartography, and authenticity receive attention. Collections, periodicals, directories, and bibliographies are noted. Duckles's *Music Reference and Research Materials* (1967) (2) includes briefly annotated citations of selected bibliographies of ethnomusicology and of ethnic and folk-music recordings.

B.2.d Folklore, Mythology, and Religion

Internationale Volkskundliche Bibliographie [International folklore bibliography] (1939–) (1) is an extensive work covering all regions and periods. The quarterly *Abstracts of Folklore Studies* (1963–) (2) consists of about 1,000 abstracts per volume of articles from all over the world. In addition, about 80 books are annotated. Each issue has an index, and there is a cumulative index for the volume in the winter issue. The latter superseded "Annual Folklore Bibliography" in the *Journal of American Folklore* (1954–62) (3), a comprehensive listing with descriptive annotations of books, parts of books, and articles. A "Folklore Bibliography" has appeared annually since 1938 in the *Southern Folklore Quarterly* (1938–) (4). It is a selective, briefly annotated list of over 1,000 books and articles arranged by subject, with an author index. Stith Thompson's *Motif-Index of Folk Literature* (1955–58) (5), subtitled "A Classification of Narrative Elements in Folk Tales, Ballads, Myths, Fables, Medieval Romances, Exempla, Fabliaux, Jest-Books, and Local Legends," is a source of information (including bibliographies) for intensive research on themes in folklore.

The *Funk and Wagnalls Dictionary of Folklore, Mythology, and Legend* (1949) (6) has entries ranging from brief definitions to review articles dealing with national folklore or subjects of central importance. Diehl's *Religions, Mythologies, Folklores* (1962) (7) is an annotated bibliography with a classified arrangement and author and title indexes. It covers selected literature on religious beliefs, mythologies, and folklores of all cultures. The introduction of the seven-volume encyclopedia *Man, Myth, and Magic* (1970–) (8) states: "The last hundred years have been the most flourishing period in the history of magic and occultism in the West since the 17th century. They have also seen the rise of the modern study of comparative religion, the modern interpretation of mythology, the attempt to test objectively such phenomena as ghosts and telepathy, and the application of modern psychology to beliefs about the supernatural. These new lights in the darkness provide the basis of our approach." The contributors are well-known authorities. Included in the broad aspects explored are "The Secret Forces," "World of Witches," and "Dawn of Belief." Over 800 articles range from "Aberdeen Witches" and "Acupuncture" to "Werewolf" and "Zulu." The book is profusely illustrated with black-and-white and colored drawings and photographs. Most articles have a brief bibliography. Cross-references are given, and there is an index.

The *Larousse Encyclopedia of Mythology* (1959) (9) has chapters on prehistoric, Egyptian, Assyro-Babylonian, Phoenician, Greek, Roman, Celtic, Teutonic, Slavonic, Finno-Ugric, ancient Persian, Indian, Chinese, Japanese, American, Oceanian, and black African mythology. The volume is illustrated with photographs and reproductions of aboriginal works of art. There is an index of names only. *Mythology of All Races* (1916–32) (10) is a comprehensive and authoritative twelve-volume collection of major mythologies, including ancient Greek and Roman, Eddic, Celtic, Slavic, Finno-Ugric, Siberian, Semitic, Indian (Hindu), Iranian, Armenian, African, Chinese, Japanese, Oceanic, North American Indian, Latin American, Egyptian, and Indochinese. The aim is to recount typical myths of various cultures, with an emphasis on facts rather than theories. Illustrations and extensive bibliographies are included, and the bibliographies feature references to articles on related topics in the *Encyclopedia of Religion and Ethics* (A.1.e:9). Volume 13 is an index. *Bulfinch's Mythology* (1970) (11) and *Lippincott's Biographical Dictionary* (A.1. d:4) are older, standard works featuring brief definitions of myths and mythological figures. Watt's *Modern Reader's Guide to Religions* (1965) (12) and Adams's *Reader's Guide to the Great Religions* (1965) (13) have chapters of interpretive descriptions of and bibliographies on the world's religions. Sir James Frazer's *The Golden Bough* (1907–35) (14), the *Aftermath* supplement (1936), and the abridged *New Golden Bough* (1959) (15) are sources of information and bibliography on primitive religion, especially the detailed index volume. The *Aftermath* supplement consists of material gathered from post-1915 studies, while the single-volume abridgment, the *New Golden Bough,* edited by Theodor Gaster, attempts to bring the original work up to date. Although some of Frazer's theories have been superseded, the material on primitive cultures is still useful, especially if the *New Golden Bough* is used as a guide. In the latter volume, a new division of subtopics has been created, and the paragraphs have been numbered to make the original easier to use.

B.2.e Linguistics

Winchell (A.1.b:13) discusses histories and handbooks in English, Germanic, Latin American, Slavic, Turkic, East African, and Oceanian linguistics. Compilations of linguistic studies appear in the annual *MLA Bibliography* (1921–) (1), though it is primarily concerned with modern literature throughout the world. Citations to books and articles in all languages are arranged in it by linguistic type, and then by subdivision, with authors' names indexed. Festschriften and other collections are listed in the first division of the *MLA Bibliography;* "F" numbers in brackets following a title refer to these items. There are no annotations, but the bibliography is noted for the small time lag between publication and listing of items. The *MLA Bibliography* has for years been issued as a supplement to *PMLA,* the journal of the Modern Language Association, and generally it has been the practice of academic libraries in the United States and Canada to bind the bibliographical supplement with the issues of *PMLA*. To make the *MLA Bibliography* more accessible, however, many of these libraries purchase an extra set of the bibliographies. A much larger number of items appears annually in *Bibliographie linguistique* (1939–) (2). In addition to bibliographical citations of books and periodical articles in all languages, it features brief annotations, reference to book reviews when available (including reviews of books noted in previous volumes), and the notation of an ab-

stract of an item in such abstract services as *African Abstracts*. The
index of authors' names is the same as in the *MLA Bibliography*.

B.2.f   Physical Anthropology

Krogman's *Bibliography of Human Morphology* (1941) (1) is
a listing of about 10,000 items, including books and articles from
periodicals. Since 1946 Krogman has edited the current literature
on physical anthropology in *Biological Abstracts* (1926–) (2).

B.2.g   Social and Cultural Anthropology

Social and cultural anthropology focuses on behavioral characteristics of humans, either from a "holistic" context (studying the
whole culture) or from a "cross-cultural" standpoint (comparing
features of one culture with those of others). There is a brief article and bibliography surveying the main features of ethnohistory
—history of the approach; sources and methods (written documents, oral traditions, field work); ethnohistory and anthropology
—within the main article "History" in the *International Encyclopedia of the Social Sciences* (A.1.e:2). Ethnohistory "has come
to mean the historical study of any non-European peoples before
and after European contact" (vol. 6, p. 440). The following article "Culture History"—"a subdivision of general history that is
concerned with the historical development of nonliterate peoples,
past and present"—covers general methodology as well as specific
methods such as verbal evidence and archaeology.

A Handbook of Method in Cultural Anthropology (1970) (1),
edited by Raoul Naroll and Ronald Cohen, includes social as well
as cultural anthropology. The volume is oriented "toward theory—
testing and theory—construction, rather than the analysis and presentation of ethnographic facts." This approach implies "a concern
with problems that tend to promote explanation applicable across
cultures." The volume is arranged in seven parts: general introduction, general problems, the field-work process, models of ethnographic analysis, comparative approaches, problems of categor-
ization, and special problems of comparative method. Specialists
cover the various kinds of methodological problems considered the
most important in cross-cultural research. Part 1 begins with general issues of epistemology, then narrows to problems of causality,
correlation, literature criticism, and "the old but still important
questions of diachronic versus synchronic analysis." The next focus is upon field-work methodology and problems of comparative
analysis. Part 2 is concerned with techniques of causal analysis.
Part 3 analyzes the uses of field work, with emphasis on the strategy of deriving theoretical generalization from empirical investiga-

tion. Part 4 considers sets of categories relevant to data on a special sector of social and cultural life, attempting to arrive at a compromise between a "holistic descriptive approach" and "specific data collection directed at theoretical goals." Leading comparative approaches are discussed in part 5, with particular attention to the methods evolved in the Human Relations Area Files (I.3:1) and related works such as the *Outline of World Cultures* (B.1.e:3), the *Ethnographic Atlas* (B.1.e:1), and Textor's *Cross-Cultural Summary* (B.1.e:7). Part 6 focuses on special problems of comparative method. At the end of each paper is a bibliography of the works discussed. Some of the papers are illustrated with tables. There are indexes of names and subjects.

Felix M. Kessing's *Culture Change* (1953) (2), *Current Sociocultural Change Literature* (H.2.b:1), and Ethel Albert and Clyde Kluckhohn's *Selected Bibliography on Values, Ethics, and Aesthetics in the Behavioral Sciences and Philosophy, 1920–1958* (1959) (3) are bibliographies worth consulting, and the *International Bibliography of Social and Cultural Anthropology* (B.1.b:4) and other works mentioned in section B.1.b should not be overlooked. In addition, substantial numbers of studies are reviewed in sections entitled "Culture Change" and "Social Organization" in volumes of the *Biennial Review of Anthropology* (B.1.b:7).

Part C

Demography

Long considered a subfield of sociology or (in its spatial aspects) a subfield of geography, demography has recently established itself as a distinct discipline. Centers for demographic research have sprung up all over the world; university departments of demography and centers for family planning and miscellaneous population studies have begun to appear in many parts of North America and in various European and Asian countries; and numerous journals, bibliographies, and other specialized demographic publications are now being issued in scores of countries.

Section I

C.1.a Atlases

There are few general atlases devoted solely to population distributions and demographic characteristics of human groups. The most useful is the Russian *Atlas narodov mira* [Atlas of the peoples of the world] (1964) (1), which has more than 100 color plates showing the locations and population densities of over 900 ethnic groups. Most of the maps are drawn on a scale of 1 to 10 million; larger-scale maps are used for small regions of great ethnic complexity. Language is the principal basis for the groupings. Text and legends are in Russian, but English equivalents of many names are provided in the index, and an English key is available. Statistical tables are included. Somewhat less handy is the loose-leaf *World Atlas of Population* (1956) (2), which, based on the first so-called world population census, shows the distribution of population in about the year 1950. Small-scale dot maps show the distribution of population for each major region of the world; choropleth maps show the population densities of other regions. Also included are statistical tables and a series of population pyramids depicting population structure by sex and age groupings for selected countries. There are introductions to each section in English and German.

For the student interested primarily in macro-regional population densities and distributions, the population maps in the *Aldine University Atlas* (A.1.a:10) and *Goode's World Atlas* (A.1.a:9) will suffice. Both use a sequence of graduated colors and shades to produce an excellent visual effect.

Two world atlases dealing with the principal diseases of mankind should be noted. The American Geographical Society's "Atlas of Diseases" (1950–55) (3), issued in separate sheets, includes maps of world or macro-regional distributions of such diseases as bubonic plague, leprosy, cholera, malaria, and yellow fever; in some instances distributions of the vectors of the disease are shown. Authoritative notes by Dr. Jacques M. May accompany each map. A more thorough and comprehensive atlas, which deals with historical as well as contemporary disease patterns, is the *Welt-Seuchen Atlas* (1952–56) (4). Its purpose is to indicate relationships between man and his diseases and the physical environment. G. Melvyn Howe's *National Atlas of Disease Mortality in the United Kingdom* (1963) (5) is easily the most outstanding among atlases limited to particular countries. Maps showing patterns of mortality from cancer, failure of the respiratory and circulatory systems, diabetes, and suicides are among those represented in the atlas.

C.I.b   General Bibliographies

Although the student will find such sources as the *International Encyclopedia of the Social Sciences* (A.1.e:2), the *International Bibliography of Sociology* (H.1.b:2), and the *Bibliographie géographique internationale* (E.1.b:6) of considerable help in tracking down demographic materials, the most useful single source is the quarterly *Population Index* (1935–) (1), which is worldwide in coverage. All items included—books, monographs, articles, and official reports—are briefly annotated. The arrangement is topical, and the 19 sections range from "general population studies and theory" through such subjects as "mortality" and "international migration" to "official statistical publications." Also included are author and geographical indexes, short articles on demographic subjects, and a variety of statistical notes. An eight-volume cumulation covering 1935 to 1968, with cumulative author and geographical indexes, was issued in 1971. The *Social Sciences Citation Index* (A.1.b:6) includes articles on demography.

The monthly *Current Publications in Population/Family Planning* (1969–) (2) selectively lists and annotates a variety of recently published works on demography, especially those connected with family planning and population control.

Of the one-volume bibliographies, the best is probably Hope T. Eldridge's *The Materials of Demography* (1959) (3), though it is now very much outdated. The work draws heavily on the *Population Index,* although the information is greatly simplified and condensed. A feature of great value is the summary listing before each chapter of items included in it. Many of the items are serials, annotations for which are lengthy when important articles and issues are specifically cited. An author index completes the volume. For regional studies of population dealing with such subjects as distribution, density, and demographic characteristics, a most valuable source is Wilbur Zelinsky's *Bibliographic Guide to Population Geography* (1962) (4). This lists some 2,563 items, more than 2,200 of which deal with major regions and countries of the world. The November 1969 issue of *Population Bulletin* (5), "A Sourcebook on Population," lists over 400 books, reports, and serials on population and related subjects.

C.1.c Biographical Dictionaries and Directories

There is as yet no biographical dictionary or directory devoted solely to demographers. For information on living or recently deceased demographers, consult such works as *American Men and Women of Science* (A.1.d:15) and the various professional directories cited in the parts of this book on sociology and geography. C. P. Hutchinson's *The Population Debate* (1967) (1), which deals with population literature of the period before 1900, includes a number of brief biographical sketches of early workers in the field, while James Bonar's *Theories of Population from Raleigh to Arthur Young* (1931) (2) deals with the main English demographers of the seventeenth and eighteenth centuries.

C.1.d Encyclopedias and Dictionaries

No specialized encyclopedia and few dictionaries of demography have appeared to date, but as with most other social sciences, excellent starting points are the *Encyclopedia of the Social Sciences* (A.1.e:1) and the *International Encyclopedia of the Social Sciences* (A.1.e:2). Both works have articles on demographic and population topics, though understandably, in view of the enormous growth of the subject between the 1930s and the 1960s, the information in the *International Encyclopedia* is much more inclusive. A group of articles under the general heading "Population" summarizes the scope and status of the field, while additional articles are provided on such subjects as census, eugenics, life tables, and migration.

Hannes Hyrenius's *Demographic Dictionary in Interlingua* (1969) (1) brings together all the demographic terms included in the *Multilingual Demographic Dictionary* issued originally by the United Nations and the International Union for the Scientific Study of Population; after coding these, it defines them in Interlingua, the language developed primarily for scientific communication.

Brief articles on population topics and useful definitions of many demographic terms are in Mitchell's *Dictionary of Sociology* (H.1. d:1), the *Dictionary of Geography* (E.1.d:9), and the *Glossary of Geographical Terms* (E.1.d:8).

C.1.e Handbooks and Yearbooks

Apart from statistical yearbooks, such as the United Nations' *Demographic Yearbook* (C.1.g:1), there are only a few useful items to be noted here. The *European Demographic Information Bulletin* (1970–) (1), issued in a number of parts annually, aims to be "more than an inter-European clearing house of information and documentation." It includes abstracts arranged by subject, articles on demographic subjects, reports on demographic trends and on activities of demographic organizations, and official announcements. Wladimir and Emma S. Woytinsky's *World Population and Production: Trends and Outlook* (1953) (2) is a compendium of information dealing with many aspects of population, natural resources, and production. Its sections cover man and his environment, world needs and resources, agriculture, energy and mining, and manufactures. There are author and subject indexes and a lengthy bibliography.

C.1.f Methodological Works

A good starting place for any discussion of demographic methodology is the *International Encyclopedia of the Social Sciences*

(A.1.e:2). Also useful is Frank Lorimer's article on demography in Hauser and Duncan's *The Study of Population* (1959) (1), which deals succinctly with the history of the subject and its evolution from seventeenth-century political arithmetic to modern demographic theory and methods and actuarial analysis. Major methodological works are cited in a selected bibliography. *Introduction to Malthus,* edited by D. V. Glass (1953) (2), has, in addition to some excellent scholarly articles, an extensive bibliography of books, pamphlets, and articles on the population question published in Britain from 1793 to 1880 and reprints of two of Malthus's works. Sydney H. Coontz's study, *Population Theories and the Economic Interpretation* (1957) (3), is a detailed review of important population theories since the time of Malthus.

Another excellent reference source is *Methods and Materials of Demography* (1971) (4), issued by the Bureau of the Census and prepared in part by the Office of Population, United States Agency for International Development. It is a two-volume work of some 900 pages, "intended to serve both as texts for courses in demographic methods and as references for professional workers who use population data." "Social Science Methodology: A Bibliography of Studies," a regular section in *Social Science Information* (B.1.f:5), should also be consulted.

C.1.g   Statistics Sources

Although census and other population statistics leave much to be desired in reliability and coverage, a great variety of statistical material on demography is available. The major international source is the United Nations' *Demographic Yearbook* (1949–) (1), which provides statistics for more than 200 countries and dependencies, compiled from official, semiofficial, and other sources. Statistical tables on world population, birthrates, infantile mortality, general mortality, life expectancy, and marriage and divorce are among the main contents. It should be noted that there is a two-to-three-year time lag in publication, so that statistics are at least that much out of date. The *Statistical Yearbook* (I.1.g:3) contains similar but less comprehensive information on population. The U.N. quarterly, *Population and Vital Statistics* (1953–) (2), is of great value for a variety of statistical information, as is the World Health Organization's *World Health Statistics Annual* (1950–) (3). Volume 1 of this work gives demographic information for many countries and territories; volumes 2 and 3 cover diseases, vaccinations, health personnel, and other such information. The *World Population Data Sheet* (1962–) (4), published annually by the Population Reference Bureau, is based on estimates provided by the Population Division of the United Nations and other official and semiofficial bodies.

Official census materials are listed in the *International Population Census Bibliography* (1965–68) (5), issued in seven volumes. The first six cover major world regions: Latin America and the Caribbean, Africa, Oceania, North America, Asia, and Europe; the seventh is a supplement for 1968. The work is limited to population censuses, but where other types of statistical materials (for example, on housing or education) are compiled as part of such censuses, these are also included. Materials are arranged alphabetically by country and chronologically for each country. Brief information on recent censuses is provided in Harold Fullard's *Geographical Digest* (E.1.e:2). The International Labor Office's *Census Publications, 1945–1954* (1955) (6) is useful for the period it covers. Methods for the taking of census and vital statistics operations are examined in two United Nations publications, the three-volume *Handbook of Population Census Methods* (1958) (7) and the *Handbook of Vital Statistics Methods* (1958–59) (8).

A valuable one-volume work, Keyfitz and Flieger's *World Population: An Analysis of Vital Data* (1968) (9), gives demographic statistics of historical and recent time periods for countries and territories with adequate data. An unusual feature is the computer analyses that provide indices of population processes and trends. Volume 1 of Kingsley Davis's *World Urbanization, 1950–1970* (1969–72) (10) contains data for three dates—1950, 1960, and 1970. The work is invaluable for the study of rural and urban populations, the size of cities, and indicators of urbanization and change. Volume 2 analyzes much of the raw data provided in volume 1, and considers changes in population distribution and future trends in world urbanization. Volume 1 of the projected multivolume *International Historical Statistics* (1968) (11) deals with active population and its structure. The text provides statistics for all countries and territories for which census materials are available, and for each individual census.

Section 2

C.2.a   Population Dynamics

Raymond Pearl's 1937 Heath Clark lectures, published under the title *The Natural History of Population* (1939) (1), represent an important contribution to the literature on human fertility. The work has an extensive bibliography. Trends in fertility are considered by Ronald Freedman in "The Sociology of Human Fertility:

A Trend Report and Bibliography" (1961–62) (2) and by a Milbank Memorial Fund study, *Thirty Years of Research in Human
Fertility: Retrospect and Prospect* (1959) (3). A companion
work, *Trends and Differentials in Mortality* (1956) (4), surveys
trends in mortality in both developed and underdeveloped countries, and a 1962 population bulletin of the United Nations, *The
Situation and Recent Trends of Mortality in the World* (C.1.b:5),
provides a detailed statistical analysis.

Research in marriage and the family is dealt with in Aldous
and Hill's *International Bibliography of Research in Marriage and
the Family* (H.2.a:1) and Mogey's *Sociology of Marriage and
Family Behavior, 1957–1968* (H.2.a:2). The regional arrangement of annotated items in the latter makes it a particularly useful
research tool.

C.2.b Migration

The literature on migration, particularly international migration, is especially rich, and numerous bibliographies and statistical
reference works are available. One of the best is J. J. Mangalam's
*Human Migration: A Guide to Migration Literature in English,
1955–1962* (1968) (1). The volume includes more than 2,000
items arranged in three sections: (1) articles, chapters of books,
and dissertations; (2) books and reports; and (3) material included in or listed in *Industry and Labor, International Labor Review,* and *Population Index.* In the first section, items are annotated and the major variables of each investigation are listed in the
subject index.

Although focusing mainly on the United States, *A Report on
World Population Migrations* (1956) (2) includes two lengthy
bibliographies with many items of wider interest. The first, "An
Introductory Bibliography for the History of American Immigration, 1607–1955," has sections on various ethnic groups, while
the second, "An Annotated Bibliography on the Demographic,
Economic, and Sociological Aspects of Immigration," has sections
on international migration, various national groups, immigration
control, and immigration policy. Brinley Thomas's *International
Migration and Economic Development: A Trend Report and Bibliography* (1961) (3) considers some of the economic implications of migration, while Ann E. Larimore's *World Urbanization
and Urban Migration: An Annotated Bibliography* (1969) (4)
covers yet another special aspect of migration.

Statistical information on international migration is included in
Walter F. Willcox's *International Migrants* (1929–31) (5). Published on behalf of the International Labor Office by the National
Bureau of Economic Research in 1929 and 1931, this two-volume

work is a mine of information on the period prior to 1924. Volume 1 contains statistics on immigration and emigration for the main countries of the world, dating from the beginning of each country's records through 1924, together with some tables of international movements. Volume 2 is a collection of interpretive studies on migration movements and other aspects of migration.

Two journals which include much useful bibliographic information, including reviews and abstracts, are *International Migration* (1961–) (6) and *International Migration Review* (1964–) (7). The *International Migration Review* annually contains references (often annotated) to some 500 articles, dissertations, books, and parts of books on interdisciplinary studies of sociological, demographic, historical, and legislative aspects of migration movements. Statistical data of migrant groups throughout the world are also given.

C.2.c Population Pressure and World Resources

One of the most useful bibliographic sources on population pressure and world resources is the Stanford Research Institutions's *Human Resources and Economic Growth: An Annotated Bibliography on the Role of Education and Training in Economic and Social Development* (1963) (1). The majority of the items listed are in English. Arthur Hazelwood's *The Economics of Underdeveloped Areas: An Annotated Reading List of Books, Articles, and Official Publications* (1959) (2) and its sequel, *The Economics of Development: An Annotated List of Books and Articles Published 1958–1962* (1964) (3), include many relevant items on population pressure and world resources.

C.2.d Population Policies and Population Control

Numerous bibliographic works on aspects of population control and policy, particularly family planning, contraception, and abortion, have appeared in recent years. David L. Kasdon's *International Family Planning, 1966–1968: A Bibliography* (1969) (1) contains 217 abstracts of books and articles, listed by author, with subject and country indexes, as well as a list of 404 journals searched. The U.N.'s *Family Planning, International Migration, and Urbanization in ECAFE Countries* (1968) (2) focuses attention on population trends and family planning. Books, articles, and reports are listed.

Two bibliographies by Christopher Tietze on fertility control are important sources. *Selected Bibliography of Contraception: 1940–1960* (1960) (3) and its 1963 supplement cover both medical and sociological literature, and *Bibliography of Fertility Con-*

trol, 1950–65 (1965) (4) examines the medical and sociological literature on such subjects as fertility control, contraception, sterilization, and abortion. Two important bibliographies dealing solely with abortion are Gunnar K. af Geijerstam's *Annotated Bibliography of Induced Abortion* (1969) (5), which includes all major works—monographs, books, and reports—on the subject, and Charles Dollen's *Abortion in Context: A Select Bibliography* (1970) (6), which focuses on books and articles in English published between 1967 and 1969. About 700 items are included, each entered under author and title.

Part D

Economics

Section 1

D.1.a   Atlases

There are several good economic atlases, notably the *Oxford Economic Atlas of the World* (1972) (1). Consult the extensive discussions of atlases in sections A.1.a. and I.1.a.

D.1.b   Bibliographies

Well-developed, inclusive bibliographies cover virtually all aspects of economics, including its international and regional (or

area) aspects. Occasionally, however, academic libraries have only
selected bibliographies.

Bibliographies of Bibliographies. Edwin T. Coman's "Economics" in Downs and Jenkins's *Bibliography: Current State and Future Trends* (B.1.b:1) discusses 104 books, articles, and serials
dealing with bibliographical resources in economics and business.
However, readers should be aware that occasionally the information in this work is incorrect or misleading, and it will often be
necessary to supplement it with other works, especially Peter Melnyk's *Economics* (1). Besterman (A.1.b:1) and the *Bibliographic
Index* (A.1.b:2) are also worth consulting, especially the latter,
since it is continuously updated. Bibliographies are indicated in
the index of the *International Bibliography of Economics* (12)
under the entry "Bibliographical Works and Economic Documentation."

Reference Works. One of the best reference sources is the *Encyclopedia of Business Information Sources* (A.1.b:7). Almost
1,500 reference works and monographs are briefly annotated in
Peter Melnyk's *Economics: Bibliographic Guide to Reference
Books and Information Resources* (1971) (1), with chapters on
"economic systems and the history of economic thought, history
of economic development (including underdeveloped areas), private and public finance, international economics, agricultural and
industrial development, transportation and communication, labor
economics, and (on a highly selective basis) population and statistics, and major reference works in commerce and marketing."
There is a selected list of periodicals and serials of value for research in economics, as well as an index of authors and institutions, titles, and selected subject headings. (Works in business administration have been, for the most park, omitted.) Items from
and on the Western world, particularly the United States, predominate, but some attention is directed to Eastern Europe, Latin
America, Asia, and Africa. In general, each chapter is arranged
as follows: current and retrospective bibliographies, dictionaries,
indexes and abstracts, handbooks and yearbooks, and monographs.
The only drawback is the lack of attention to sources of historical
statistics. Arthur Maltby's *Economics and Commerce* (1968) (2)
is subtitled "The Sources of Information and Their Organization."
Designed as an introduction to the literature of economics for British library-science students, it contains useful descriptions of economic works. Topics covered include literature on the scope of
economic and commercial activity, encyclopedias and dictionaries,
directories and similar reference works, retrospective and current
bibliographies, government publications and the economist, sources

of economics statistics, gaps in economics documentation, and major economic organizations and their work.

The Use of Economics Literature (1971) (3) is perhaps even more useful than Maltby, particularly since more attention is given U.S. and other non-British sources. Edited by John Fletcher, it represents an attempt by librarians and economists to "give economists a guide to what material there is on the various branches of the subject, what is important and valuable, and what level it best serves, what tools are available to assist the researcher in making a more extensive and intensive survey of the literature of his specialized field, and where the material can be found." Chapter 1 discusses British and American libraries with strong economics collections and suggests procedures for a literature search on a new topic. Chapter 2 briefly outlines the organization of libraries. The seven following chapters examine reference works, including bibliographies, periodicals, unpublished papers and theses, British and U.S. government publications, publications of international organizations, and sources of statistics. Finally, fourteen chapters by specialists briefly review such subdivisions of the discipline as the history of economic thought, economic history, mathematical economics, econometric theory and method, economic-development growth and planning, business cycles, short-term economic stabilization, prices and incomes, labor economics and industrial relations, industrial economics, agricultural economics, monetary economics, public finance, international economics, and economic sociology. "These [chapters] are not intended to be comprehensive reviews of the subject, or surveys of the literature, but rather to reflect the author's personal view of that literature, and note the sources of information and bibliographical tools which he has found most useful." Although it suffers from a lack of annotation, E. L. Fundaburk's projected five-volume *Reference Materials and Periodicals in Economics* (1971–) (4) promises to be quite comprehensive. Volume 1, on agriculture, has over 4,800 entries. Other volumes will focus on general economics, general business, industry and commerce, specific industries in mining and manufacturing, and specific industries in the services. "Emphasis in selection was placed upon identifying a wide scope of national materials typical of the types of reference works which have been and are being developed in various countries." Works included range through the seventeenth, eighteenth, and nineteenth centuries, but most attention is placed on the twentieth century. Volumes are arranged in four large divisions. Part 1 consists of bibliographies, catalogs, indexes, abstracts, and digests; part 2, dictionaries, encyclopedias, registers, atlases, almanacs, and biographies; part 3, guides, manuals, statistics sources, and yearbooks. Part 4 comprises a listing of periodical bibliographies, indexes, catalogs, abstracts, and digests, and an alphabetical list of periodicals. There are subject, place-of-publication, author-and-publisher, date-of-publication (arranged chronologically), and abbreviated-title indexes.

General Bibliographies. In addition to Melnyk (1), the *ABS Guide to Recent Publications in the Social Sciences* (A.1.b:8) and the *London Bibliography of the Social Sciences* (A.1.b:5) are worth consulting for selected works in economics. The following works are devoted exclusively to economics. Harvard University's Graduate School of Business Administration issues with the aid of a computer a *CORE Collection* (1970–) (5), a selection of about 1,600 recommended titles. The volume is arranged alphabetically by author in part 1 and by subject in part 2. Although most of the titles focus on the United States, attention is directed to other parts of the world, under such subject headings as agriculture, automation, balance of payments, minorities, and planning. *Business Periodicals Index* (1958–) (6) is an excellent complement to the Harvard *CORE Collection,* although U.S. titles predominate among the 170-odd journals indexed. The range of subjects is indicated by the subtitle: "A Cumulative Subject Index to Periodicals in the Fields of Accounting, Advertising, Banking and Finance, General Business, Insurance, Labor and Management, Public Administration, Taxation, Specific Businesses, Industries and Trades." *Economics Selections: An International Bibliography* (1953–) (7) is a quarterly listing by subject of over 300 new books. The emphasis is on English-language works, but important works in other languages are noted. Each title is briefly annotated and graded to indicate the level for which it is intended. This series was known as *Economics Library Selections* from 1954 to 1965 and as *International Economics Bibliography* in 1966. The editors attempt to include all new books and monographs over sixty pages in length; reprints (including paperbacks) and new editions; bibliographies; reference works; biographies and new journals citing works of interest to economists; books from other disciplines (such as mathematics, statistics, history, and geography); and textbooks. The *Cumulative Bibliography of Economic Books* (*1954/62*–) (8), published in 1965, comprises citations (minus annotations) of *Economics Selections* (known then as *Economics Library Selections*). It is arranged by subject, with an author index. Future cumulations are planned.

The title of the *Journal of Economic Abstracts* was changed to *Journal of Economic Literature* (1962/63–) (9) in March 1969. (Among economic indexes this one lists articles and books with the least time lag between publication and listing.) Before

January 1969, the *Journal of Economic Abstracts* consisted of 300-word abstracts of articles selected from about 150 international economics journals. The abstracts are arranged by journal title; each issue has a subject index, and there is an annual author index. With the change in title, the *Journal of Economic Literature* enlarged its scope to include annotated citations of books in addition to the abstracts of articles. There are ten sections of book classification: general economics, including theory, history, systems; economic growth, development, planning; statistics; monetary fiscal theory and institutions; international economics, administration, business finance, and so forth; industrial organization, technological change, industry studies; agriculture; national resources; manpower, labor, population; and welfare programs, consumer economics, urban and regional economics. Over 800 books (including reprints), institutional reports, and government publications are critically annotated, with an indication of the intended audience. The tables of contents of about 170 international journals are reproduced, with abstracted articles designated by large black dots. The articles are arranged according to a more elaborate classification system than that for books, and all articles are listed in the "Subject Index of Articles in Current Periodicals," again with abstracted articles indicated by dots. The selected abstracts, prepared by the authors of the articles, are arranged in the classified system and have been reduced to 100 words. Over 1,200 articles are abstracted annually. In each issue, abstracts are indexed by author, and there is an annual author index for abstracts, but titles are not indexed. The short time lag between publication and listing articles is also a feature of *Social Sciences Citation Index* (A.1.b:6).

The American Economic Association's *Index of Economic Journals* (1886–) (10) is an excellent aid to research, providing an uninterrupted, classified arrangement of the development of the discipline. Eight volumes have appeared, covering material up to 1967, and more are planned. Each volume is in two parts. Part 1 is arranged by subject according to a special classification scheme consisting of twenty-three main classes, with nearly 700 subclasses. Part 2 is a listing of articles alphabetically by author, then chronologically. Thus it is possible to trace articles by a particular economist or on a particular topic over a great many years. As a further aid to finding articles, there are geographical symbols in the left-hand margin of the classified section. (A table of these symbols is inside the back cover.) The industry classification in section 15.5 includes all major studies of each industry (for example, on prices, production, trade, and labor conditions). In two classes, "Economic History" and "General Contemporary Economic Conditions: Policy and Planning," and in some subdivisions of other classes, entries are arranged geographically in order to bring together material on the same area. Accompanying the 1964–65 volume, for the same years, is an *Index of Economic Articles in Collective Volumes* (1964–) (11), covering festschriften, conference reports with individual papers, collected essays (excluding those indexed in the *Index of Economic Journals*), readings in special fields of economics, hearings and studies of congressional committees, and translations of foreign articles. A list of books indexed appears at the beginning of the volume. The format is the same as the *Index of Economic Journals*.

The annual *International Bibliography of Economics* (1955–) (12) is one of the most comprehensive sources. A classified subject arrangement is used. Broad topics covered in pure and applied economics include methods, history of economic thought, economic history, economic activity, organization of production, production (goods and services), prices and markets, money and finance, income and income distribution, demand (use of income), social economics and policy, and public economy and international economics. Each broad topic is subdivided. For example, "Economic Activity" consists of headings for individual nations, arranged by world region, as well as such headings as estimation and forecasting of national income and capital; national capital or wealth; regional planning; and growth, maturity, and stagnation. The editors attempt to include the most significant economic publications, "scientific in character" (except theses, dissertations, and newspaper articles) from all countries and in all languages. About 1,500 journals from all over the world are searched, and each volume contains roughly 8,000 items. There are author and subject indexes. Although items are not annotated, occasionally book reviews are indicated. When an entry is preceded by "Bibl." and a Roman and an Arabic numeral, it indicates a review for a book listed in a preceding volume (meaning that for book reviews later volumes should be consulted as well as the one listing a book).

A specialized bibliography, Albert and Kluckhohn's *Selected Bibliography on Values, Ethics, and Aesthetics in the Behavioral Sciences and Philosophy* (*1920–1958*) (B.2.g:3), contains over 160 briefly annotated citations of books and articles focusing on "values, ethics, and aesthetics" in economics.

Reviews of Research.   Bert F. Hoselitz's *Reader's Guide to the Social Sciences* (A.1.b:9) reviews over 340 monographs on the history and theory of economics, directing attention to the scope of the discipline, early works, mercantilism, scientific economics, national differences, and methodology. Among the features of economic theory described are theory of value and price and theory of production, income and employment, monetary theory, economic fluctuations, and international economics. In the discussion of the application of economic theories, Hoselitz surveys works on agricultural economics, problems of labor and management, entrepreneurship, banking, public finance, planning, and international problems. Finally he focuses on the comparison of the development of economic institutions, or economic history.

A more detailed source of reviews of economics research, the three-volume *Surveys of Economic Theory* (1965–66) (13) is the result of a joint effort of the *American Economic Review* and the *Economic Journal*. Review articles by specialists analyze items on money, interest, and welfare; growth and development; and resource allocation. The first chapter of volume 2 is Harry Johnson's "Monetary Theory and Policy," a survey of 129 titles on the quantity of money in the economic system and monetary policy for the control of this supply to achieve the objectives of general economic policy. In chapter 2, Martin Bronfenbrenner and Franklyn D. Holzman's "Survey of Inflation Behavior" discusses 183 items concerned with "the positive theory of open inflation," including level of employment, rate of growth, and income distribution. In the remaining chapters, G. L. S. Shackle is arbitrarily more selective in choosing 50 titles for discussion of "recent theories concerning the nature and role of interest," and E. J. Mishan covers 250 titles on welfare economics appearing between 1939 and 1959.

Volume 2 includes surveys of the theory of economic growth, comparative advantage and development policy, pure theory of international trade, and regional economics. On the theory of economic growth, F. H. Hahn and R. C. O. Matthews cover over 250 articles and books published during the preceding twenty-five years. The emphasis is on models of economic growth. Hollis B. Chenery analyzes 66 works on resource allocation in underdeveloped economies, considering "the extent to which the allocation principles derived from trade theory and from growth can be reconciled . . . without losing their operational significance"; comparing approaches to the measurement of optimal resource allocation in terms of logical consistency and applicability to different conditions; and discussing procedures of determining investment policy in underdeveloped countries. Jagdish Bhagwati assesses the literature on the theory of international trade, discussing 148 studies focusing on "empirical verification of testable propositions, through measurement of the gains and losses from changes in trade policy and through the formulation of analytical and operational models to assist the developmental planning that is becoming a key characteristic of developing nations." John R. Meyer notes 130 studies of regional economics. Sections deal with defining a region, "policy-problem stimuli," the theoretical foundations of regional economics, and emerging approaches to regional economics.

In volume 3, Herbert A. Simon discusses 71 works on theories of decision making in economics and behavioral science, including such topics as "How Much Psychology Does Economics Need?" "The Utility Functions," and "The Goals of Firms." Robert Dorfman, in a chapter entitled "Operations Research," notes 40 studies. J. R. Hicks analyzes techniques for the preceding fifteen years on linear programming, activity analysis, input-output, and theory of gains. Robert Ferber's "Research on Household Behavior" focuses on 170 studies of theories of spending and saving, determinants of asset holdings and specific expenditures, and decision processes. A. R. Prest and R. Turvey discuss 90 studies of cost-benefit analysis, outlining the development and scope of the subject; the principles of cost-benefit analysis; and the application of cost-benefit techniques to such problems as water-supply projects, transport, land usage, health, education, and research. Additional volumes are planned.

Social Science Information (B.1.f:5) regularly lists surveys of research in economics.

D.1.c Biographical Dictionaries and Directories

Biographical information on deceased economists can be found in *Palgrave's Dictionary of Political Economy* (D.2.a:1) and the *Encyclopedia of the Social Sciences* (A.1.e:1), while the *International Encyclopedia of the Social Sciences* (A.1.e:2) includes articles on a few prominent contemporary economists, as well as those deceased. The *International Encyclopedia of the Social Sciences* includes biographies only of persons distinguished for writing or research; the *Encyclopedia of the Social Sciences* includes persons active in business or government affairs. Section 4.8 of the AEA's *Index of Economic Articles in Collective Volumes, 1964–1965* (D.1.b:11) and *Index of Economic Journals* (D.1.b:10) provide references to biographical material on economists. Biographical information on other individuals associated with economics is noted in other sections of these sources (e.g., bankers in section 9, businessmen in section 14, labor leaders in section 19). Brief biographical information for about 14,000 members of the American Economic Association appears in the *Handbook* (1938–) (1) of the Association. It includes members in academic institutions, government service, business firms, and nonprofit organizations.

D.I.d Encyclopedias and Dictionaries

As an indication of the significance for economists of the *International Encyclopedia of the Social Sciences* (A.1.e:2), four articles appeared in the 1969–70 issues of the *Journal of Economic Literature* (D.1.b:9) reviewing the encyclopedia's treatment of economic history, the history of economic thought, public finance, and international economics. Articles in the early work tend to be historical-descriptive; in the later work, articles are more analytical, and there is considerably less attention to economics. (The principal editors of the original *Encyclopedia* were economists, while the editor of the more recent work is a sociologist.) Articles include economic history (in the larger topic "History"), economic growth, industrialization, entrepreneurship, agricultural history, price history, and business history, as well as such peripheral topics as the history of statistical method, consumer sovereignty, and the study of technology. There are articles on the economic thinkers of the ancient and medieval periods as well as on the mercantilist, physiocratic, socialist, historical, Austrian, and institutional schools of economics. In addition, the work includes surveys of economic theory, statistics, econometrics, international trade, finance, economic growth, population, and social economy. Articles in applied economics discuss government budgeting, budgeting as a political process, public expenditures, taxation, personal and corporate income taxes, local finance, public finance in communist nations, and fiscal policy. Articles on international economics examine central banking, foreign aid, international monetary economics, international trade controls, international economic unions, the international trade of communist countries, and the international monetary system.

The *McGraw-Hill Dictionary of Modern Economics* (1973) (1) includes about 1,300 terms and descriptions of some 200 private, public, and nonprofit organizations and institutions; tables and graphic representations; and references to other sources such as economic texts and significant articles. Terms and organizations are arranged alphabetically in two parts. The suggested sources for more information on each term and organization make this the most useful dictionary of economics. Philip A. S. Taylor's *New Dictionary of Economics* (1966) (2) is a briefer work, but provides definitions of terms, especially European ones, not included in the American dictionary. B. J. Horton stresses that the *Dictionary of Modern Economics* (1948) (3) is designed "primarily for the layman and incidentally for the college student." It provides definitions of terms often encountered "in books and articles on modern economic society, those which contributed to the understanding of the historical factors of the past which have molded the present, and those which are used extensively in business and economic affairs." In addition, there are brief descriptions of factors and institutions that have influenced economics, such as laws having a direct bearing on commercial and industrial activities, Supreme Court decisions, government agencies, and private organizations with economic interests. Also included are brief biographies of prominent economists. Horton is worth consulting if the *McGraw-Hill Dictionary of Modern Economics* does not have the required information.

D.I.e   Handbooks and Yearbooks

The best sources to consult for handbooks and other works with miscellaneous data are the *Encyclopedia of Business Information Sources* (A.1.b:7) and Melnyk (D.1.b:1). The *Financial Times Yearbook: Business Information* (1969–) (1) contains a description of the economic structure of 25 major countries (the United States, West Germany, the United Kingdom, France, Japan, Canada, Italy, the Netherlands, Belgium, Sweden, Switzerland, Australia, Spain, Denmark, South Africa, Norway, Austria, Yugoslavia, Finland, Greece, Ireland, Portugal, New Zealand, Turkey, and Iceland). The emphasis is on the industrial and financial framework in which business operates. Brief information on environmental factors, national income, and financial structure is provided for each country. Separate tables provide comparisons between units, such as the relation of population density to the direct tax burden of salary earners. There is a chapter on the history and characteristics of international economic blocs and organizations, as well as an English-German-French vocabulary of business terms. Sources indicated are mainly official national or international publications.

A recommended purchase is *The Student Economist's Handbook* (1967) (2), by Ralph Andreano et al., which includes instructions in the use of statistics, the library, and government publications, as well as annotated lists of bibliographies, economics journals, and bibliographies of statistical sources arranged by subject.

D.I.f   Methodological Works

Economics Selections (D.1.b:7); the *Index of Economic Journals* (D.1.b:10) and its companion, *Index of Economic Articles* (D.1.b:11); and the *International Bibliography of Economics* (D.1.b:12) contain sections on methodological works. Over 120 articles and books on the application of survey methods to the study of economics are discussed by James N. Morgan in *Survey*

Research in the Social Sciences (B.1.f:3). Morgan states that "new techniques of sampling human populations, eliciting information from them, and analyzing the rich data which result, provide the economist today with information about consumers and businessmen and about the forces that affect their economic difficulties." Morgan's chapter considers such issues as existing methods (household surveys, business behavior); how survey data are used in economics (behavioral theory in economics, short-run changes in behavior, middle-range changes in behavior, use of survey data in structural models, long-term changes, testing economic hypotheses); some methodological-developments problems and prospects; and accuracy and validity of data (methods of analysis, new sources and types of survey data, and so on). Note the description of coverage of studies in methodology in "Social Science Methodology: A Bibliography of Studies," a regular feature of *Social Science Information* (B.1.f:5).

D.1.g   Statistics Sources

Two reference works edited under the supervision of Paul Wasserman have greatly facilitated the finding of statistics: *Statistics Sources* (A.1.h:1) and the *Encyclopedia of Business Information Sources* (A.1.b:7). Consult section A.1.h if information on features of particular statistical reference works is required. The single-volume *Cross-Polity Time-Series Data* (I.1.g:7) contains statistics on a wide range of subjects from the early 1800s to the late 1960s.

Section 2

D.2.a   Economic History

Works introduced in this section trace the development of agriculture, industry, trade, and social conditions. (See section D.2.b for the history of economic thought.) The *Encyclopedia of the Social Sciences* (A.1.e:1) and the *International Encyclopedia of the Social Sciences* (A.1.e:2) are recommended for beginning research in economic history. For example, brief articles (with bibliographies) survey the main features of economic history and business history within the main article "History" in the *International Encyclopedia of the Social Sciences* (A.1.e:2). The somewhat dated *Palgrave's Dictionary of Political Economy* (1925–26) (1) is a three-volume work with articles on economic history, definitions, discussions of economic terms and categories, and the development of economic thought. Treated with the same prudence as *Larned* (F.1.d:3) and the eleventh edition of the *En-*

cyclopaedia Britannica (F.1.d:5), it is a useful research aid. The articles are extensive, arranged alphabetically, and written by specialists. The work deals mainly with Britain, the United States, and English-speaking British colonies. There are many biographical articles, including some for persons (such as Martin Luther and Charles Bradlaugh) only indirectly associated with economics. Survey articles direct attention to the economic thought of the "principal countries of the world": the United States, Austria, Holland, England, France, Germany, Italy, and Spain. Volume 1 of the latest edition contains an appendix updating the original articles. An asterisk (*) after a term in the main body of the set indicates a cross-reference to the appendix for further information. Each article has a bibliography, and there is a detailed table of contents and an index for all volumes.

Melnyk (D.1.b:1) notes several bibliographies of economic history. The *Index to Economic History Essays in Festschriften, 1900–1950* (1953) (2), edited by E. Schleiffer and R. Grandall, is a slight volume arranged by broad subjects, with an index of authors and proper names. In addition to good general bibliographies of history, which treat economic history as one historical theme, the American Economic Association's *Index of Economic Journals* (D.1.b:10), the *International Bibliography of Economics* (D.1.b:12), category 2 of *Technology and Culture* (F.2:4), and the *London Bibliography of the Social Sciences* (A.1.b:5) are excellent sources. For example, chapter 5 of each volume of the AEA's *Index of Economic Journals* (D.1.b:10) is devoted to articles on economic history, including subdivisions such as "Empirical Studies," followed by period and geographical divisions. A list of other history classes and subclasses is noted in the classification schedule of each volume. *Economics Selections* (D.1.b:7) notes titles in economic history, including reprints of older works. Examples of general historical bibliographies worth consulting for items in economic history are the American Historical Association's *Guide to Historical Literature* (F.1.b:2), the *International Bibliography of Historical Sciences* (F.1.b:4), and *Historical Abstracts* (F.1.b:10).

Historical statistics generally are not widely available. Several countries, including the United States, Great Britain, and Canada, have published volumes devoted to their own statistics, and a few works on overseas trade statistics have appeared. These will be discussed in appropriate area parts. Older works recognized as reliable sources are Mulhall's *Dictionary of Statistics* (3), Webb's *New Dictionary of Statistics* (4), and the eleventh edition of the *Encyclopaedia Britannica* (F.1.d:5). The fourth edition of Michael G. Mulhall's *Dictionary of Statistics* (1899) (3) was reprinted in 1969, and can be found in many academic libraries. Over 800 pages long, it provides statistics on a broad range of subjects from A.D. 300 to 1898. A complement to this edition, compiled by A. D. Webb and entitled *New Dictionary of Statistics* (1911) (4), brings the coverage up to 1909. Mulhall's work is arranged alphabetically by subject (although there are two separate alphabetized sections) and includes an extensive subject index, as well as a bibliography of sources. Occasionally, sources of statistics are indicated. Webb's compilation is similar in arrangement to Mulhall's but unlike the latter, indicates sources for all information cited. The eleventh edition of the *Encyclopaedia Britannica* (F.1.d:5) is a good, though little-known, source of statistics. *Cross-Polity Time-Series Data* (I.1.g:7), a compilation of historical statistics produced with the assistance of data-processing techniques, is generally easy to use.

D.2.b Economic Theory (Including the History of Economic Thought)

The focus in this section is the theory of the science of economics, including the history of economic thought, as it affects population, production, value, distribution, money and banking, and international trade. As with economic history, the points at which to begin research are *Palgrave's Dictionary of Political Economy* (D.2.a:1), the eleventh edition of the *Encyclopaedia Britannica* (F.1.d:5), the *Encyclopedia of the Social Sciences* (A.1.e:1), and the *International Encyclopedia of the Social Sciences* (A.1.e:2). Also as with economic history, there are few bibliographies exclusively devoted to the topic. In addition to Melnyk (D.1.b:1), the following are recommended. The critical survey and bibliography by Oreste Popescu (1964) (1) on the historiography of economic thought is arranged in the following parts: "Introduction"; "General History of Economic Thought"; "Stages of the History of Economic Thought"; and "Critical Guide for a General Bibliography of the History of Economics, 1768–1963." Over 170 titles are covered, most of them extensively annotated; the contributions of Blanqui, MacCulloch, Twiss, Cossa, Whittaker, Oser, and Schumpeter are given special attention. This is an invaluable aid to anyone concerned with the history of economic thought.

The scope of H. E. Batson's *Select Bibliography of Modern Economic Theory, 1870–1929* (1930) (2) is limited in that money and banking are excluded and no attempt has been made to cover descriptive economics or economic history. Part 1 is arranged by subject, and each citation is accompanied by a critical annotation; part 2 comprises a listing of the works of prominent English, American, German, and French economists. Significantly, the editors have attempted to make a complete listing of each author's work. The most useful part of the volume is the assessment given each work in part 1. Supplementing Batson is an issue of *Economics Selections,* series 2, "Economic Theory and History of Thought" (1960) (3), a brief, annotated list of 250 selected books in three sections: general treatises, monographs, and collected essays in economic theory; history of economic thought; and methodology. An author index is included. This list is also part of the *Cumulative Bibliography* (D.1.b:8).

D.2.c   Commerce (Industry, Marketing, Transport, and Other Aspects of Applied Economics)

The works discussed in this section are merely a representative selection of those available. Melnyk (D.1.b:1), the *Encyclopedia of Business Information Sources* (A.1.b:7), and Fundaburk (D.1.b:4) list many others. Most of the titles are issued by the Gale Research Company of Detroit, Michigan in their Managament Information Guide series. The complete list, consisting of 21 titles with others projected, can be consulted in the firm's catalog in *PTLA* (A.1.b:30). *Accounting: Information Sources* (1970) (1) surveys over 2,400 reference works, general books, and periodicals on a wide range of U.S. accounting topics, including accounting practices in many types of businesses. There are author, title, and subject indexes. Woy's *Business Trends and Forecasting* (1965) (2) is a selective listing, with annotations, of reference works and monographs on the business cycle, theory and technique of forecasting, and similar topics, as well as sources of important data and bibliographies. A glossary of terms, some with extensive definitions, and an author, title, and key-word index are also included. "Deceptive packaging" and "labels and labeling—laws and regulations" are among the topics covered in Gwendolyn Jones's *Packaging Information Sources* (1967) (3), an annotated guide to the literature, associations, and educational institutions concerned with containers and packaging in the United States. There are author-title and subject indexes. Randle's *Electronic Industries: Information Sources* (1967) (4) is a guide to data sources with general electronic references, followed by basic and introductory sources on specific techniques, devices, and applications including management and production methods. Topics covered in Vara's *Food and Beverage Industries: A Bibliography and Guidebook* (1970) (5), include organization and historical development, agriculture, population, transportation, marketing, advertising and selling, and science and technology in the United States. There is also a chapter on world food-supply problems. Metcalf's *Transportation: Information Sources* (1965) (6), is one of several bibliographies on aspects of transportation; others are noted in section E.2.c. Metcalf covers a wide range of topics and sources in English. The volume is well indexed by author, title, and subject. A specialized aspect of transportation receives attention in Flood's *Research in Transportation* (1970) (7), a bibliography arranged in three parts: legal source materials, legal research procedures, and an annotated list of sources for research. The subtitle of McDermott and Coleman's *Government Regulation of Business Including Antitrust: Information Sources* (1967) (8), "A Comprehensive Annotated Bibliography of Works Pertaining to the Antitrust Division, Department of Justice, and the Major Regulatory Agencies of the Federal Government," lists everything in the book except its author, industry, and government-reports indexes. Volume 8 of the *Universal Reference System* (G.1.b:7) is a bibliography of "Economic Regulation, Business, and Government."

D.2.d   Agricultural and Land Economics

In general, for research concerned with agriculture and land economics such as forestry and mining, most attention should be directed to area studies parts and part I, as most problems in agricultural economics are related to particular geographical regions. The *Encyclopedia of Business Information* (A.1.b:7), Winchell (A.1.b:13), Walford (A.1.b:12), and Melnyk (D.1.b:1) are good sources for general and specialized reference works and bibliographies. Several volumes in Fundaburk (D.1.b:4) apply.

D.2.e   Private and Public Finance (Including Social Economics and Policies)

James Woy's *Investment Information* (1970) (1) is a subject index of sources of financial statistics of U.S. and foreign markets published on a daily, weekly, or monthly basis in the United States. *Ethics in Business Conduct* (1970) (2) is subtitled "Selected References from the Record-Problems, Attempted Solutions, and Ethics in Business Education from 1900 to 1970 in the U.S." There are author and subject indexes. Knox's *Public Finance Information Sources* (1964) (3) is an annotated guide in the broad field of public finance and taxation. Most of the material was published in the early 1960s, but important older studies are also included. Chapter 9, "International Public Finance," covers over 30 areas and countries throughout the world. There are author and subject indexes.

D.2.f   International Economics

Lora Wheeler's annotated bibliography of information sources in *International Business and Foreign Trade* (1968) (1) is arranged in nineteen sections. Attention is directed first to general books on theory, international investment, organization and management, finance, problems associated with exporting and importing, insurance, legal aspects and taxation, personnel, international marketing, and advertising. Next are annotated citations of books concerned with investment conditions, international commerce, regulations, and business customs in some 25 areas and countries throughout the world. Over 100 reference works and services are noted, including handbooks, dictionaries, sources of statistics, and directories. Works on labor conditions in foreign countries are described. Over 30 U.S. government, national, and international organizations assisting in international commerce are discussed. There is an author-title-institution index.

The International Monetary Fund's *International Financial Statistics* (1948–) (2) is a monthly report providing statistics on exchange rates, international liquidity, bank reserves, life insurance, interest, prices, production, international transactions, balance of payments, government finance, and national accounts for each country. Quarterly figures are given for the past five years, and annual figures for the years from 1960. In addition to statistics for each country, tables are provided indicating exchange transactions, the par value of currency loans, gold production, international liquidity, interest rates, exchange rates, commodity prices, and world trade.

D.2.g   Labor Economics

An issue in *Economics Library Selections,* series 2 (D.2.b:3), "The Economics of Labor, Including Social Security and Welfare Benefits" (1961), is an annotated list of over 200 books on such topics as the labor force, unemployment and productivity, and wages and wage theory. This list is also part of the *Cumulative Bibliography* (D.1.b:8). There is an author index. V. L. Allen's *International Bibliography of Trade Unionism* (1968) (1) is a classified bibliography of over 1,600 books and articles in many languages published since 1940 on all the industrialized areas of the world. The classification scheme includes bibliographies, anthologies, research guides, and source material; methodology; general descriptive regional studies, with sections on developing and industrialized economies; histories concerned with international and comparative aspects, as well as individual unions, movements, and ideologies; organization; conflict; and unions in their environment. The latter sections are arranged topically. An author index is included. World labor statistics are well covered in the *Yearbook of Labor Statistics* (1936–) (2). It includes figures for 170 countries or areas on employment, hours of work, consumer-price indexes and retail prices, family-living studies, industrial injuries, unemployment, wages and labor income, social security, industrial disputes, and migration. The *Yearbook* is supplemented by the quarterly *Bulletin of Labor Statistics* (1965–) (3), as well as by the *Supplement to the Bulletin of Labor Statistics* (1965–) (4), issued ten times a year, which provides data available since the latest quarterly *Bulletin*.

Part E

Geography

Section 1

E.1.a Atlases and Gazetteers

Atlases cover every region of the world and virtually every human activity, natural resources, and all other geographical distributions that can be mapped. (See section A.1.a for a discussion of world atlases and relevant area-studies parts of this work for discussions of regional atlases.) A good single-volume descriptive bibliography of twentieth-century maps and atlases is given in *A List of Geographical Atlases in the Library of Congress, with Bibliographical Notes* (A.1.a:12); the British Museum's *Catalog of Printed Maps, Charts, and Plans* (A.1.a:13); and the American Geographical Society's *Index to Maps in Books and Periodicals* (A.1.a:14). A record of the atlases, maps, charts, and globes published each year can be found in the *Bibliographie cartographique internationale* (1938–) (1). As with the better-known *Bibliographie géographique internationale* (E.1.b:6), all citations are in the original language, with annotations in French. The arrangement is by continent and country, and there are subject and author indexes.

While most good atlases provide adequate indexes of place names cited, the student often needs additional information. This may be found in a number of general gazetteers or in various general encyclopedias. The most valuable single-volume listing of place names is the *Times Index-Gazetteer of the World* (1965) (2), which gives location by latitude and longitude. It encompasses close to 350,000 names of towns and other settlements, as well as a great many physical and other geographical features. Far more detailed is the Official Standard Names Gazetteer series (1955–) (3), published by the United States Board on Geographic Names of the Department of the Interior. Over 100 volumes in this series have appeared.

The *Columbia-Lippincott Gazetteer of the World* (1962) (4) is the best single-volume source in English. Also useful is *Webster's Geographical Dictionary* (1967) (5), subtitled "A Dictionary of Names of Places with Geographical and Historical Information and Pronunciations." In addition, the *Encyclopaedia Britannica* (A.1.e:5), the *Encyclopedia Americana* (A.1.e:6), the *Columbia Encyclopedia* (A.1.e:7), and other such works should not be overlooked for this type of information.

E.1.b Bibliographies

Bibliographies of Bibliographies. No satisfactory bibliography of geographical bibliographies exists. The best available is provided by Nordis Felland in Downs and Jenkins's *Bibliography: Current State and Future Trends* (B.1.b:1), a survey of 32 bibliographies —retrospective and current—concerned with geography, its subdivisions, and geographical regions. Richard Gray's *Serial Bibliographies in the Humanities and Social Sciences* (A.1.b:3) lists periodicals regularly or irregularly publishing bibliographies of geographical works. Besterman (A.1.b:1) and the *Bibliographic Index* (A.1.b:2) are other useful sources, especially the latter, which brings to light many bibliographies on minor topics. The Association of American Geographers' *Geographical Bibliography for American College Libraries* (3) cites many general and special bibliographies.

Reference Works. Although out-of-date in a number of respects, J. K. Wright and E. T. Platt's *Aids to Geographical Research* (1947) (1) is one of the most useful guides to geographical research. In addition to hints on geographical research, bibliogra-

phies, serials, atlases, gazetteers, and various other classes of geographical literature are carefully considered and appraised. The
lengthy introductory section is followed by sections dealing with
general, topical (systematic), and regional aids. Chauncy D. Harris's *Bibliographies and Reference Works for Research in Geography* (A.1.b:14) is a valuable supplement to Wright and Platt.
More limited in value is C. S. Minto's *How to Find Out in Geography* (1966) (2), subtitled "A Guide to Current Books in English" and arranged according to the Dewey decimal classification
system. Some 650 books are commented on.

Walford (A.1.b:12), Winchell (A.1.b:13), and White's *Sources
of Information in the Social Sciences* (A.1.b:10) should also be
consulted.

General Bibliographies.   The most useful bibliography for basic
geographical research at the undergraduate level is the Association
of American Geographers' *Geographical Bibliography for American College Libraries* (1970) (3). Some 1,760 works are described in four parts: "General Aids and Sources"; "History, Philosophy, and Methods"; "Works Grouped by Topic"; and "Works
Grouped by Region." Serials as well as books and monographs
are listed, mainly English-language works but with a judicious
smattering of publications in other languages.

Altogether different in scope and a major research aid for the
graduate student is the *Research Catalog of the American Geographical Society* (1962) (4), which lists all accessions of the
society from 1923 to 1961. Sixteen volumes, including a one-volume map supplement, give full citations to more than 219,000
items. The arrangement is primarily a complex regional/topical
one, full understanding of which is essential for effective use. An
extensive description of the system is given in the first volume. In
volumes 1 and 2, general, systematic, and methodological works
are cited and classified according to a decimal system. For the regional works, which occupy volumes 3–15, a regional classification system is used. The world is divided into 52 regions, each
represented by a number, while subregions of each of these are
identified by letters. (The western part of the United States, for
example, is region 10, and the states of Oregon and Washington
are subregion 10a.) This classification appears on the upper left-
hand side of the cards. Maps showing the regions and their subdivisions are conveniently placed in each volume. Within divisions,
works are listed chronologically. There is no author or title index.

Current Geographical Publications (1938–) (5), also issued by
the American Geographical Society, is organized in a similar fashion, but with the systematic and regional classifications somewhat

abridged. These appear in the right-hand margin of each page, a feature which permits users to find quickly all the items of each issue on a particular subject. Published ten times a year and listing approximately 7,000 items annually, this work has an annual subject index, as well as author and area indexes. Occasionally items are annotated, and the level for which a work is intended is indicated. In addition to the kinds of material included in the *Research Catalog,* issues of *Current Geographical Publications* occasionally contain citations of chapters or sections of books. It should be noted that all items listed in *Current Geographical Publications* until 1962 were included in the *Research Catalog,* thus eliminating the need to consult annual volumes from 1938 to 1962.

In many respects the most satisfactory general bibliography of current geographical literature is the *Bibliographie géographique internationale* (1891–) (6), published annually by the Association de Géographes Français, in collaboration with the American Geographical Society, the Royal Geographical Society, and a number of other national geographical associations. The arrangement is workmanlike and generally satisfactory. The first and smaller part is devoted to systematic studies, including the history of geography, history of cartography, historical geography, physical geography, human geography, and general reference and methodological works. The second part deals with the continents and their individual countries and territories; the arrangement of materials for each of these follows an easily comprehended topical scheme. The titles of all books and articles are given in their original language, with brief, initialed annotations in French. There is an author but no title index.

Other valuable sources include two British publications. *New Geographical Literature and Maps* (1951–) (7), issued twice yearly by the Royal Geographical Society, lists all accessions to its library—books, atlases, and maps—and includes full citations of all articles in some twenty major British and foreign geographical periodicals, as well as selected items from more than 100 others. The arrangement follows fairly closely that in the book-review section of the Society's *Geographical Journal.* The first section lists regional works, classified by continent and country; it is followed by sections on various systematic fields of the discipline and a final one on atlases and maps. There are no indexes. The other British publication, *Geographical Abstracts* (1966–) (8), appears in four series: Geomorphology, Biogeography, Economic Geography, and Social Geography and Cartography. Each series appears six times a year. Brief abstracts of articles of geographical interest and content, selected from well over 100 journals in more than a dozen languages, together with a smaller number of abstracts of important books, make this a major research aid in tracking down current geographical literature. Regional and author indexes appear for each series in the last issue of the year. Comprehensive subject and author indexes produced by computers are compiled periodically.

Finally, *PAIS* (A.1.b:15), C. L. and A. G. Vinge's *United States Government Publications for Teaching and Research in Geography* (A.1.i:1), and the *Social Sciences Citation Index* (A.1.b:6) should not be overlooked.

Reviews of Research. Geographers, it seems, have been far less eager than their fellow social scientists to publish regular reviews of research completed or in progress. In an attempt to rectify this omission, a new British periodical, *Progress in Geography* (1969–) (9), now appearing twice yearly, is devoted exclusively to review articles. It is expected that each volume will contain five to eight review papers, ranging in length from 10,000 to 15,-000 words. Methodological developments, environmental perception, voting patterns, climatic geomorphology, regional taxonomy, geographic space perception, urban growth, climatology, and coastal geomorphology are some of the topics dealt with in the first two issues.

A number of one-volume works are useful for their appraisals of research in various topics up to their date of publication. These include *Geography in the Twentieth Century* (E.1.f:12), *American Geography: Inventory and Prospect* (E.1.f:13), *Problems and Trends in American Geography* (E.1.f:15), and *Trends in Geography* (E.1.f:16).

Many of the presidential addresses presented to the Association of American Geographers and published in the *Annals* of the Association are useful for their reviews of current and past research. Important also are the "Review Articles" which have appeared at irregular intervals in the *Annals*. Norton Ginsburg's chapter on geography in Hoselitz's *Reader's Guide to the Social Sciences* (A.1.b:9) appraises more than 100 significant geographical titles covering a wide range of topics.

Periodicals. The major bibliographical source for information on geographical periodicals and other serials is Chauncy D. Harris and Jerome D. Fellmann's *International List of Geographical Serials* (1972) (10). More than 1,600 serials, both current and defunct, are cited and briefly annotated as to language, dates of publication, periodicity, and the like. Chauncy D. Harris's shorter *Annotated World List of Selected Current Geographical Serials in English* (1964) (11) lists five "key American and British periodicals" and a further 56 English-language publications, mainly by country. An appendix lists and annotates 55 foreign-language serials which contain occasional articles in English or regularly publish English abstracts of articles.

E.1.c Biographical Dictionaries and Directories

Stamp's *Dictionary of Geography* (E.1.d:9) includes brief biographical information on many leading geographers, both past and present. Longer biographical articles on a select number of prominent world geographers can be found in the *Encyclopedia of the Social Sciences* (A.1.e:1) and the *International Encyclopedia of the Social Sciences* (A.1.e:2). T. W. Freeman's *A Hundred Years of Geography* (1962) (1) has a section on "Short Biographies of Geographers" which includes close to 100 famous names. Brief sketches of many North American geographers are included in the Social and Behavioral Sciences volumes of *American Men and Women of Science* (A.1.d:15).

The *Directory* (1970) (2) of the Association of American Geographers lists the names and addresses of the more than 6,700 persons who were members of the Association on 28 February 1970. Brief biographical information is given for more than 90 percent of the members. In addition to listing members of geography departments in academic institutions, the annual *Directory of College Geography of the United States* (1949–) (3) contains information on courses and areas of specialization at all four-year institutions offering the subject. A similar source of information is the Association of American Geographers' *Guide to Graduate Departments of Geography in the United States* (1968) (4). The most comprehensive directory of world geographers and of geographical departments and institutions is *Orbis Geographicus: World Directory of Geography* (1952–) (5). Volume 1 covers societies, institutes, and agencies; volume 2 is devoted to individual geographers, listed by country. A new edition of volume 2 is under way.

Obituary notices, as well as biographical articles, are regularly listed in the A.G.S. *Research Catalog* (E.1.b:4), *Current Geographical Publications* (E.1.b:5), *Bibliographie géographique internationale* (E.1.b:6), and *New Geographical Literature* (E.1.b:7).

E.1.d Encyclopedias and Dictionaries

In general, the encyclopedias related to geography offer lengthy articles on important topics while the dictionaries give brief definitions of terms and short explanations of a variety of phenomena. The two most authoritative encyclopedias dealing with aspects of

the discipline are the *Encyclopedia of the Social Sciences* (A.1.
e:1) and the more recent *International Encyclopedia of the Social
Sciences* (A.1.e:2). Since they are invaluable for defining technical terms, for investigating the scholarship and scope of the published research in the field, and for obtaining information on persons who have made major contributions, many research activities
can begin here. There are articles in the *Encyclopedia,* for instance,
on such terms as culture, determinism, and migration, as well as
longer articles on such subjects as cultural geography, demography, human geography, and economic geography. Progress in each
field is considered up to the 1930s. The *International Encyclopedia* deals with such subjects as area, diffusion, ecology, enclaves
and exclaves, environmentalism, industrial concentration, population, and water resources, while other articles note progress since
the 1930s in such fields as cultural, economic, political, social, and
statistical geography. In addition, a number of one-volume encyclopedias should be cited. The *Larousse Encyclopedia of World
Geography* (1965) (1) is an English adaptation of a larger work
originally published in French. More than 60 scholars from many
countries contributed articles on various regions and countries.
Many colored and black-and-white photographs, together with
over 100 black-and-white maps, greatly enhance the value of the
work. The volume is indexed. A companion volume, the *Larousse
Encyclopedia of the Earth* (1961) (2), covers the earth's history
and physical characteristics, and is similarly well illustrated. R.
Kay Gresswell's *Standard Encyclopedia of the World's Rivers and
Lakes* (1965) (3) covers briefly lakes, rivers, swamps, and man-
made lakes. A series of one-volume encyclopedias, edited by
Rhodes W. Fairbridge, on aspects of geology and related earth
sciences contains much of interest to the geographer. The articles,
which are generally extensive, are written by scholars, and each
has a short bibliography of suggested sources of further information and cross-references to related articles. Volumes that have
appeared to date are the *Encyclopedia of Oceanography* (1966)
(4), the *Encyclopedia of Atmospheric Sciences and Astrogeology*
(1967) (5), and the *Encyclopedia of Geomorphology* (1968)
(6). Additional volumes in this series will be listed in the Reinhold Book Corporation's catalog in *PTLA* (A.1.b:30).

A work that is likely to take its place as a major source is the
Westermann Lexikon der Geographie (1968–) (7), a projected
five-volume set. An encyclopedia and gazetteer, the work has been
put together by a team of more than 100 geographers and other
scholars.

There are now available a large number of useful dictionaries
of geography, of which Stamp's *Glossary of Geographical Terms*

(1966) (8) is generally regarded as the most authoritative. Many geographical terms are defined, with information as to origin and differences of usage. Somewhat wider in scope and including short notices of persons and places, as well as geographical societies and journals, is Stamp's *Dictionary of Geography* (1966) (9). Less well-balanced than the Stamp volumes, and leaning heavily towards physical rather than human and cultural geography, are F. J. Monkhouse's *Dictionary of Geography* (1970) (10), W. G. Moore's *Dictionary of Geography* (1967) (11), and J. C. Swayne's *Concise Glossary of Geographical Terms* (1963) (12). All three are the work of British geographers. The only recent American dictionary of this sort is the paperback *Dictionary of Basic Geography* (1970) (13) by Allen A. Schmieder et al. Written with the beginning student in mind, it ranges through the major subfields of the discipline. Very clear illustrations and maps add greatly to its value. A much earlier work is Alexander Knox's *Glossary of Geographical and Topographical Terms* (1904) (14).

Occasionally it is necessary to find the English meaning of foreign geographical terms and names. *The Glossary of Geographical Names in Six Languages* (1967) (15) indicates alternate spellings in English, French, Italian, Spanish, German, and Dutch of over 4,000 place names. The main part of the glossary lists most common names with other forms following, while a comprehensive index leads users from a less common to the more common form. The researcher delving into the very rich literature of German geography will find the volume by Eric Fisher and Francis E. Elliot, *A German and English Glossary of Geographical Terms* (1950) (16), invaluable.

E.I.e Handbooks and Yearbooks

Probably the most useful single work to geographers in this category is the *Statesman's Yearbook* (1864–) (1), a statistical and historical annual that long ago earned the reputation of being the handiest and most accurate of yearbooks. Data on international organizations, individual countries and internal subdivisions, and colonial and other possessions are systematically arranged, and provide information on economic and social conditions, political organization and structure, and prominent government officials. Lists of each nation's diplomatic representatives and select bibliographies are other important features. There is an index of names, places, and major commodities.

The *Annual Register* (A.1.g:4), though directing more attention to political events, has much ready information on countries and places of the world, and the *Worldmark Encyclopedia of the Nations* (I.1.d:1) includes maps, statistical tables, and bibliographies.

The *Geographical Digest* (1963–) (2) is a small volume containing a variety of demographic, economic, and other current information for all parts of the world. Two other works that provide a variety of current geographical information are John Laffin's *New Geography* (1966–) (3) and C. B. Muriel Lock's *Geography: A Reference Handbook* (1972) (4). The first, an annual, includes entries dealing with regional and systematic topics. The second book attempts "not to maintain a balanced coverage either regionally or thematically, but to draw attention to the outstanding scholars whose achievements have helped to shape the modern concept of geographical studies, and to some of the organizations and sources of the greatest continuing significance within the framework of world geography."

Still of considerable use is the Geographical Handbook series (1941–46) (5), issued by the Naval Intelligence Division of the British Admiralty. Some 58 volumes cover 31 countries or geographical regions in a detailed manner, including sections on their history, political institutions and government, economic conditions, and physical and human geography.

E.I.f Methodological Works

The methodology of modern geography has undergone frequent change since the days of Alexander von Humboldt and Karl Ritter in the early nineteenth century. A full study of the methodology of geography would demand consultation of many different types of works, some of them dealing with the contributions of individual geographers, others with trends in the several branches of the discipline, and a select few with its underlying philosophy.

Of particular note is Richard Hartshorne's *The Nature of Geography* (1939) (1), which despite its turgid style and many outmoded ideas, remains a major source book. In its original version some 400 different methodological works by German, French, British, and American geographers were cited, and in the revised version a further 128. Hartshorne's later book, *Perspective on the Nature of Geography* (1959) (2), is a shorter restatement of the subject, but one in which the interpretation of a number of key concepts and methods is markedly modified. The serious student will do well to consult both these works, as well as D. W. Harvey's *Explanation in Geography* (1969) (3), which not only examines the role of explanation in geography with reference to both past and present methodologies but also adds much needed comment on some of the latest developments. R. J. Chorley and Peter Haggett's *Models in Geography* (1967) (4) is another work of vital importance to the understanding of current methodology. An earlier work also worthy of attention is Isaiah Bowman's *Geography in Relation to the Social Sciences* (1934) (5).

Short appraisals of the discipline, aimed particularly at the professional geographer and the graduate student, are E. A. Ackerman's *Geography as a Fundamental Research Discipline* (1958) (6), the National Research Council's *The Science of Geography* (1965) (7), and *Geography* (1970) (8), edited by Edward J. Taaffe for the 1967–69 Behavioral and Social Sciences Survey. More useful to the undergraduate student are two other short works—J. O. M. Broek's *Compass of Geography* (1966) (9) and S. W. Wooldridge and W. G. East's *The Spirit and Purpose of Geography* (1967) (10)—which consider the philosophy of the subject, its methods, and certain recent trends.

Part 1 of Robert W. Durrenberger's *Geographical Research and Writing* (1971) (11) discusses such matters as the nature of geographical research, the identification of problems, the development of research plans, research methods, and the preparation of manuscripts. Part 2, "Aids to Geographical Research," discusses in six chapters general guides, bibliographies, and sources of information; special indexes, abstracts, and bibliographies; major sources of statistical information; map sources; sources of photographs; and selected periodicals. In all, some 622 bibliographic and other reference works are cited. There are title and subject indexes.

Works dealing more specifically with trends and developments in the major branches of the subject are abundant. *Geography in the Twentieth Century* (1957) (12), edited by Griffith Taylor, includes chapters by distinguished geographers from Canada, Czechoslovakia, Poland, the United Kingdom, and the United States. Its subtitle, "A Study of Growth, Fields, Techniques, Aims, and Trends," sufficiently explains its purpose, and it covers most major aspects of the subject. *American Geography: Inventory and Prospect* (1954) (13), edited by Preston E. James and Clarence F. Jones for the Association of American Geographers, surveys the achievements of the various branches of the subject. Except for the introduction, each chapter contains an extensive bibliography. T. W. Freeman's *A Hundred Years of Geography* (E.1.c:1) has useful chapters on the evolution of the subject and on trends in its major fields. Perhaps the most useful and important work cited in this section is *Frontiers in Geographical Teaching* (1965) (14), edited by R. J. Chorley and Peter Haggett and written mainly by a number of Britain's younger geographers. Its emphasis is on techniques. The first seven chapters deal with major concepts in the discipline as a whole and in certain of its subfields, and the next six with various techniques now being employed in the subject. Each chapter ends with a well-selected list of readings. *Problems and Trends in American Geography* (1967) (15) is somewhat less useful, though it should not be ignored. The most recent publication of this sort is another collection of essays, *Trends in Geography: An Introductory Survey* (1969) (16). A regular feature of *Social Science Information* (B.1.f:5) is "Social Science Methodology: A Bibliography of Studies."

E.1.g   Statistics Sources

In addition to the statistical sources listed in I.1.h, only two works need be cited here. Chisholm's *Handbook of Commercial Geography* (1966) (1), edited by Dudley Stamp and S. Carter Gilmour, provides a wealth of information on commodities, manufactures, trade, and transportation across the world. Statistical tables, maps, and a comprehensive index make it a useful research aid for the beginning student. H. V. Warren and E. F. Wilks's *World Resources Production: Fifty Years of Change* (1966) (2) has tables and graphs on production rates of 32 agricultural and mineral commodities, with brief descriptive notes for each item. Appendix A, "Documentation for Table 2," indicates the 127 sources used in obtaining the information.

Section 2

For convenience, the subfields of geography are here arranged in broad groups. "Exploration and Travel" considers the history of exploration and cartography, and travel in its varied aspects; "Human Geography" deals with historical, political, cultural, population, and settlement geography; "Economic Geography" with agricultural, industrial, commercial, and transportation geography; "Urban Geography and Planning" with urban, economic, and settlement geography; recreation; and regional, urban, and resource planning; and "Environmental Studies" with such matters as conservation of natural resources and pollution. Physical geography—properly classified as an earth science—is not treated separately here, although a few works in physical geography are cited where pertinent (for example, under such headings as "Environmental Studies" and "Urban Geography and Planning").

E.2.a   Exploration and Travel

While exploration is frequently treated as a branch of history, when coupled with travel it may be considered a subfield of geography. A wealth of literature exists on these subjects, though there are few useful general guides.

In addition to the many excellent maps of exploration which appear in the historical and geographical atlases listed elsewhere in this volume, two atlases devoted exclusively to the history of the world's exploration should be noted. *Discovery and Exploration: An Atlas-History of Man's Journeys into the Unknown* (1968) (1), by Frank Debenham, covers the world from ancient times to the present day. Contemporary maps from many eras, as well as numerous contemporary drawings, are reproduced in facsimile, while the routes of the major explorers of each continent and region are shown in a series of specially drawn maps. The European explorations are particularly well treated. The Russian-language *Atlas istorii geograficheskikh otkrytii i issledovanii* [Atlas of the history of geographical discoveries and explorations] (1959) (2) covers explorers' routes, the extent of geographical knowledge at particular dates, and political geography from ancient times to the present. Another valuable work is R. A. Skelton's *Explorers' Maps: Chapters in the Cartographic Record of Geographical Discovery* (1958) (3).

On the general history of exploration, the *Concise Encyclopedia of Explorations* (1969) (4) contains short sketches of the most important explorers as well as brief articles on group expeditions and major regions of exploration such as Antarctica, Arabia, and central Australia. I. A. Langnas's *Dictionary of Discoveries* (1959) (5) is a somewhat similar compilation, but differs sufficiently so that both may be consulted with profit. Most useful for the European discoveries of late medieval and modern times is Wilcomb E. Washburn's brief bibliographical essay, *The Age of Discovery* (1966), one of the Service Center for Teachers of History series (O.2.e:8), which expertly surveys more than 100 significant monographs and articles devoted to European expansion. A much older work by P. Lemosof, *Le livre d'or de la géographie* (1902) (6), available in many college libraries, contains brief biographical sketches of the main explorers to the end of the nineteenth century.

Since 1847, the Hakluyt Society of London has published more than 250 volumes of carefully edited and annotated original works of early exploration and travel in all parts of the world. The Society's *Prospectus* (1956) (7) lists all volumes issued to that date. The later supplementary lists should be consulted for details on recent issues.

For travel, the indispensable aid is E. G. Cox's *Reference Guide to the Literature of Travel* (1935–49) (8), which covers materials published up to 1800. Volume 1 deals with the Old World, volume 2 with the New World, and volume 3 with Great Britain. The last volume has, in addition, chapters on maps and charts, general reference books, and bibliographies. The entries are arranged chronologically under area and subject headings, and in general, are carefully annotated. For travel literature published since 1800, see the various general bibliographies of history and geography listed in the chapters on those disciplines.

E.2.b   Human Geography

Special atlases dealing with peoples of the world, language, religion, population, and settlement are numerous. The best general atlases covering certain of these themes are the *Atlas narodov mira* (C.1.a:1) and Friedrich Burgdörfer's *World Atlas of Population* (C.1.a:2). However, for most human geographic themes the *Aldine University Atlas* (A.1.a:10) and *Goode's World Atlas* (A.1. 2:9) will suffice. Historical-geographic matters are best covered, though not always satisfactorily, in various historical atlases. Of these the most highly recommended are *Shepherd's Historical Atlas* (F.1.a:1), *Muir's Historical Atlas: Ancient, Medieval, and Modern* (F.1.e:2), the *Rand McNally Atlas of World History* (F.1.a:3), and, probably best of all, *Westermanns Grosser Atlas zur Weltgeschichte: Vorzeit, Altertum, Mittelalter, Neuzeit* (F.1. a:4).

Geographical Abstracts D: Social Geography and Cartography (E.1.b:8) and such general bibliographies as *Current Geographical Publications* (E.1.b:5), *New Geographical Literature and Maps* (E.1.b:7), the *Bibliographie géographique internationale* (E.1.b:6), and the A. G. S. *Research Catalog* (E.1.b:4) should be consulted.

No general bibliography of historical geography has appeared to date; the best selective listing is in Andrew H. Clark's paper on "Historical Geography" in *American Geography: Inventory and Prospect* (E.1.f:13). Unfortunately, this is now out of date. Population geography has fared better with the publication of Zelinsky's *Bibliographic Guide to Population Geography* (C.1.b:4), which lists more than 2,000 items from all major regions of the world. For settlement geography there is a useful work by Gwendolyn Bell and others: *Annotated Bibliography of the Patterns and Dynamics of Rural Settlement* (1968) (1). More valuable still is the *Ekistics Index* (1955–) (2), a computer-produced monthly listing of selected articles on the problems and science of human settlements. More than 40 international journals are regularly searched, and each issue abstracts about 400 articles. Selection is based largely on the probable interest of articles to planners, architects, social scientists, and others concerned with developments in the field of ekistics. Like most computer-produced bibliographies, the *Ekistics Index* is formidable on first sight; however, detailed instructions on how to use it are given on the inside cover of each issue. Arrangement is by subject—geographical and topical.

Of all the branches of human geography, political geography

has produced the most varied and helpful bibliographies. Extensive annotated bibliographies are included in Roger E. Kasperson and Julian V. Minghi's *The Structure of Political Geography* (1969) (3), which has sections on "heritage," "structure," "process," "behavior," and "environment." Brian R. Goodey's *The Geography of Elections: An Introductory Bibliography* (1968) (4), which lists more than 750 items, is arranged in two main sections; the first deals with general and methodological works, the second with election studies of individual countries. An author index is provided. Louis C. Peltier's *Bibliography of Military Geography* (1962) (5) covers yet another aspect of political geography, mainly from English, French, and German sources.

E.2.c Economic Geography

A large body of reference literature exists for this branch of the discipline; consequently, it is necessary to be highly selective. The best general economic atlas is the *Oxford Economic Atlas of the World* (D.1.a:1), and this, with its associated series, the *Oxford Regional Economic Atlases* (I.1.a:1–7), comprises a reasonably comprehensive and detailed cartographic survey of world economic distributions, production, and commercial transactions. An earlier work, Norton Ginsburg's *Atlas of Economic Development* (1961) (1), covers some of the same ground and can also be consulted with profit.

The Economic Geography series of *Geographical Abstracts* (E.1.b:8) is the most useful current bibliographic source.

Agricultural geography, formerly covered by only one special English-language atlas—volume 1, *The Agricultural Resources of the World,* of William van Royen's *Atlas of the World's Resources* (1952–54) (2)—is now provided with the magnificent four-volume *World Atlas of Agriculture* (1969) (3). Volume 1 covers Europe, the USSR, and Asia Minor; volume 2, South and East Asia and Oceania; volume 3, the Americas; and volume 4, Africa. Sponsored by the International Association of Agricultural Economists, the atlas is largely the work of eminent geographers and agricultural economists from more than twenty countries. Sixty-two maps of land utilization and four volumes of monographs illustrate the agricultural economy of the various countries and territories shown. Each monograph is divided into five parts, which consider, in turn, physical environment and communications; population; exploitation of resources; land utilization, crops, and animal husbandry; and agricultural economy. Widest in scope of the current bibliographies is the *Biological and Agricultural Index* (1916–) (4), which covers subjects ranging from soil science and plant physiology to rural sociology. An excellent general guide is

Blanchard and Ostvold's topically organized *Literature of Agricultural Research* (1958) (5). Edgar T. Thompson's *The Plantation: A Bibliography* (1957) (6) is a comprehensive work covering a narrow theme. *Biological Abstracts* (B.2.f:2) should also be consulted for its many references to agricultural literature. A large number of articles and books on agricultural geography are cited and annotated in the International Geographical Union's *Selected Bibliography of the Humid Tropics* (1959) (7), while *Tropical Abstracts* (1946–) (8) regularly features extended sections on agriculture and agricultural research.

The geography of mineral production is covered in volume 2, *The Mineral Resources of the World,* of William van Royen's *Atlas of the World's Resources* (2). Plates and accompanying text deal with geological, technological, economic, and other aspects of mineral production. Jackson and Penn's *Dictionary of Natural Resources* (1969) (9) is useful for its short definitions of mineral terms and its descriptions of important developments in the field of mineral exploitation and production. More valuable to the advanced student is volume 2 of Guides to Information Sources in Science and Technology, *A Guide to Information Sources in Mining, Minerals, and Geosciences* (1965) (10). Part 1 lists organizations by geographic area, together with address, purpose, function, publications, and related information; part 2 is a listing by subject of reference works. There are separate indexes to each part. Besides the multivolume *World Trade Annual* (I.1.g:8), two other publications contain generally reliable statistics on world mineral production: volume 4 of the United States Bureau of Mines' *Minerals Yearbook* (I.1.g:16) and the British government's *Statistical Summary of the Mineral Industry* (I.1.g:17).

Marine resources are well covered in F. E. Firth's *The Encyclopedia of Marine Resources* (1969) (11), a substantial volume dealing with marine life and minerals and related industries. Most articles contain useful bibliographies. The work is well illustrated with black-and-white maps, photographs, and diagrams; and has a satisfactory index.

Manufacturing geography is covered briefly in an early work of Chauncy Harris, *A Bibliography of the Geography of Manufacturing* (1952) (12), and in more detail, but with a narrower focus, in Stevens and Brackett's *Industrial Location: A Review and Annotated Bibliography of Theoretical, Empirical, and Case Studies* (1967) (13). More than 900 books and articles are cited.

Of all the branches of economic geography, transportation seems best served with bibliographical aids. Roy I. Wolfe's *Annotated Bibliography of the Geography of Transportation* (1961) (14) covers books and articles published prior to 1960; Gunnar Olsson's *Distance and Human Interaction: A Review and Bibliography* (1965) (15) is particularly important for its attention to theory and the use of models in transportation studies; William R. Siddall's *Transportation Geography: A Bibliography* (1969) (16) deals with transportation literature published in English between 1950 and 1963; and Black and Horton's *Bibliography of Selected Research on Networks and Urban Transportation Relevant to Current Transportation Geography Research* (1968) (17) covers publications issued between 1965 and 1968. For current items in transportation the most useful source is *Current Literature in Transportation* (1958–) (18). Other sources are Metcalf (D.2. c:6) and Flood (D.2.c:7).

The geography of world trade is covered in Andreas Grotevald's *Selective Annotated Bibliography of Publications Relevant to the Geographic Study of International Trade* (1960) (19).

E.2.d   Urban Geography and Planning

Although urban mapping is an ancient craft, and modern street maps and city plans are in worldwide use, few atlases of urban places have appeared to date, and none covering the urban geography of the world. Many general world atlases, however, include fairly large-scale maps of selected cities, as for example the maps of London, Paris, New York, and other cities in *The Times Atlas of the World* (A.1.a:1).

Fortunately, bibliographic guides to urban geography are more readily available. John W. Sommer's *Bibliography of Urban Geography* (1966) (1) lists articles on urban geography in geographical journals between 1940 and 1965. The arrangement is regional, with author and subject indexes. Berry and Pred's *Central Place Studies: A Bibliography of Theory and Application* (1961) (2) is an annotated listing of more than 1,000 items, and together with its 1965 supplement, comprises the most important single bibliographic aid in urban geography. *The Study of Urbanization* (1965) (3) contains three chapters especially important to the urban geographer; each surveys the research literature published prior to 1965 in its respective field.

There are individual bibliographies of urban and regional planning, and one continuing series of planning bibliographies. Caroline Shillaber's *References on City and Regional Planning* (1960) (4) is a selected listing of major items of particular use to the research worker and planner. Another useful and relatively short bibliography is Francis Chapin's *Selected References on Urban Planning Methods and Techniques* (1963) (5). This has sections on such topics as the urban economy, activity systems, land-use planning, and the urban environment. A much more extensive listing is provided in Bestor and Jones's *City Planning: A Basic Bibliography of Sources and Trends* (1962) (6), which includes sections on industrial areas, land use, community facilities, and commercial activities. The International Union of Local Authorities published *Metropolis: A Select Bibliography of Administrative and Other Problems in Metropolitan Areas* (1967) (7). The items are arranged first by country, then under twelve headings: administration and organization, finance, culture and education, social welfare, health, planning and urbanism, transport and traffic, social aspects, economy, population, geography, and history. No materials on the United States or Canada are included. The United States is the principal focus of Melville C. Branch's *Comprehensive Urban Planning* (1970) (8), a "selective annotated bibliography with related materials," including 1,500 items arranged by subject. There are three categories: items dealing directly with comprehensive urban planning, items indirectly related to comprehensive urban planning, and items dealing with the environment. Background materials covering such topics as early city-planning literature, social problems affecting urban growth, economic geography, public administration, and the like are also included. Bibliographies and other bibliographic sources are cited, and there are subject and title indexes.

Researchers using Branch's *Comprehensive Urban Planning* will encounter among the 1,500 items cited a number of references to the Exchange Bibliographies (1958–) (9), published at fairly regular intervals by the Council of Planning Librarians (CPL). This series, now numbering more than 400, covers a broad range of topics relating to planning. A separately prepared index lists the bibliographies in the series by both number and title, and by author and subject.

In its "Urban Information Clearinghouse" section *Urban and Social Change Review* (1967–) (10) features brief annotated references to periodicals; books, monographs, and reports; bibliographies and documents; information retrieval systems; information reference services; simulation games; and so forth. At the end of each issue of the bimonthly *Journal of the American Institute of Planners* (1925–) (11) is a bibliography of selected articles from about twenty planning journals. The arrangement is by journal title and there is no index.

E.2.e Environmental Studies

Recent years have witnessed a deluge of environmental literature of every sort, much of it of little permanent value. Guides and handbooks have been followed by bibliographies of the whole field or of special parts of it. In general, the literature has tended to be somewhat more concerned with pollution and environmental deterioration than with conservation and the proper use of resources.

General bibliographies are now quite numerous. "The Environmental Crisis" (1970) (1) is an annotated listing of paperbound books on environmental quality, pollution, and the population explosion. Some 1,500 works are cited in *Science for Society: A Bibliography* (1970) (2), published by the American Association for the Advancement of Science. Emphasis is on the application of science and technology to human problems, notably environmental demographic ones. Robert W. Durrenberger claims that *Environment and Man: A Bibliography* (1970) (3) is a basic list of works concerned with environment and man's relation to it. There are over 2,000 books and articles (most published since 1960) arranged by author with a subject index. The most important source of information on current environmental literature is the semimonthly *Environment Information Access* (1971–) (4). Coverage includes abstracts of articles selected from 1,000 periodicals, federal and state government publications (including congressional hearings), legislation, research reports of environmental-protectionist groups, and conference papers. Books are reviewed rather than abstracted. Abstracts are entered under the following classifications: air pollution, chemical and biological contamination, energy, environmental action, environmental design, food, land use and misuse, noise pollution, nonrenewable resources, oceans and estuaries, population planning and control, radiological contamination, recreation, renewable resources, solid waste, transportation, water pollution, weather modification and geophysical change, and wildlife. Shorter additional sections on government affairs, research activities, control products, and scheduled conferences are regular features. Separate indexes cover subject terms, subjects, industries, and authors.

The Environment Index (1971–) (5) is an annual subject, industry, and author index to *Environment Information Access*. In addition, there are indexes of books, U.S. legislation, and environmental-control patents issued by the U.S. Patent Office. The monthly *Environment Reporter* (1970–) (6) notes current developments in environmental management, as well as texts of federal and state legislation, and Supreme Court and other federal and state court decisions concerned with environmental law. More attention is given this topic in numbers 334 and 366 of the CPL's *Exchange Bibliography* (E.2.d:9). The *Annual Review of Ecology and Systematics* (1970–) (7) covers such topics as statistical plant ecology, mineral cycling, and contemporary systematic philosophies. Volume 1 of *Advances in Environmental Sciences and*

Technology (1969–) (8) covers such topics as water pollution, air pollution, ecology and environment, public health, and food contamination.

Three guides to the environment should also be noted: Mitchell and Shilling's *Ecotactics: The Sierra Club Handbook for Environmental Activists* (1970) (9), Paul Swatek's *The User's Guide to the Protection of the Environment* (1970) (10), and the U.S. Sport Fisheries and Wildlife Bureau's *Handbook of Toxicity of Pesticides to Wildlife* (1970) (11). The first two, aimed primarily at the general public, are sponsored by environmental groups, but their purposes are somewhat different. The *User's Guide* essentially provides the facts about consumer products and their ecological effects. *Ecotactics,* intended as a guide for activists, provides information on sources of materials and on the many professional groups, societies, and government agencies engaged in environmental action and control. The third work is directed more to personnel engaged in research and wildlife management, though it will be useful to the student seeking information on pesticides, their relative toxicity, ecological effects, chemical compositions, and trade names.

The annual *Conservation Directory* (1956–) (12) provides information about organizations, agencies, and officials concerned with natural-resource use and management. While it deals mainly with the United States and Canada, it also includes a certain amount of international information. The arrangement of materials is by geographic region.

Abstracts of recent articles and other works on recreation are included in *Environment Information Access* (4) and in *Geographical Abstracts C: Economic Geography* (E.1.b:8). A useful survey and listing of recreational literature is Roy I. Wolfe's "Perspective on Outdoor Recreation: A Bibliographic Survey" (1964) (13). Volume 27 of the Study Reports of the Outdoor Recreation Resources Review Commission, entitled *Outdoor Recreation in the United States: Its Literature and History* (1962) (14), includes a "basic listing, description, and assessment of some of the more important references." Both the literature on resources for recreation and the literature of uses of these for recreation are critically assessed. Separate bibliographies on leisure and on intergovernmental problems are provided, as well as a section on the historical development of outdoor recreation, with a chronology of significant events from 1710 to 1962. James R. and Marjorie J. Pinkerton's *Outdoor Recreation and Leisure* (1969) (15) updates and expands *Outdoor Recreation Literature*. It has two parts: (1) reference guides, such as bibliographies and other research aids; and (2) a selected bibliography of books, articles, and government publications related to outdoor recreation, with emphasis on the 1960–66 period. An author and title index is included.

A number of reference works deal with pollution in general and in its various forms. *Pollution Abstracts* (1970–) (16), which appears six times a year, is the most useful source of bibliographical information on pollution in all its aspects. The major section of the serial is devoted to abstracts of current items—books, articles, reports, and other materials. The first part of each issue is taken up with general, nontechnical items on air pollution, water pollution, land pollution, and general pollution; the second, with technical items on air, fresh-water, marine, land, and noise pollution, as well as sewage and waste treatment. Among additional features is a section on contracts and patents in the field of pollution.

Walter C. McCrone's *The Particle Atlas: A Photomicrographic Reference for the Microscopical Identification of Particulate Substances* (1970) (17) enables identification of the various particles involved in air pollution. More than 500 colored micrographs are included. The United States National Air Pollution Control Administration's *Guide to Research in Air Pollution* (1970) (18) lists and describes a large number of domestic and foreign research projects actively under way during 1969, while Patricia A. Burd's *Index to Air Pollution Research: A Guide to Current Government and Industry Supported Research* (1968) (19) covers the previous period. *Air Pollution Abstracts* (1969–) (20), issued by the British government, covers selected books and articles.

Water pollution is well documented by *Water Pollution Abstracts* (1927–) (21), issued monthly by the Department of the Environment of the United Kingdom. Annual author or title indexes are provided. The arrangement is topical and the coverage worldwide. R. Keith Stuart's *Water Pollution Control: Waste Treatment and Water Treatment: Selected Biological References* (1966) (22) lists, but does not annotate, some 2,300 items. Its sections deal with pollution in fresh waters, pollution in marine waters, waste treatment and water treatment, and reporting aspects for biological data. A more narrowly focused bibliography is Evelyn Sinha's *Coastal/Estuarine Pollution: An Annotated Bibliography* (1970) (23). The *Water Resources Research Catalog* (1965–) (24), of which six volumes have been issued, is a listing of water research projects, including many concerned with water pollution, in progress in the United States and various foreign countries. Reports on many of these projects make up a large proportion of the respective volumes.

Herbert F. Lund's *Industrial Pollution Control Handbook*

(1971) (25) has information on all aspects of industrial pollution, including water-quality criteria, the monitoring of gaseous pollutants, radioactive wastes, and plant layout and the problems of contamination control. The 26 chapters by 34 experts are arranged in three sections: Evolution of Industrial Pollution Control, Pollution Control by Industry Problem, and Pollution Control Equipment and Operation.

Part F

History

Introductory Note

For centuries in Europe and America the only history considered worthy of intensive research was that of the Western world. Only recently have there appeared histories on Africa and Asia written from the standpoints of these areas. Previously they were considered, if at all, only in connection with European penetration and occupation. Thus we have such historical divisions as ancient, classical, medieval, and Renaissance, all referring to periods in the development of Western society. Entirely different situations existed in other parts of the world during these same periods, and these are now beginning to receive the attention they deserve. In most works discussed in this chapter, however, primary attention is focused on the history of the West. An outstanding example is the chapter on history in White (A.1.b:10), a book we have recommended in other parts of this volume. White collaborated with Dr. James P. Shenton of Columbia University on this chapter, and while acknowledging the soundness of the writing, one hesitates to consider it well-balanced when no attention is directed to geographical areas outside the Western world, or even to Latin America;

Walford (A.1.b:12) provides a much more balanced treatment. Because of this bias (termed "Europocentrism"), we recommend that persons doing research on geographical areas outside the Western world focus most of their attention on the materials discussed in appropriate area parts, using this part on general historical materials as a secondary source of information. Readers will note, however, that there are certain aspects of the general works that must be considered for an overall view. Concomitant with this suggestion is, of course, the expectation that those doing research in ancient, medieval, or modern history of the Western world will turn to the appropriate area-studies parts.

The arrangement of this part deviates from the established format, but it need not be confusing. In order to facilitate finding the required items for a particular period, materials in section 1 are arranged by historical periods. Section 2 is confined to reference works on the history of science and technology.

Section 1

F.1.a   Atlases and Gazetteers

Lock's *Modern Maps and Atlases* (A.1.a:11) discusses over twenty atlases published in the Western world that cover the mapping of history. *Shepherd's Historical Atlas* (1965) (1), now in its ninth edition, is perhaps the best known and most widely used general historical atlas. More than 200 pages of generally clear and reasonably uncluttered maps and over 100 pages of index make it one of the most comprehensive historical atlases available; the coverage spans the whole earth, and the time ranges from the early Mediterranean and Middle Eastern world to the 1960s. Almost as well-known and just as venerable is *Muir's Historical Atlas: Ancient, Medieval, and Modern* (1964) (2). Close to 100 pages of maps cover all periods from the second millennium B.C. to the 1960s, emphasizing political and military affairs. Another useful general historical atlas is the Rand McNally *Atlas of World History* (1965) (3), edited by R. R. Palmer, and including more than 100 maps with valuable accompanying textual comment. An outstanding German historical atlas is the *Westermanns Grosser Atlas zur Weltgeschichte: Vorzeit, Altertum, Mittelalter, Neuzeit* (1968) (4). This covers much the same time span as the Shepherd, Muir, and Rand McNally atlases, but its range of maps is considerably wider. In addition to the usual political and military maps, there are various economic and cultural maps, including some urban maps and a few dealing with such topics as ethnic groups. The maps are unusually clear and well designed, and there is some accompanying explanatory text.

Two atlases by Martin Gilbert are useful for research in modern history. His *Recent History Atlas* (1969) (5) has 121 black-and-white maps on the historical issues of world significance from 1870 to the present. Maps of political and military episodes predominate, but there are also a number depicting population and economic conditions, including one on world health, literacy, and incomes since 1960. There are descriptive notes for each map, but unfortunately, there is no bibliography or index. Gilbert's *First World War Atlas* (1970) (6) consists of 159 black-and-white maps on aspects of the war, including military operations, diplomatic factors, technical developments, and economic conditions. Gilbert claims that at least two maps (no. 34: A Plan for the Middle East, 1915; and no. 44: British Defenses against a Possible German Invasion, 1915) are based on materials not previously available and that other subjects have never been mapped before. Maps are arranged in the following categories: prelude to war, 1914, the early months of the war, 1915, 1916, the war in the air, the war at sea, 1917–18, the world at war, and aftermath. A selective critical bibliography consisting principally of the works— official histories and general treatments—used in compiling the atlas is also provided, and there is an index.

F.1.b Bibliographies

Except for the history bibliographies selected from Besterman (A.1.b:1) and published separately, there is no universal bibliography of bibliographies in history. Besterman covers materials up to 1965. The *Bibliographic Index* (A.1.b:2), the *International Bibliography of Historical Sciences* (4), and *Historical Abstracts* (10) are worth consulting within the limits of their coverage for bibliographies on historical subjects. The *Bibliographic Index* is especially useful for minor topics. However, in general, bibliographies are more likely to be found in connection with area-studies parts.

Several bibliographies that attempt to cover aspects of history are Poulton's *The Historian's Handbook* (1), the AHA *Guide to Historical Literature* (2), the *Annual Bulletin of Historical Literature* (3), the *International Bibliography of Historical Sciences* (4), and Irwin's *Guide to Historical Reading: Nonfiction* (5). They differ, however, in the types of material included, the criteria for selection, and other matters.

Helen Poulton's *The Historian's Handbook* (1972) (1) is a generally reliable guide to 700-odd reference sources in history. World coverage is attempted, and some of the works discussed, especially such legal sources as Price and Bitner (O.2.g:19) and Ford (L.2.g:12–16), do not usually receive attention in guides to historical-research materials. Coverage also is given to non-English

sources. There are author and title indexes. Unfortunately for beginning researchers, rather than being organized according to geographical area, the book is arranged by type of reference work
(e.g., bibliographies, encyclopedias and dictionaries, almanacs and
statistical handbooks, biographical materials, and primary sources
and dissertations). The most useful source for material issued up
to the late 1950s is the AHA's *Guide to Historical Literature*
(1961) (2). Specialists have selected and briefly annotated over
20,000 items, mostly monographs, but including also significant
articles and other important historical materials. The volume is
arranged in broad divisions: Introduction and General History,
Historical Beginnings, Middle Period in Eurasia and Northern
Africa, Asia since Early Times, Modern Europe, The Americas,
Africa, Australasia and Oceania, and The World in Recent Times.
Each of these divisions is subdivided into regional and national
groups. A standard sequence within each subdivision has been
followed, but not rigidly imposed: bibliographies, libraries, and
special museum collections; encyclopedias and works of reference;
geographies, gazetteers, and atlases; anthropologic, demographic,
and linguistic works; printed collections of sources; general histories; histories of periods, areas, and topics; biographies; government publications; and periodicals. Sections and subsections are
identified by letters, with each entry given a number preceded by
the letters of the section in which it appears. These symbols are
used in the index and for cross-references. The index combines in
one listing authors and broad subjects, and this is occasionally
misleading or difficult to use. It is recommended that students
make greater use of the subject arrangement. This is the best single-volume bibliography in English for references to printed collections of sources; note, however, The Consolidated Treaty Series (G.2.c:16), the League of Nations Treaty Series (G.2.c:13),
and the United Nations Treaty Series (G.2.c:14).

The purpose of the *Annual Bulletin of Historical Literature*
(1912–) (3) is stated in the preface of volume 1: "The principal
books which have appeared during the year are noticed, special
stress being laid on the new evidence brought forward in them,
and on fresh interpretation of existing evidence. Reference is also
made to some articles . . . which modify the generally received
opinion on important points. Each section is contributed by a recognized authority." Each volume is in sections, beginning with a
general one on the philosophy of history, historiography, and
method; through prehistory, ancient history, and the Middle Ages;
to modern times, where there are separate sections on "Europe
and the Wider World" and the Americas. The approximately 700
items noted annually are mainly in English, with occasional French,

German, and other foreign works, and with most emphasis on
Europe. There is an author index for volumes 1–22; later volumes
have annual author indexes. An attempt is made to include source
material and bibliographical and other reference works, as well as
general and specialized studies. Volumes published since 1960 partially supplement the AHA's *Guide to Historical Literature* (2).
The *International Bibliography of Historical Sciences* (1926–)
(4) is a descriptive bibliography of books and articles arranged
as follows: General Historical Bibliographies; Auxiliary Sciences;
Manuals and General Works; Prehistory; the Ancient East; Greece;
Rome, Ancient Italy, and the Roman Empire; The Church to
Gregory the Great; Byzantine History since Justinian; The Middle
Ages; Modern History; Modern Religion; Modern Culture; Modern Economic and Social History; Modern Legal and Constitutional History; and International Relations. (Items for Asia, Africa, and America are limited to the period of colonization.) It
attempts to be a selective, general bibliography "comprehending
the whole field of historical sciences" and to direct attention to
"international or national bibliographies dealing with one of the
historical disciplines" and bibliographies of special subjects. At
the beginning of a division, bibliographies are indicated by an asterisk, and collections of documents and other historical texts by
two asterisks. Exceptions are made for Greek, Roman, Early
Church, Byzantine, and medieval history; each of these chapters
has a subdivision devoted to collections of sources. References to
related items in other sections or in previous volumes are indicated
by "Cf. no. ———." Book reviews are noted, including those for
items in preceding volumes. It will be necessary to supplement this
source with more specialized bibliographies. Each volume contains
over 7,500 items.

Recognized by librarians as an authoritative list of over 1,500
"popular" histories of the ancient world, Europe, Asia, Africa, the
Pacific, the United States, Canada, and Latin America, Leonard
B. Irwin's *Guide to Historical Reading: Nonfiction* (1970) (5) is
generally neglected in academic research. The work is principally
recommended as a source when a general knowledge of a particular
period or geographical area is required. "Popular" is defined as a
recent, reliable history written in a readable style, and about half
the titles included are for high-school readers. Examples of titles
falling within the criteria are Carl Bridenbaugh's *Vexed and Trou-
bled Englishmen, 1590–1642* (1968), "a careful and realistic look
at the people of England of the early 17th century, from whom
came the first American settlers, [as well as] a broad and imagina-
tive portrayal of the society which supplied the beliefs, traditions
and background of early America"; two of Basil Davidson's ex-

cellent works, *Black Mother: The Years of the African Slave Trade* (1961) and *The Lost Cities of Africa* (1959); Hubert Cole's *Christophe, King of Haiti* (1967), a biography of a neglected black figure in the history of the New World; and Timothy Severin's *Explorers of the Mississippi* (1967), with "stories of not only LaSalle, Joliet and Marquette, but also of numerous other lesser-known persons—priests, voyagers, charlatans, and others, each of whom sought something from the great river." Author and title indexes are included. The four volumes of the *Bibliography of Historical Works Issued in the United Kingdom* (1947) (6), (1957) (7), (1962) (8), and (1967) (9) are listings arranged by subject of over 10,000 books on world history published between 1940 and 1965. Finally, the *Social Sciences Citation Index* (A.1.b:6) can be a valuable research aid.

Coverage of the modern world is provided by the quarterly *Historical Abstracts, 1775–1970* (1955–) (10). Volumes 1 to 16 contain about 4,000 abstracts per year of articles on world history from 1775 to 1945. With volume 17, *Historical Abstracts* was separated into two sections: *A, 1775–1914* and *B, 1914–1970*. The expansion in scope and chronology of coverage doubled the number of abstracts. Arrangement in all volumes is as follows: part 1, general items, including bibliography, methodology and research, historiography, and philosophy of history; part 2, international relations, wars and military history, political history, social and cultural history, economic history, religions, and sciences and technology. Part 3 is in seven sections, each devoted to specific geographical areas and countries. Abstracts concerning U.S. and Canadian history are in *America: History and Life* (O.2.e:6). As well as indexes for each issue, there are annual subject and author indexes, and five-year cumulative indexes. In current indexes, author, biographical, geographical, and subject entries are combined.

Janet Ziegler's *World War II: Books in English, 1945–65* (1971) (11) is a subject arrangement of over 4,500 titles. The introduction published in 1965 is a valuable survey of bibliographical coverage of the war; unlike the main part of the work, it includes bibliographies in books and serials in languages other than English. (Oriental language barriers prevented more than a survey of "useful U.S. compilations of Oriental publications.") The main text covers broad categories: General Works, Prelude to the War (Origins and Outbreak), Military Aspects, Political Aspects, Economic and Legal Aspects, Social Impact, Position of the Neutral Countries, and War Crimes Trials (including the Eichmann trial). Subdivisions in chapter 1 include general and specific bibliographies, guides to collections and archives, chronologies, general accounts, pictorial histories, altas histories, and historiography.

Chapter 2, on the prelude to the war, first lists general treatments, then titles on Europe and the Far East. The chapter on military aspects has numerous subdivisions, including memoirs and biographies, strategy, espionage, unit histories (by country), campaigns (land, aerial, and naval), and underground and resistance movements. Subdivisions in the chapter on social impact include information about prisoner-of-war, concentration, and relocation camps; demographic changes; displaced persons; relief activities; the arts and war; and radio and press censorship. The only drawback is the lack of annotations. There is an index of authors and major series.

Quarterly coverage of publications from all countries on World War II is given in the *Revue d'histoire de la deuxième guerre mondiale* (1950–) (12).

F.1.c   Biographical Dictionaries and Directories

Sources of biographical information in history are Slocum (A.1.d:9), Mason (G.2.c:2), and the AHA *Guide to Historical Literature* (F.1.b:2). The *Guide to Historical Literature* cites important biographical studies as well as biographical dictionaries. Information on 9,500 North American historians is provided in volume 1 of the *Directory of American Scholars* (1942–) (1).

F.1.d   Encyclopedias and Dictionaries

The *Encyclopedia of the Social Sciences* (A.1.e:1) contains articles on such historical factors as bolshevism, GOSPLAN, imperialism, fascism, the Russian Revolution, and German National Socialism. In the *International Encyclopedia of the Social Sciences* (A.1.e:2), historical events are referred to only in connection with the social sciences. There are, however, over 120 pages of discussion on historiography and history. Historiography is treated in six parts; after "The Rhetoric of History," African, Chinese, Islamic, Japanese, and South and Southeast Asian historiography are surveyed in individual articles with bibliographies by specialists. There are articles on 39 prominent historians. The History section includes The Philosophy of History, History and the Social Sciences, Ethnohistory, Culture History, Social History, Intellectual History, Economic History, and Business History, each prepared by a specialist and including a bibliography.

Aside from historical articles in general encyclopedias, William L. Langer's single-volume *Encyclopedia of World History* (1968) (1) is the only current world historical encyclopedia in English. Combining a geographical and chronological arrangement, it consists of over 1,300 pages of highly compressed descriptions of historical events and persons. Except for a brief, general introductory section on the beginning of the nineteenth century, scant attention is given anything other than political and military events. Cross-references are provided, and there are 183 pages of index, as well as over 100 genealogical tables and 50 black-and-white historical maps. There are no bibliographies. The editors have attempted "to compile a handbook . . . so arranged that the dates stand out while the material itself flows in a reasonably smooth narrative."

Joseph Dunner's *Handbook of World History: Concepts and Issues* (1967) (2) aims to provide information on the origin and application of historical concepts considered keys to the explanation of present-day sociopolitical life. There are over 300 articles, by more than 100 contributors, ranging from twenty pages for "Parliamentarism" and "Zionism" to short paragraphs on "Aggrandizement" and the "Cordon Sanitaire." Some articles have brief bibliographies.

Among the older encyclopedias of universal history are the *New Larned History* (1922–24) (3) and the ninth, eleventh, twelfth, and thirteenth editions of the *Encyclopaedia Britannica*. Although outdated in many respects, the *New Larned History,* and the ninth and eleventh editions of the *Encyclopaedia Britannica* can still provide valuable information if prudently used.

The *New Larned* reflects the modern approach toward history as not merely recounting "past politics" but encompassing fine-arts, literary, economic, religious, social, and scientific topics. The set consists of selections from prominent historians' works, newspapers, propaganda, official statements and correspondence, and related materials, together with chronologies, brief biographical sketches, definitions, and so forth, related to significant historical events. Three features are provided: a single, alphabetical arrangement of major and minor subjects; extensive narrative descriptions of the history of individual countries; and "easy tracing of the inter-relations of history." In general, the arrangement of a subject is chronological, but occasionally an alphabetical, topical, or other logical arrangement is required. For example, the treatment of World War I consists of over 1,000 pages, including a chronological table of events, with a classification system of numerals and letters. Where appropriate, certain subjects are treated in groups (for example, there are entries for "abdications," "armistices," and "massacres"), and there are numerous cross-references. Sources for quoted material are cited in full. The last volume includes citations of over 5,000 works from which selections were made. Among the titles are such works as the *Encyclopedia of Religion and Ethics* (A.1.e:9), the *Annual Register* (A.1.g:4), and *The Statesman's Yearbook* (E.1.e:1). Among the historians quoted are Herodotus, Froissart, Machiavelli, Voltaire, Gibbon, Macaulay, Ranke, Treitschke, Stubbs, Renan, Lavisse, Aulard, Ferrero, Breasted, Parkman, Rhodes, and Bancroft. Authorities in other fields who are cited include Franz Boas and R. A. Lowie in anthropology, William Graham Sumner in sociology, and James Bryce in political science. As an example of coverage, there are 334 pages of French history, beginning with a description of the country's geography, climate, area, and population, and covering its history from the ninth century A.D. to 1922. Among other features are genealogical tables for the Carolingians, Anjous, and Bonapartes; small, colored maps of France in 1154, 1180, 1314, and 1369; a black-and-white map of Paris in 1789; maps of the battles of Trafalgar, Austerlitz, and Waterloo; and texts of the constitutions of France from 1875 to 1919. Noting that historians generally do not like to deal with recent events, often characterizing them as "present politics" or "history in the making," the editors adopted the following policy: "So far as practicable the material used for the history of latter years is taken from official sources; i.e., from statements of fact that are made with official responsibility, in despatches, reports, diplomatic correspondence and other state papers published with governmental sanction"— thus presenting researchers with a repository of primary sources. In the *American Historical Review* of January 1923, however, historian Arthur I. Andrews expressed reservations about some of the authorities selected, mentioning especially Mark Twain on Austria-Hungary and Lothrop T. Stoddard (a well-known polemicist for Nordic supremacy) on nationalities in 1914.

Although there are more extensive descriptions of the various editions of the *Encyclopaedia Britannica,* the short one in Walford (A.1.b:12) is sufficient for determining its usefulness for research in history or other social sciences. Scholars generally agree that the ninth edition (1875–89) (4) and the eleventh edition (1910–11) (5) are the most valuable. (The twelfth and thirteenth editions each contain the eleventh edition with supplements.) The articles on some areas, including Africa, Southeast Asia, and Latin America, suffer from the limited information available when the sets were published, but other articles on subjects for which there was considerable factual data available are almost as useful today as when they were written.[1]

Another factor that cannot be overlooked is that older works such as the ninth and eleventh editions of the *Encyclopaedia Britannica* and the *New Larned History* reflect the morals and mores of the age in which they were written. For example, in the Victorian era the use of the word *homosexual* was regarded as in bad taste; hence, biographies of persons who were either known or alleged homosexuals ignored the issue or stated it in euphemistic terms. On the subject of Negroes, it is startling to encounter today the following statement from an article in a reference work:

> Mentally the negro is inferior to the white. The remark of F. Manet- ter, made after a long study of the negro in America, may be taken as generally true of the whole race: "The negro children were sharp, intelligent and full of vivacity, but on approaching the adult period a gradual change set in. The intellect seemed to become clouded, animation giving place to a sort of lethargy, briskness leading to indolence. We must necessarily suppose that the develop- ment of the negro and white proceeds on different lines. While with the latter the volume of the brain grows with the expansion of the brainpan, in the former the growth of the brain is on the contrary arrested by the premature closing of the cranial sutures and lateral pressure of the frontal bone." This explanation is reasonable and even probable as a contributing cause; but evidence is lacking on the subject and the arrest or even deterioration in mental development is no doubt very largely due to the fact that after puberty sexual matters take the first place in the negro's life and thoughts. At the same time his environment has not been such as would tend to pro- duce in him the restless energy which has led to the progress of the white race; and the easy conditions of tropical life and the fertility of the soil have reduced the struggle for existence to a minimum. But though the mental inferiority of the negro to the white or yellow races is a fact, it has often been exaggerated; the negro is largely the creature of his environment, and it is not fair to judge of his mental capacity by tests taken directly from the environment of the white man, as for instance tests in mental arithmetic; skill in reckoning is necessary to the white race, and it has cultivated the faculty; but it is not necessary to the negro. [*Encyclopaedia Britannica,* 11th ed., vol. 19, pp. 344–45]

In spite of such statements long since proven incorrect, it cannot be denied that the eleventh edition of the *Encyclopaedia Britan- nica* is an excellent source to consult, and is the only one for in- formation on some subjects. Articles on historical events and institutions are often accompanied by detailed maps, plates, or diagrams, and statistics (occasionally voluminous) are included where appropriate. Finally, most articles have excellent bibliogra- phies of works published before 1910.

Following is an analysis of the treatment given two terms, "an- archism" and "eugenics," in the ninth and eleventh editions of the *Encyclopaedia Britannica* and in the *New Larned History,* the *Encyclopedia of the Social Sciences,* and the *International Ency- clopedia of the Social Sciences.*

Anarchism is a political theory advocating abolition of all laws of the state and their replacement by voluntary agreements be- tween functional, local groups. Unfortunately, as a modern movement it has attracted many who are prone to insanity and violence. Anarchism has no alphabetical entry in the ninth edition of the *Encyclopaedia Britannica,* but there is an entry in the index for it, referring to the article on socialism. The author of the article on anarchism in the eleventh edition of the *Encyclopaedia Britannica* demonstrated a broad knowledge of the origins and growth of the movement up to 1910, and the article is accompanied by an excellent bibliography, including many works in languages other than English. The entry for anarchism in the *New Larned History* consists of selections from histories, the writings of propagandists (such as Emma Goldman), newspaper accounts, and so on. Anarchism in the *Encyclopedia of the Social Sciences* is longer, bringing the narrative up to the 1930s, with a good bibliography.

Eugenics is the science which seeks to understand all influences that can improve the inherited qualities of future generations. It became prominent toward the end of the nineteenth century. The early eugenics movement had an insecure scientific foundation, with supporters attracted by elitist sentiments and racial prejudice. Although coined by Sir Francis Galton in 1883, years before the appearance of the ninth edition of the *Britannica,* the term was not yet prominent enough to be included in it. There is a brief article in the eleventh edition. The writer, while giving a good, clear description of eugenics, wisely refrained from making any claims about the efficacy of its application. It is quite evident that a controversial term like eugenics points up a difficulty which editors of works such as the *New Larned History* encounter. In making selections from what are considered authoritative works, it is virtually impossible for a person with a limited knowledge of the information associated with a new term to distinguish objective exposition from polemics. For example, several of the selections on the term in the *New Larned* are from writers actively supporting the racist eugenics movement. The *Encyclopedia of the Social Sciences* gives a historical, scientific account; the author does not hedge on his skepticism of the efficacy of eugenics. A substantial bibliography, divided into exposition and criticism, is included. In the *International Encyclopedia of the Social Sciences,* the author of the eugenics article is not bothered by the indeterminate situation associated with the term in the 1930s or earlier. While acknowledging the potential of the practice of eugenics, he notes that considerably more data and research are required, along with the recognition that certain adverse factors cannot be ignored.

What is suggested by the above examples is that for terms, events, places, and people requiring only narrative descriptions, the ninth and eleventh editions of the *Encyclopaedia Britannica* and the *New Larned History* are still fairly reliable, but that articles on terms such as eugenics, requiring more than narrative descriptions, are not as reliable and in some cases may be downright misleading.

The *Harper Encyclopedia of the Modern World* (1970) (6) covers the period from 1760 to the present. It was edited by Richard B. Morris and Graham W. Irwin, with consultant editors for sections on Africa; China; Class, Labor, and Social Thought; [the] Communist World; Constitutional Development; Economic Development and Technology; Europe to 1914; Europe since 1914; India; Japan; Latin America; [the] Middle East; Science; and Southeast Asia. The book is in two parts: a "Basic Chronology" of political, military, and diplomatic history by state, region, and area; and a "Topical Chronology" of economic, social, and constitutional history, and the history of science, thought, and culture. Considerable attention is given to economic development and technology in the "Topical Chronology," where the subject matter is handled by time segments for major world areas, arranged according to their relative status on the economic-development scale. Headings within subsections follow the same order throughout: agriculture (and animal husbandry), raw materials, labor, energy, manufacturing and industry, transportation, communications, finance, foreign trade and investment, business organization, government policy, and "other factors." This arrangement enables the reader to trace a theme for one country, a group of countries, or the whole world from 1760 to the present. There are over 200 pages of index, and 52 black-and-white maps. There are no systematic bibliographies, but sources are cited for statistical tables and charts.

A. W. Palmer's *Dictionary of Modern History* (1962) (7) covers the period 1789–1945. Although "British affairs predominate," there are numerous entries of varying length on North America, Latin America, Western and Eastern Europe, and the Far East (but few on Africa). Biographies are included, but there are no bibliographies.

Ernest and Trevor Dupuy's *Encyclopedia of Military History* (1970) (8) is an excellent work on a neglected subject. It covers world military history from 3500 B.C. to A.D. 1965. Each chapter opens with a descriptive essay on the military trends of the period covered, including outstanding leaders; the development of military tactics, strategy, and weaponry; and so on. This is followed by a chronological survey of the principal wars of the period. The remainder of each chapter comprises a combined geographical and chronological treatment, with descriptions, of the significant military events of particular areas. The 117-page index is divided into "general," "battles and sieges," and "wars." There are over 80 black-and-white maps, and a bibliography of selected books on military history from ancient to modern times. Material on World

War I in the *New Larned History* (3) has been noted. The four-volume *Ten Eventful Years* (1947) (9) gives encyclopedic coverage to events and issues in the decade 1937–46. It is the work of 800 contributors from 45 countries. Articles vary in length from 30 or 40 pages for significant topics to a few hundred words for minor ones, and most have brief bibliographies. Topics include biography and literature, economics and geography, politics and government, science and medicine, and military events. Statistics are provided where appropriate. There are many illustrations, especially photographs, and an index.

Although outdated in many respects, Haydn's *Dictionary of Dates and Universal Information Relating to All Ages and Nations* (1910) (10) is useful as far as it goes. Recently reprinted, it consists of over 10,000 alphabetically arranged entries of people, places, events, associations, and so on. Where appropriate, certain subjects are treated in groups (for example, "abdications," "assassins," and "battles"). An index of names and subjects is included.

F.1.e   Handbooks and Yearbooks

In a scheme that combines a chronological arrangement and six parallel columns, S. H. Steinberg's *Historical Tables, 58 B.C.–A.D. 1963* (1964) (1) gives brief facts about historical events. The columns are labeled Western and Southern Europe; Central, Northern, and Eastern Europe; Countries Overseas; Constitutional History and Natural Science; and Cultural Life. Preference is given to events of the British Commonwealth and the United States. R. L. W. Collison's *Newnes' Dictionary of Dates* (1966) (2) is in two sections: an alphabetical arrangement of people, places, and events, with dates and a chronological listing of significant events. Haydn's *Dictionary of Dates* (F.1.d:10) is more comprehensive.

The "primary object" of Miriam Allen DeFord's *Who Was When?* (1950) (3) "is to ascertain who were the contemporaries of any celebrated person from 500 B.C. to 1949 A.D." The text is arranged in parallel columns, with such headings as Government and Law; Travel and Exploration; Literature; and Industry, Commerce, Economics, Finance, Invention, and Labor. All names are indexed together with birth and death dates of prominent contemporaries. Neville Williams's two-volume *Chronology* (1967, 1969) (4, 5) covers the period from 1492 to the late 1960s. Events in the arts and in science and technology are included, as well as political history. Each volume has an index of persons, places, and subjects. An added feature in the second volume is the inclusion of very brief statistics. There is an obvious bias toward the Western world.

F.I.f Historiography and Methodological Works

Barzun and Graff's *The Modern Researcher* (1970) (1), recently issued in an expanded edition, is generally acknowledged as the outstanding handbook on research and writing, with much valuable information on historical methodology. Part 1 deals with "first principles," exploring the difference between "research" and historical "reporting," and discussing general features of methodology and attitude. Part 2 discusses such aspects of historical research as fact-finding, note-taking, verification, and truth and causation. Part 3 focuses on such problems of writing as organization, style and the elimination of jargon, sentence structure, and the use of footnotes and bibliography. The book is lively, lucid, and full of sensible suggestions throughout. The bibliography, arranged by subject, includes books and articles on historical method, truth and causation, schools of thought, and the great historians, as well as titles on writing and composition. There is an index.

Among the categories of section A, part 1, of the AHA's *Guide to Historical Literature* (F.1.b:2) are manuals of historical method, persistent problems (causal analysis, explanation, continuity and change, logic), the meaning of man's past (theories of history), the scope and function of historical literature, and the doctrine and practice of historiography. Almost 500 annotated citations are interspersed among the categories. Lists of historiographical works are included among the chapters on geographical divisions.

The first two parts of the *Harvard Guide to American History* (O.2.e:5) should be noted. Part 1, "Status, Methods, and Presentation," explores such topics as theories of historical interpretation, principles of historical criticism, statistics and history, history and contemporary social research, along with suggested opportunities for research, methods of note-taking, and the mechanics of citation. Most topics include extensive bibliographies. Part 2, "The Materials of History," focuses on such problems as nondocumentary sources, maps and history, and the use of manuscripts. It also has bibliographies. *Approaches to History* (1962) (2), edited by H. P. R. Finberg, is a very useful guide by a number of distinguished British historians. Separate chapters survey the methods, trends, and some achievements of political, economic, social, universal, and local history; historical geography; the history of art; the history of science; and archaeology and place names. There are no formal bibliographies, but useful bibliographical details are included in each chapter.

Historical Studies Today (1972) (3), which originally appeared as the Winter and Spring 1971 issues of *Daedalus,* is devoted to current developments and trends in historiography, and contains

23 articles with such titles as "Is Politics Still the Backbone of History?" "From Social History to the History of Society," "Local History," "Quantitative History," "The Use and Abuse of Psychology in History," "Economic History and Economic Theory," and "History of War." Editor Felix Gilbert notes that although fashions in historical scholarship do not change rapidly, a revolution has occurred in historical scholarship, particularly in its focus. Social history, for example, has become the history of society, and "new fields have gained prominence: demography and kinship, social classes and social groups, modernization and industrialization, social movements and movements of social protest"—reflecting a new interpretation of the proper concern of historical research and indicating its debt to other disciplines.

The history of historical writing is covered in two works by leading American historians: James Westfall Thompson's monumental two-volume *History of Historical Writing* (1942) (4) and Harry Elmer Barnes's one-volume work of the same title (1962) (5). Both can be highly recommended for their balanced surveys of historical writing from the Greek period to the present. Barnes's history, published originally in 1937, was revised to some extent in 1962, and a number of titles were added to the bibliographies.

Introductory works on historical method are numerous; three of these, along with a work on the use of computers, will be mentioned.

The *Guide to Historical Method* (1969) (6) of Robert J. Shafer et al. is designed for history students. Chapters explore "The Nature of History," "Ideas and History," "Historical Evidence," "Collecting Historical Evidence," and "Using Evidence" ("external" and "internal" criticism, "synthetic operations," and "communications"). Appendix B, "Bibliographic Aids for Selective Countries," is a descriptive guide, of uneven quality, to selected titles on the United States, Great Britain, France, Germany, Mexico, and Kenya. Appendix C is a list of additional readings on historical method. A short work by G. Kitson-Clark, *Guide for Research Students Working on Historical Subjects* (1968) (7), prepared for graduate students at Cambridge, is quite helpful to other students. Direct and sensible advice on such topics as choice of subject, reviewing the evidence, and research notes is followed by three appendixes; the first covers books on historical research; the second is on the search for materials, discussing libraries, bibliographies, catalogs, and archival and other primary evidence; and the third covers working tools, reviewing a variety of reference materials.

Aimed more at the uncommitted and less advanced undergraduate is Walter T. K. Nugent's *Creative History: An Introduction to Historical Study* (1967) (8), which examines such topics as the meaning of history, reasons for studying history, library techniques, historical imagination, and quantification and uniqueness in history. Short book lists are given in many of the chapters, and there is a brief bibliography at the end of the book.

Charles M. Dollar and Richard J. Jensen describe their *Historian's Guide to Statistics* (1971) (9) as "a practical guide to the use of quantitative methods and computers in historical research." The first chapter examines the purpose and methods of quantitative research. Chapters 2–4 cover the statistical techniques of greatest value in dealing with historical data, and the principles of electronic data-processing and their application in historical research are discussed in chapters 5 and 6. Chapter 7, in three parts, is a "Guide to Resources of Value in Quantitative Historical Research." Part 1, "Guide to Published Data," lists general guides and international sources, American sources (general and sources of American election statistics), and sources for other countries. Part 2 is a list of social-science machine-readable data archives in the United States. Part 3, dealing with "scholarly literature (mostly from social sciences with special emphasis upon writings of the 1960s"), is arranged in three broad sections: (1) "Methodology," consisting of titles on historiography, research design, statistics, recommended statistics texts, electronic data-processing, geography, content analysis and information retrieval, and clustering methods; (2) "Political Studies," which lists works on methods, comparative and international political science, elections and parties, legislatures and roll calls, and collective biography; and (3) works on economic history; education and human capital; demography and population; urbanization and community; and mobility, conflict, stratification, and organizations.

F.1.g   Statistics Sources

The important sources of historical statistics are noted in the last paragraph of section D.2.a. The *Cross-Polity Time-Series Data* (I.1.g:7) is a good single-volume source. The increasing numbers of compilations of historical statistics on particular countries or regions are discussed in appropriate area-studies parts. Similar in approach to Taylor (G.1.h:2) and *Cross-Polity Time-Series Data,* Singer and Small's *The Wages of War, 1816–1965; A Statistical Handbook* (1972) (1) is a computer-produced compendium of data designed to identify variables most often associated with the eruption of war in the past 150 years. It examines 93 wars, with attention given to the factors of conflicts that result in war or in less violent solutions. Such data as trends and fluctuations in the frequency, magnitude, and intensity of wars are arranged systematically in many tables.

Section 2

F.2   History of Science and Technology

Thomas S. Kuhn declares that "though the history of science remains a small field, it has expanded more than tenfold in the last fifteen years. . . ."[2] The following are titles of some reference works useful for the history of science and technology and related disciplines, especially economic history and geography. *Isis* (1913–) (1), a quarterly devoted to the history of science and its cultural influences, includes an annual bibliography of about 2,500 entries. Various historical, philosophical, literary, and medical journals are searched for appropriate articles, and important books are also included. Many entries are annotated, and reviews are noted. The bibliography is arranged in four main categories, with most citations coming under "Histories of the Special Sciences" and "Chronological Classifications." The coverage is international, with abundant Russian and Japanese titles, but fewer from Chinese sources. There is an index of authors in each annual bibliography. In 1972 all separate bibliographies up to 1965 were cumulated, with an index including names of individual scientists and other personalities mentioned in the bibliographies as well as entries relating to institutions and societies. Subsequent parts will be arranged in order of periods and subjects. George Sarton's *Introduction to the History of Science* (1927–48) (2) is more like an encyclopedia than a history. According to the AHA *Guide to Historical Literature* (F.1.b:2), "it is indispensable for the period from classical times to the beginning of the 14th century. Sarton, a pioneer historian of science, covers world culture and treats science in its widest context. Unsurpassed for biographical and bibliographical data." A general index in volume 3 lists the main personalities covered in volumes 1 and 2, and is relatively inclusive for the third volume.

History of Science (1962–) (3), an annual review of literature, research, and teaching, provides critical reviews of problems in research in specific fields and from recent publications. Volume 1 includes a study of outstanding problems and sources for research in the history of the physical sciences in the first half of the nineteenth century, a critical review of recent Newtonian research, a study of the problems concerning the relations between science and technology in the eighteenth century, and a survey of recent publications in the history of medicine. A recent volume contains the first part of a study by Walter Pagel, "William Harvey Revisited"; an essay on Aztec science and technology; and a survey of sources and modern studies in the history of optical instruments. Most articles have extensive bibliographies.

The annual "Current Bibliography in the History of Technology" has appeared in the quarterly *Technology and Culture* (1959–) (4) since 1964. The 1964 cumulation covered articles and books of the year 1962, but there was no index; the author index in the 1965 cumulation covered the previous year as well. A cumulative subject index was provided for the first four annual bibliographies in the spring 1967 issue. The early cumulations contained over 400 entries, but the bibliographer, Jack Goodwin, noted that they were far from comprehensive, lacking especially items from Soviet and Eastern European sources. Current volumes have over 700 items. At first a classification scheme incorporating fifteen categories was used. The categories included

general and collected works (including works covering two or more special subjects)

documentation (bibliography; economic, business, political, and social history; travels and description; general relationships between technology and culture)

civil engineering (buildings, bridges, and tunnels; water supply and sewerage; urban engineering; surveying; instruments and maps)

transportation (ships; navigation and charting; canals and boats; roads and vehicles; railroads and vehicles; aircraft and spacecraft)

energy conversion (hydraulic engineering; internal-combustion engines; steam engines; steam-electric central stations; electrical-power transmission; lighting; heating and ventilating)

material and processes (metal, chemical, and wood industries, including paper and printing)

mechanical and electromechanical technology (tools, office machines, and so on; mechanical power transmission; weights and measures)

communication and records (except printing)

agricultural and food technology

industrial organization (management and mass-production techniques)

military technology

In later issues the following six chronological divisions were added: (1) the twentieth century and works relating to more than one division; (2) prehistory, antiquity, and primitive societies; (3) the Middle Ages; (4) from the Renaissance to the seventeenth century; (5) the eighteenth century; and (6) the nineteenth century. Items are arranged according to the previously described classification scheme within the chronological divisions. The annotations are informative, and bibliographies and reviews are noted.

In his preface, Eugene S. Ferguson states that the *Bibliography of the History of Technology* (1968) (5) attempts to provide "a reasonably comprehensive introduction to primary and secondary sources in the history of technology," excluding works on the history of science. The bibliography ranges from general titles to such specialized topics as the interrelationships of technology and culture and the development of the industrial assembly line. Annotations for the approximately 3,100 items include "scope" and "possible uses." Indexes to government publications, patents, catalogs of illustrations, and manuscripts are also described. There are author and subject indexes. This is a remarkably erudite book, a model of its type.

Especially designed for students and the general reader, K. J. Rider's annotated *History of Science and Technology: A Select Bibliography for Students* (1970) (6) attempts to "demonstrate the richness and variety of the material available for study. Preference has usually been given to narrative histories and works illustrating the scientific or technical development of their subjects, though highly specialized or technical works have been excluded." The section on the history of science includes bibliographies, histories, museums, and associations, but with most attention given to histories by countries, periods, and subjects. The technology section receives similar treatment but covers more subjects, including agriculture, engineering, firearms, printing, and transportation. There are name, title, and subject indexes.

The five-volume work by Charles Singer et al., *A History of Technology* (1956–64) (7), is the standard work on technology from its beginnings to 1900 (although coverage is generally confined to the Middle East, Europe, and the United States). Ferguson (F.2:5) notes that "just as a wise reader frequently turns first to a good encyclopedia when he prepares to enter a subject he is unfamiliar with, so the student of the history of technology should permit individual chapters of this work to give him an overview and a point of departure." A dissenting voice comes from M. I. Finley in a paper, "Archaeology and Society," published in *Historical Studies Today* (F.1.f:3). Finley cites the first two volumes of Singer as examples of

> the perverse refusal by some distinguished experts in the history of technology to permit either the historian or his documentation to make a contribution. They prefer to write the history of technology largely, if not solely, from the artifacts. . . . [More reliable, he suggests, are] the painstaking, often unrewarding, but always more fruitful and more accurate studies during the past decade or so, by scholars who combine the archaeological and documentary evidence in an investigation of agricultural technology in Gaul and other parts of the western Roman Empire.

The chapter by A. Rupert Hall on the history of science and technology in *Approaches to History* (F.1.f:2) should not be overlooked.

Part G

Political Science

Section 1

G.1.a Atlases and Gazetteers

Andrew K. H. Boyd's *Atlas of World Affairs* (I.1.a:8) is discussed in part I. *Shepherd's Historical Atlas* (F.1.a:1) is one of several historical atlases useful for political science. Others are introduced in section F.1.a. *Shepherd's* has detailed, colored maps showing political and military activities and colonization from 1450 B.C. to A.D. 1964. Occasionally research in political science requires gazetteer information; among the most useful sources are the *Times Index-Gazetteer of the World* (E.1.a:2), the *Columbia-*

Lippincott Gazetteer of the World (E.1.a:4), and *Webster's Geographical Dictionary* (E.1.a:5).

G.1.b   Bibliographies

Bibliographies of Bibliographies. Volume 3 of the *Universal Reference System* (7) lists roughly 2,400 selected bibliographies on a wide range of topics in political science and related disciplines to be found in books, journals, and government publications. Besterman (A.1.b:1), the *Bibliographic Index* (A.1.b:2), and Gray's *Serial Bibliographies in the Humanities and Social Sciences* (A.1.b:3) are also recommended, particularly because researchers will find these titles easier to use than the *Universal Reference System*. Bibliographies are indicated in the index of the *International Bibliography of Political Science* (4) under the entry "political science, works of reference."

Reference Works. Clifton Brock's *The Literature of Political Science: A Guide for Students, Librarians, and Teachers* (1969) (1) is perhaps the most useful reference work for undergraduate research. Brock concentrates on fewer titles but directs more attention to library procedures and has more description of important works. Particularly helpful are the illustrations of pages from such reference works as the *U.S. Government Publications: Monthly Catalog,* the *U.N. Documents Index* (G.2.b:14), and the *Statistical Abstract of the United States* (O.1.g:2). The illustrations give a practical demonstration of how to use these works. Brock's guide has two sections. The first includes discussions of card-catalog features, periodical indexes and abstracts, searching for book reviews, sources of statistics, and using publications of the federal government, the U.N., and related organizations. The second section includes descriptions of general political-science bibliographies, as well as recommended sources for research on American government and politics, political behavior and public opinion, public administration, and so on.

Robert Harmon's *Political Science: A Bibliographical Guide to the Literature* (1965) (2) and Lubomyr Wynar's *Guide to Reference Materials in Political Science* (1966–68) (3) may seem pedestrian when compared to Brock's lively narrative, but each covers a larger number of monographs and reference works than Brock does. Wynar's work is in two volumes: the first is devoted to general social-science reference sources, general political-science reference sources, and reference works and monographs on political theory and ideology; the second has chapters on international relations, public administration, political behavior, and comparative politics, as well as on government publications of international organizations and world nations and reference sources in law. The emphasis is on English-language publications, but important items in other languages are noted. All citations are briefly annotated, and there is an index for each volume. Harmon's *Political Science* .lists reference works and general monographs on comparative government, state and local government, political parties, public opinion and electoral processes, political theory, public administration, and international relations. Headnotes are provided for each category, and some titles are annotated. A supplement brings coverage up to January 1, 1967, and some sections covered in the original volume are treated more extensively in the supplement. (A second supplement has also been published.) Harmon's first volume was criticized for uneven coverage and poor organization. Walford (A.1.b:12), Winchell (A.1.b:13), White (A.1.b:10), and Lewis (A.1.b:11) are worth consulting.

General Bibliographies.   The *ABS Guide to Recent Publications in the Social and Behavioral Sciences* (A.1.b:8), the *London Bibliography of the Social Sciences* (A.1.b:5), and the PAIS *Bulletin* (A.1.b:15) provide selective coverage of materials in political science. More extensive coverage is provided in the *International Bibliography of Political Science* (1953–) (4) and *International Political Science Abstracts* (1951–) (5). The first is an annual, with about 5,000 significant articles, monographs, and publications of international and national governments. The editors claim that only works of "true scientific character" are included, while journalistic or polemical ones are excluded. About 1,400 periodical articles are regularly searched for articles. Beginning with the fourth volume, items abstracted in *International Political Science Abstracts* are indicated. Each volume is arranged according to a detailed classification scheme of six major categories: general political science, including methodological works, reference works, and bibliographies; political thought, including ideologies; government and public administration; governmental process; international relations; and area studies. Each category is subdivided into areas, including regions and countries. Occasionally book-review citations are given. Reviews for titles listed in previous volumes are noted. There are author and subject indexes. The quarterly *International Political Science Abstracts* is more selective in coverage, being limited to 150 periodicals. The same arrangement is used as that for the *International Bibliography of Political Science*. Each issue has a subject index, and there are annual cumulative subject and author indexes.

A "current contents" type of bibliography, *ABC POL SCI* (1969–) (6), reproduces in advance of publication the tables of contents of 260 journals in political science, public administration, law, and related fields. Each issue has an author index (cumulated twice yearly), with an annual subject index. The virtue of this type of bibliography is the access it provides to the contents of a large number of journals, eliminating the necessity of scanning individual journals. Although based on different principles than *ABC POL SCI,* the *Social Sciences Citation Index* (A.1.b:6) also provides access to recent articles.

Considerable controversy is associated with the *Universal Reference System* (1967–) (7), a ten-volume work with annual supplements. It is an attempt to produce, with the assistance of data-processing techniques, a large bibliography in political science. Its main feature is a large, multifaceted index, giving more approaches to the contents of works than other bibliographies. The main criticisms of *URS* have been that it is limited to a select number of English-language publications, mostly monographs, and that for all the effort of production, it still requires supplementing. In the 995-page index of volume 1, titles are arranged chronologically under subject headings. A code of letters and numbers in the index entry directs users to an annotated listing in the numerically arranged "Catalog of Documents." Other codes in the indexes indicate the form of the work (i.e., "S" for short article, "B" for book), as well as the major "facets," or subjects, of a particular title. At the front of each volume is an explanation on how to use the *URS,* a topical and methodological index, and an alphabetical table showing frequency of occurrence of "descriptors." A volume is devoted to each of the following topics: international affairs; legislative process, representation, and decision-making; bibliography of bibliographies in political science, government, and public administration; administrative management; public and private bureaucracy; current events and problems of modern society; public opinion, mass behavior, and political psychology; law; economic regulation; public policy and the management of science; and comparative government and cultures. It is recommended that *URS* be used jointly with other bibliographies, including another computer-produced bibliography, the *Peace Research Abstracts Journal* (G.2.d:12). The latter is easier to use, and covers a range of subjects far broader than the title suggests. According to the editors, broad coverage is required because issues affecting peace are so nebulous. Consequently, abstracts of items on world affairs or the domestic affairs of particular nations which might be of value to the peace researcher are included. The extent of *PRAJ* coverage is exemplified by the following items: an abstract of the NATO *Agreement between the Parties to the North Atlantic Treaty for Cooperation Regarding Atomic Information* (1964) "specifying the types of atomic information that will be communicated to NATO countries by the U.S. and other NATO members possessing such information"; an abstract of a document published in the *Peking Review* by the Chinese Ministry of Foreign Affairs on October 8, 1969, replying to a Soviet statement of June 13, 1969; the contents of selected writings on the Chinese approach to negotiations published as hearings of the U.S. Senate Subcommittee on National Security and International Operations; an abstract of a bibliography published by the U.S. Army on U.S. civil-defense activities, 1960–67; an abstract of a "portrait" in a German periodical of the powerful Arab guerrilla organization Al Fatah; abstracts of translations of captured Viet Cong documents published by the RAND Corporation; and an abstract of a Dutch account of the struggle against Portuguese colonialism.

The *Index to Legal Periodicals* (1908–) (8) lists by subject, with author index, all articles, comments, and notes in the principal American and British Commonwealth periodicals, significant articles of bar journals, and other publications. There is also a "Table of Cases Commented Upon" and an index to book reviews, arranged by author. It is cumulated annually and triennially. The quarterly *Index to Periodical Articles Related to Law* (1959–) (9) excludes articles indexed in the *Index to Legal Periodicals.* It lists articles selected from general and other nonlegal journals that focus on law and its influence on agriculture, economics, social issues, and international affairs.

Chapter 7 of *Historical Abstracts* (F.1.b:10) focuses on political science, including a subdivision on international relations. Ethel Albert's *Selected Bibliography on Values, Ethics, and Aesthetics in the Behavioral Sciences and Philosophy, 1920–1958* (B.2.g:3) contains more than 140 annotated citations of books and articles on political science, public administration, and government.

Reviews of Research. Chapter 4 of Hoselitz's *Reader's Guide to the Social Sciences* (A.1.b:9) comprises a critical review by Heinz Eulau of over 650 published monographs. The emphasis is on recent American works, but included are studies ranging back to the beginning of this century. In the first section, the analyses are divided into such categories as politics as science, the state of affairs; political theory, the lost frontier; the core of political science, the study of government; the party and the vote; and the behavioral breakthrough. The second section is a continuation of his earlier review essay in the chapter "Political Science" in *A Reader's Guide to the Social Sciences* (1959). The earlier essay covers the literature through 1956, while the revised chapter covers books that appeared after that date. In it works are categorized by subjects such as political theory, political man, comparative politics, and international politics.

The stated purpose of the *Political Science Annual* (1966–) (10) is "to contribute periodic inventories of selected aspects of political science"; in fact, the work attempts to synthesize the results of "scattered" research. Each section is written by a specialist and includes a bibliography of works discussed. The chapters in volume 1 are "Political Socialization," by Richard E. Dawson; "Legislative Institutions and Processes," by Heinz Eulau and Katherine Hinckley; "An Application of the Policy Sciences Orientation: The Sharing of Power in a Psychiatric Hospital," by Harold D. Lasswell and Robert Rubenstein; and "Public Opinion and Opinion Change," by Bernard C. Hennessy. Dawson indicates that although the concept of political socialization is relatively new, a considerable body of literature exists. He discusses over 130 research studies relating both to the individual or socio-psychological level and the societal or system level. Eulau and Hinckley cover about 120 studies published between 1961 and 1964, focusing both on the activities inside legislatures, such as party caucuses and investigative committees, and forces outside, such as electoral constituencies, district parties, and pressure groups. Lasswell and Rubenstein discuss 50 research studies. Hennessy covers about 180 articles and books with the following objectives: to identify "problem areas," referring "to standard and/or current provocative work"; and "to consider, in more detail and with greater speculative license than reviewers usually claim, the special problems having to do with opinion change and the links between opinion change and policy change." There is an index for the whole volume. Volume 2 has been criticized as being uneven. There are chapters on education and political behavior, community-power studies, international law, and international organization.

A special supplement of the *American Behavioral Scientist* (1963) (11) provides a review of the literature of political science and jurisprudence from a "behavioristic" point of view. Among the topics treated are working specifications of the field; schools, methods, and techniques; results achieved; contemporary controversy; and problems of terminology. There is a bibliography of selected books and journals. Each volume of D. C. Heath's Problems in Political Science series (1967–) (12) covers a particular topic and includes different interpretations of specialists. Among existing titles are *The Representative: Trustee? Delegate? Politician?* (1967); *Free Speech and Political Protests* (1967); *Western Europe: What Path to Integration?* (1967); *Karl Marx: Scientist, Revolutionary, or Humanist?* (1969); and *The CIA:*

Problems of Secrecy in a Democracy (1968). New titles will be found listed in the D. C. Heath catalog in *PTLA* (A.1.b:30). *Social Science Information* (B.1.f:5) regularly lists surveys of research in political science.

G.1.c   Biographical Dictionaries and Directories

Biographies of prominent political scientists are included in the *Encyclopedia of the Social Sciences* (A.1.e:1) and the *International Encyclopedia of the Social Sciences* (A.1.e:2). The Social and Behavioral Sciences volumes of *American Men and Women of Science* (A.1.d:15) lists a number of political scientists, and the American Political Science Association issues irregularly a *Biographical Directory* (1945–) (1) of members. Biographical information on prominent statesmen and politicians is found in the *Almanac of Current World Leaders* (1957–) (2), the *International Yearbook and Statesmen's Who's Who* (A.1.d:6), and the *New York Times Biographical Edition* (A.1.d:13). The *Almanac of Current World Leaders,* arranged by country, gives information on government officials down to the cabinet level. It is issued three times a year, with monthly supplements. A good source for biographical information on deceased persons is the *New York Times Obituary Index* (A.1.d:12). In addition to *Biography Index* (A.1.d:10) and Slocum (A.1.d:9), chapter 12 of Mason's *Research Resources* (G.2.c:2), "Biographical Reference Publications," is an annotated list of biographical sources arranged in five sections (United States, continents and regions, countries, international and professional groups, and specialists in the social sciences).

G.1.d   Encyclopedias and Dictionaries

The *Encyclopedia of the Social Sciences* (A.1.e:1) and the *International Encyclopedia of the Social Sciences* (A.1.e:2) are good starting points for research on specific topics. Among the articles relating to political science in the *Encyclopedia of the Social Sciences* are "The Press," "The Philippine Problem," and "League of Nations," as well as "Common Law," "Constitutional Law," "Fascism," and almost 100 pages on "Government." In the *International Encyclopedia of the Social Sciences,* besides "Political Science," there are articles on "International Law," "International Relations," "Political Behavior," "Political Theory," and on prominent contributors to the development of the discipline.

Gould's *Dictionary of the Social Sciences* (A.1.e:4) and Zadrozny's *Dictionary of Social Sciences* (A.1.e:3) include political-science terms. Joseph Dunner has edited the *Dictionary of Politi-*

cal Science (1964) (1) and the *Handbook of World History: Concepts and Issues* (F.1.d:2). In the first work, about 200 specialists provide "concise definitions and descriptions of nations, terms, events, and personalities used most frequently in the writings of political scientists." In the second about 200 specialists have contributed signed articles, some with bibliographies appended, on a broad range of terms related to "present-day sociopolitical life." Besides definitions of political terms, issues, and so on, Walter Thiemer's *Encyclopedia of Modern World Politics* (1950) (2) has brief political histories of nations and biographical sketches of political leaders. Maurice Cranston and Sanford Lakoff edited *A Glossary of Political Ideas* (1968) (3), in which 15 contributors define 51 abstract terms and list suggestions for further reading. The terms range from "Anarchism" and "Authority" through "Ideology" and "Imperialism" to "Syndicalism" and "Utopia." Rudolph Heimanson's *Dictionary of Political Science and Law* (1967) (4) focuses mainly on American political terms, though there are some definitions of general items. Finally, because political science is rife with acronyms and code names, attention is directed to the *Code Names Dictionary* (A.1.e:13) and the *Acronyms and Initialisms Dictionary* (A.1.e:14).

G.1.e   Handbooks and Yearbooks

Among the most useful yearbooks for research in political science are the *Annual Register* (A.1.g:4), *The Statesman's Yearbook* (E.1.e:1), and *The Europa Yearbook* (I.1.e:1). Others are noted in section I.1.e.

G.1.f   Newspapers and News Digests

In section I.1.f, extensive discussion of newspapers and news digests is provided, and almost inevitably, such discussions emphasize political issues. Not mentioned in I.1.f are two news-digest services issued by the same firm. *Deadline Data on Foreign Affairs* (1965–) (1), published on 5 by 8-inch cards rather than in the standard news-digest loose-leaf format, gives information on the national and international affairs of individual countries as well as on international events. *Deadline Data* is an information-retrieval system providing quick reference to world events. Currently there are over 12,000 cards on more than 300 subjects, with weekly supplements. Subject headings are organized alphabetically and chronologically. Subjects are traced historically, and sources are indicated. Interpretive editorial comments are identified. *On Record* (1963–) (2) is based on *Deadline Data;* each issue focuses on a particular country or event and contains background information and a chronological summary of events.

G.I.g   Methodological Works

Over 120 articles and books on the application of survey methods to the study of politics are discussed by Herbert McCloskey
in *Survey Research in the Social Sciences* (B.1.f:3). McCloskey
notes that "within two decades the survey method has become the
most important research procedure in the 'behavioral' study of
politics, and is being increasingly adopted by 'non-behaviorists' as
well" (p. 65). "Traditional political science has relied principally
upon documentary sources, reportage, anecdotal data, subjective
and unsystematic observation, individual interpretations, narrative
treatment, and the philosophical examination of analytical and
normative statements. The behavioral study of politics has stressed
direct observation, objective measurement, systematic data collection, the operationalizing of concepts, quantification, a deliberate
search for regularities and variations, and systematic comparison
across groups and cultures in an effort to ascertain the limits of
generalization" (p. 65). McCloskey discusses such issues as the
nature and types of surveys; survey methods and the science of
politics (establishing the facts, increasing the range and amount
of information, the adoption of the scientific posture); the substantive contributions of surveys (public opinion, participation,
voting, political elites and leadership, political ideology and extreme belief, political socialization, psychology and politics, political institutions, comparative and international studies); new applications for survey research (political leadership, internal party
affairs, the relation of belief to action, historical trends and analysis); the contribution of surveys to theory; and limitations and
problems in the use of political surveys.

Heinz Eulau and James G. March edited *Political Science*
(1969) (1), a "comprehensive review and appraisal" of political
science, with attention directed toward what political science is
about; its relevance for public policy; the changing frontiers of
theory; and research, the prospects of research, and so on. Political science is one of the disciplines in "Social Science Methodology:
A Bibliography of Studies," a regular feature of *Social Science Information* (B.1.f:5).

G.I.h   Statistics Sources

Recent interest among political scientists, as well as scholars in
related disciplines, in studies of cross-cultural comparisons has
resulted in the compilation of a number of computer-produced
volumes of statistical data. Often these are useful as sources of
statistics for all types of research. Perhaps the best example of the
broad uses possible is the *Cross-Polity Times-Series Data* (I.1.

g:7), a volume compiled expressly for comparative historical studies. An earlier compilation of data along similar lines is the *Cross-Polity Survey* (1963) (1), which compares 115 independent nations in terms of 57 characteristics.

The *World Handbook of Political and Social Indicators* (1972) (2) contains quantitative data up to 1972 on 136 countries. Arrangement of the five main parts is as follows: category 1 is on "political structure and performance," and data on such factors— some extremely subjective—as the age of national institutions, education expenditure, party fractionalization, press freedom, and electoral irregularities—are given. Protest demonstrations, riots, armed attacks, deaths from domestic violence, external interventions, and regular and irregular executive transfers are among the issues discussed in category 2. The largest group is category 3, "social patterns," which provides data on literacy for 1950 and 1960, urbanization, concentration of population, vital statistics, mail per capita, and income and land distribution. In category 4, concern is for "national resources and development," including population density and growth rates, GNP and growth rates, scientific capacity, energy consumption, and so on. Attention is directed to "external relations" in category 5, where diplomatic representation, foreign aid, and foreign trade and mail are among the factors tabulated. Sources are given, along with discussions of applications of and references to examples of aggregate data analysis.

Section 2

G.2.a Comparative Politics

The area-studies section of this volume contains the bulk of information sources useful for comparing political systems. Brock (G.1.b:1), Harmon (G.1.b:2), and Wynar (G.1.b:3) have chapters on comparative politics, while *Comparative Political Studies* (I.2.f:1) features an annotated list of books and articles in two issues of each volume.

G.2.b International Organizations

This section, as well as the next, cover topics that have received much attention from scholars, who have devoted to them a large number of bibliographies and reference works. This section is arranged as follows: works on international organizations in general; then the League of Nations, the United Nations, and related organizations. (Regional organizations receive more attention in the appropriate area-studies parts.) Bibliographies are listed first, followed by handbooks and other miscellaneous guides. Besides

Brock (G.1.b:1), Harmon (G.1.b:2), and Wynar (G.1.b:3), consult the Union of International Associations' *Select Bibliography on International Organization, 1885–1964* (1965) (1), compiled by Georges P. Spaeckaert. This is an annotated listing of over 1,000 books in several languages on international organizations in general, as well as on 214 individual organizations. Brock (G.1. b:1) notes that "other bibliographies provide better coverage of major organizations such as the U.N. but Spaeckaert lists books on many lesser-known, non-governmental organizations." Each issue of the quarterly *International Organization* (1947–) (2) has a selected bibliography of books and articles in various languages, arranged under the following headings: general (political, economic, and social); U.N. (political and security questions, economic and social questions, administrative and budgetary matters, legal questions); and legal issues. A bibliography of studies published from 1945 to 1966 entitled *International Organization* (1969) (3) was compiled by Harold S. Johnson and B. Singh. The table of contents gives some idea of the scope: Approaches to the Study of International Organization, Foundations of the International System, Participants in International Organization, International Institutionalization, Dynamics of International Organization, Progress of International Organization. A list of bibliographical aids is included.

Although the multivolume *League of Nations and United Nations Monthly List of Selected Articles: Cumulative, 1920–1970* (1971–) (4) is arranged awkwardly and has no annotations, subject indexes, or lists of periodicals indexed, it promises to be an important research aid. It cumulates the League of Nations' *Monthly List of Selected Articles* (1929–45), the U.N.'s *List of Selected Articles* (1949–63), and *Current Issues* (1965–70). Articles are confined to the activities of the League of Nations, the United Nations, and their specialized agencies, concerning political, legal, economic, and social problems. The lack of an adequate introduction to the set requires the user to learn through using it. In general, it is arranged first by subject, then by country in intervals of about four years, with articles listed chronologically under each heading. *Current Issues and New Publications in the Dag Hammarskjold Library* merged into *Current Bibliographical Information* (1971–) (5).

Jacob Robinson's *International Law and Organizations* (1967) (6) contains over 2,000 annotated citations in many languages. Encyclopedias, dictionaries, bibliographies, yearbooks, periodicals, and collections of documents are included; private international law and international relations are excluded. Perhaps the most useful feature for undergraduate research is the list of sources of biographical information on individuals prominent in international law, including those who influenced its growth—jurists, lawyers, Nobel Peace Prize winners, and racial leaders who espoused non-violence. The format of the biographical chapter is similar to Arnim (A.1.b:4). Amos J. Peaslee's *International Governmental Organizations: Constitutional Documents* (1965–68) (7) contains in four volumes texts of charters and related items. The *Yearbook of International Organizations* (1948–) (8), the monthly *International Associations* (1947–) (9), and *Who's Who in International Organizations* (1962–) (10) are published by the Union of International Organizations. The *Yearbook* gives names of members and officers, brief histories, descriptions of the structures and activities, and publications of both intergovernmental and nongovernmental international organizations. Information on organizations is updated in the issues of *International Associations*. *Who's Who in International Organizations* is a directory of officers of these organizations. Volume 1 of *The Europa Yearbook* (I.1. e:1) provides information on international organizations ranging from the U.N. to the Asian Development Bank to bilateral agreements such as the St. Lawrence Seaway and the Columbia River treaties. Data include a list of member nations, structure of organization, activities, a list of conventions and agreements, statistical tables, budgets, texts or summaries of constitutions or other statutes, and publications. A special section lists under 17 headings (including agriculture, forestry and fisheries, education, social welfare, transport, and youth and students) smaller international and nongovernmental organizations.

Alice H. Flynn's *World Understanding* (1965) (11) is an annotated bibliography of selected books on the U.N. and its work, arranged by subject, with an author index. The *Monthly List of Books Cataloged in the Library of the United Nations* (1946–) (12) is a more comprehensive source of books on issues of concern to the League of Nations and the U.N. Approximately 3,500 titles are briefly annotated annually. (Official publications are excluded.) There is an annual author index. J. Douma's *Bibliography on the International Court of Justice, 1918–1964* (1965) (13) is a bibliography of over 3,000 selectively annotated articles, books, and official publications. The table of contents allows a systematic approach to the Permanent Court of International Justice, established under the League of Nations, and the present International Court of Justice. A comprehensive list of U.N. publications is in the *United Nations Documents Index* (1950–) (14). *Publications Issued by the League of Nations* (1935) (15) and its supplements (1936 and 1937) cover the League's publications in a similar manner. The U.N.'s *Publications Catalog* (1967) (16)

and its supplement (1968–69) describe all sales publications of
the U.N., including publications, issued from 1945 to 1969, of the
International Court of Justice (excluding mimeographed documents prepared by the Economic Commission for Europe). Researchers requiring considerable working knowledge of the publications of the League of Nations or the U.N. should consult Hans
Aufricht's *Guide to League of Nations Publications* (1951) (17)
(reprinted in 1966), the briefer *Sources of Information: A Handbook on the Publications of the League of Nations* (1939) (18)
by A. C. von Breycha-Vauthier, or Winton's *Publications of the
United Nations System* (1972) (19). Aufricht's *Guide to League
of Nations Publications,* the definitive bibliography of the League,
provides a concise historical outline of its activities. It comprises
a selective, annotated list, with extensive headnotes for each subdivision, covering publications of the Permanent Court, the International Labor Organization, the International Institute of Intellectual Cooperation, and so on. Three types of annotations are
used: brief descriptions; tables of contents; and footnote references to related documents, articles, or books, and other pertinent
information. Part 4 is in the form of brief statements of facts,
issues, or procedures, accompanied by footnotes indicating the
principal documents related to these questions. The appendixes
contain more than 240 pages of documents on the League of Nations, the International Labor Organization, the Permanent Court
of Justice, and finally the transfer of the League of Nations' assets
and functions to the U.N. There is an index. The aim of Breycha-
Vauthier's *Sources of Information* is to indicate where and how
material can be located on political, economic, legal, and social
problems, as well as military, health, and transport questions.
"Since League documents as a rule contain detailed references to
earlier related material, it is comparatively easy to collect all information published by the League on a given question, once the
most recent central documents have been traced" (introduction).
This brief book mentions such central documents and makes suggestions for further research. Winton's *Publications of the United
Nations System* is in three parts. Part 1 outlines each organization
and its publications, giving aims, member states, principal organs
in its structure, and the nature of its official records, as well as
guides, bibliographies, and constitutions; there are cross-references
to publications in parts 2 and 3. The divisions in part 2—ranging
from "agriculture," "the arts," "bibliographies and documentation
services," and "cartography" to "science and technology," "social
science," "transport," and "treaties and international agreements"
—each comprise descriptions of statistical publications, directories,
collections of laws and treaties, dictionaries, abstracts, catalogs,

and so on. Part 3 is a comprehensive list of periodicals, yearbooks, and "recurrent surveys," with brief descriptions giving such information as year of first issue, analysis of content, and so on.

Volume 1 of the *Worldmark Encyclopedia of the Nations* (I.1.d:1) is an authoritative guide to the structure and activities of the U.N. and related bodies, including aims, membership, and bibliographical information. At the end is a useful table indicating membership (as well as purpose) of regional intergovernmental organizations throughout the world. *Everyman's United Nations* (1948–) (20) is a biennial official handbook containing extensive descriptions of the U.N.'s purposes and work, along with information about related intergovernmental agencies. There is a general index. The *Yearbook* (1947–) (21) of the U.N. is a record of the U.N., its specialized agencies, and General Agreement on Tariffs and Trades (GATT). Topics ranging from political and security questions to matters of trusteeship and administration are treated in detailed essays, with references to documents and previous *Yearbooks;* the texts of (and vote on) resolutions of that year are included. For example, the section on legal questions provides the texts of decisions and dissenting opinions on cases taken to the International Court of Justice. Tables and lists of data (especially offices and officers) are included. Each volume has subject and name indexes. The *Annual Review of United Nations Affairs* (1949–) (22) is a briefer treatment than the *Yearbook,* with emphasis on the role of the Secretary General.

Bibliographies of the Commonwealth of Nations will be discussed in section L.2.g. H. Duncan Hall's *Commonwealth: A History of the British Commonwealth of Nations* (1971) (23) has an excellent select bibliography of primary and secondary sources and a discussion of bibliographies concerning internal Commonwealth relations.

G.2.c International Relations

The titles introduced in this section represent a selected number of the best of their type; there are many others. Two excellent guides to sources of information in the study of international relations exist. Janusa K. Zawodny's *Guide to the Study of International Relations* (1966) (1) contains well-annotated citations to over 500 important bibliographies, periodicals, dictionaries, handbooks, and guides for the study of international relations. The arrangement is by type of source (e.g., encyclopedias, documents, statistical abstracts). It is indexed by subject and title. Brock (G.1.b:1) suggests that Zawodny is the best starting place for research in international relations, but John Brown Mason, in *Research Resources: Annotated Guide to the Social Sciences*

(1968–) (2), has reservations. In the first volume of Mason's *Research Resources,* entitled *International Relations and Recent History,* over 1,200 books and periodicals (including newspapers) are listed and extensively annotated. The book comprises six parts. Part 1 introduces indexes and abstracts, general and specialized, not only in international relations but also in related subjects in the social sciences, and for geographical areas. In parts 2 and 3, a similar treatment is given periodicals and reference books. (The excellent list of biographical-reference publications in part 3 has been mentioned previously.) Part 4 is an extensive listing of national and trade bibliographies of various countries, and it is of interest principally to persons involved in extremely intensive research. Part 5 is a listing of U.S. government publications. Part 6 takes up newspapers and related publications, including one of the best discussions available of translations of the foreign press. There are indexes of names and titles. *The Foreign Affairs Fifty-Year Bibliography* (1972) (3) is a reassessment by 400 authorities of 2,000-odd books on international issues published between 1920 and 1970. Comments are longer and more critical than similar retrospective bibliographies, often with comparisons of other titles on the same subjects. There are author and title indexes.

Reviews of published research in international affairs are available in the *Yearbook of World Affairs* (1947–) (4). Each volume has two sections. The first consists of long descriptive and interpretive articles on major world developments written by specialists. (Since topics vary from year to year, the examination of a number of volumes is suggested.) The second part comprises a series of bibliographic essays dealing with economic, legal, sociological, and other aspects of world affairs. About 600 books on world affairs are reviewed annually (an index of titles appears at the front of each volume). There is a general index to articles and bibliographical essays.

In Jack Plano and Ray Olton's *International Relations Dictionary* (1969) (5), terms are arranged under broad categories: Geography and Population; International Economics; War and Military Policy; Ideology and Communications; Nationalism, Imperialism, and Colonialism; Nature and the Role of Foreign Policy; National Political Systems; Diplomacy; Disarmament and Arms Control; International Law; and International Organization. In addition to defining the terms, the book explains their significance in the context of the category in which they appear. For example, in the section on American foreign policy, the "Bricker Amendment" is defined as a move in 1953 and 1954 to amend the U.S. Constitution so that external treaties would not have an internal effect on the United States, its significance being that it reflected apprehension over U.N. activities and that it was an attempt to reverse the trend toward strong executive leadership in U.S. foreign affairs. There is an index for main entries and for other terms. A. M. Hyamson's *Dictionary of International Affairs* (1947) (6) includes entries on nations, treaties, organizations, and related matters. The more significant terms and treaties receive longer treatment, while historical information is given for states and nationalities. Gunther Haensch's *Dictionary of International Relations and Politics* (1965) (7) provides a slightly different, but extremely useful, type of information, noting differences between British and American English and the equivalent terms of German, French, and Spanish as spoken in various countries. The main section is arranged by subject, allowing users to familiarize themselves with terms within a particular context, such as countries within a region, international law, international organization and administration, or political and diplomatic history. There are indexes arranged by language.

The most authoritative review of world events is the annual *Survey of International Affairs* (1925–) (8). Coverage varies according to events, but generally attention is directed to major geographical divisions of the world. The volume covering 1961 was issued in 1965, indicating a substantial time lag. A companion series, *Documents on International Affairs* (1929–) (9), contains documents, speeches, and communiqués. The arrangement of documents corresponds to the arrangement of chapters in the *Survey* of the same year. The *Survey* volumes are indexed; the *Documents* volumes list documents in chronological order at the end of the book. Using *Keesing's Contemporary Archives* (A.1.g:5) jointly with the *Survey* and *Documents* is recommended, since they provide excellent coverage of world events during the 1930s, 40s, and 50s.

Among the myriad guides, handbooks, yearbooks, and miscellaneous items on international affairs is a series known as the *International Review Service* (1954–) (10). Recent topics were "China: Representation in U.N." (1969), "Czechoslovakia Invasion" (1968), "Industrialization of Underdeveloped Countries" (1969), "Suez Canal" (1969), and "U.N. Emergency Force" (1969). Issues appear several times a year, with one issue summarizing U.N. activities for the previous year.

Locating texts of documents such as peace treaties and other multipartite agreements in the English language has provided considerable difficulty for students. Several sets of translated treaties, as well as indexes to locations of treaties, have recently appeared, making the task easier. It is noted in section I.1.g that *Keesing's Contemporary Archives* is a good source of texts of documents and speeches, but its index is occasionally difficult to use. Concise summaries of the most important multilateral treaties in force as of April 1968 are in *Treaties and Alliances of the World* (1968) (11), but more important, this work provides access to *Keesing's*. Beginning with the Declaration of Paris of 1856, early international agreements and their later expansion are briefly traced up to World War II. The chapters that follow focus on the treaties emanating from World War II, the U.N., the integration of Europe, OECD, NATO, the Communist world, the French Community, the Commonwealth, the Americas, the Middle East, Africa, Asia, and the "Third World." Citations in *Treaties and Alliances of the World,* given in square brackets, refer to the consecutive pagination of *Keesing's* from July 1, 1931 to 1968. Membership of international groupings is easily determined from the many maps and tables in each chapter. A useful index is included.

The *Index to Multilateral Treaties* (1965) (12) lists chronologically 3,859 multilateral treaties, including agreements between international organizations, from 1596 to 1963. Symbols for each treaty indicate sources for the complete text. Several important declarations have been listed (although they are not actual treaties), as well as draft treaties unsigned at time of publication. Uniform model statutes, submitted for adoption by national legislatures of a particular region, are also included. A partial list of sources consulted appears in the "List of Abbreviations"; other titles are cited in full in the index itself. Treaties are arranged chronologically. In general, entries include a consecutive identification number, the date of signature, a brief descriptive title in English, the place of signature if the treaty is commonly identified by that name, the area in which the treaty applies, and sources for and the language of the full text. The League of Nations Treaty Series (1920–45) (13) and the United Nations Treaty Series (1946–) (14) are large compilations of treaties of the twentieth century. The League's Treaty Series consists of 205 volumes of over 4,800 documents registered with the Secretariat. Documents are published in English and French as well as in the original language. There are general indexes. The United Nations Treaty Series consists of treaties and international agreements registered or filed with the U.N. Secretary since December 14, 1946. The texts are reproduced in their original language as well as in English and French. Other information provided includes date of ratification, amendments, and so on. Both of these sets are partially indexed in the *Index to Mutilateral Treaties* (12). Unfortunately, neither *Major Peace Treaties of Modern History, 1648–1967* (1967) (15), edited by Fred L. Israel, nor The Consolidated Treaty Series (1969–) (16), compiled and edited by Clive Parry, is indexed in the *Index to Multilateral Treaties.* Hence it may be necessary to consult these volumes as well when searching for texts of treaties. In four large volumes, *Major Peace Treaties* consists of over 100 treaties, including 17 concerned with the United States, from the Delaware Indian Treaty of 1778 to the Treaty of Paris of 1898. Forty pages of maps are included to show boundaries and locations, as well as to illustrate territorial acquisitions. A "conceptual and analytical index" appears at the end of volume 4. Introductions to each section summarize the contexts of the treaties. Parry's *Consolidated Treaty Series* is a much more ambitious undertaking (when completed, the set will comprise about 140 volumes covering 1648 to 1918). It includes treaties in their original language accompanied by translations in French or English if such translations can be located. Each volume covers about two years. Unfortunately, only information indicating sources is included; there is no descriptive or interpretative information.

The bimonthly *International Legal Materials: Current Documents* (1962–) (17) is designed to provide access to significant documents of public or private international matters that are unlikely to appear elsewhere. Documents are arranged under the headings Judicial and Similar Proceedings, Legislation and Regulations, and Treaties and Agreements. Sources are indicated. Generally excluded are materials such as U.S. tax laws, and articles, speeches, commentaries, and reports by individuals and private organizations. Occasionally, when the actual document is not available, unofficial typescript versions or excerpts are used. Treaties published in *International Legal Materials* are indexed in *PAIS* (A.1.b:15) under the heading "Treaties," as well as other headings indicated with a "See also" reference and entries with a "Treaties" subheading.

The following publications of the U.S. Department of State are especially useful. *Treaties in Force* (1929–) (18) is an annual list of treaties and other international agreements of the United States. Each volume is in two sections: first, a list of bilateral treaties and agreements; second, multilateral treaties and agreements by subject. Both lists indicate where texts of the treaties and agreements are located. The texts of all treaties, conventions, executive agreements, and so on to which the United States is a party are contained in volumes of the series *United States Treaties and Other International Agreements* (1950–) (19). Before 1950, this material appeared in U.S. *Statutes at Large* (O.2.g:13), but fortunately the U.S. Department of State is now publishing a multivolume set consisting of volumes of multilateral treaties and other agreements, arranged chronologically, and volumes of bilateral treaties and other agreements, arranged by country. The title of

the set is *United States Treaties and Other International Agreements of the United States of America, 1776–1949* (1968–) (20). It is kept up to date by weekly issues of the Department of State *Bulletin* (1939–) (21).

Great Britain's Foreign Office has issued *British and Foreign State Papers* (1841–) (22) and *Documents on British Foreign Policy, 1919–1939* (1947–) (23). The former consists of over 160 volumes of bilateral treaties and agreements. The volumes are arranged chronologically, with subject indexes. *Documents on British Foreign Policy, 1919–1939* consists of over 30 volumes.

The U.S. Department of State has issued 19 volumes of translated *Documents on German Foreign Policy 1918–1945* (1957–) (24), selected from the archives of the German foreign ministry and Reich Chancellery. See Brock (G.1.b:1) for more information on this series.

For intensive research needs, attention should be given Toscano's *History of Treaties and International Politics* (1966) (25). Treaty collections dating from the fifteenth century are covered, but more consideration is given those concerned with the two World Wars, in the over 1,100 works described and assessed. In addition, various types of diplomatic documents (formal and informal) and memoirs of over 600 statesmen of 18 nations, including the United States, most European countries, and Turkey, China, and Japan are discussed extensively. According to Quincy Wright, Toscano "not only appraises the influence of the memoir writer and the value of his writings for understanding the international transactions in which he was engaged, but often narrates particular transactions and comments on the motives for decisions and their wisdom as indicated by subsequent history."[1]

G.2.d Military Policies and the Search for Peace

Brassey's Annual (1886–) (1) is the oldest continuing assessment of military and strategic affairs. Each volume comprises about 30 articles by military officials and other specialists. Among recent articles are "British Defense Policy," "The First Twenty Years of NATO," "The Czechoslovak Crisis of 1968," "The Evolution of the Warsaw Pact," "Soviet Strategy in the Nineteen Seventies," "Soviet Armored Fighting Vehicles," "A Century of Warship Development," "The Arab-Israeli War—1967," "The Evolution of Chinese Air Power," and "China—The Great Proletariat Cultural Revolution." Each volume has an alphabetically arranged selection of about 250 significant books "of service interest," as well as numerous tables, maps (some of which fold out), and photographs. There is no general index. Sellers's *Reference Handbook of the*

Armed Forces of the World (1966–) (2) contains brief information on defense budgets, manpower, and equipment of the armed forces of each country. The most authoritative annual publication, issued by the Institute of Strategic Studies in London, is *The Military Balance* (1958–) (3), which provides annual estimates of the nature and size of the principal military forces. Volumes are arranged in three sections: the Communist countries, the Western alliances, and the nonaligned countries. Comparative tables on expenditures for defense, nuclear power, and related issues are provided.

There are numerous works on various aspects of military operations and strategy. Peter B. Riddleburger's *Military Roles in Developing Countries* (1965) (4) is an annotated bibliography, arranged by region. *CINFAC Bibliographic Review* (1966–) (5) is a bibliography on counterinsurgency, unconventional warfare, and psychological operations; supplements are issued biannually. It is the result of a merger of three separate annotated bibliographies: Carl Berger and Howard C. Reese's *Psychological Operations* (1960) (6), D. M. Condit's *Counterinsurgency Bibliography* (1963) (7), and Hope Miller's *Selected Bibliography on Unconventional Warfare* (1961) (8). Kurt Lang directs attention to different aspects of the military. His *Military Institutions and the Sociology of War* (1972) (9) consists of a classified bibliography, with brief annotations, preceded by a long narrative section discussing over 1,300 items. Crawford's *The Social Sciences in International and Military Policy* (1965) (10) is an annotated bibliography of articles, reports, and books focusing on the role of social-science research in international relations and military policies since 1945. *The Role of the Military in the Less Developed Countries* (1964)—briefly covering the development of the military in Africa, the Middle East, Asia, and Latin America—is an example of the kind of bibliographies issued by the U.S. government. This and other, similar bibliographies issued by the U.S. Army or the State Department are listed in Body (O.3:4) and Wynkoop (O.1.b:1).

Toward a Genuine World Security System (1964) (11) is an annotated bibliography of over 350 books and articles on "world law, world order and world peace," arranged under 16 headings. It can be supplemented and updated by the *Peace Research Abstracts Journal* (1964–) (12) and *Peace Research Review* (1967–) (13). *Peace Research Abstracts Journal* is a computer-produced work, with abstracts arranged in categories: Military Situation; Limitation of Arms; Tension and Conflict; Ideology and Issues; International Institutions and Regional Alliances; Nations and National Policies; Pairs of Countries and Crisis Areas; International Law, Economics, and Diplomacy; Decision Making and Communications; and Methods and Miscellaneous. Each category is further subdivided. For example, Nations and National Policies is arranged by country; Pairs of Countries and Crisis Areas, by countries or regions; and International Law, Economics, and Diplomacy is divided into such subdivisions as International Law— General, Connally Reservation and Compulsory Jurisdiction of World Court, Economic Aid and Development, Population Explosion and Control, and Oil, Iron, and Other Commodities in International Affairs. It is issued monthly. Only two or three categories appear in each issue, with full coverage provided on a six-month schedule. All categories and subdivisions are identified by a combination of Roman and Arabic numerals, called "system numbers." Materials abstracted are selected from sources in English and other languages, these sources including books and articles, government publications, and publications of international organizations, newspaper articles, films, and tapes. Significant items ranging back as far as ten years are often included. The abstracts vary in length from a single sentence to 500 words.

Three approaches to searching through *PRAJ* are suggested. Each issue has an author index, and a cumulated author and subject index is issued annually. When the subject is known, its "system number" can be traced through the two or three issues where it appears each year. The annual subject index directs attention to articles with minor treatment of a subject. Occasionally, corporate (or institutional) authors are not listed in author indexes, making it necessary to trace through categories in various issues. The "Coding Manual" which accompanies each set is easy to use if difficulty is encountered in other approaches. See the discussion above of the suggested joint use with the *Universal Reference System* (G.1.b:7) and other general bibliographies.

Each issue of the *Peace Research Review* (1967–) (13) contains review articles critically examining material published on one topic, with extensive bibliographies. Among recent articles are Alan Newcombe's "Initiatives and Responses in Foreign Policy," John Raser's "Theories of Deterrence," J. Lawler and J. Lanlict's "International Integration in Developing Regions," and William Ackhardt's "Ideology and Personality in Social Attitudes." *Arms Control and Disarmament* (1965–) (14) is a quarterly bibliography, with abstracts of recent books, articles, and related material, that focuses on arms control and disarmament. Each issue has a classified arrangement, with author and subject index, and there is an annual cumulated index.

Albert Legault's *Peace-Keeping Operations* (1967) (15) is an annotated bibliography of several hundred articles, books, and government publications on "peace-keeping operations," particularly those related to the U.N. April Carter's *Nonviolent Action: Theory and Practice* (1966) (16) lists 277 items in English on nonviolent-resistance movements and theorists of nonviolent action. World military history is briefly covered in Dupuy's *Encyclopedia of Military History* (F.1.d:8). About 300 military and political terms are defined in Schwarz and Hadik's *Strategic Terminology: A Trilingual Glossary* (1966) (17). Equivalent terms in English, French, and German are given, as well as examples of how the terms are used by authorities.

G.2.e   Political Behavior

Two significant works reviewing research studies in human behavior, Berelson and Steiner's *Human Behavior* (H.1.d:6) and Gardner Lindzey's *Handbook of Social Psychology* (H.1.d:3), have sections on political behavior. Bruce L. and Chitra M. Smith's *International Communication and Political Opinion* (1956) (1) is an extensive bibliography, with brief annotations, emphasizing works on propaganda and public opinion. This material is updated in each issue of *Journalism Quarterly* (1930–) (2) in the section "Articles on Mass Communication in U.S. and Foreign Journals." Beck and McKechnie's *Political Elites* (1968) (3) is "a select computerized bibliography" of over 4,000 studies of political elites throughout the world. Section 1 is a "Keyword Title Listing" of the material, while section 2 indicates the relation of each title to seven aspects of elite studies, such as "General Elite Theory" and "Composition of Elites." Section 3 is an author index. *International Guide to Electoral Statistics* (1969–) (4) is a projected multivolume set on election studies. Volume 1 covers the multiparty countries of Western Europe. Subsequent volumes will include Canada, Israel, Japan, the United States (to 1920), Turkey, the Philippines, the majority of the remaining Commonwealth countries, and Latin America. Data for each country are arranged according to a standard format. First, there is a chronology of the development of the electoral system; recorded national elections are arranged according to dates coinciding with the extension of suffrage or other changes in the electoral system. Information on each period includes franchise qualifications, voter-registration procedures, and rules for absentee ballots, as well as electoral procedures (whether the vote is for one candidate or several, whether there is a run-off after the initial election, and so on). The second part consists of bibliographical and other information on data sources in the first part. In the third part, attention is directed to completed analyses. In the fourth section are tables of national-

election results. For example, information on the United Kingdom
includes a chronology of the electoral system from the Reform
Bill of 1832 to 1958; statistical sources and analyses; and bibliographies of official sources, including poll books (noting especially
J. R. Vincent's *Pollbooks: How Victorians Voted* [1967], an excellent analysis of a mine of data), and unofficial sources, such
as the statistical tables in *Dod's Parliamentary Companion* (L.1.
c:10), *Vacher's Parliamentary Guide* (1832–), *Whitaker's Almanack* (A.1.f:1), and Frederick H. McCalmont's *Parliamentary
Poll Book of All Elections* (1910), with constituency results from
1832 to January 1910, as well as secondary authorities and analyses
(87 items are cited); and tables of descriptions of election results
for the years 1900–1966.

G.2.f   Political Philosophy and Ideology

Little academic attention is currently being directed to political
philosophy and ideology. The reason for this situation is in part
explained by Professor Eulau (see section G.1.b). Research on
political thought should begin with the *Encyclopedia of the Social
Sciences* (A.1.e:1), the *International Encyclopedia of the Social
Sciences* (A.1.e:2), and the *Encyclopedia of Philosophoy* (A.1.
e:8). Among articles in *Marxism, Communism, and Western Society* (M.1.d:3) are: Alliances, Systems of; Bourgeoisie; Capital;
Balance of Power; Counter-Revolution; Democracy; Dictatorship;
Disarmament; Genetics; Historical Materialism; Maoism; Marxism; Marxism-Leninism; Sino-Soviet Dispute; Stalinism; Titoism;
and Trotskyism.

Volume 1 of Wynar's *Guide to Reference Materials* (G.1.b:3)
has a chronological listing of the most prominent political theorists and exponents of political ideology and their works, accompanied by a list of authoritative critical treatments and reference
works. Harmon (G.1.b:2) provides a similar list. He evidently
recognized the need to expand the treatment given political thought
in his first volume, for in the supplement substantially more titles
are listed, including a section on studies of American, Argentinian,
Chinese, French, German, British, East Indian, Italian, Japanese,
Middle Eastern, Russian, and Spanish political thought. Bibliographies, dictionaries, and biographical dictionaries are also included.

G.2.g   Public Administration

Comparative Public Administration (1960) (1) is a selective
annotated bibliography of over 900 books and articles. Great Britain's Ministry of Overseas Development has issued *Public Admin-*

istration: A Select Bibliography (1967) (2), an unannotated list of over 900 books, pamphlets, and articles. Compiled to assist new institutes of public administration in Africa, it emphasizes materials on that area. Each quarterly issue of the *International Review of Administrative Sciences* (1928–) (3) has a "bibliographical section" containing brief abstracts of recent books on administration and a list of selected articles. Articles from over 160 periodicals are indexed by subject in *Public Administration Abstracts and Index of Articles* (1957–) (4). The periodicals are from many countries, but predominantly the United States, Great Britain, and India. Substantial abstracts are provided for about 20 significant articles in each issue. Each volume of *Bibliography on Planned Social Change* (I.2.g:3) has a substantial number of items on political issues of developing countries. Each issue of the bimonthly *Journal of the American Institute of Planners* (E.2.d:11) has a bibliography of about 20 articles from planning journals. Arrangement is by journal title, and there is no index. Biographical data on people involved in public administration is available in the *Society Directory* (1955–) (5) of the American Society for Public Administration, Comparative Administration Group, and the *Directory of Organizations and Individuals Professionally Engaged in Governmental Research and Related Activities* (1935–) (6).

Part H

Sociology

Section 1

H.1.a Atlases and Gazetteers

Strictly speaking, there is no atlas or gazetteer devoted exclusively to sociology, but occasionally it is necessary to use one for sociological reference. In general, the atlases recommended in other parts of this handbook, especially parts A and I, will be satisfactory. The *Atlas narodov mira* (C.1.a:1) might prove useful.

H.1.b Bibliographies

Bibliographies of Bibliographies.   Bibliographies of sociology and related topics are listed in Besterman (A.1.b:1) [if published before 1965], the *Bibliographic Index* (A.1.b:2), *Sociological Abstracts* (H.1.b:1), and the *International Bibliography of Sociology* (H.1.b:2). Bibliographies are indicated in the index of the *International Bibliography of Sociology* under the entry "Sociology, reference works."

Reference Works.   Reference works in sociology are included in White (A.1.b:10), Walford (A.1.b:12), Winchell (A.1.b:13), and section A of the *International Bibliography of Sociology* (2).

General Bibliographies.   Among bibliographies in the social sciences with general coverage which have entries for sociology are White (A.1.b:10), the *London Bibliography of the Social Sciences* (A.1.b:5), PAIS *Bulletin* (A.1.b:15), the *ABS Guide to Recent Publications in the Social and Behavioral Sciences* (A.1.b:8), and *Social Sciences Citation Index* (A.1.b:6).

Sociological Abstracts (1952–) (1) annually contains over 5,000 abstracts of books, sections of books, and articles. Abstracts of books include chapter and appendix titles, as well as descriptions of content. Issues are arranged in an elaborate classification scheme. Among the divisions are methodology and research technology; sociology; history, theory, and the sociology of knowledge; social psychology; group interactions; culture and social structure; complex organizations (management); social change and economic development; mass phenomena; political interactions; social differentiation; community development and rural sociology; urban sociology; sociology of religion; social control; demography and human biology; the family and socialization; sociology of health and medicine; and social problems and social welfare. Cross-references are given for previous, related abstracts. Although the classification scheme is different from that of the *International Bibliography of Sociology* (2), it usually is not difficult to select the equivalent categories for each of the schemes and to search the contents of volumes of both titles systematically for the required topics.

(Many items not included in *Sociological Abstracts* are listed in the annual *International Bibliography of Sociology* [2], especially studies concerned with geographical areas outside North America.) Each monthly issue of *Sociological Abstracts* has an author index, and there are annual cumulative author and subject indexes. Unfortunately, the indexes are somewhat confusing and difficult to use. Incidentally, since many periodicals and related materials in sociology are closely related to psychology, *Psychological Abstracts* (1927–), a larger service, often provides abstracts for research studies not found in *Sociological Abstracts*. Further, the cumulative author and subject indexes for *Psychological Abstracts* provide a rapid means of finding abstracts.

The *International Bibliography of Sociology* (1959–) (2) currently includes over 5,000 citations of articles, books, and related works considered important, regardless of the country of origin or the language in which they are drafted. Volumes 1–4 appeared in *Current Sociology* (1951–54). Items are arranged according to an

elaborate classification scheme. Section A, History and Organization of Social Studies, includes historical development, current
trends, reference works and bibliographies, and professional activities and biographical notices. Section B, Theories and Methods
of Sociology, has subdivisions on definitions and fundamental problems, scope, methodology, general theoretical systems, and analysis
of basic sociological concepts. The subdivision on methodology is
further divided in such categories as historical methods, statistical
methods, sampling techniques in fieldwork, and test models and
scales, and thus is a useful updating of *Sociological Measurement*
(H.1.f:1) and other works in H.1.f. Section C, Social Structure,
contains such subdivisions as demography, age groups, geographical and ecological factors, culture and personality, social com-
plexes and social groups, social stratification (and social mobility),
marriage and family, ethnic groups, economic institutions, labor
organizations, and political and religious institutions. Among the
subdivisions of section D, Social Control and Communication, are
customs; morals; religion; mythology; law, opinion, and attitudes;
ideologies; language; mass media; and education. Social Change,
section E, focuses on issues such as the "influence of technology
on social change," "social factors of economic development," and
the "history of human societies." Section F, Social Problems and
Social Policy, lists studies of the practical application of research
findings, in determining the roots of problems and in providing
remedies. Among the subdivisions on social problems are poverty
and unemployment, sexual abnormalities, drug addiction and alcoholism, crime and delinquency, and punishment and penal institutions; in the subsection on social policy are such topics as family
protection, health insurance, social service, and community organization and services. About 1,500 journals from all over the
world are searched. There are author and subject indexes. Occasionally the existence of book reviews is indicated, although without annotation. A citation preceded by "Bibl." and both Roman
and Arabic numerals indicates a review for a book listed in a previous volume. This means that for book reviews later volumes
should be consulted as well as the one where a book is listed.

A regular feature of *Humanitas* (1965–) (3), issued three times
a year, is a bibliography of works on the themes of symposia held
at the Institute of Man at Duquesne University. Each symposium
has a central topic "selected for its basic relevance to a better understanding of man, and for its historical timeliness in regard to
problems of humanization and of dehumanization of mankind and
to contribute to the growth of a comprehensive theory of man that
is open and in harmony with the new insights, perspectives and
data of sciences such as psychology, sociology, cultural anthropology, aesthetics, political science and philosophical anthropology."

Over 200 items are listed in each bibliography, and selected titles have extensive summaries in a special section. Topics covered to date include Anxiety, Automation and Leisure, Autonomy and Community, Changing Nature of Man, Creativity, Crisis of Values in Contemporary Culture, Dehumanizing Trends in Contemporary Cultures, Love and Violence, Motivation and Human Need, Neurosis and Personal Growth, Personality and Aesthetics, Personality and Play, Society and Self Emergence, Self-Destruction and Self-Creation, Human Response to a Functional World, and Creative Response to Custom and Tradition. Albert and Kluckhohn's *Selected Bibliography on Values, Ethics, and Aesthetics in the Behavioral Sciences and Philosophy* (B.2.g:3) covers sociology.

Reviews of Research. The chapter "Sociology," by Peter Blau and Joan Moore, in Hoselitz's *Reader's Guide to the Social Sciences* (A.1.b:9) covers almost 200 works, focusing on the development of the discipline, along with a survey of contemporary sociological literature in selected areas (social theory, methods of data collection and analysis, social psychology, demography and human ecology, social differentiation in community and nation, and format organization). White (A.1.b:10) provides a briefer survey in a different format. Robert Faris edited the *Handbook of Modern Sociology* (1964) (4), a massive volume examining such aspects of sociological research as demography, ecology, labor force, small groups, collective behavior, race and ethnic relations, political sociology, and sources and types of data. Unfortunately, crime, delinquency, and the generic aspects of social change are not covered. A list of all works discussed, along with a name and subject index, is given at the end of the volume. *Social Science Information* (B.1.f:5) regularly lists surveys of research in sociology.

H.1.c   Biographical Dictionaries and Directories

In addition to the entries in *American Men and Women of Science* (A.1.d:15), biographical information on sociologists can be obtained from the American Sociological Association's *Directory of Members* (1950–) (1), issued every few years. This has brief directory information (excluding writings) on about 8,500 members. A few biographies of sociologists are noted in section A of the *International Bibliography of Sociology* (H.1.b:2), and over 70 biographical articles are included in the *International Encyclopedia of the Social Sciences* (A.1.e:2).

H.1.d   Encyclopedias and Dictionaries

In the *Encyclopedia of the Social Sciences* (A.1.e:1), there are 28 articles relating to sociology, while the *International Encyclo-*

pedia of the Social Sciences (A.1.e:2) includes approximately 200 articles and over 70 biographies. A major criticism of the latter has been that it is overwhelmingly concentrated on the United States. In other respects, it is a fairly reliable source for information.

Gould's *Dictionary of the Social Sciences* (A.1.e:4) and Zadrozny's *Dictionary of Social Science* (A.1.e:3) are useful. Mitchell's *Dictionary of Sociology* (1968) (1) and Theodorson's *Modern Dictionary of Sociology* (1969) (2) are recent volumes. Mitchell is considered the better, having about 300 terms and biographical sketches of prominent sociologists. In general, after a short description, it gives the uses of a term and a brief list of authorities to consult for a more detailed discussion. Theodorson includes about 3,000 entries, with brief definitions of terms used in sociology as well as in cultural anthropology, psychology, statistics, economics, political science, and philosophy. Occasionally he refers to the work of an authority that will provide more extensive explanations. Critics indicate that some terms (e.g., "sociology, industrial" and "surplus value") are inadequately or even misleadingly defined.

The five-volume *Handbook of Social Psychology* (1968–70) (3) provides a massive amount of information. Edited by Gardner Lindzey and Elliot Aronson, the present edition was compiled by 68 contributors, including political scientists, sociologists, anthropologists, and psychologists. The titles of individual volumes illustrate the broad coverage: *Historical Introduction and Systematic Positions, Research Methods, The Individual in a Social Context, Group Psychology and Phenomena of Interaction,* and *Applied Social Psychology.* Each chapter includes a bibliography. A separate cumulative author and subject index has also been published. Alfred M. Freedman et al. edited the *Comprehensive Textbook of Psychiatry* (1967) (4), a large, single-volume, encyclopedic compilation of information on neurophysiology and neuropharmacology as well as individual and group behavior. Each article is by an authority and has a bibliography. Another specialized source is *The Encyclopedia of Sexual Behavior* (1967) (5), edited by Albert Ellis and Albert Abarbanel. The work of over 90 contributors, mostly from the United States, it attempts to be "comprehensive, authoritative, inclusive of wide-ranging viewpoints, and truly international." The scope of its articles—with brief bibliographies—includes emotional, psychological, sociological, legal, anthropological, geographical, and historical aspects of sexuality.

Human Behavior (1964) (6), by Berelson and Steiner, is intended to present a "simplified" distillation of the findings of 650 works in the behavioral sciences, in language that can be comprehended by nonspecialists. Emphasis is on the major aspects of human behavior to which scientific study has been devoted. Predominantly, findings are based on Western culture, particularly as related to the United States. Included among chapter titles are "The Individual" (behavioral development, perceiving, learning and thinking, motivation); "The Family"; "Face-to-Face Relations in Small Groups"; "Organizations"; "Institutions" (religious, economic, political, educational, military); "Social Stratification"; "Ethnic Relations"; "Opinions, Attitudes, and Beliefs"; "The Society" (demography, geography, social change, social conflict, social disorganization); and "Culture." In general, material in chapters is arranged uniformly: first, definitions of key terms; then a major section on findings, given as numbered statements followed by illustrative data; finally, a list of sources. For research purposes, three approaches are possible: individual chapters, on broad subjects; the subject index, referring to narrower topics; or the "bibliographical index," indicating the pages where the findings of particular researchers are discussed. This work can be supplemented by *Sociological Abstracts* (H.1.b:1), the *International Bibliography of Sociology* (H.1.b:2), and *Social Sciences Citation Index* (A.1.b:6).

H.1.e   Handbooks and Yearbooks

The *Handbook for Social Research in Urban Areas* (1964) (1), edited by Philip M. Hauser, contains suggestions for designing and conducting research for such problems as analyzing area units, basic statistics, field and case studies, social organization, migration and acculturation, and so on. Bibliographies of additional sources are included.

Sociology (1969) (2), edited by Neil J. Smelser and James A. Davis, gives a review and appraisal of the discipline and suggests a method of strengthening it. Among topics are examinations of the scope of sociology; its developing areas; its development as an academic discipline; its applications; manpower and resources in sociology; and recommendations for strengthening undergraduate education, graduate education, and sociological knowledge.

H.1.f   Methodological Works

Sociological Measurement (1967) (1), by Charles M. Bonjean et al., is

an inventory of scales and indices from *American Journal of Sociology, American Sociological Review, Social Forces* and *Sociometry* between 1954 and 1965. Although the distinctions are not rigidly imposed, index is taken to mean combining several indicators into

one measurement and scale "a special type of index designed to reflect only a single dimension of a concept." Every use of a scale or
index is noted, categorized and, in some cases, the measuring instru-
ment is thoroughly described. The result is an extensive bibliography
which locates any use of any scale or index during the period.
Heavily used measures (achievement motivation, California F Scale,
etc.) are described technically. [*Social Science Quarterly*, September
1968, p. 392]

Charles Y. Glock states in "Survey Design and Analysis in Sociology," the first chapter in *Survey Research in the Social Sciences*
(B.1.f:3), that "defining sociology broadly, there is no other discipline that has adopted survey methods as enthusiastically or used
them as extensively." Glock notes that, although not revised since
1955, H. H. Hyman's *Survey Design and Analysis: Principles,
Cases, and Procedures* "continues to be the standard reference."
He notes further that survey designs in sociology can be identified
according to whether their purpose is descriptive or explanatory,
and whether or not they include an interest in change. He discusses
static designs and those intended to deal with change, as well as
the "cross-sectional survey" and its variations. In the final section,
consideration is given to two designs for studying change: trend
and panel. In all, 84 works are discussed. The Holland and Steuer
Mathematical Sociology (1970) (2) is a bibliography of 340 English-language articles and books on the application of mathematics to sociology. There are subject and author indexes.

Sociological Methodology (1969–) (3) proposes to be an annual examination of developments in methodology in the discipline. There are 13 contributors in the first volume. Four articles
focus on aspects of "causal inference" (two of which are "Principles of Path Analysis" and "Problems in Analysis and Causal Inference"). "Logic and Levels of Scientific Explanation" and "Ecological Variables" are titles among the four general papers, while
shorter items are concerned with "Testing a Measurement Model,"
"Use of Ad hoc Definitions," and "Probabilities from Longitudinal
Records." Each article has a bibliography of works discussed, and
there is a name and subject index. The works of about 180 sociologists are described. Sociology is one of the disciplines included
in "Social Science Methodology: A Bibliography of Studies," a
regular feature of *Social Science Information* (B.1.f:5).

H.1.g   Statistics Sources

Sources of statistics discussed in A.1.i should not be overlooked.
Among the best sources of population, vital statistics, and related
social data are the statistical publications of the various countries.
Foreign Statistical Documents (I.1.g:1) provides a list of the var-

ious types and scope of publications of each country. *Statistics Sources* (A.1.h:1) and to a lesser extent the *Encyclopedia of Business Information Sources* (A.1.b:7) give greater detail about the contents of these publications. (The latter two are limited to English-language sources.) Publications containing data of social concern include the *Compendium of Social Statistics* (I.1.g:6) and the *World Health Statistics Annual* (C.1.g:3). Another type of statistical compilation, exemplified by the *Cross-Polity Time-Series Data* (I.1.g:7) and the *World Handbook of Political and Social Indicators* (G.1.h:2), is often useful for sociological research.

Section 2

H.2.a Social Structure

This section is arranged in the following sequence: marriage, family, and socialization; social organization and social stratification; and religion.

The *International Bibliography of Research in Marriage and the Family* (1964) (1) is an extensive bibliography of over 12,000 research studies on marriage and the family published between 1900 and 1964. The work is arranged in five sections: a "key-word-in-context," or KWIC, index; a subject index; a "complete reference list" (an alphabetically arranged list of items in the bibliography); an "author list"; and a list of periodicals. A code combining letters and numbers directs users from entries in other sections to the "complete reference list." In the subject index, items are classified according to 12 divisions and 131 subdivisions, including such headings as macroscopic studies of marriage and family as an institution; family transactions with groups; mate selection; marriage and divorce; reproductive behavior; family and sex; special problems (disorganization, economic stress, mentally ill, juvenile delinquency, mobility, and so on); applied fields (education for marriage and parenthood, sex education, marriage counseling, therapy); subcultural group membership and the family (ethnic groups in the United States, family and social class); and trends in marriage, fertility, and divorce rates. An "Aids for Research" section lists family-research methodologies, critiques and analyses of research literature, and bibliographies.

John Mogey's *Sociology of Marriage and Family Behavior, 1957–1968* (1971) (2) comprises a trend report and a selectively annotated bibliography of over 2,000 items from 39 countries, and is a continuation of a cumulation in *Current Sociology* (vol. 7, no. 1 [1958]) of over 900 items of the 1945–56 period. It is intended as a critical review of the world literature (excluding the United States) on the sociology of the family, although it acknowledges that "coverage of India, Southeast Asia, parts of Africa and some countries of Europe is inadequate" because of the difficulty of obtaining data. Editors throughout the world were asked to include empirical research findings using clearly specified concepts; case studies with definite conclusions; statistical descriptions with clearly defined categories; anthropological descriptions of family behavior or family typologies; historical descriptions of family types; studies using such family variables in relation to such other variables as income, consumer behavior, migration, illegitimacy, juvenile delinquency, and so forth; and chapters, sections of books, and articles about the family, including data about families in community and other microsociological research. Excluded are studies using individual variables (such as sex or age) and nonsystematic works. Annotations describe problems of research, the concept used, the research design, data collection, data analysis, and findings. A subject index arranged in an elaborate scheme provides access to all entries.

Similar in intent to Berelson's *Human Behavior* (H.1.d:6) but narrower in scope, William J. Goode's *Social Systems and Family Patterns* (1971) (3) is an inventory of research findings on the family as a social institution (including the relation of the family to other social institutions) in most world urban areas of the twentieth century. The over 8,000 propositions are cast in the form of correlations among factors internal to the family unit (e.g., as the group becomes acculturated, the status of the wife becomes more egalitarian; the divorce rate is low in patrilineal systems where the bonds that tie a woman to her husband are extremely strong; the mother's power in decision making does seem to be influenced by class status). Propositions include reference to the over 1,600 studies listed at the end of the volume. Joint use with Aldous and Hill's *International Bibliography of Research in Marriage and the Family* (1) and Mogey's *Sociology of Marriage and Family* (2) is suggested.

Christensen's *Handbook of Marriage and the Family* (1964) (4) is similar in intent and format to the *Handbook of Modern Sociology* (H.1.b:4). The chapters, arranged in five broad categories, examine developments and trends of research on marriage and the family. "Theoretical Orientations" comprises one chapter on the history of family studies and four chapters examining theoretical aspects (institutional, structural-functional, interactional and situational, and developmental). "Methodological Developments" covers prediction studies, field surveys, experimental research, demographic analysis, and measuring families. "The Family in Its Societal Setting" and "Member Roles and Internal Processes" focus on substantive findings on such issues as subcultural variations, sexual behavior, the premarital dyad, and the adjustment of married mates. "Applied and Normative Interests" includes chapters on family-life education, marriage counseling, and divorce, as well as one on "the intrusion of values." Works of over 1,600 researchers are discussed. There are author and subject indexes. *The Encyclopedia of Sexual Behavior* (H.1.d:5) includes articles such as the following on marriage and the family: Divorce, Sexual and Affectional Functions of the Family, Laws on Marriage and Family, Marriage, Marriage Conciliation, Marriage Counseling, and Education for Marriage and Family Living.

Straus's *Family Measurement Techniques* (1969) (5) is a bibliography of 319 well-annotated family-measurement instruments developed between 1935 and 1965. In addition to reports by developers of these techniques, references are given for uses by later researchers. There are indexes of test titles, authors, subjects, and family roles. A more specialized aspect of family life receives attention in *International Family Planning, 1966–1968* (C.2.d:1).

"Sociology and Social Psychology" is one division in *Child Development Abstracts and Bibliography* (1927–) (6). About 180 abstracts selected from over 100 U.S. and foreign journals appear annually. There are six issues per year, with annual author and subject indexes.

The *Handbook of Socialization Theory and Research* (1969) (7), edited by David A. Goslin, is the work of 38 contributors, who approach socialization from divergent theoretical perspectives as well as from significantly different levels of analysis. Sociological and anthropological frames of reference are provided, along with more traditional developmental-psychological points of view. Attempts were directed toward integrating sociological, anthropological, and psychological conceptions of the social learning process, with the primary concerns of "discovering how individuals learn to participate effectively in social interaction, why some individuals have difficulties and what makes some groups function better than others." After a lengthy introduction, the volume is arranged in four broad parts. The first, "Theoretical Approaches to the Socialization Process," comprises chapters on such topics as "The Concept of Internalization" and "Culture, Personality, and Socialization: An Evolutionary View." Among the chapters of part 2, entitled "Content of Socialization," are "The Acquisition of Language" and "Development of Interpersonal Competence." Part 3, "Stages of Socialization," has chapters on childhood, adolescence, occupation, marriage and parenthood, and the middle and later years, as well as such titles as "Three Faces of

Continuity in Human Development," "The Social and Socializing Infant," and "Childhood Socialization." Part 4 comprises chapters on socialization as related to correctional institutions, blind children, physical disability in children, the mentally retarded, and American minority peoples. There are author and subject indexes.

Social stratification, as well as social mobility and the correlates of stratification, are covered in Glenn's *Social Stratification* (1970) (8), a classified bibliography of over 4,000 English-language articles and monographs published between 1940 and 1968. Unfortunately, there are no annotations. About 35 bibliographies on social stratification or related topics are also included. The *Handbook of Organizations* (1965) (9), edited by James G. March, and similar in intent and format to the *Handbook of Modern Sociology* (H.1.b:4), contains chapters by specialists focusing on developments and trends in research on social organizations, stressing in particular foundations, methodologies, theoretical-substantive areas, specific institutions, and applications. Works of over 2,400 people are discussed. There are author and subject indexes. Each of the main divisions in Mendes's *Bibliography of Community Organizations* (1965) (10) ("Community Organization as Technique," "Theoretical and Empirical Foundations," and "Citizen Participation in Voluntary Democratic Associations") has several subdivisions listing significant books, articles, and government publications.

Although it suffers from a lack of annotations, Berkowitz and Johnson's *Social Scientific Studies of Religion* (1967) (11) is the most substantial bibliography of the sociology of religion. It is a classified arrangement of over 6,000 books and articles in English after 1945. The first three divisions concern definitions, descriptions, and the history and development of religions. The next four focus on the relation of religion to other social institutions and behavior, religion and social issues, religion and social change, and the impact of religious belief on behavior. The last two divisions list textbooks, readers (including methodological statements about the study of religion), and over 90 bibliographies, encyclopedias, and dictionaries of religion. There is an author index.

H.2.b   Social Change

According to editors Edward Knop and Kathryn Aparicio, *Current Sociocultural Change Literature* (1967) (1) is the first "systematic topical codification and annotation of literature bearing on generic sociocultural change" since Keesing's *Culture Change* (B.2.g:2). "Keesing's comments on the sources he cites are thorough and perceptive, and serve well to outline the development of professional interest in change. The Keesing work, however, was

intended as a scholarly treatment of the nature of change literature throughout the years, and not as a 'working bibliography' for
change researchers. It is the intention of this volume to supersede
Keesing's contribution by providing the student of social and cultural change with a thorough—though not exhaustive—annotated
and topically organized listing of about 2,000 English-language
items spanning the years 1950 to 1966, in anthropology and sociology, as well as psychology, economics, political science, and
social work." Works are arranged in the following categories: (1)
"Change in Selected Dimensions of Diverse Sociocultural Settings,"
with research describing changes in institutional, structural, and
ideo-psychological dimensions of life in advanced and transitional
urban-industrial and folk-agrarian settings; (2) "The Process of
Sociocultural Change and Stability," including theory, innovation,
diffusion, assimilation, and social control; (3) "Special Problems
as Concomitants of Change," such as social disorganization, mar-
ginality, alienation, and personal deviance; (4) "Planned Change,"
emphasizing community development, economic and technological
development, education and occupational retraining, and public
health; (5) "Methods of Studying Change," describing "materials
containing principles, procedures, and outstanding examples of
historical analysis, ethnographic comparisons, and empirical analysis." Articles and books most likely to be in moderate-sized academic libraries were included, while dissertations, theses, U.S.
government publications, and articles in obscure journals were excluded because of their general unavailability. The lack of indexes
can be overcome by reading chapter headnotes.

   Community Development Abstracts (1964) (2), a volume prepared by the editors of *Sociological Abstracts* (H.1.b:1) contains
over 1,000 abstracts of articles, monographs, and related items
published between 1954 and 1964 on social action and change;
urbanization; group behavior; and political, economic, and educational aspects of community development. There are author, subject, and "nation-tribe-society" indexes. (A second volume covering up to 1968 is forthcoming.)

   Garth Jones et al.'s *Planning Development, and Change* (1970)
(3) focuses primarily on planned organizational change. There are
1,500 items, but the work suffers from an almost complete lack
of annotations, especially concerning the usefulness of some of the
bibliographies listed. According to the *Peace Research Abstracts
Journal* (G.2.d:12), Henry Bienen's *Violence and Social Change*
(1968) (4) covers "in varying degrees of depth, ghetto violence
(but not racial violence *per se*); internal war (including counterinsurgency, civil war, riots, and coups); revolution, as distinct
from the two previous headings; theoretical works in the structure

of violence, typologies of violence, and romantic treatments; and finally, totalitarianism. The linkage of domestic violence with international conflict is omitted, as is discussion of the tools or instrumental characteristics of violence. . . . particularly of interest for exploring the problems of modernization in rapidly changing societies." Part of Spitz's *Developmental Change* (1969) (5) and the three-volume *Bibliography on Planned Social Change* (I.2.g:3) are devoted to social factors and problems in developing countries. Frederick Frey's *Survey Research in Comparative Social Change* (1969) (6) is an annotated bibliography of about 1,600 articles in English-language journals reporting the results of sample survey research in developing countries and cross-national research in developing and developed countries.

H.2.c   Public Opinion, Communication, and Mass Media

Bruce and Chitra Smith's *International Communication and Political Opinion* (G.2.e:1) and the *Journalism Quarterly* (G.2.e:12) are good sources for information on propaganda and mass communication. "Decision-Making and Communications" is the heading for section 9 of the *Peace Research Abstracts Journal* (G.2.d:12). The value of consulting this source as well as the more obvious ones listed in section G.1.b is that one often finds previously unconsidered items, accompanied by excellent descriptive annotations. Tracing the results of public-opinion polls, either to determine the opinions expressed or to discover the instruments used, is relatively easy in *PAIS* (A.1.b:15). Editors of *PAIS* use the entry "Public Opinion" as a "see reference" only, since public-opinion polls are more appropriately placed under particular subjects. For example, in the volume for 1970, under the entry "Public Opinion," "see references" direct searchers to about 30 topics, including Alcoholism, Employment—Negroes, Law Enforcement, Marijuana, Medicine, Pollution, Riots, Social Problems, and numerous polls associated with the Vietnam War.

H.2.d   Social Deviance, Social Control, and Social Policy

In this section the concern is with social problems in general, but inevitably, issues in the United States predominate. While the *International Bibliography of Sociology* (H.1.b:2), *PAIS* (A.1.b:15), and the PAIS *Foreign Language Index* (A.1.b:16) give greater coverage to social problems outside the United States, in *Sociological Abstracts* (H.1.b:1), in 1967, there was roughly a 2:1 ratio in favor of the United States over all other foreign studies. Among the foreign studies, those concerned with Britain and Canada predominated. The *Mental Health Book Review Index* (A.1.c:3) should not be overlooked.

William Pinson's *Resource Guide to Current Social Issues* (1968) (1) has briefly annotated citations of books, pamphlets, government publications, and films on over 40 topics of social concern, including abortion, alcoholism, divorce, narcotics, and pornography. Unfortunately, the usefulness of this source is limited somewhat by its emphasis on religious materials and its uncritical attitude toward the bias of some of the sources it lists. Although designed for libraries, *IRC Recommends* (1969–) (2) can be useful to individual researchers looking for "fugitive" materials that in general are difficult to locate. *IRC Recommends* is a loose-leaf service evaluating materials such as films, pamphlets, and books concerned with mental health, family living, and social problems. Among the subjects covered are child care, preadolescence, young adults, marriage, self-understanding, aging, alcoholism, drug abuse, mental illness, retardation, physical handicaps, suicide, and urban problems. About 200 items are reviewed each year.

The six-volume *Encyclopedia of Mental Health* (1963) (3) authoritatively defines approximately 150 terms. Each term is intensively explored. The format consists of answering hypothetical questions related to a particular term. Occasionally suggestion is made in the text of a definition of which authorities to consult for additional information. Volume 6 includes a selected bibliography of about 200 books and articles, brief definitions of about 1,000 additional terms, and indexes of names and subjects. "Abortion," "Adolescent Sexuality," "Aging and Sex," "Contraception," "Extramarital Sex Relations," "Homosexuality," "Illegitimacy," "Laws on Sex Crimes," "Marriage Conciliation," "Marriage Counseling," "Sexual Perversions," "Planned Parenthood around the World," "Population and Sex," "Prostitution," "Separation," "Standards of Sexual Behavior," and "Venereal Diseases" are some of the articles in the *Encyclopedia of Sexual Behavior* (H.1.d:5).

The *Encyclopedia of Social Work* (1929–) (4) is the new title given the Social Work Yearbook series, of which 14 were published between 1929 and 1960. Excellent for tracing the development of social work in the United States, the yearbooks noted developments and trends of social work and social security in authoritative articles—including bibliographies—on a broad range of topics. Each volume includes a directory of international, governmental, and voluntary social-work organizations. The *Encyclopedia of Social Work* is of similar format but includes also a section of statistics on U.S. social-welfare and demographic trends, and biographies of prominent people associated with social work.

The *Handbook on the Study of Social Problems* (1971) (5), edited by Erwin O. Smigel, with 28 expert contributors, is con-

Social Science Research Handbook

cerned with the difficulties encountered when dealing with social problems, particularly the multiplicity of definitions of social problems. The book attempts to clarify the reasons for these disagreements about definitions and to distinguish social problems from aspects of social disorganization, social deviance, and individual disorganization. Five categories of social problems are noted: "recurrent," "rerecognized," "current," "refashioned," and "unrecognized." Crime is considered a recurrent problem. Pollution, however, is a current problem because it "is one that has recently been labeled, is generally acknowledged, and is receiving societal attention." A refashioned problem "is a recurrent one that has been redefined"; an unrecognized problem (e.g., poverty), one that has "not yet become visible to a significant population." No unifying theory for the study of social problems is found, but a number of chapters suggest various approaches to solving social problems, including those involving "action"; social planning and social control; and conservative, liberal, and radical thinking. Certain chapters—on crime, education, industry, physical health, mental health, race relations, and religion—were included "to demonstrate the position, trend, and deficiencies in a particular field and to provide a basic bibliography." The attention given to bibliographies is a valuable feature, with at least one for each chapter, often annotated. An index of names and subjects is included.

Few bibliographies, outside of those encountered in the authoritative texts in the field, exist on "social control." *Sociological Abstracts* (H.1.b:1) and the *International Bibliography of Sociology* (H.1.b:2) should not be overlooked as excellent sources.

The reprinting of the Kuhlman and Culver bibliographies on crime and criminal justice makes available an almost complete access to studies of these subjects. Kuhlman's *Guide to Material on Crime and Criminal Justice* (1929) (6), is a descriptive, classified catalog of over 13,000 books, monographs, pamphlets, and articles relating to all phases of crime and criminal justice in the United States to 1927. The reprint contains an author index, originally published separately. Culver's two-volume *Bibliography of Crime and Criminal Justice* (1949) (7), with 22,000 entries, brings the coverage to 1937, "including the addition of the more important foreign references." These volumes—along with Dorothy Culver Tompkins's *Sources for the Study of the Administration of Criminal Justice, 1938–1948* (1949) (8), with 2,500 entries; her *Administration of Criminal Justice, 1949–1956* (1956) (9), with 3,000 entries; and her *The Offender: A Bibliography* (1963) (10), with 3,500 entries—explore a broad range of subjects relating to the causes and problems of crime in society and to the treatment of criminals. *Crime and Delinquency Abstracts*

(1961–) (11) contains about 2,000 abstracts per year of articles, monographs, and unpublished reports pertaining to crime and delinquency. Each issue has an author and subject index, and there are annual cumulative indexes.

More selective than *Crime and Delinquency Abstracts, Crime and Delinquency Literature* (1968–) (12) annually contains about 1,200 abstracts on articles from 140 journals on such subjects as law and the administration of justice, law enforcement and the police, correction, juvenile delinquency and the delinquent, crime and the offender, drug abuse, and related social issues. Perhaps more useful is the regular review by a specialist of the body of literature on a particular social problem. Topics examined include the mentally retarded offender, victimless crime, criminal justice programs in model cities, modern correctional design, strategies for decreasing jail populations, public opinion and correctional reform, halfway houses, criminal statistics, problems in police-community relations, and gun control and the informer. *Excerpta Criminologica* (1961–) (13), another abstracting service concerned with criminology, is international in scope, with about 25 percent of the items from the United States. Subjects include psychopathology; anthropology, sociology, and social work; special offenses; prediction; prevention; and treatment. Chambliss and Seidman's *Sociology of the Law* (1970) (14) and bibliographies in issues of *Law and Society Review* (O.2.g:38) are useful for recent materials. In the former volume, articles and books are arranged under such divisions as law and morality; social welfare and labor law; penology; criminology and criminal justice; abortion, drugs, crime, and medical jurisprudence; the impact of legal systems; and comparative legal systems and international law.

A Dictionary of Words about Alcohol (1968) (15), by Mark Keller and Mairi McCormick, gives about 2,000 definitions of terms concerned with the consumption of alcoholic beverages. Authorities are often cited, and about 200 authoritative works are listed at the end. Those needing a comprehensive work should consult the *International Bibliography of Studies on Alcohol* (1960–) (16), "a broad multidisciplinary and interprofessional bibliography" concerned with the social uses of alcohol. Volume 1 contains 25,000 items in a chronological and alphabetical arrangement, and volume 2 has subject and author indexes. Supplementary volumes are planned. The *Quarterly Journal of Studies on Alcohol* (1940–) (17) annually abstracts about 400 reports; items not abstracted are listed in a "Current Bibliography." Access to abstracts and bibliography is provided by the annual "Current Literature Subject Index" in the *Quarterly Journal of Studies on Alcohol*. Quinquennial and decennial cumulations are also published.

A retrospective international bibliography covers the literature from 1471 to 1900.

In Richard Lingeman's *Drugs from A to Z* (1969) (18), the so-called mind drugs are described from pharmacological and sociological points of view, including the curious origins of certain terms. Important words (for example, heroin and marijuana) receive several pages of treatment. Quotations following definitions are intended to illustrate usage and implications, or "provide a subjective description of the effects of a drug."

The *Bibliography on Drug Dependence and Abuse, 1928–1966* (1966) (19), issued by the National Clearinghouse for Mental Health Information, contains over 3,000 selected books, articles, legal documents, and reports of Congressional hearings and investigations concerned with drug dependence and abuse from 1928 to early 1966. Items are arranged in the following categories: general discussions, reviews, and history; incidence and prevalence; sociological factors; treatment and rehabilitation; attitudes and education; pharmacology and chemistry; psychological factors; and production, control, and legal factors. James R. Gamage and E. L. Zerkin compiled *A Comprehensive Guide to the English Language Literature on Cannabis (Marijuana)* (1969) (20). Joseph Menditto's *Drugs of Addiction and Non-Addiction: Their Use and Abuse* (1970) (21) contains 6,000 general and scientific books, dissertations, and articles in thirteen categories, including amphetamines and stimulants, barbiturates and tranquilizing drugs, LSD, marijuana, addiction, rehabilitation, narcotics, trade, legislation, narcotics and crime, and a narcotics bibliography. There is an author index. This work is to be updated annually in *Drug Abuse Bibliography* (1970–) (22).

Poverty and Human Resources Abstracts (1966–) (23) annually contains about 300 abstracts of articles, government reports, and books on such topics as characteristics and conditions of the poor and causes and remedies of poverty. For the most part the work focuses on the United States, and thus provides some periodic updating of Tompkins's *Poverty in the United States during the Sixties* (O.2.h:2). In addition to abstracts, each issue lists over 100 unannotated items. The abstracts are indexed, but the unannotated items are not. Each issue has one or two review articles. (For example, in the November–December 1966 issue, John Erlich discussed about 135 works concerned with organizing the poor.)

Bahr's *Disaffiliated Man* (1970) (24) is an annotated bibliography of about 300 items designed to provide access to studies on problems of homelessness and chronic drunkenness. It is apparently the only such work in this specialized field.

Part I

Area Studies: General Works

Introduction

A powerful stimulus exists for research relating to specific geographical areas, particularly the so-called underdeveloped areas, to be interdisciplinary. Sociologists, anthropologists, and geographers, for example, make wide use of each other's research. In view of this fact, handbook users are urged to use the materials discussed in this part that relate to their field of interest and to refer to earlier parts for further information. Although an attempt has been made to indicate items of greatest value for particular research needs, it is not possible to mention each item whenever it becomes pertinent. Instead, we urge readers to frequently review related sections when investigating a problem. For example, the Human Relations Area Files (I.3:1), usually associated with anthropology, might also contain information vital to demography, political science, or history. AUFS *Reports* (I.1.e:14), a collection of reports covering a broad range of topics, is often overlooked because its title fails to suggest its scope. Sections J.1.e and K.1.3 describe the *Africa Research Bulletin* (J.1.f:2) and the *Asia Research Bulletin* (K.1.f:4). These excellent news digests are in two sections: "Political, Social, and Cultural" and "Economic, Financial, and Technical." The latter section is not a usual feature of news digests and hence is likely to be neglected unless it is kept in mind as a useful source for economic information.

Section I

I.1.a   Atlases

Atlases dealing with individual continents are few, nor are there many covering other macro-regions. Besides the *Oxford Economic Atlas of the World* (D.1.a:1), the Oxford Regional Economic Atlases comprise a very useful series, providing authoritative information on such subjects as natural resources, agriculture, manufacturing, trade, and communications. Seven have appeared up to the present: *The USSR and Eastern Europe* (1956) (1), *Western Europe* (1971) (2), *The Middle East and North Africa* (1960) (3), *Africa* (1965) (4), *United States and Canada* (1967) (5), the *Oxford Economic Atlas for India and Ceylon* (1953) (6), and the *Oxford Economic Atlas for Pakistan* (1955) (7). Each atlas contains a statistical appendix and a bibliography of selected sources. More modest in format, and relying on black-and-white maps, is the Praeger series of atlases on world affairs. Seven volumes are now available: *An Atlas of World Affairs* (1965) (8), *An Atlas of Middle Eastern Affairs* (1964) (9), *An Atlas of African Affairs* (1965) (10), *An Atlas of Latin American Affairs* (1965) (11), *An Atlas of European Affairs* (1964) (12), *An Atlas of Soviet Affairs* (1965) (13), and *An Atlas of North American Affairs* (1969) (14). World atlases are discussed in section A.1.a. Turn to appropriate area studies parts for regional atlases or those concerned with individual countries.

I.1.b   Bibliographies

Very few bibliographies attempt broad coverage of the published research in the social sciences of the world, an undertaking that would require a massive effort. The titles discussed in this

section are among the most familiar. Using them jointly with bibliographies on specific geographical áreas is recommended.

The Developing Nations (1965) (1), by Eloise G. ReQua and
Jane Statham, "a guide to information sources concerning their
economic, political, technical, and social problems," brings together about 800 items dealing with underdeveloped areas, the
processes of economic development and social change, and problems of foreign-aid policy. It is concerned with regions and areas
rather than specific countries, and consists of annotated citations
of books, articles, and documents in the English language in classified arrangement, with an author-title index. This bibliography is
supplemented to a limited extent by the quarterly *Journal of Developing Areas* (1966–) (2), which regularly carries a section entitled "Bibliography of Periodicals and Monographs," listing by
region articles and books on developing areas. Each issue contains
about 1,000 unannotated citations, including AUFS *Reports* (I.1.
e:14), arranged under such headings as general Anglo-America;
Latin America; Western Europe; Eastern Europe and the Soviet
Union; Asia (general, East Asia, South Asia, and Southeast Asia);
Africa (general, North Africa and the Middle East, and sub-Saharan Africa); and Oceania. There are no indexes.

Slightly narrower in areas covered, the AUFS *Select Bibliography* (1960–) (3), with supplements, now contains over 10,000
annotated citations of books on the economics, history, anthropology and sociology of Asia, Africa, Eastern Europe, and Latin
America.

The U.S. Army has published *Africa, Problems and Prospects:
A Bibliographic Survey* (1967) (4); *Latin America and the Caribbean: Analytical Survey of Literature* (1969) (5) and the earlier *Latin America, Hemispheric Partner: A Bibliographic Survey*
(1964) (6); the two-volume *Middle East, Tricontinental Hub: A
Bibliographic Survey* (1965–68) (7); the two-volume *Communist
China* (1966–71) (8); *USSR: Strategic Survey* (1969) (9) and
its updating volume, *Communist Eastern Europe* (1971) (10);
and *Pacific Islands and Trust Territories* (1971) (11). Each volume has annotated citations for about 800 items, including books,
articles, and government publications. Bibliographies are aug-
mented by appendixes, including charts, tables, and envelopes of
large colored maps detailing military, political, and economic conditions.

The "Annotated Bibliography of Major U.N. Publications and
Documents on Development Planning, 1955–1968" (1969) (12)
is a compilation of over 100 general-planning studies. Subjects
include the methodology of development planning (general-planning methodology, aggregative models, input-output, linear pro-

gramming, and commodity-balance techniques); investment criteria; sectoral planning (industry-agriculture, trade and finance, social sectors); and economic integration and multinational planning.

I.1.c   Biographical Dictionaries and Directories

Volumes described in section A.1.d, especially *International Who's Who* (A.1.d:6), *Who's Who in the World* (A.1.d:7), *Biography Index* (A.1.d:10), and the *New York Times Biographical Edition* (A.1.d:13), are useful for general coverage of prominent people throughout the world. For political figures, the *Almanac of Current World Leaders* (G.1.c:2), the *International Yearbook and Statesmen's Who's Who* (I.1.e:3), and chapter 12 of the first volume of Mason's *Research Resources* (G.2.c:2) are the recommended titles among those discussed in section G.1.c.

I.1.d   Encyclopedias and Dictionaries

The best in this field is the *Worldmark Encyclopedia of the Nations* (1972) (1), a five-volume work containing brief economic, political, historical, geographical, and sociological information about countries and international organizations throughout the world. Prepared by a number of distinguished contributors, it includes information for each national entry arranged uniformly under such headings as location, size, and extent; topography; climate; population; ethnic groups; language; religion; history; government; political parties; judicial system; armed forces; migration; economic policy; press; dependencies; and bibliography.

I.1.e   Handbooks and Yearbooks

Among the most useful yearbooks are the *Annual Register* (A.1.g:4), *The Statesman's Yearbook* (E.1.e:1), and *The Europa Yearbook* (1959–) (1). *The Europa Yearbook,* the *Political Handbook of the World* (1927–) (2), and the *International Yearbook and Statesmen's Who's Who* (1953–) (3) are noteworthy for their similarities as well as their distinctive features. *The Europa Yearbook* was originally entitled *Europa Yearbook* (1926–29), later *Europa* (1930–37), and then *Orbis: Encyclopedia of Extra-European Countries* (1938–45). *Orbis* includes information on countries outside of Europe. It started as a loose-leaf service; bound volumes began to be issued in 1959, at which time it was renamed *The Europa Yearbook;* two volumes per year have been issued since 1960. Volume 1 contains surveys of economic, political, and social conditions, as well as directories of political, industrial, financial, cultural, educational, and scientific organizations of European countries; volume 2 contains similar information on the countries of Africa, the Americas, Asia, and Australasia. For each country there is an introductory survey, indicating geographical features, recent history, government, economic affairs, social welfare, education, currency, and so on, with statistical tables. This is followed by a brief description of the structure of the government and judicial system and a directory of government officials and political parties. Next is a directory of newspapers, periodicals, and other media, including such information as circulation figures and political affiliation, and a list of diplomatic representatives and addresses. The texts of new constitutions and related documents are also provided. Although briefer, the information in the *Political Handbook of the World* (2) is more subjective and gives more attention to certain factors. (For example, opposition parties, including illegal ones, are extensively described.) Each volume has a directory of international organizations and a chronology of political developments. The *International Yearbook and Statesmen's Who's Who* (3) has brief directory information on international organizations and national units, but most of each volume is devoted to biographical sketches.

Perhaps the most useful series of handbooks is issued by the Praeger publishing firm. Each volume consists of three or four parts. Part 1 provides brief statistical and other factual data on each country; part 2 contains authoritative surveys by experts of each country; in part 3, authorities examine such topics as religion, art, literature, minorities, and mass media; and part 4 contains the texts of selected documents. Each article has a bibliography and tables and maps where appropriate. Already published are *Africa: A Handbook* (1966) (4); *Latin America and the Caribbean* (1968) (5); *The Middle East* (1971) (6); *Western Europe* (1967) (7); *Asia* (1966) (8); *The Soviet Union and Eastern Europe* (1970) (9); and *Australia, New Zealand, and the South Pacific* (1970) (10). *The United States and Canada* (11) is in preparation.

U.S. Army Area Handbooks (1957) (12) are fairly comprehensive surveys of about 60 countries or areas throughout the world. Attention is directed to social, political, and economic conditions, with emphasis on security policies. The surveys range from 300 to over 800 pages, with extensive bibliographies and numerous maps and charts. The U.S. Department of State's *Background Notes on the Countries of the World* (in continuous revision) (13) are often useful. Consisting of fewer than ten pages, each includes information on a country's land, people, history, government, political conditions, economy, and foreign relations. One of

the best sources for empirical studies, American Universities Field
Staff *Reports* (1952–) (14) currently comprise over 1,000 brief,
authoritative reports on social, political, and economic aspects of
15 regions or subregions throughout the world by experts stationed in the field.

I.I.f   Newspapers and News Digests

A brief survey is provided in *The Foreign Press* (1970) (1),
which aims "to present a panoramic picture of the world's press
systems with a minimum of distortion and to bring to the student
who desires a more intensive study many excellent sources for further investigation."

Although researchers on Eastern Europe, China, or other areas
where the predominant language is non-Western realize that the
most valuable information may be published in local newspapers
and periodicals, they may discount the possibility of using these
sources because of the language obstacle. Except for a small group
of scholars working in these areas, there is little awareness of the
extent to which foreign-language newspapers and periodicals are
translated, principally under the sponsorship of the U.S. government, but also as a regular serevice of the diplomatic offices of
foreign governments stationed in these countries. Mason (G.2.
c:2) and Brock (G.1.b:1) have sections devoted to descriptions
of and information on access to translations of foreign materials.

The *New York Times* (A.1.g:1) and the *Times* of London
(A.1.g:3) are perhaps the most widely used newspapers for research on world affairs, but features of the *Christian Science Monitor* (O.1.f:2) and other newspapers discussed by Mason (G.2.
c:2) are worth noting.

Dennis L. Wilcox's *English-Language Dailies Abroad* (1967)
(2) is a guide to 202 daily newspapers in non-English-speaking
countries. The author notes that "this guide gives not only the
name of the newspaper, its circulation, and founding date but information about readership, circulation patterns, advertising ratio,
news emphasis, wire services used, editorial policy," and so on.
(The Bahama Islands, Barbados, Bermuda, Guyana, Canada, Jamaica, the Leeward Islands, Trinidad, the United States, the U.S.
Virgin Islands, Ireland, the United Kingdom, Australia, and New
Zealand are excluded.) *Keesing's* (A.1.g:5) is the best news digest
that attempts to cover world affairs.

I.I.g   Statistics Sources

The *Encyclopedia of Business Information Sources* (A.1.b:7)
and *Statistics Sources* (A.1.h:1) should be consulted. *Foreign Sta-*

tistical Documents (1967) (1) lists statistical publications on general matters, including international trade and agriculture, for more than 250 different countries, territories, and other political units.

For information on various cultural, political, and social matters, the best general source is UNESCO's *Statistical Yearbook* (1963–) (2), which provides information on such matters as education, news media, and cultural events. *The Statesman's Yearbook* (E.1.e:1) should also be consulted.

The most authoritative and generally useful collection of international statistics is found in the U.N.'s *Statistical Yearbook* (1949–) (3). It comprises demographic, economic, and social data on nearly 300 countries and territories. [Its predecessor was the *Statistical Yearbook* of the League of Nations (1926–44) (4).] The *Monthly Bulletin of Statistics* (1947–) (5), also published by the U.N., contains the most recent information.

The second *Compendium of Social Statistics* (1967) (6) was issued as a joint undertaking of the U.N., the ILO, the FAO, UNESCO, and WHO. Included among the statistical tables are those showing population and vital statistics; health conditions; food consumption and nutrition; housing, education, and cultural activities; labor force and conditions of employment; income and expenditures; and consumer prices. The *World Health Statistics Annual* (C.1.g:3) is a three-volume work, giving demographic information for many countries and territories of the world, along with data on diseases, vaccinations, health personnel, and so on.

For quick reference, and provided that no more than summary figures are needed, the *Cross-Polity Time-Series Data* (1971) (7) is a useful source of comparative historical statistics on over 150 countries. The data have been compiled with the assistance of data-processing techniques from a variety of standard sources. The data for the 102 variables, including such ratios as "per capita" and "per square mile," are arranged in ten "segments," or categories. Beginning dates vary according to the availability of statistics, and the statistics do not go beyond 1966. Categories include area and population; political information (type of regime, number of coups d'etat, parliamentary responsibility, legislative selection) from 1815; population of urban cities to 10,000 from 1815; national-government revenue and expenditures; railroad mileage from 1860; telegraph, postal, and telephone services from 1860; educational data from 1860 and literacy figures from 1929; energy production and consumption; newspaper circulation and publishing; gross national product; number of physicians from 1946; and domestic upheaval (assassinations, strikes and revolutions, political-party competition) from 1946. Most data are given in units, but some require presentation on a "more or less" basis, or the use of an arbitrarily chosen code to indicate type of leader, legislative selection, and so on.

The *Geographical Digest* (E.1.e:2) contains a wide variety of statistical information in capsule form on population, production, trade, and communications, among other things. Detailed demographic statistics for most countries and regions of the world are best provided in the U.N.'s *Demographic Yearbook* (C.1.g:1), but see also *Population and Vital Statistics* (C.1.g:2), a quarterly publication of the U.N.

For international economic information, there are many excellent sources. The *World Trade Annual* (1964–) (8) is a four-volume compilation of statistics showing the amount and value of commodities imported and exported by countries throughout the world. The *Commodity Yearbook* (1939–) (9) contains statistics for 107 commodities (mainly for about two decades), with tables showing world production, average prices, and U.S. and foreign trade. The *Quarterly Economic Review* (1956–) (10) includes statistical information on certain economic indicators and foreign trade, among other items, for sixty-two countries or areas. The United Nations' *Yearbook of International Trade Statistics* (1950–) (11) and the *Trade Yearbook* (1947–) (12) of the Food and Agricultural Organization (FAO) are the most authoritative sources for matters of international trade. Agricultural statistics are provided in FAO's *Production Yearbook* (1948–) (13) and the same agency's *State of Food and Agriculture* (1947–) (14). *World Crop Statistics: Area, Production, Yield, 1948–64* (1966) (15) is a very useful compilation and summary of facts and figures on all major crops and important agricultural regions. Animal and crop distributions and areas of intensive agricultural activity are graphically represented in the Oxford Regional Economic Atlases (I.1.a:1–7).

Two valuable sources of information on mineral production and sales are the U.S. Bureau of Mines' *Minerals Yearbook* (1933–) (16), volume 4 of which deals with international data, and the United Kingdom Overseas Geological Surveys' *Statistical Summary of the Mineral Industry: World Production, Exports and Imports* (1913/1920–) (17). The latter work covers five-year periods and is regularly updated.

Two older works, *World Population and Production* (C.1.e:2) and *World Commerce and Governments* (1955) (18), are still of considerable value and should not be overlooked.

A useful work covering the North Atlantic area is Bernard Mueller's *Statistical Handbook of the North Atlantic Area: Western Europe, Canada, United States* (1965) (19). It includes statistics on population, employment, public and private expenditures, productivity, national output, resources, and foreign trade.

Section 2

I.2.a Anthropology

Anthropology does not lend itself to being treated in this type of format except perhaps as comparative anthropology. Comparative anthropology is the main concern of the Human Relations Area Files (I.3.1) and its related publications. In Naroll (B.2. g:1), Timothy O'Leary notes several subject bibliographies concerned with comparative aspects of anthropology, but most of the items he discusses relate to individual geographic areas. Note, however, that distinguishing features of anthropology and sociology, as well as other disciplines, are becoming increasingly obscure. See Marsh's *Comparative Sociology* (I.2.g:1), the *Bibliography on Planned Social Change* (I.2.g:3), and *Current Sociocultural Change Literature* (H.2.b:1).

I.2.b Demography

Demography is adequately covered in part C, with *Population Index* (C.1.b:1) particularly recommended. Bibliographies and related works devoted to specific areas are discussed below.

I.2.c Economics

In general, section I.1.g, part D, and the economics sections in the parts to come should be consulted. Fundaburk (D.1.b:4) promises to be a comprehensive bibliography, though critics suggest this work is not well organized. The economic structures of 25 major countries are described in the *Financial Times Yearbook* (D.1.e:1). The *F and S Index International* (1967–) (1) closely resembles *F and S Index of Corporations and Industries* (O.2.c:1); about 250 foreign and U.S. trade journals are covered. Continuously updated, *I, L, & T: Investing, Licensing, and Trading Conditions Abroad* (1965–) (2) is a loose-leaf service concerned with investment conditions in over 50 countries. Information is arranged uniformly under such headings as political forecast; market forecasts; amount of foreign investment; state role in industry; rules of competition; price controls; taxes; labor (unions and work stoppages, wages and fringe benefits); and foreign trade. Economics is a concern of the *Bibliography on Planned Social Change* (I.2.g:3).

I.2.d   Geography

As a discipline, geography is concerned to a large extent with limited geographical areas or regions. The organization of the *Bibliographie géographique internationale* (E.1.b:6), the AGS *Research Catalogue* (E.1.b:4), and *Current Geographical Publications* (E.1.b:5) bear this out. Evidently, a bibliography of comparative geography does not exist. It is therefore suggested that handbook users consult part E and the appropriate sections of the area-studies parts. Geography is a concern of the *Bibliography on Planned Social Change* (I.2.g:3).

I.2.e   History

Part F, especially the AHA *Guide to Historical Literature* (F.1.b:2), the *Annual Bulletin of Historical Literature* (F.1.b:3), and *Historical Abstracts* (F.1.b:10), along with appropriate sections of the area-studies parts below, should be consulted. See the "Introductory Note" of part F for a discussion of the treatment of history in this handbook.

I.2.f   Political Science

Brock (G.1.b:1), Harmon (G.1.b:2), and Wynar (G.1.b:3) have chapters on comparative politics. A quarterly journal devoted exclusively to the field, *Comparative Political Studies* (1968–) (1), features an annotated list of books and articles in two issues of each volume. Amos J. Peaslee compiled *Constitutions of Nations* (1965–68) (2), a three-volume work in five parts, containing constitution texts in English, together with summaries, annotations, bibliographies, and comparative tables. *Social Conflict* (1966) (3) is a keyword-in-context bibliography consisting of 1,300 citations drawn from the main behavioral-science journals, mostly over the period 1950 to 1966, concerning the literature on social conflict in developing areas. The *Bibliography on Planned Social Change* (I.2.g:3) is concerned with politics.

I.2.g   Sociology

In part H it was noted that most sociological research is concerned with the United States, but attention is increasingly being directed to other places. Robert M. Marsh, in the preface of *Comparative Sociology* (1967) (1), states that "what is needed in sociology and anthropology is a systematic specification of which theories and propositions hold for all societies, which for only certain types of societies, and which for only individual societies.

Comparative sociology is *central* to this task of universalizing sociological theory and continually reassessing its propositions in this light." The first part of Marsh's book is concerned with sociological data from two or more societies. Assuming that societies can be systematically compared in terms of a small number of variables, he presents a scheme for codifying such data, using the variable "degree of structural differentiation." Part 2 examines 90 cross-societal studies published between 1950 and 1963, conducted by sociologists, social anthropologists, and social psychologists. Propositions of major subsystems of society are tested; the subsystems are kinship, family, and marriage; polity and bureaucracy; social stratification and mobility; ecology, urban sociology, and demography; and cultural-value orientations. After discussing the substance, theory, and methodology of each study, the book codifies its propositions according to their relationship to degree of differentiation. Part 3 focuses on certain problems of methodology and research techniques in comparative analysis. Part 4 suggests further developments in the codification scheme for comparative analysis and emphasizes the close links between evolutionary theory and comparative sociology. A sample of 581 primitive, historical, and contemporary national societies is presented in the appendixes. The book also contains an annotated bibliography, including almost 1,000 cross-societal studies published between 1950 and 1963. *Current Sociocultural Change Literature* (H.2. b:1) has a similar concern. The *International Bibliography of Sociology* (H.1.b:2) and *World Agricultural Economics and Rural Sociology Abstracts* (1959–) (2) are among other recommended sources. The arrangement of the three-volume *Bibliography on Planned Social Change* (1967) (3) is rather complex. Volume 1 is confined to periodical articles; volume 2, books and book-length monographs; and volume 3, government and U.N. publications, as well as conference proceedings. In volume 1, articles were selected from over 200 international journals in English, mostly published between 1955 and 1965. About 90 percent of the articles are abstracted, and 900, considered most relevant, were "reviewed for the purpose of extracting the most important propositions." A subject code consisting of six categories (geography, economics, agriculture, social change, education, and politics and government) and appropriate subdivisions is provided for access to articles. In many cases sufficient information may be obtained by consulting the combination of abstract and proposition if the article is not available. Over 600 books and government publications are listed in each of the remaining volumes which, although partially abstracted, lack the propositions and elaborate indexing of the first volume.

One of the few works attempting world coverage in sociology is John Mogey's *Sociology of Marriage and Family, 1957–1968* (H.2.a:2).

Section 3

I.3   Human Relations Area Files

The Human Relations Area Files (1949–) (1), a unique type of reference work, comprises a vast collection of data on human cultures (historical, contemporary, and primitive). Some idea of the scope of this collection has already been indicated in B.1.e. It consists of primary and secondary source materials on 220 ethnic groups and 66 national societies throughout the world, and provides materials for undertaking research on individual cultures or of making cross-cultural comparisons. Essentially, it is a system of organizing data about a people, the environment in which they live, their behavior, and their culture. It consists of 286 individual files, with nearly 2.5 million file pages. Note, however, that HRAF should be used with caution. G. W. White points out these limitations: (1) its lack of theoretical material and (2) its reliance on the manipulation of data by others.[1] Another major concern is the danger of inexperienced researchers selecting facts about particular cultures without fully understanding the context in which they exist. Remember that the complete text of all items deposited in the Files can be found in category 116 of each culture. Unfortunately, approaching this vast collection of data through the *Outline of World Cultures* (B.1.e:3) and the *Outline of Cultural Materials* (B.1.e:5) is unnecessarily confusing. The person supervising the use of the HRAF in your library can quickly demonstrate how to use the material. HRAF has 23 major universities and the Smithsonian Institution as its voting membership, in addition to over 140 associate members in the United States and abroad who receive microfiche copies of the files.

Part J

Africa and the Middle East

Section 1

J.1.a Atlases

In addition to the special atlases listed here, consult section I.1.a for a list of useful general atlases. The *Atlas of Middle Eastern Affairs* (I.1.a:9) and *Atlas of African Affairs* (I.1.a:10) focus on recent political, social, and economic conditions. Horrabin's *Atlas of Africa* (1960) (1) has 50 maps accompanied by brief descriptions of Africa from prehistoric times to independence and discussions of "problems of tomorrow." Martin's *Africa in Maps* (1962) (2) consists of 58 maps without text. However, the maps are larger and more detailed than Horrabin's, and greater emphasis is placed on current social and economic conditions. The maps in both volumes are in black and white. The small *Atlas of the Arab World and the Middle East* (1960) (3) deals with physical and cultural aspects of the Middle East from Morocco to Iran. Explanatory text and photographs accompany the maps. The Israeli-produced *Atlas of the Middle East* (1964) (4), though somewhat larger, with 40 pages of general, physical, and thematic maps, unfortunately has text and map legends in Hebrew only. Despite its heavy economic emphasis, the *Oxford Regional Economic Atlas of the Middle East and North Africa* (I.1.a:3) is very useful. In the *Atlas of Israel* (1970) (5) more than 200 maps and diagrams make up the 71 sheets, arranged in 15 sections, covering cartography, geomorphology, geology, climate, hydrology, botany, zoology, land utilization, history, population, settlement, and so on. Considerable background information on the explanation of the maps and diagrams is given. Among existing African atlases are the *Atlas of Kenya* (1962) (6), *Atlas du Maroc* (1954–) (7), and *Atlas of Tanganyika, East Africa* [now called Tanzania] (1956) (8). The *West African International Atlas* (1968–) (9) is concerned with the area from the Atlantic and the Gulf of Guinea to Lake Chad. Other national atlases are described in Lock (A.1.a:11), and bibliographies of African atlases are given in Conover and Duignan (J.1.b:4).

J.1.b   Bibliographies

Following the bibliographies covering Africa in general are listed those devoted specifically to the Middle East and North Africa and to Sub-Saharan Africa.

Bibliographies of Bibliographies.   Garling's *Bibliography of African Bibliographies* (1968) (1) consists of about 900 items arranged by country under general regional headings and alphabetically by author within each country. It is unannotated, but notes the number of entries in each bibliography where possible. Although not strictly a bibliography of bibliographies, J. D. Pearson's *Oriental and Asian Bibliography* (1966) (2), subtitled "An Introduction with Some Reference to Africa," directs attention to the scope and range of Oriental, Asian, and African studies, as well as to organizations focusing on these areas; manuscript collections, reference books, periodicals, and bibliographies; and libraries and archives, together with special problems affecting them. Angela Molnos's *Sources for the Study of East African Cultures Development* (1968) (3) lists 796 social-scientific bibliographies, abstracts, reference works, directories, and so on with special reference to Kenya, Tanzania, and Uganda, covering the years 1946–66. Topics include administration, agricultural development, archaeology, health, history, economics, education, politics, sociology, and related subjects. The work is arranged alphabetically by author. Besterman (A.1.b:1) and the *Bibliographic Index* (A.1.b:2) are worth consulting.

Reference Works.   Sections of Walford (A.1.b:12) and Winchell (A.1.b:13) are devoted to reference works on Africa. Careful, extensive annotations make the Conover and Duignan *Guide to African Research* (1971) (4) the most useful source. It updates and expands Conover's *Africa South of the Sahara,* which covered material up to 1963. Arranged in four parts, it includes over 3,000 "primary" entries, and references to 1,500 additional works. Part 1 discusses research organizations, libraries, archives, and other research agencies in Europe and Africa. Reference works are outlined in part 2, with particular attention to bibliographies, serials, government publications, dissertations, atlases, and maps. Parts 3 and 4 are concerned with research on such subjects as art, politics, science, and sociology, arranged in over thirty categories and with studies of regions and countries. In the November 1968 issue of *Current Bibliography of African Affairs* (7) about 110 items are annotated by Daniel G. Matthews in "African Bibliography Today: Selected and Current Bibliographical Tools for African Studies, 1967–1968." Economics, fine and performing arts, history, juvenile literature, politics and government, and recent studies are among the topics. Bibliographies of African government publications are listed inside the back cover of *Sub-Saharan Africa: A Guide to Serials* (17).

General Bibliographies.   Conover and Duignan (4) is the best source with which to begin research on Africa. Paden and Soja's four-volume *The African Experience* (1970) (5), an interdisciplinary approach to the continent, includes essays by specialists in five divisions (African Society and Culture, Perspectives on the Past, Process of Change, Consolidation of Nation States, and Africa and the Modern World); a syllabus of 100 "topic summaries" or "modules"; and an annotated bibliography of over 4,000 items. The bibliography is in two sections, with an author index. Section 1 lists books and articles arranged according to 100 subdivisions, while section 2 consists of case studies [including titles in the Ethnographic Survey of Africa series (J.2.a:1) on the 46 countries or dependent states and territories]. Items within each of the 100 categories are arranged uniformly: the most significant works, titles suggested for further reading, works on the theory of the subject, less accessible sources, and case studies. Articles published in volumes of collected studies, occasional book reviews, and publications of governments and nongovernmental organizations, as well as items in HRAF (I.3.1) are included. Volume 2B has articles on reference works concerned with Africa, developments in African publishing, African journals and newspapers, African-language publications (including lists of works in Hausa and Swahili), audiovisual aids, and the use of computers in compiling bibliographies.

Planned as an updating of Conover's *Africa South of the Sahara,* Gutkind and Webster's *Select Bibliography on Traditional and Modern Africa* (1968) (6) contains over 2,900 citations of books and articles, including those in collected volumes published between 1962 and 1968. It is indexed by author, subject, and key word. Part 1 includes chapters on geography, population, archaeology and prehistory, races, migrations, history, ancient and modern kingdoms, the slave trade, social systems, land tenure, and law. Chapters in part 2 cover continuity and change, particularly in respect to imperialist occupation; the growth of nationalism; problems of modernization; literature; art; and international relations. The last chapter lists 72 bibliographies.

Besides containing references to books and articles on African countries and related topics, the bimonthly *Current Bibliography of African Affairs* (1962–) (7) features an extensive bibliographical essay on a special subject, book reviews, and a list of forthcoming publications. The AUFS *Select Bibliography* (I.1.b:3), the *London Bibliography of the Social Sciences* (A.1.b:5), and Mason (G.2.c:2) have sections devoted to Africa. *African Affairs for the General Reader* (1967) (8) lists, with annotation, about 1,600 recommended books, pamphlets, and periodical articles on all aspects of the continent; it is one of several bibliographies published by the African Bibliographic Center. Other publications of this organization are listed in Conover and Duignan (J.1.b:4). Titles in the International African Institute's Africa Bibliography series A are *West Africa* (1958) (9), *Northeast Africa* (1959) (10), *East Africa* (1960) (11), and *Southeast Central Africa and Madagascar* (1961) (12). In preparation are volumes on Africa (general), North Africa, West Central Africa, and South Africa. Each volume lists about 750 books and articles, arranged geographically and by subject, with indexes of authors and of ethnic and linguistic names. Emphasis is on ethnography, sociology, and linguistics. In the Institute's Africa Bibliography series B, each volume deals with a special subject. The U.S. Army's *Africa, Its Problems and Prospects* (I.1.b:4), *The Developing Nations* (I.1.b:1) by ReQua and Statham, and the *Journal of Developing Areas* (I.1.b:2) are concerned with African issues.

Monroe Nathan Work's *Bibliography of the Negro in Africa and America* (1928) (13) lists more than 17,000 selected books, pamphlets, and articles—about half of them on Africa—in a classified arrangement with an author index. The existence of a bibliography of pre-1928 periodical articles is noteworthy, since the articles are easily obtained through the photocopying service of a library's interlibrary-loan facilities. Work is supplemented from 1932 to the 1960s by the long bibliographical sections in the *Journal of Negro Education* (1932–) (14).

Reviews of Research. The *African World* (1965) (15), edited by Robert Lystad, is a survey of social-science research, including comprehensive review articles by specialists of recent research on 18 topics, ranging from law, education, and politics to literature and the arts. Historical and sociocultural, physio-biological, and psycho-cultural approaches are represented. Each chapter has an extensive bibliography, and the volume is indexed. Volume 1 of *The African Experience* (J.1.b:5) attempts a comprehensive, interdisciplinary introduction to African studies. In each of 31 essays a specialist discusses current research, considers the interdisciplinary relevance of each topic, and suggests topics for future research. Part 1, "African Society and Culture," and part 2, "Perspectives on the Past," focus on traditional aspects, including implications for contemporary problems, from such perspectives as traditional society, economic systems, major themes in African history, and the impact of colonialism. Part 3, "Processes of Change"; part 4, "Consolidation of Nation States"; and part 5, "Africa and the Modern World," identify contemporary issues and problems from such perspectives as personality, education and elitism, urbanization, African concepts of nationhood, the development of political and legal systems, international relations, Africa and Islam, the confrontation with South Africa, and Afro-American relations. *Expanding Horizons in African Studies* (1968) (16) consists of interpretative essays by scholars assessing the future directions of disciplinary and interdisciplinary research.

Periodicals. The Library of Congress's *Sub-Saharan Africa: A Guide to Serials* (1970) (17) is a guide to a selected number of monographic series, annual reports of institutions, yearbooks, directories, and periodicals in Western languages or in African languages using the Roman alphabet. As an aid to obtaining photocopies of articles, periodicals held in libraries in the United States and Canada are indicated. In addition, information is given as to where several hundred periodicals are abstracted or indexed. Descriptions of 492 periodicals covering Africa south of the Sahara are contained in *African Studies: World List of Specialized Periodicals* (1970) (18). Arrangement is by country of origin, with geographical, institutional, and title indexes. A brief analysis of each title, along with editorial information, addresses, frequency of issue, and so on, is also provided.

Middle East and North Africa. All fields of North Africa and the Middle East are well covered in Pearson's *Index Islamicus* (1958–) (19). The main volume comprises a classified listing of over 26,000 items. Supplements bring the coverage up through 1970, and more are planned. The U.S. Army has published two editions of its *Middle East, Tricontinental Hub: A Strategic Survey* (I.1.b:7). The 1968 edition contains only material published since 1965. Ettinghausen's *Selected and Annotated Bibliography of Books and Periodicals in Western Languages Dealing with the Near and Middle East, with Special Emphasis on Medieval and Modern Times* (1954) (20) is a briefly annotated list of about 2,000 items. Each issue of the quarterly *Middle East Journal* (1947–) (21) contains a bibliography of about 250 periodical articles which deal with the Middle East since the rise of Islam; encompassed are North Africa and Muslim Spain, the Arab world, Israel, Turkey, Afghanistan, the Transcaucasian states of the Soviet Union, Iran, Pakistan, and Turkestan. Arrangement is by subject; geography, history, economic and social conditions, science, philosophy and religion, language, law, literature and the arts, biography, bibliography, and book-review citations, as well as AUFS *Reports* (I.1.e:14), are included. Articles in languages other than English are so indicated.

Sub-Saharan Africa. Besides Conover (J.1.b:4), Forde's *Selected Annotated Bibliography of Tropical Africa* (1956) (22) is a good introductory guide. It includes sections on geography, ethnography, sociology and linguistics, administration and government, economics, education, missions, and health, listing the significant studies of African problems in all languages. There are no indexes. The annual *U.S. and Canadian Publications on Africa* (1960–) (23) lists books, pamphlets, and periodical articles on Africa south of the Sahara. It is arranged by subject and by country, and lists bibliographies appearing in books and periodicals, as well as theses and dissertations. One of the largest bibliographies appears quarterly in *Africa* (1928–) (24), which notes each year over 2,000 books, sections of books, periodical articles, pamphlets, and reports in many languages. Emphasis is on ethnography, sociology, and linguistics, but history, economics, politics, and related subjects are included. There is a classified arrangement, and occasionally items are briefly annotated. In 1971 the bibliography began to be published separately as *International African Bibliography* (1971–) (25). *African Abstracts* (1950–) (26), a quarterly review of ethnographic, social, and linguistic studies appearing in current periodicals, abstracts in each issue over 200 periodical articles. The arrangement and emphasis are similar to the bibliography section associated with *Africa*. Each issue of the quarterly

African Affairs (1901–) (27) has a bibliography of about 100 books, and articles in "non-African periodicals." There is no subject arrangement, and the emphasis is on the humanities.

J.1.c   Biographical Dictionaries and Directories

Only nine of the many biographical dictionaries and directories relating to Africa are noted here. Eight are dictionaries of biographies of prominent Africans, and the ninth is a directory of social scientists specializing in African studies. See sections A.1.c and I.1.c for biographical dictionaries and directories that include Africans. The annual *Middle East and North Africa* (J.1.e:8) and *Africa South of the Sahara* (J.1.e:9) include biographical data on prominent persons. *The New Africans* (1967) (1) has biographical sketches of 600 prominent Africans, as well as brief histories of each independent country south of the Sahara. Ronald Segal's *African Profiles* (1962) (2) is a revised edition of his *Political Africa* (1961) (3), a "who's who" of personalities and parties. Biographical data is provided on 400 Africans and 100 political parties. Brief biographies of 28 African statesmen and politicians are provided in *The New Leaders of Africa* (1961) (4) by Rolf Italiaander. *Who's Who* volumes exist for East Africa (1963–) (5) and Southern Africa (1907–) (6). More substantial biographies are in Rosenthal's *Southern African Dictionary of National Biography* (1966) (7). It includes about 2,000 brief biographies of persons now deceased who were notable in the history of the Republic of South Africa, South West Africa, Rhodesia, Zambia, Malawi, Mozambique, Swaziland, Bechuanaland, and Basutoland. The first volume of the *Dictionary of South African Biography* (1968–) (8) contains 368 biographies of black Africans and Europeans. The complete set is planned to include over 2,500 persons notable in the history of South Africa. The editors have not used either an alphabetical or a chronological arrangement, but an index is provided, and subsequent volumes will have cumulative indexes. There is a bibliography for each article, and notes on iconography are often included. Each quarter the *Middle East Journal* (J.1.b:21) refers to 20 to 40 biographical articles on people involved in Middle Eastern affairs. *Social Scientists Specializing in African Studies* (1963) (9) has brief biographical information on over 2,000 African specialists in the United States and elsewhere.

J.1.d   Encyclopedias and Dictionaries

As yet, no encyclopedia covers Africa exclusively. The *Encyclopedia Africana* (1), being prepared in Accra is proposed to be a single volume consisting of "the work as far as possible of Afri-

can scholars distinguished in their own fields of study."[1] General
encyclopedias such as those listed in section I.1.d have articles on
Africa. Eric Rosenthal's *Encyclopedia of Southern Africa* (1965)
(2) has information on the history, biogeography, and related
topics of countries and territories of southern Africa, as well as
maps and illustrations. The *Encyclopedia of Islam* (1954–) (3)
is considered the most important reference work in English on
Islamic subjects. Scholarly articles focus on such topics as religious
beliefs, institutions, manners and customs, tribes, industries, sciences, and artistic production, as well as biography, history, geography, economics, and social topics. Geographical material includes separate articles on towns and larger political divisions of
the former Ottoman Empire and other regions in which Islam is
prominent. The *Shorter Encyclopedia of Islam* (1965) (4) reprints the articles from the first edition and supplement of the
Encyclopedia of Islam (1913–33) that relate particularly to the
religion and law of Islam. A few new entries have been added and
all bibliographies have been updated. Included is a "Register of
Subjects" giving the English translation of Arab headings and an
alphabetical index of articles. Stephan and Nandy Ronart's two-
volume *Concise Encyclopedia of Arabic Civilization* (1960–66)
(5) is useful for brief information on people, places, institutions,
and events. The first volume focuses on the "Arab East" (the
Arabian peninsula, Egypt, Iraq, Jordan, Lebanon, and Syria), and
the second on the "Arab West" (North Africa [except Egypt] and
the Iberian peninsula). Each volume is designed to be used inde-
pendently, but the first has more information on issues relating to
Islam in general. The articles range from a few lines to several
pages. There are no indexes; however, in addition to "see" references, asterisks following words and phrases in the text indicate
the existence of additional articles. Levine and Shimon's *Political
Dictionary of the Middle East in the Twentieth Century* (1972)
(6) has 760 brief, authoritative articles on historical, political,
social, and military aspects and on the roles of major powers, and
biographies of prominent twentieth-century figures. The *Encyclopedia Judaica* (A.1.e:12) should not be overlooked.

J.1.e   Handbooks and Yearbooks

The best-known and most widely used handbook is Colin Legum's *Africa: A Handbook* (I.1.e:4). Two hardcover editions
have appeared, the latest in 1966. A paperback version of the
1966 edition appeared in 1970. [Michael Adams's *The Middle
East: A Handbook* (I.1.e:6) is a volume in the same series with
a similar format.] Legum is also associated with a new, ambitious

annual, *African Contemporary Record* (1969–) (1). Each volume is in three parts. Part 1 has articles on current issues such as
the Nigerian civil war, South African gold and world liquidity, the
East African community, and the Soviet Union and Africa. Part 2
is a chronicle of major events in 49 countries, and part 3 is a collection of documents about Africa issued in 1967 and 1968. There
are 18 maps. U.S. Army Area Handbooks (I.1.e:12) are published for many countries of Africa and the Middle East including
Afghanistan, Algeria, Angola, Burundi, Cyprus, Ethiopia, Iraq,
Jordan, Kenya, Lebanon, Liberia, Libya, Morocco, Mozambique,
Nigeria, Rwanda, Saudi Arabia, Senegal, Somalia, Sudan, Syria,
Tanzania, Turkey, Uganda, the United Arab Republic, and Zambia.

AUFS *Reports* (I.1.e:14) cover Southwest Asia, North Africa,
Northeast Africa, East Africa, Central and Southern Africa, and
West Africa. The AUFS *Reports* on Southwest Asia, North Africa,
and Northeast Africa are indexed in the *Middle East Journal*
(J.1.b:21). The U.S. Department of State's *Background Notes on
the Countries of the World* (I.1.e:13) exist for over 50 African
and Middle Eastern countries. Volumes on Africa or the Middle
East in the Geographical Handbook series (E.1.e:5) cover Algeria, the Belgian Congo, French Equatorial Africa and Came-
roons, French West Africa (two volumes), Iraq and the Persian
Gulf, Morocco (two volumes), Palestine and Transjordan, Persia,
Syria, Tunisia, Turkey (two volumes), and Western Arabia and
the Red Sea. The annual *Africa* (1969–) (2) contains details of
each African country—population, political affairs, educational
system, economy, and so on—and a number of feature articles on
such current developments as administration, geography, economic
conditions, and politics. The illustrations and colored maps of 47
nations are especially useful. There is no index. Three earlier
works are Violaine Junod's *Handbook of Africa* (1963) (3),
John Hatch's *Africa Today and Tomorrow* (1965) (4), and
Helen Kitchen's *Handbook of African Affairs* (1965) (5). Although no attempt is made to interpret or analyze the data, *The
Handbook of Africa* contains documented information on each of
the fifty-odd political units of Africa. Appendixes include essays
on colonial policies, regional groupings, metropolitan aid to Africa, British and French marketing systems, and tables of measures
and currency. There is no index. In addition to an outline of basic
facts about Africa, *Africa Today and Tomorrow* includes a selective chronology of events in African history, and statistical and
governmental information on African states. Lord Hailey's revised
African Survey (1957) (6), though reflecting a British-colonial
attitude, is a useful source of information on political, legal, eco-

nomic, social, and educational policies and conditions in Africa up
to 1956. Among its chapters are "The Physical Background," "The
African Peoples," "The African Languages," "Population Records," "Systems of Government," "The Non-European Immigrant
Communities," "Law and Justice," "Water Supply and Irrigation,"
and "Projects of Economic Development." There is an index.
[See the brief account of the book in Conover (J.1.b:4).] *An
Atlas of African Affairs* (I.1.a:10) has data up to 1965. George
H. T. Kimble's two-volume work, *Tropical Africa* (1960) (7),
is an intensive study by a professional geographer. Volume 1 sur-
veys "Land and Livelihood"; volume 2, "Society and Polity."

A number of yearbooks focus on regional aspects of the African continent and neighboring areas. *The Middle East and North
Africa* (1948–) (8) and *Africa South of the Sahara* (1971–) (9)
contain surveys of developments in economics, history, and education; concise information about constitutions and political conditions; directories of industrial, financial, cultural, and educational
organizations; and biographical directories. Much of this data is
also included in *The Europa Yearbook* (I.1.e:1). *West Africa
Annual* (1962–) (10), the *Yearbook and Guide to East Africa*
(1950–65) (11), and the *Yearbook and Guide to Southern Africa* (1901–) (12) are oriented toward business and travel. Basic
political and economic data on countries of each region are provided, but more attention is directed to travel routes, hotels, and
so on. East Africa and Southern Africa were combined in one
volume until 1949; in 1965 the East Africa volume ceased publication. As well as general small colored maps, both volumes feature numerous maps of cities and towns.

J.I.f   Newspapers and News Digests

African and Middle Eastern newspapers and related matters are
reviewed in Merrill's *The Foreign Press* (I.1.f:1). *Africa: A Guide
to Newspapers and Magazines* (1969) (1) is in German and English. Information in chart form includes the name of the newspaper or periodical, frequency of publication, political affiliation,
and language, as well as data useful to advertisers. Africa receives
a good deal of attention in *Keesing's Contemporary Archives*
(A.1.g:5) and is covered by three news-digest services. The *Africa Research Bulletin* (1964–) (2) appears in two separate sections: *A*, "Political, Social, and Cultural"; and *B*, "Economic, Financial, and Technical." Each section appears monthly, with a
digest of press articles and other sources on current events in
Africa relating to its field. About 100 African and world newspapers and other sources are surveyed for material. Names of information sources are provided, but not dates and pages of issues.

References to earlier news items are included. Each section has semiannual and annual indexes. The *Africa Diary* (1961–) (3) and *African Recorder* (1962–) (4) are both published in India. The *Africa Diary,* issued weekly, is a news digest of events in individual countries and in Africa as a whole. The *African Recorder* is a fortnightly, summarizing and quoting from major newspapers. Included is a section covering news from European and other foreign sources. Both are indexed. The *Mideast Mirror* (1948–) (5), issued weekly, consists of summaries, edited from news reports, of developments in the Middle East. Its quarterly index is arranged by country.

J.1.g   Statistics Sources

The most accessible statistical source is the U.N. Statistical Office's *Statistical Yearbook* (I.1.g:3), supplemented regularly by its *Monthly Bulletin of Statistics* (I.1.g:5). The Africa Institute in Pretoria publishes *Africa at a Glance* (1967–) (1), a regularly updated "quick reference" of maps, tables, and graphs containing information on economic, social, and educational statistics. The Africa Institute's separately issued Africa: Maps and Statistics series (1962–) (2) has information on the topics *Population* (1962); *Vital and Medical Aspects* (1962); *Cultural and Education Aspects* (1963); *Transport and Communications* (1963); *Water and Power* (1963); *Agriculture and Forestry* (1963); *Livestock Farming and Fishing* (1964); *Mining, Industries, and Labor* (1964); *Trade, Income, and Aid* (1964); and *Political Development* (1965). Similar publications are listed regularly in the Africa Institute's monthly. Joan Harvey's *Statistics Africa* (1970) (3) provides information on published statistics (and indicates the availability of unpublished statistics) for the African continent and nearby islands. After a list of information sources for the whole continent, countries are listed alphabetically, with statistical publications arranged in the following groups: general, production, external trade, internal distribution, and population and standard of living. Over 600 items are annotated, with indexes of titles and organizations. *Statistics Sources* (A.1.h:1) and the *Encyclopedia of Business Information Sources* (A.1.b:7) are useful, and historical statistics are available in *Cross-Polity Time-Series Data* (I.1.g:7).

Section 2

J.2.a   Anthropology

Collections of Data. Information on over sixty African and Mid-

dle Eastern cultures exists in the Human Relations Area Files
(I.3:1). Included are the following:

AFRICA

Africa
Bambara
Dogon
Mossi
Mende
Tallensi
Twi (Ashanti, Fanti,
  Akan)
Katab
Nupe
Tiv
Yoruba
Fang
Nuer
Shilluk
Ganda
Dorobo
Kikuyu
Luo
Masai
Chagga
Ngonde (Ngone,
  Nyakyusa)

Azande
Mongo (Nkundo, Mongo,
  Ekonda)
Rundi (Ruanda, Rundi)
Mbundu
Bemba
Ila
Ngoni
Thonga
Yao
Bushmen (Kung, Auin,
  Heikum)
Hottentot (Nama,
  Lorana)
Lovedu
Tanala
Somali
Amhara
Hausa
Tuareg (Ahaggar, Ayr)
Wolof
Senegal
Rif

MIDDLE EAST

Middle East
Iran (Qashqu, Jurds,
  Bakhtiaris)
Kurd
Turkey
Syria (Druze)
Rwala
Lebanon
Jordan
Iraq
Kuwait
Saudi Arabia (Badu,
  Anazah, Sa'ar,
  Salubba)

Bedouin
Maritime Arabs
Trucial Oman
Yemen
Aden
Hadhramaut
Fellahin
Siwans
Kanuri
Shluh
Bahrain

The Ethnographic Survey of Africa series (1954–) (1), edited
by Daryll Forde, is an excellent source of information on tribes

or groups of people, comprising over 50 monographic volumes. They are listed in Conover and Duignan (J.1.b:4) and in Paden and Soja (J.1.b:5). Written by experts, the volumes present a brief critical treatment of existing knowledge of tribal groupings, distribution, physical environment, social conditions, political and economic structure, religious beliefs, cult practices, technology, and art. Each contains a substantial bibliography. Tribes in the following regions are covered: Western Africa (27 volumes), North-eastern Africa (3 volumes), East Central Africa (18 volumes), Madagascar (1 volume), West Central Africa (4 volumes), Congo (5 volumes), and Southern Africa (4 volumes).

Bibliographies. Gibson notes the existence of 872 bibliographies in "A Bibliography of Anthropological Bibliographies: Africa" (1969) (2). This bibliography is "intended to provide an up-to-date guide to the many regional and topical bibliographies useful in African anthropological research, as well as to some more general lists that devote significant sections to African anthropological topics." It comprises ethnology and ethnography, social anthropology, culture history, archaeology, prehistory, folklore, linguistics, race, and ancient man; such subdivisions as primitive art, oral literature, law, race relations, and social and cultural change; and the neighboring fields of history, sociology, psychology, economics, political science, education, human geography, and medicine. Annotations indicate number of entries, coverage, scheme of classifications, and the existence of annotations or indexes. The index includes, in a single listing, subjects, authors, institutions, and journals responsible for the bibliographies. In Lystad (J.1. b:15), P. H. Gulliver discusses 105 articles on anthropology; Robert Gray surveys 33 studies on the anthropological aspects of medical research. As well as Harvard University's *Peabody Museum Catalog* (B.1.b:2), Wilfred D. Hambly's *Source Book for African Anthropology* (1937) (3), with its supplement, "Bibliography of African Anthropology, 1937–1949" (1952) (4), and H. A. Wieschoff's *Anthropological Bibliography of Negro Africa* (1948) (5) are highly regarded older works. Hambly's *Source Book* was reprinted in 1969. Four sections treat the results of anthropological research in Africa to 1936, including (1) physiography, biology, archaeology, physical anthropology, and linguistics; (2) the continent in terms of culture-area concepts; (3) the nature of Negro culture; and (4) the European period of African development. A selective listing of over 2,600 books and periodical articles is included; the bibliographical supplement covers the years 1937–49. Wieschoff is arranged by tribes, with over 12,000 references to English, French, and German books, sections of books, and articles.

Henry Field's ten-volume *Bibliography of Southwestern Asia, 1940–1959* (1953–62) (6) is arranged in two major sections: "anthropogeography" and natural history. Anthropogeography includes anthropology, ethnology, sociology, linguistics, demography, archaeology, and so on. The 31,000-odd citations, unannotated, are arranged by author, with a cumulative subject index for volumes 1–5 only. *Circum-Mediterranean Peasantry: Introductory Bibliographies* (1969) (7) serves as a guide to the geographical, sociological, and anthropological literature on peasants and peasantries, rural producers, the societies in which they live, and urban migration. The bibliographies on various groups are comprehensive, but limited to French and English titles. Gaps exist, however, particularly in relation to eastern European countries (Greece, Yugoslavia, and Albania) and Turkey and Egypt, where much active research and publishing is now going on. All countries "with littorals on the Mediterranean Sea" are included (Spain, France, Italy, Yugoslavia, Albania, Greece, Turkey, Syria, Lebanon, Israel, Jordan, Egypt, Libya, Tunisia, Algeria, Morocco, and the islands of Corsica, Sardinia, the Balearics, Malta, Crete, and Cyprus), along with Portugal, "which shares the pattern but not the shoreline." The preface also surveys such topics as the "Mediterranean pattern," geographical factors, and major anthropological contributions. There are chapters on each of the countries, all including a headnote discussing important works and an unannotated list of books and articles. *The Central Middle East* (1971) (8) is in five chapters, each devoted to a specific area: the Nile valley, the Arab Levant, southern Mesopotamia, the Arabian peninsula, and the industrially based state of Israel. Each chapter is written by a specialist, and provides "the serious student of the cultural anthropology of this central sector of the Middle East with an overview of the major regions and socio-cultural types and a guide to the adequacies or inadequacies of the major published research on the area. All of the chapters and bibliographies, originally composed and compiled between 1960 and 1962, have been updated to 1967, and some additions and revisions have been made for this new issue in 1971." Editor Sweet notes in the preface, however, that "a new synthesis, taking into account the withdrawal of colonial administrators, the establishment of sovereign governing systems, and the introduction and proliferation of international commercial and industrial mechanism, awaits systematic anthropological study."

Subfields of Anthropology

Archaeology.   The *COWA Bibliography* (B.2.a:1) has area reports 9–14 on Africa and 15–20 on Asia. J. D. Clark's *Atlas of*

African Prehistory (1967) (9) is the work of many scholars. There are 12 base maps of ecology and palaeoecology and 38 transparent overlay maps of political boundaries and cities, cultural distributions, fossil-fauna sites, fossil-man sites, and so on. The maps are accompanied by a volume consisting of commentaries, a gazetteer, and related information. Creighton Gabel's "African Prehistory" in the 1965 *Biennial Review of Anthropology* (B.1.b:7) is a review of the published research. The 193 items are arranged under such topics as areal syntheses, terminology, absolute chronology, paleontology, human origins, pleistocene archaeology, neolithic and agricultural origins, and the introduction of iron. A number of review articles relating to African anthropology appear in Lystad (J.1.b:15). J. Desmond Clark discusses 66 studies on African prehistory.

Art. The *Encyclopedia of World Art* (B.2.b:1) includes many survey articles with lengthy bibliographies, and black-and-white and colored plates of art and related subjects of Africa and the Near East.

Linguistics. Murphy and Goff's *Bibliography of African Languages and Linguistics* (1969) (10), includes 1,218 selected items. Bibliographies of over 200 languages are represented, including dialects of Arabic, Hamitic, Malagasy, Afrikaans, and Creole, as well as the so-called Negro-African languages. A general section, divided into such topics as bibliography, general studies, regional studies, phonology and orthography, language learning, and languages in education, precedes chapters on non-Bantu, Bantu, and other languages of Africa. The International African Institute's Handbook of African Languages series (1948–) (11) consists of volumes surveying African languages; they parallel the Institute's Ethnographic Survey of Africa series (J.2.a:1); listed in Conover-Duignan (J.1.b:4) and Paden-Soja (J.1.b:5), volumes in this latter series provide information on geographical distribution, population statistics, linguistic classification, and basic bibliographies. Joseph Greenberg reviews 135 studies in African linguistics in Lystad (J.1.b:15); a briefer review by Jack Berry is in volume 1 of Paden (J.1.b:5). About 380 studies on linguistics appear annually in the sections "Sub-Saharan Africa" and "Afro-Asiatic" of the *MLA Bibliography* (B.2.e:1), and a much larger number appear in the sections "Sub-Saharan languages of Negro Africa," "Asiatic and Mediterranean," and "Hamito-Semitic" of the annual *Bibliographie linguistique* (B.2.e:2).

Ethnomusicology. D. L. Thieme's *African Music* (1964) (12), an annotated list of 597 sources discussing the music of sub-Saharan Africa in books and articles since 1950, is indexed by author and tribe. L. J. P. Gaskin's *Select Bibliography of Music in Africa* (1965) (13) lists some 3,000 books and articles. Alan P. Merriam reviews 43 studies on African music and dance in Lystad (J.1.b:15), and Klaus Wachsmann approximately the same number in Paden and Soja (J.1.b:5).

Mythology. Volumes 5–7 and 12 of *Mythology of all Races* (B.2.d:10) deal with myths of Semitic, Egyptian, and African peoples. A substantial bibliography of African folklore has appeared annually since 1967 in the "African Literatures" section of *MLA Bibliography* (B.2.e:1). In Lystad (J.1.b:15), Bascom reviews 56 studies on folklore and literature, stressing such subjects as the social roles of folklore, and studies of African verbal art.

J.2.b Demography

The *Demographic Yearbook* (C.1.g:1) has census figures for African countries. The *Population Index* (C.1.b:1) includes a number of studies devoted to Africa, and the November 1969 special issue of the *Population Bulletin* (C.1.b:5), an annotated list of selected books on population, includes Africa. In Lystad (J.1.b:15), 86 demographic studies and reports are reviewed by Frank Lorimer, William Brass, and Etienne van de Walle. Attention is directed to population, development of demographic statistics, methods of collecting demographic statistics, analysis of demographic trends, and demographic aspects of migration.

J.2.c Economics

The annual *International Bibliography of Economics* (D.1.b:12) includes items on African and Middle Eastern economics. Andrew M. Karmack's bibliographical essay in Lystad (J.1.b:15) assesses items on economics and economic development. Arnold Rivkin's "Economic Systems Development" in Paden (J.1.b:5) treats such topics as "Economy Building in Africa," "Problems of Development Planning," "International Aid and Currency Relations," and "Outlook for African Development." The *Economic Survey of Africa since 1950* (1959) (1) is comprehensive for the decade that it covers. Attention is directed to structural aspects, growth trends, and the development of external trade and capital formation, including development plans and the financing of investments. This is supplemented by the *Economic Bulletin for Africa* (1961–) (2), issued once or twice annually, with articles on current economic trends and problems of trade. *Economic Developments in the Middle East* (1949–) (3) is an annual review that supplements the *World Economic Survey*. Two magazines issued by commercial banks are reliable sources for information on economic conditions in Africa and other areas. Their chief virtue is that data appear in them more quickly than in U.N. publications. *Barclays International Review* (1946–) (4), formerly known as the *Overseas Review,* is issued monthly, with an annual survey of trade and economic conditions in the territories in which the Barclays Bank group is represented: Botswana, Cameroun, Cyprus, Ghana, Gibraltar, Israel, Kenya, Lesotho, Malawi, Malta, Mauritius, Mozambique, Nigeria, Seychelles, Sierra Leone, South Africa, South West Africa, Swaziland, Uganda, and Zambia. As well as the latest production statistics for each country, issues contain commentary on other aspects of the countries included. The *Standard Bank Review* (1919–) (5) covers nations in eastern, southern, and western Africa where the Standard Bank organization is represented. A separate *Annual Economic Review* of each nation is also published. The *Oxford Regional Economic Atlas: Africa* (I.1.a:4) and the *Oxford Regional Economic Atlas: The Middle East and North Africa* (I.1.a:3) include many reliable maps in color and a substantial amount of information in summary or tabular form. Africa and the Middle East receive considerable attention also in ReQua and Statham's *The Developing Nations* (I.1.b:1). Edmund Neville-Rolfe's *Economic Aspects of Agricultural Development in Africa* (1969) (6) is an annotated listing of selected reports and studies of forty African countries for the years 1960–69. Jane Martin's *Bibliography on African Regionalism* (1969) (7) lists selected books, periodicals, periodical articles, and documents published between 1960 and 1968. The focus is on supranational political and economic developments, and sections are included on case studies of East, West, and North Africa. Each of the six parts begins with a bibliographical essay, followed by an alphabetically arranged list of titles. Section 6 suggests aids to further research. There is no index.

J.2.d Geography

John W. Sommer's *Bibliography of African Geography, 1940–1964* (1965) (1), lists 1,725 articles from 58 journals, primarily in English or French. It is arranged in the following sections: human geography, economic geography, physical geography, and general African. Sanford H. Bederman's *Bibliographic Aid to the Study of the Geography of Africa* (1970) (2), the AGS's *Research Catalog* (E.1.b:4), and *Current Geographical Publications* (E.1.b:5) should be consulted for additional material on African geography. Henry Field's ten-volume *Bibliography of Southwestern Asia, 1940–1959* (J.2.a:6) covers the "anthropogeography," mostly periodical articles, of the Middle East.

J.2.e History

The increasing attention directed to Africa by historians—African and non-African—has resulted in a large number of books and an increasing number of historical journals devoted to Africa. Recent volumes reflect an "African-oriented" outlook rather than a European or North American one. There are brief articles (with bibliographies) surveying the main features of African and Islamic historiography within the main article "Historiography" in the *International Encyclopedia of the Social Sciences* (A.1.e:2). Philip Curtin's *African History* (1964) is one of the AHA's Service Center for Teachers of History series (O.2.e:8). Using such terms as "cultural arrogance" and "racism," Curtin explains how attitudes of superiority among "progressive" white societies arose during the industrial revolution (1750–1900). In all, he mentions about 150 books and articles concerned with aspects of African civilization, principally history. Combining topical and chronological approaches, the work discusses the emergence of African history (the discovery of historical Africa, teaching materials); pre-colonial Africa (new techniques and new sources, conventions [contents and periodization], the problem of "lag," the problem of the Bantu Migration, communication and isolated development [forests and southern savanna, some myths and mythmakers], tribes, cultures, and states); and Africa and the Europeans (the slave trade; new interpretations of the "pre-colonial century," 1780–1880; the "scramble" and its causes; and the impact of European rule). Curtin speculates about technological development in Africa, particularly relating to the problem of so-called lag. He concludes that "the lag in African development, as seen at the nineteenth-century confrontation with Europe, had two components. First was the ancient lag behind the Near Eastern civilization, which was shared for a time by northwest Europe. The second was the European advance, which carried the West further ahead technologically than either the Sudan or the Near East. This second component has no direct relation to African history. It was produced by unusual achievements in Europe, not unusual failures outside Europe. . . . Only Europe's unusual dynamic at its breakthrough into industrialism made Africa and other civilizations of the world appear static" (p. 29). In the *Cambridge History of the British Empire* (1929–59) (1), volumes 1, 2, 3, and 8 are on Africa. Each volume includes chapters by specialists, focusing on social, economic, and cultural aspects. A widely acclaimed feature is the large bibliography of each volume, listing archive materials, official papers, and so on, as well as secondary sources.

Africa and the Middle East are blessed with several good historical atlases. J. D. Fage's *Atlas of African History* (1958) (2) features 62 black-and-white maps of the continent and neighboring areas from A.D. 410 to 1957. A more recent work is Harry Gailey's *History of Africa in Maps* (1967) (3). Harry W. Hazard's *Atlas of Islamic History* (1954) (4) covers the period from A.D. 600 to 1953. Facing each map are summaries of important historical events. A conversion table of Christian and Muslim dates and an index of place names are included. Another recommended work is Roolvink's *Historical Atlas of the Muslim Peoples* (1957) (5). The African Bibliographic Center's *Black History Viewpoints* (1969) (6) is an introductory bibliographical guide to current resources on Afro-American and African history. Daniel G. Matthews's *Current Themes in African Historical Studies* (1970) (7) contains extensive bibliographies of medieval West Africa and the African diaspora, as well as on trends in African historical studies, 1967–69.

Many pages in the American Historical Association's *Guide to Historical Literature* (F.1.b:2) are devoted to Africa and the Middle East. The AHA *Guide* is partially updated with Robert O. Collins's "African History in the 1960's: Enthusiasm, Vitality, and Revelations" (1967) (8), a bibliographical essay noting 35 monographs. In the *Annual Bulletin of Historical Literature* (F.1.b:3), a great many monographs receive scholarly assessment. For premodern Islamic history, Sauvaget's *Introduction to the History of the Muslim East* (1965) (9) is a valuable research aid. Arranged in three categories ("The Sources of Muslim History," "Tools of Research and General Works," and "Historical Bibliography"), it discusses some 1,800 works in many languages. Bernard Lewis and P. M. Hold have edited *Historians of the Middle East* (K.2.e:11), a volume with 41 contributors. Another noted historiography of the Middle East is F. Rosenthal's *History of Muslim Historiography* (1952) (10). Robin Winks's *Historiography of the British Empire* (1966) (11) has chapters relating to Africa and the Middle East. A comparative examination of various interpretations of African history is provided by Clarence G. Contee in "Current Problems in African Historiography" (1967) (12).

Two bibliographical essays appearing in *Current Bibliography on African Affairs* (J.1.b:7) should be noted: "Black is Black? A Selected and Introductory Bibliographical Guide to Current Resources on Relations between the Black American and African" (1968) and Anne M. Forrester's "Black America Views Africa: A Selected Bibliography of Perspective" (1968). Seven problems of African history receive attention from historians in Robert O. Collins's *Problems in African History* (1968) (13).

Emerging Themes of African History (1968) (14), edited by
Terence O. Ranger, comprises papers on such topics as the his-
toriographical tradition of African Islam, the periodization of
African history, the use by historians of ethnographic data, and
African resistance to and rebellion against colonial rule.

J.2.f Contemporary Literature and Fine Arts

The main purpose of the Oriental and African sections of the
Penguin Companion to World Literature (L.2.f:1) is "to provide
a handy and readable 'Who's Who' of the most significant writers
of Asia and Africa, from ancient times to the present day." Each
brief entry includes important facts of the author's life and a concise guide to outstanding works, as well as critical studies thereof.
Janheinz Jahn's *Bibliography of Creative African Writing* (1971)
(1) is the most ambitious treatment of contemporary African literature. Published books, performed plays, and completed manuscripts are included. Arrangement is by geographical area, with an
author index. Creative works of literature in English by black
African writers, along with relevant criticism, are listed in Barbara
Abrash's *Black African Literature in English since 1952: Works
and Criticism* (1967) (2). A substantial bibliography of criticism
of African literature has appeared annually since 1967 in the
MLA Bibliography (B.2.e:1).

In Lystad (J.1.b:15), Sieber's article "Visual Arts" focuses on
traditional tribal art, suggesting that it is pertinent to the study of
contemporary arts; 22 studies are reviewed. Alan P. Merriam reviews 43 studies on African music, stressing such issues as music
and dance as artistic product and as behavior, and their relationships with other disciplines. William Bascom discusses 56 studies
on African folklore and literature, and briefly considers a number
of sub-Saharan African authors and their works.

Evelyn S. Brown's *Africa's Contemporary Art and Artists*
(1966) (3) is a review of creative activities in painting, sculpture,
ceramics, and crafts of more than 300 artists working in the modern industrialized societies of sub-Saharan Africa. Institutions and
cultural organizations are included. Lionel J. P. Gaskin's *Bibliography of African Art* (1965) (4) lists over 5,350 items, in such
categories as general, regional, handbooks, bibliographies, and
special numbers of periodicals. There are geographical-and-ethnic
and subject indexes.

J.2.g Political Science

The *International Bibliography of Political Science* (G.1.b:4)
and its companion *International Political Science Abstracts* (G.1.

b:5) have sections devoted to African politics. Harvey Glickman reviews about 700 studies of African political affairs in Lystad (J.1.b:15).

The U.S. Army's Area Handbooks (I.1.e:12) relating to Africa and the Middle East provide general background information and extensive bibliographies on a number of nations. The U.S. Army's *Middle East, Tricontinental Hub: A Strategic Survey* (I.1.b:7) is a good starting point for research on political issues of the area. The quarterly *Chronology of Arab Politics* (1963–) (1) is based on Arabic sources, by country, with an annual index. Although volumes of the annual *Middle East Record* (1960–) (2) appear several years after the year covered, it provides a comprehensive survey of political developments.

Political affairs in sub-Saharan Africa have been covered in several works. Patrick J. McGowan's *African Politics* (1970) (3) is a substantial volume subtitled "A Guide to Research Resources, Methods, and Literature." William and Judith Hanna's *Politics in Black Africa* (1964) (4) is a selective bibliography of English and French periodical literature, listing about 1,200 articles arranged by subject. Herbert J. Spiro's *Politics in Africa* (1962) (5) discusses the "new look" in African politics, with emphasis on nationalism. There are bibliographies for each chapter and an author-subject index. Claude Wauthier's *The Literature and Thought of Modern Africa: A Survey* (1967) (6), an updated version of his *L'Afrique des africains, inventaire de la négritude* (1963), discusses the works of many African writers on independence. The second edition of Harold F. Alderfer's *Bibliography of African Government, 1950–1966* (1967) (7) is a listing of several thousand books and articles on government, politics, and public administration, arranged by country, with an author index.

The African Bibliographic Center's *The Sword and Government* (1967) (8) is a selected list, in two parts, of books and articles on African military affairs. The U.S. Army's *Africa: Problems and Prospects* (I.1.b:4) includes a summary of the armed forces of African states. Literature on Communist activities in Africa and the Middle East is discussed in Hammond's *Soviet Foreign Relations and World Communism* (M.2.g:3), the *Yearbook on International Communist Affairs* (M.2.g:4) and D. G. Matthews's "Soviet View of Africa: A Select Guide to Current Resources for Study and Analysis" (1967) (9). Ronald Segal's *African Profiles* (J.1.c:2) is an important source for information on political parties and on 400 political figures. Segal is updated by Sidney Taylor's *The New Africans* (J.1.c:1).

J.2.h Sociology

There is a powerful stimulus for interdisciplinary research on Africa. Geographers, anthropologists, and political scientists tend to overlap into the preserve of sociologists in African and Middle Eastern studies, as indicated by the abundance of HRAF material on Africa and the Middle East (see section J.2.a). Urbanization, the sociology of religion, and race relations are among the prominent subjects of research. *African Urbanization* (1965) (1) is a brief list of selected books, articles, and reports. Ruth P. Simms's *Urbanization in West Africa* (1965) (2) is a review of current literature. Eva L. Deregowska's bibliography on *Some Aspects of Social Change in Africa South of the Sahara* (1967) (3) includes 600 items relating to social change, conflict, stability, social stratification, elites, women, tribalism, and so on, with author and country indexes. Leo Kuper's review article "Sociology: Some Aspects of Urban Plural Societies" in Lystad (J.1.b:15) discusses 47 items, mostly empirical studies, stressing such issues as cultural and social pluralism, tribal or ethnic cleavage or integration, race, class, and voluntary association. Several essays in *The African Experience* (J.1.b:5) are related to sociological issues. The annual *International Bibliography of Sociology* (H.1.b:2) includes a substantial number of items on Africa and the Midlde East.

Part K

Asia

Section 1

K.1.a Atlases

Only general atlases are considered in this section; for historical atlases see K.2.e. Although no single atlas in English is devoted to the whole of Asia, there are a number of atlases that deal with certain of its subregions, as well as others that cover many of its individual countries. Southwest Asia and the Middle East are well covered in a number of recent atlases, noted above in part J. The *Atlas of Southeast Asia* (1964) (1) is the sole English-language atlas covering the region. The atlas includes almost 70 regional and thematic maps, as well as an illustrated historical introduction. Former French possessions in Asia, including French Indochina and Syria, are mapped in the *Atlas des colonies françaises, protectorats et territoires sous mandat de la France* (1934) (2).

Atlases dealing with the individual countries of China, India, Israel, Japan, Korea, Pakistan, Saudi Arabia, and Turkey vary greatly in quality and coverage. One of the most ambitious is the five-volume *National Atlas of China* (1959–62) (3). General physical maps and more detailed demographic, economic, and other thematic maps cover all regions of China. The *People's Republic of China* (1971) (4) comprises a series of 17 double-folio maps. Very useful also to the American student is Harold Fullard's small paperback atlas, *China in Maps* (1968) (5), which includes a number of general historical and regional maps as well as some thematic maps dealing with agriculture, industry, and resources. Mention should be made of John Lossing Buck's classic work, *Land Utilization in China* (1937) (6), volume 2 of which is an atlas comprising 184 maps and 13 aerial photographs.

What promises to be one of the most elaborate and useful national atlases is the *National Atlas of India* (1957–) (7), which was first published in a Hindi edition. It includes 26 maps, each on the scale of 1 to 5,000,000, showing certain physical, economic, and cultural aspects of the country. A much-enlarged English-language edition has been in preparation since 1959 but is still far from complete. In the meantime, the now very much outdated *Oxford Economic Atlas for India and Ceylon* (I.1.a:6) will likely be found the most useful source of much fairly detailed cartographic information on the country.

Japan is the Asian country best served with atlases. *Teikoku's Complete Atlas of Japan* (1969) (8) is a very useful general and economic atlas covering most aspects of the country's geography and economic activity. More recently the International Society for Educational Information of Tokyo has produced the *Atlas of Japan: Physical, Economic, and Social* (1970) (9), which contains 73 maps, together with explanatory notes. K. Aki's earlier *Economic Atlas of Japan* (1954) (10), though published only in Japanese, is a valuable atlas despite its now much-outdated information. It is best used in conjunction with Ginsburg and Eyre's *Key to the Economic Atlas of Japan* (1959).

Unfortunately, the *Standard Atlas of Korea* (1960) (11), is available only in a Chinese-language edition. Some use, however, might be made of this and other foreign-language atlases with the help of Olson and Whitmarsh's *Foreign Maps* (1944) (12), chapter 5 of which includes extended glossaries of topographic and other terms used on maps in a number of Asian and other languages. Pakistan is well covered by the *Oxford Economic Atlas of Pakistan* (I.1.a:7). The peninsula of Indochina is excellently covered in the U.N.'s *Atlas of Physical, Economic, and Social Resources of the Lower Mekong Basin* (1968) (13). Maps, statistical information, and explanatory text cover physical, economic, and social aspects of the four countries—Vietnam, Laos, Cambodia, and Thailand—that border the river.

K.I.b Bibliographies

Reference Works. According to G. Raymond Nunn, his *Asia: A Selected and Annotated Guide to Reference Works* (1971) (1) is the first attempt to present in an integrated fashion a selection of the whole literature on Asia. It annotates 975 books and periodicals, of which two-thirds are in English. Criteria for selection included the comprehensiveness and quality of the work, and avoidance of duplication. Primarily the concern is with modern issues. The guide selectively updates and supplements the excellent bibliographies of Teng Su-Yu and Knight Biggerstaff's *Annotated Bibliography of Selected Chinese Reference Works,* Peter Berton and Eugene Wu's *Contemporary China: A Research Guide* (K.1. b:22), and the *Guide to Japanese Reference Books.* Nunn's earlier volumes, *South and Southeast Asia: A Bibliography of Bibliographies* and *East Asia: A Bibliography of Bibliographies,* are both superseded. After a general section, arrangement is by region and country, then by type of reference work, subdivided by subject when appropriate. Within these divisions titles appear chronologically. There is an author-title index.

Maureen L. P. Patterson, in "Bibliographical Controls for South Asian Studies" (1971) (2), describes 113 titles, with particular reference to the availability, comprehensiveness, and reliability of Eastern and Western sources. The paper is recommended for people requiring intensive knowledge of South Asia. Donald Clay Johnson's *Guide to Reference Materials on Southeast Asia* (1970) (3) is an important and extensive guide, based on the collections in the Yale and Cornell University libraries, that arranges more than 2,200 items.

General Bibliographies. The most valuable and authoritative general bibliography on Asia is the one produced by the Association of Asian Studies as the final number of its *Journal of Asian Studies* (1941–) (4) and issued in October of each year. Some 3,000 to 5,000 items dealing with the Asian continent, its regions, and individual countries are listed. Material on India, Pakistan, Ceylon, and Nepal has been included since 1956. The arrangement is regional and alphabetical, and an author index is provided. A cumulative bibliography based on the journal's listings has been issued by the firm of G. K. Hall; it is the *Cumulative Bibliography of*

Asian Studies, 1941–1965: Association of Asian Studies, Author and Subject Bibliography (1970) (5). In the subject volumes, items are arranged primarily by country or region in alphabetical order, with special subjects listed alphabetically under each region or country.

Eleazar Birnbaum's *Books on Asia from the Near East to the Far East* (1971) (6) is a selected, annotated listing of some 2,000 works written in either English or French and currently in print. *Asia: A Guide to Basic Books* (1966) (7) provides an introduction to paperback books on Asia, with sections on South Asia, Southeast Asia, and East Asia and their respective countries. India, China, and Japan are those most fully considered.

The American University Field Staff's *Select Bibliography: Asia, Africa, Eastern Europe, Latin America* (I.1.b:3) is a recommended source. The U.S. Army's two-volume *Communist China* (I.1.b:8) emphasizes security issues.

By and large, the South and Southeast Asian areas are far better provided with good bibliographical references than is the Middle East. *South Asia: An Introductory Bibliography* (1962) (8) by Maureen L. P. Patterson and Ronald B. Inden lists well over 4,000 items on India, Pakistan, Ceylon, and Nepal, arranged in six sections. Each section is subdivided according to a threefold scheme: chronological, topical, and geographical. There are no annotations, but author and title indexes are provided. Kennedy G. Tregonning's *Southeast Asia: A Critical Bibliography* (1969) (9) is a selected, graded, and annotated listing of more than 2,000 items covering Burma, Thailand, Cambodia, Laos, North and South Vietnam, Malaysia, Indonesia, and the Philippines. The items are arranged first by country and then by subject, and there is clear indication as to the relative authoritativeness of the items. An older work by John F. Embree, *Books on Southeast Asia: A Select Bibliography* (1956) (10), is also worth noting. For research in earlier writings on Southeast Asia the major work is Henri Cordier's *Bibliotheca Indosinica* (1912–15) (11), which lists books, articles, documents, maps, and official reports on the whole Indochinese area (here including Assam, Burma, and Malaya). J. Irikura's *Southeast Asia: Selected Annotated Bibliography of Japanese Publications* (1956) (12) reviews nearly 1,000 books on the social sciences.

Bibliographical works on a number of individual countries should also be noted: Donald N. Wilbur's *Annotated Bibliography of Afghanistan* (1962) (13), Fred Egger's *Selected Bibliography of the Philippines* (1956) (14), and Frank N. Trager's *Annotated Bibliography of Burma* (1956) (15). J. Michael Mahar's *India: A Critical Bibliography* (1964) (16) is a valuable selected, graded, and annotated bibliography dealing with most aspects of India and the Indian people. An author index is provided. *Index India* (1967–) (17) is a quarterly list of articles, editorials, notes, letters, and other materials on Indian subjects.

Karl J. Pelzer's *West Malaysia and Singapore: A Selected Bibliography* (1971) (18) is an updated and expanded version of his *Selected Bibliography on the Geography of Southeast Asia: Part III, Malaya* (K.2.d:1). It covers anthropology, economics, geography, political science, and sociology, as well as history and the natural sciences. Approximately 4,300 books and articles are listed. There is an author index. Among the chapters is a list of about 80 bibliographies.

A. R. Ghani's *Pakistan: A Select Bibliography* (1951) (19), which lists some 9,000 items on the history, geography, natural resources, and political and economic activities of that country, has been severely criticized for its slipshod editing. Updating this work to some extent is *Books From Pakistan Published during the Decade of Reform, 1958–1968* (1968) (20). It should be noted, however, that works on Pakistan published elsewhere are not listed, while works published in Pakistan but not concerned with Pakistan are listed. Regular supplements to the latter work are planned; the first, covering the years 1969–70, has already appeared. Linda G. Schappert's *Sikkim, 1800–1968: An Annotated Bibliography* (1968) (21) is a listing of nearly 340 items on the history, culture, topography, and resources of that small country.

Bibliographical materials on the Far East are primarily concerned with China and Japan. Widely recognized as the best introductory bibliography to modern China is Berton and Wu's *Contemporary China: A Research Guide* (1967) (22). Coverage is largely restricted to works on mainland China issued after 1949 and to works on Taiwan issued after 1945. Most significant bibliographical and reference works available in English or Chinese are carefully annotated. Two appendixes cover research libraries and institutions, and dissertations and theses. Subject and author-title indexes are provided. Equally important is Charles O. Hucker's *China: A Critical Bibliography* (1962) (23), which grades and annotates some 2,285 selected books, articles, and other published items. In general, items are listed in order of importance. Fairbank and Liu's *Modern China: A Bibliographical Guide to Chinese Works, 1898–1937* (1950) (24) has sections dealing with general reference works, general history, government and law, historical studies by period, foreign affairs, economic data and studies, social problems, cultural movements and education, intellectual and literary history, and selected newspapers and learned journals. A much more comprehensive listing of works on China in Chinese is provided in the Hoover Institution's thirteen-volume *Library Catalog: Catalog of the Chinese Collection* (1969) (25). Author, title, and subject cards of books, pamphlets, and other research material are interfiled alphabetically. Another major work for more advanced research on aspects of imperial China is Henri Cordier's five-volume *Bibliotheca Sinica: Dictionnaire bibliographique des ouvrages relatifs à l'empire chinois* (1878–1924) (26). Tung-li Yuan's *China in Western Literature* (1958) (27) is subtitled "A Continuation of Cordier's *Bibliotheca Sinica*." Some 18,000 books are listed in 28 broad subjects, with appropriate subdivisions, followed by sections which cover the various regions of China. An author index is provided.

Index Sinicus: A Catalog of Articles Relating to China in Periodicals and Other Collective Publications, 1920–1955 (1964) (28) provides coverage of periodicals, festschriften, and other collective works and congresses. The items are arranged in 27 parts, which cover topical and regional subjects, including foreign relations; national minorities; philosophy and religion; and Central Asia, Hong Kong, and Macao.

Bernard S. Silberman's *Japan and Korea: A Critical Bibliography* (1962) (29) is the best introductory bibliography in English for both countries. The 1,615 items on Japan and the 318 items on Korea have been carefully selected, graded, and annotated. Those on Japan are organized into ten sections, including land and people, art and literature, and education and population. The works on Korea are somewhat similarly arranged. Henri Cordier's classic work, *Bibliotheca Japonica* (1912) (30), parallels his works on China (K.1.b:26) and Indochina (K.1.b:11).

K.1.c Biographical Dictionaries and Directories

In addition to general biographical works cited in part A, many of which include biographical information on major Asian statesmen, scholars, and other notable persons, a number of more detailed works on individual countries are available.

For China there are biographical dictionaries covering periods from the remote and legendary past to the present. Widest in range is H. A. Giles's two-volume *Chinese Biographical Dictionary* (1898, reprinted in 1964) (1), which deals with all periods to the end of the nineteenth century. Though regarded as a standard reference work, it is not entirely reliable, being outdated in some of its contents and incorrect in certain details. The Library of Congress's two-volume *Eminent Chinese of the Ch'ing Period (1644–1912)* (1943–44) (2) is a detailed biographical dictionary of approximately 800 eminent Chinese and Mongols of the period. H. L. Boorman's four-volume *Biographical Dictionary of Repub-*

lican China (1967–70) (3) has important biographical articles on prominent Chinese figures of the period from 1911 to 1949. The Communist period is covered by a number of works, including *Who's Who in Communist China* (1966–) (4). *Who's Who in China: Biographies of Chinese Leaders* (1918–) (5), now in its fifth edition, should also be consulted. Biographical sketches previously published in the *China Weekly Review* comprise the volume. Donald W. Klein and Anne B. Clarke's two-volume *Biographic Dictionary of Chinese Communism, 1921–1965* (1971) (6) has 433 lengthy biographical articles on major figures in Chinese communism through the mid-1960s.

The 3-volume *Japan Biographical Encyclopedia and Who's Who* (1958–) (7) includes short biographical sketches of more than 15,000 eminent Japanese, whose names are given in both Japanese characters and romanized equivalents. Chronological tables, a list of emperors, a table of major eras of Japanese history, and lists of Japanese cabinets and diplomats are among the many other items included. It might be noted also that volume 2 of Goedertier's *Dictionary of Japanese History* (K.2.e:6), the first volume of which appeared in 1968, is devoted to biographies of eminent Japanese, living and dead.

Buckland's *Dictionary of Indian Biography* (1906) (8) and the annual *Times of India Directory and Yearbook* (1914–) (9), which includes a who's who of important Indian figures, are the most useful biographical reference works for India.

Other current biographical directories for individual Asian countries are *Who's Who in Malaysia* (1956–) (10) and the *Asia Who's Who* (1957–) (11); the latter, providing short biographical sketches of more than 2,000 Asians, is, of course, of more general use.

K.I.d   Encyclopedias and Dictionaries

One of the major encyclopedias dealing with Asia, and the most important single reference work on Islam, is the *Encyclopedia of Islam* (J.1.d:3). Authoritative, signed articles by leading scholars in the field deal with all aspects of the Moslem religion, and also with the history and geography, and social, political, and economic institutions of the various Islamic countries, as well as with the tribes, manners and customs, art, music, and other aspects of the Islamic world. The *Shorter Encyclopedia of Islam* (J.1.d:4) includes, among other material, all articles contained in the first edition and later supplements of the *Encyclopedia of Islam* on the religion and laws of Islam. Most of this material is printed in its entirety.

For China there is the *Encyclopedia Sinica* (1917) (1), which, though occasionally outdated in its explanation of terms and in its interpretation of historical events, is still of some value. *The Chinese Readers' Manual* (1874) (2), by William Frederick Mayers, is an encyclopedic handbook of biographical, historical, mythological, and general literary reference.

The government of India's four-volume *Gazetteer of India* (1965–) (3) promises to be an encyclopedic treatment of India's land, people, and institutions. Volume 1, the work of an impressive list of leading scholars and other experts, deals with the "Country and People." Volume 2 will deal with "History and Culture," volume 3 with "Economic Structure," and volume 4 with "Administration and Public Welfare."

Two useful dictionaries are Yule and Burnell's *Hobson-Jobson: A Glossary of Colloquial Anglo-Indian Words and Phrases* (1903) (4) and Janey Chen's *Practical English-Chinese Pronouncing Dictionary* (1970) (5), which provides English, Chinese characters, romanized Mandarin, and Cantonese in one listing.

K.I.e   Handbooks and Yearbooks

Two works cover the whole Asian continent. *Asian Annual* (1954–) (1), arranged alphabetically by country, provides comprehensive and up-to-date coverage of such matters as population and resources, economic output by sector, government organization and personnel, and trade and transportation. Equally valuable, though not a regular annual production, is *Asia: A Handbook* (I.1.e:8).

Covering major regions of Asia are two Europa yearbooks, *The Middle East and North Africa* (J.1.e:8) and *The Far East and Australasia* (1969–) (2). The arrangement of materials is somewhat similar in the two, though *The Far East and Australasia* is more elaborately arranged. Part 1 deals with general topics, part 2 with South Asia as a region and with its individual countries and territories, part 3 with Southeast Asia, and parts 4 and 5 with East Asia and with Australia and the Pacific respectively. Reference materials (including a who's who), directories of organizations, lists of weights and measures, and selected bibliographies are provided in part 6. Much of the data is duplicated in *The Europa Yearbook* (I.1.e:1). Harold C. Hinton's *The Far East and South Pacific, 1969* (1968) (3) provides statistical data, maps, and brief historical and social information on 19 independent countries and a number of smaller territories and dependencies of the area. Harvey S. Olson's *Orient Guide* (1962) (4) is a travel guide which provides general information on the Far East and parts of the Pacific, and more detailed information on individual countries.

A great deal of varied information is provided in a number of well-known series. The U.S. Army's Area Handbooks (I.1.e:12) are available for the following countries: Burma; Cambodia; Communist China; India; Indonesia; Japan; Korea; Laos; Malaysia and Singapore; Nepal, Sikkim, and Bhutan; North Vietnam; Pakistan; the Philippines; South Vietnam; Thailand; and Vietnam. More modest in scope is the Background Notes on the Countries of the World series (I.1.e:13).

Much more extensive in coverage are the Asian volumes of the Geographical Handbook series (E.1.e:5). China is covered in three volumes and the Netherlands East Indies and Turkey in two each. Single volumes deal with Indochina, Iraq and the Persian Gulf, Palestine and Transjordan, Persia, Syria, and Western Arabia and the Red Sea. Aimed largely at the traveler and regularly updated are the Fodor Guides (1962–) (5), which are available for many countries, including India and Japan.

A number of handbooks and yearbooks are available for individual countries of Asia. China and India are particularly well supplied with such reference works, though some of them leave much to be desired in terms of reliability and authority. The *China Year Book* (1921–39) (6), an unofficial publication, was for long the most respected source of information on all aspects of China. *China Yearbook* (1943–) (7), published in Taiwan by the Nationalist government, regularly covers from 1937 such matters as the government and its functions, national defense, international affairs, the national economy, social affairs, education, and culture. There are also special sections on the Chinese Communist regime, chronological tables, and a who's who combined with obituary notices. Communist China is treated more intensively in two other yearbooks: *Communist China* (1955–) (8) and *Communist China Yearbook* (1962–) (9). The annual volumes of the first publication summarize events in that country and give details of party, foreign, and military affairs. The second work has chapters on various aspects of Communist China, such as major meetings and statements; people's communes; the economy, education, and culture; and foreign relations. It also includes a directory of leaders and a diplomatic list. *Contemporary China: Economic and Social Studies, Documents, Bibliography, and Chronology* (1955–) (10) is purportedly an annual collection of articles and documents, but only six issues appeared between 1955 and 1968. Its title explains its scope. Nagel's encyclopedic guide, *China* (1968) (11), provides copious information on many aspects of China.

Among the numerous handbooks and yearbooks devoted to India, four are of considerable value. *India: A Reference Annual* (1953–) (12) is an official publication which contains statistical and other data on many aspects of Indian life, as well as brief information on political and social developments. Election statistics and short bibliographies are included as appendixes. *The Times of India Directory and Yearbook* (K.1.c:9) provides a variety of information on economic, political, and cultural aspects of India for officials, businessmen, and tourists. Lists of firms and organizations, and a who's who of Indian leaders are other regular features. The *Hindustan Yearbook and Who's Who* (1933–) (13) covers a similar range of material and includes a section called "India at a Glance" which provides useful information in capsule form. The most venerable handbook on India is Murray's *Handbook for Travellers in India, Pakistan, Burma, and Ceylon* (1859–) (14). Introductory information on all aspects of Indian life is followed by detailed descriptions of each region of the four countries. A directory of place names and an index are also provided.

Japan Handbook (1966) (15) claims to be "a wealth of useful data on Japan for everyday reference." It has sections on such topics as geography and climate, history, education, religion, government, agriculture, finance, labor, industry, transportation, and communications, as well as an extensive statistical section. Herschel Webb's *Research in Japanese Sources* (1965) (16) is another useful source. *Twenty Years of Pakistan, 1947–1967* (1967) (17) was compiled by the Pakistani government to mark Pakistan's first twenty years of independence. Its 32 sections review most aspects of Pakistani life and society, and include a biographical directory and a useful working bibliography. *Pakistan Year Book* (1969–) (18), a continuation of *Twenty Years of Pakistan,* aims to provide a year-by-year review of the nation's life and achievements. Select bibliographies are also provided. *Singapore Yearbook* (1966–) (19) is another official publication which provides a variety of information on many aspects of the history, peoples, and economy of the country.

K.1.f Newspapers and News Digests

A most useful listing of the newspapers of Asia is provided in Feuereisen and Schmacke's *Die Presse in Asien und Ozeanien* (1968) (1), which is printed in both German and English and arranged alphabetically by country or territory. Name, address, circulation, frequency of issue, class of reader, format, and information on printing methods and advertising are tabulated for each newspaper of the continent. A more detailed bibliographical reference work is King and Clarke's *Research Guide to China-Coast Newspapers, 1822–1911* (1965) (2), which includes an annotated list of China-coast newspapers and biographies of China-coast editors and publishers.

The *Asian Recorder* (1955–) (3) is a weekly digest of outstanding events listed and described under each country or territory. Quarterly and annual indexes are provided.

The *Asia Research Bulletin* (1971–) (4) provides a monthly analysis of political, economic, and social issues from over 300 English-, Chinese-, Malay-, and Thai-language newspapers, periodicals, and official publications of South and Southeast Asia. In addition, important events and issues are treated more extensively in survey articles. Statistical tables from official sources are a regular feature. Sources are indicated. Cross-references, including references to other sources, as well as monthly, quarterly, and annual indexes, are provided. *Asian Survey* (1961–) (5) consists of topical papers in the social sciences on South and Southeast Asia. Special January and February issues review events and issues of the previous year for each country of the region. The *Asia Letter* (1964–) (6) is published weekly, with occasional supplementary special reports and surveys. Written by American foreign correspondents with long experience in Asia, it claims to provide an authoritative analysis of Asian affairs. The *SEATO Record* (1960–) (7) features significant events in Southeast Asia, as well as activities of SEATO and its member nations.

Mention should be made here also of news digests on the People's Republic of China. The American consulate-general in Hong Kong has for some years issued a series of publications of considerable value for the study of China's political and economic conditions; these include the *Survey of China Mainland Press* (1950–) (8) and *Selections from China Mainland Magazines* (1965–) (9). Consult Brock (G.1.b:1) or Mason (G.2.c:2) for more details on these publications and translations of mainland-Chinese materials.

K.1.g   Statistics Sources

The most useful source of Asian statistics is the annual *Economic Survey of Asia and the Far East* (1948–) (1), which can be supplemented by the quarterly *Economic Bulletin for Asia and the Far East* (1957–) (2). Both publications give statistics on resources, production, and trade for each country of the continent. The U.N.'s *Statistical Yearbook* (I.1.g:3), *Monthly Bulletin of Statistics* (I.1.g:5), and *Demographic Yearbook* (C.1.g:1); FAO's *Production Yearbook* (I.1.g:13), *Trade Yearbook* (I.1.g:12), and *Commodity Yearbook* (I.1.g:9); and the *Statesman's Yearbook* (E.1.e:1) are other sources of information for Asia as a whole and for its individual countries and territories. Quick access to these titles is provided by the *Encyclopedia of Business Information Sources* (A.1.b:7) and *Statistics Sources* (A.1.h:1). *Cross-Polity Times-Series Data* (I.1.g:7) is useful for historical statistics, as well as other statistical information.

Statistics for individual countries are provided in various official and unofficial annual and occasional publications. Among useful works of this kind are the *Japan Statistical Yearbook* (1949–) (3) and the *Pakistan Statistical Yearbook* (1952–) (4).

A number of the yearbooks cited in section K.1.e, particularly those on India, contain statistical data.

Section 2

K.2.a   Anthropology

Collections of Data.   Information on over eighty cultures is deposited in HRAF (I.3:1). The arrangement below is according to the *Outline of World Cultures* (B.1.e:3).

ASIA

Korea	Vietnam
Ainu	Malaya
Okinawa	Malays
Formosa	Semang
Formosan Aborigines	Thailand (Akha, Miao)
(Atayal, Ami)	Central Thai
Taichung Peasants	Burma
Sino-Tibetan Border	Burmese
(Chiang, Mewu Fantzu)	Kachin
Lolo	Karen
Miao (Hainan, Hunan,	Garo
Cowry Shell, Flowery,	Khasi
Ch'uan)	Afghanistan
Monquor	(Afghan, Pathan,
China	Hazara)
North China	Kashmir
Northwest China	Dard
Central China	Kashmiri
East China	Burusho (Hunza)
Southwest China	India (Hindus, Chamar)
South China	Bihar
Manchuria	Coorg
Mongolia	East Panjab
Inner Mongolia	Gujerati
(Chahar, Suiyan,	Kerala (Nayar)
Ningsia)	Telugu
Outer Mongolia	Uttar Pradesh
Sindiang	Bhil
Tibet (A Mdo Pa)	Gond (Muria, Raj, Maria)
West Tibetans (Ladakhi)	Kol
Lepcha	Santal
Southeast Asia	Toda

Indochina   Sinhalese
Cambodia   Vedda
Laos   Andamans (Onge, Jarawa)

Anthropological reference materials on certain regions of Asia
and particular aspects of Asian life are numerous. One major work
is Embree and Dotson's *Bibliography of the Peoples and Cultures
of Mainland Southeast Asia* (1950) (1). This covers such topics
as physical anthropology and demography, archaeology, ethnology,
cultural history, social organization, law and religion, language,
literature, and folklore. It includes individual sections on the Chinese and Indians in Southeast Asia, as well as sections on all major
regional groups of peoples and tribes. A critical listing of bibliographies, lists of periodicals cited, and a list of useful journals on
Southeast Asia are additional features.

More recent is Frank LeBar's "Ethnography of Mainland Southeast Asia: A Bibliographic Survey" (1966) (2). The focus is on
descriptive ethnography; theoretical and linguistic studies are not
included. The author evaluates about 150 books and articles, examining first introductory studies and surveys and then studies of
Burmese, Chinese, and other tribes. Equally important is Elizabeth von Fürer-Haimendorf's *Anthropological Bibliography of
South Asia* (1964) (3), which has 20 sections covering 19 regions and the area as a whole. Each section is arranged in three
parts. Part A lists works published before 1940; part B, books
published between 1940 and 1954; and part C gives data on field
research carried out during the years 1940–54. Both parts A and
B of each section are arranged under six headings: cultural and
social anthropology, material culture and applied arts, folklore and
folk arts, prehistoric archaeology, physical anthropology, and mis-
cellanea. A second volume, arranged somewhat similarly (though
the regional sections are treated in terms of current administrative
units), covers the years 1955–59, and a third volume the years
1960–64.

A number of works in the HRAF Country Survey series provide copious anthropological reference materials on individual
countries, including North Borneo, Brunei, and Sarawak (1956)
(4); Thailand (1966) (5); Cambodia (1959) (6); China (1960)
(7); Laos (1967) (8); Afghanistan (1962) (9); Indonesia
(1963) (10); and Pakistan (1964) (11). Published by the same
organization are two other important works. Raymond Kennedy's
Bibliography of Indonesian Peoples and Cultures (1962) (12),
which concentrates on anthropological and sociological aspects, is
listed island by island and arranged by language groups; Frank
M. LeBar's *Ethnic Groups of Mainland Southeast Asia* (1964)
(13) is an important work on the many hill and valley peoples of

mainland Southeast Asia, with comprehensive bibliographical references.

Minority Groups in Thailand (1970) (14) provides basic facts about the social, economic, and political institutions and practices of 19 groups. *Laos Project Paper* (1961–) (15) is an annotated bibliography on the peoples of Laos and northern Thailand, based mainly on English, French, and Japanese sources published since 1945. J. M. Kanitkar's *Bibliography of Indology* (1960) (16) claims to be a basic book on all aspects of Indian culture. There are nine regional sections and a tenth which covers India as a whole. More than 2,000 separate items are listed.

For bibliographical and other information on the religions of Asia, consult Charles J. Adams's *Reader's Guide to the Great Religions* (B.2.d:13), and Harold Watts's *Modern Reader's Guide to Religions* (B.2.d:12). More specialized is Christmas Humphrey's *Popular Dictionary of Buddhism* (1962) (17), which briefly defines some 1,000 terms associated with the religion.

K.2.b Demography

In addition to the U.N.'s *Demographic Yearbook*s (C.1.g:1), one other work provides important demographic information on Asia. *The Population of Asia and the Far East, 1950–1980* (1959) (1), published by the Bureau of Social Affairs of the U.N., is a country-by-country analysis of population numbers, rates of growth, and projections of future population. Sources of statistical information cited, as well as other references, are provided. Often *Statistics Sources* (A.1.h:1) and the *Encyclopedia of Business Information Sources* (A.1.b:7) are valuable aids.

K.2.c Economics and Economic History

Although the literature of economics and economic history is well represented in numerous general bibliographies on the Asian continent and its regions, there are few specialized bibliographical works.

Nai-Ruenn Chen's *The Economy of Mainland China, 1949–1963* (1963) (1) is a bibliography of materials in English on China's resources, production, and trade. Included is a list of United States Joint Publications Research Service reports, issued monthly and providing translations of articles from major Chinese journals. Consult Brock (G.1.b:1) or Mason (G.2.c:2) for more information on translations of Chinese and other Asian materials. Two other recent works on China are valuable reference sources, though neither is primarily a bibliographical work. *An Economic Profile of Mainland China* (1968) (2) consists of studies prepared for the Joint Economic Committee of the United States Congress. Volume 1 covers the general economic setting and the various economic sectors; volume 2, population and manpower resources, and external relations. *Economic Trends in Communist China* (1968) (3) is a comprehensive survey of the Chinese economy and its history and development. Agriculture, industry, and foreign trade are emphasized, and statistical materials are abundantly provided.

K.2.d Geography

A number of useful bibliographies exist on Asia's geography. Widest in scope is Karl J. Pelzer's *Selected Bibliography on the Geography of Southeast Asia* (1949) (1), which was issued as a companion to Embree and Dotson's *Bibliography of the Peoples and Cultures of Mainland Southeast Asia* (K.2.a:1). Volume 1 deals with Southeast Asia in general, volume 2 with the Philippines, and volume 3 with Malaya. Volume 2 is supplemented by the *Bibliography of Philippine Geography, 1940–1963* (K.2.d:5). Pelzer has recently revised and greatly enlarged volume 3 of this work in his *West Malaysia and Singapore* (K.1.b:18).

Well over 2,000 items on the geography of South Asia are listed in Ernst Reiner's "Vorderindien, Ceylon, Tibet, 1926–1953" (1954) (2), which occupies the first 186 pages of the 1954 *Geographisches Jahrbuch*.

Three other bibliographies treat individual countries of Asia. For China there is *The Geography of China: A Selected and Annotated Bibliography* (1967) (3). The items, annotated at length, include popular works, maps, and films, as well as scholarly books, monographs, and articles. Japan is well treated in Hall and Noh's *Japanese Geography: A Guide to Japanese Reference and Research Materials* (1956) (4), which lists journals, maps, and atlases, as well as books and articles. This work also includes some information on English abstracts of Japanese articles and articles on Japan in Western languages. Robert Huke's *Bibliography of Philippine Geography, 1940–1963* (1964) (5) is a selected list of more than 1,200 items. It was designed to supplement volume 2 of Pelzer's *Selected Bibliography on the Geography of Southeast Asia* (1).

K.2.e History

Atlases. Two general atlases on the Islamic world are H. W. Hazard's *Atlas of Islamic History* (J.2.e:4) and Roelof Roolvink's *Historical Atlas of the Muslim Peoples* (J.2.e:5).

Adolph Herrmann's *Historical and Commercial Atlas of China*

(1935–37), published originally by the Yenching Institute at Harvard, was reissued in a revised edition as *An Historical Atlas of China* (1966) (1), edited by Norton Ginsburg. All periods of Chinese history, from Neolithic to contemporary times, are dealt with. M. A. Beek's *Atlas of Mesopotamia: A Survey of the History and Civilisation of Mesopotamia from the Stone Age to the Fall of Babylon* (1962) (2) includes 22 diagrammatic maps, as well as photographs, drawings, and almost 150 pages of text.

Handbooks and Dictionaries. One of the most valuable general guides is the *Handbook of Oriental History* (1951) (3). Jan M. Pluvier's *Handbook and Chart of South-East Asian History* (1967) (4) provides brief notes on each territory and lists of rulers and administrators.

Sachidananda Bhattacharya's *Dictionary of Indian History* (1967) (5) has 2,785 entries on persons, places, institutions, and literary and historical events. Joseph M. Goedertier's *Dictionary of Japanese History* (1968) (6) includes over 1,100 concise definitions and explanations. Paul Yachita Tsuchibashi's *Japanese Chronological Tables from 601 to 1872* A.D. (1952) (7) deals with the conversion of Japanese dates to the Western calendar.

Two series of books may also be mentioned here. Problems in Asian Civilization (1963–) (8) is a valuable collection of brief analytical essays. A full list of titles in the series will be found in the Heath catalog in *PTLA* (A.1.b:30). The Legacy series has a number of volumes on Asia, including *The Legacy of China* (1964) (9) and *The Legacy of India* (1938) (10). Bibliographical references are seldom extensive, but other features make these volumes useful reference works.

Bibliographies. Covering every region of the continent except parts of Siberia is the four-volume *Historical Writing on the Peoples of Asia* (1961–62) (11). Volume 1 deals with the historians of India, Pakistan, and Ceylon; volume 2, with those of Southeast Asia; volume 3, with those of China and Japan; and volume 4, with those of the Middle East. Each volume consists of a series of essays grouped by time period and/or language, and each essay deals with a particular historical topic or problem. Another broad work in this field is Winks's *The Historiography of the British Empire* (J.2.e:11), a series of essays attempting to provide a critical assessment of recent writing, with attention directed particularly towards "newer" interpretations. The chapters relating to Asia cover India, Pakistan, Ceylon, Burma, and Malaysia. The bibliographical citations are given as footnotes, but there is a detailed index of authors, anonymous titles, and subjects. Brief articles (with bibliographies) survey the main features of Chinese, Islamic, Japanese, and South and Southeast Asian historiography within the main article "Historiography" in the *International Encyclopedia of the Social Sciences* (A.1.e:2).

Two works give detailed bibliographical information on the history of Southeast Asia. Hay and Case's *Southeast Asian History: A Bibliographical Guide* (1962) (12) provides a short listing of about 700 of the more important works on Southeast Asia, its countries, and its regions. Gayle Morrison's *Guide to Books on Southeast Asian History, 1961–1966* (1969) (13) covers the same regions, providing lists essentially supplementary to those in the Hay and Case work. Another valuable work is Margaret H. Case's *South Asian History, 1750–1950: A Guide to Periodicals, Dissertations, and Newspapers* (1968) (14). It has three parts, with numerous subdivisions in the first two. Part 1 deals with articles, part 2 with dissertations, and part 3 with newspapers. The newspapers are arranged by country and city (or locale). In Downs and Jenkins's *Bibliography: Current State and Future Trends* (B.1.b:1), Ernest Wolff examines bibliographies and related materials in "Far Eastern History," focusing on China, Japan, Korea, and Taiwan; he notes especially the usefulness of Hummel's *Eminent Chinese of the Ch'ing Dynasty* (K.1.c:2) and Boorman's *Biographical Dictionary of Republican China* (K.1.c:3) as valuable sources of bibliographies as well as biographies. Allan Burnett Cole's *Forty Years of Chinese Communism: Selected Readings with Commentary* (1962) is number 47 in the Service Center for Teachers of History series (O.2.e:8).

Other sources are Jean Sauvaget's *Introduction to the History of the Muslim East* (J.2.e:9) and Paul H. Varley's bibliographical guide, *A Syllabus of Japanese Civilization* (1968) (15), which is arranged by periods from about 50,000 B.C. to the present day. Each section includes a brief chronology, a list of recommended readings, and study or discussion questions. Also included are a glossary of terms and various maps.

K.2.f Literature

A good recent treatment of Asian literature and authors is the *Penguin Companion to World Literature* (L.2.f:1). Winchell (A.1.b:13) describes a select number of other works concerned with aspects of the various types of Asian literatures, but the authors consider the approach of Walford (A.1.b:12) more satisfactory for research connected with the social sciences. Intensive research needs are best served by the *Journal of Asian Studies* (K.1.b:4) and the *MLA Bibliography* (B.2.e:1).

K.2.g Political Science

Only a few bibliographical and other reference works dealing
with the political institutions and organizations of the Asian continent have appeared to date. *Government and Politics of India
and Pakistan, 1885–1955* (1956) (1) is a bibliography of works
in Western languages on the politics of the two countries. Chun-tu
Hsueh's *The Chinese Communist Movement, 1921–1949* (1960)
(2) is an annotated bibliography of selected materials housed in
the Chinese collection of the Hoover Institute on War, Revolution, and Peace, at Stanford. A second volume covers the years
1937–49. *China and United States Far East Policy, 1945–1966*
(1967) (3) is a review of the events, personalities, and issues
affecting United States involvement with China, Formosa, Korea,
and Vietnam. Hammond (M.2.g:3) and the *Yearbook on International Communist Affairs* (M.2.g:4) are useful for tracing Communist activities throughout Asia.

K.2.h Sociology

Bibliographies of sociological studies of Asia are rare. To com-
pensate for this inadequacy, it is recommended that appropriate
sections of the *International Bibliography of Sociology* (H.1.b:2)
and the annual bibliography in the *Journal of Asian Studies* (K.1.
b:4) be examined. Items in section K.2.a include sociological
studies.

Part L

Western Europe

Section 1

L.1.a Atlases

As in the other regional parts, only general atlases are cited here; historical atlases are considered in section L.2.e. The difficulties of selection are much greater for Europe than for other continents, and all that can be claimed is that the list is a reasonably representative one. For further information, the reader is strongly urged to consult C. B. Muriel Lock's *Modern Maps and Atlases* (A.1.a:11), which devotes 130 pages of text to the maps and atlases that have appeared on Europe and its individual countries and regions.

Apart from the major world atlases, such as the *Times Atlas of the World* (A.1.a:1), the Italian *Atlante Internazionale* (A.1.a:2), and the Soviet *World Atlas* (A.1.a:3), which devote a high proportion of their pages to Europe, general atlases covering Europe as a whole have seldom been issued. Pounds and Kingsbury's *Atlas of European Affairs* (I.1.a:12) is one of the few currently available; however, its use as a reference work is limited. Place names are few, and detail of èvery sort is kept to a minimum. A number of road atlases do better with place names; most show not only the basic road networks of each country but also the classes of roads, together with more detailed maps of important tourist districts and major cities. Two of the best are the *Collins Road Atlas of Europe* (1965) (1), with more than 200 six-color maps, and *The Road and Travel Atlas of Europe* (1961) (2), which has nearly 100 maps. An extended commentary and an index in English, French, German, and Italian make it one of the most widely used road atlases in Europe.

The *Oxford Regional Economic Atlas of Western Europe* (I.1. a:2) and *The Atlas of Social and Economic Regions of Europe* (1964–) (3) are, in some ways, comparable volumes. The latter is concerned solely with the non-Communist nations of Europe and will comprise eventually about 100 maps with texts and keys in German, English, and French. Western Europe is well treated in the *Atlas of Western Europe* (1963) (4). Central Europe, which takes in many of the countries of Western Europe, is covered by two general atlases. The *Atlas Östliches Mitteleuropa* (1959) (5) provides maps on the history, geology, physical features, and natural resources of the region, with captions in English, French, and German; the *Atlas of Central Europe* (1963) (6) shows all areas on a scale of 1 to 1 million or larger, and has a gazetteer/index of more than 37,000 entries.

Official national atlases, or atlases of commensurate stature and authority, are available for many countries of Western Europe. Although the standard of these varies considerably in terms of coverage, cartographic quality, and current reliability, all provide detailed information on their respective countries. A good many have appeared in loose-leaf format, and some of these are still far from complete. For a description of these, see Lock (A.1.a:11), the Library of Congress's *List of Geographical Atlases* (A.1. a:12), or the British Museum's *Catalog of Printed Maps* (A.1. a:13). Among the Western European countries for which national atlases have been produced are Austria (1961–) (7), Belgium (1950–64) (8), Denmark (1949–61) (9), Finland (1960) (10), France (1951–58) (11), West Germany (1965–) (12), Great

Britain and Northern Ireland (1963) (13), and Italy (1940) (14).

In addition to the national atlases, there are a growing number of atlases dealing with special aspects of individual countries, and an even larger number of general, country atlases and regional atlases. One of the most valuable and scholarly of these is the *Atlas der Deutscher Agrarlandschaft* (1962–65) (15), aimed at mapping all aspects of German agriculture. J. T. Coppock's *Agricultural Atlas of England and Wales* (1964) (16) is a similar though less comprehensive work, as is Axel Sømme's *Atlas of Norwegian Agriculture* (1950) (17). The *Atlas industriel de la France* (1960) (18) is one of the few atlases that treats another major group of economic activities.

The *Reader's Digest Complete Atlas of the British Isles* (1966) (19) and the *Reader's Digest Atlas de la France* (1969) (20) contain a great variety of cartographic and photographic information, accompanied by explanatory text, on most aspects of the respective countries.

Among outstanding regional atlases are three recent French works: *Atlas de la France de l'Est* (1959–) (21), *Atlas du Nord de la France* (1961–) (22), and *Atlas de Normandie* (1965–70) (23). Three of Western Europe's largest cities are covered in comprehensive fashion in elaborate atlases: *The London Atlas* (1968–69) (24), *Atlas de Paris et de la région parisienne* (1967) (25), and the *Atlas von Berlin* (1962) (26).

L.1.b   Bibliographies

The sheer volume and variety of bibliographical materials available for the study of Western Europe probably account for the almost total lack of bibliographies of bibliographies and for the relative scarcity of general bibliographies for the region. Besterman (A.1.b:1) and the *Bibliographic Index* (A.1.b:2) should be consulted for bibliographies on Europe. Moreover, do not overlook the fact that many of the works mentioned in preceding chapters are predominantly concerned with Europe. Paul E. Vesenyi's *European Periodical Literature in the Social Sciences and the Humanities* (1969) (1) is designed to assist scholars in locating articles published in Europe on these subjects. Gray (A.1.b:3) provides the same approach but more selectively. The *Internationale Bibliographie der Zeitschriften Literatur* (A.1.b:19) is the largest index of European periodicals. The quarterly *British Humanities Index* (A.1.b:18) is one of three separate indexes introduced to replace the *Subject Index of Periodicals* (1915–61). *British Education Index* (1962–) and *British Technology Index* (1962–) are the others. Two current bibliographies which go beyond the con-

fines of history and the humanities deserve mention. *L'année philologique* (1928–) (2) annually lists the literature on classical
Greece and Rome, and the *Quarterly Checklist of Renaissance
Studies* (1958–) (3) covers the Renaissance. *Atlantic Studies*
(1964–) (4), a semiannual listing of research planned or in progress, and the U.S. Department of State's annual *External Research: Western Europe, Great Britain, and Canada* (1958–) (5)
provide coverage of many research projects in the social sciences
connected with, or being conducted in, Europe.

A useful, but now considerably outdated introductory bibliography is the Library of Congress's *Introduction to Europe: A Selected Guide to Background Reading* (1950) (6) and its 1955
supplement. Approximately 1,500 items are classified and annotated. A briefer list is *Books Dealing with Europe* (1965) (7),
aimed largely at the professional educator and teacher. Some 250
books and pamphlets—predominantly in English, French, and
German—are briefly annotated. There are sections on geography,
history, philosophy, culture, education, European integration, and
"Europe and the wider world." Problems of Europe and efforts
to bring about European integration are more fully explored in
Pehrsson and Wulf's *European Bibliography* (1965) (8), devoted
almost entirely to Western European countries. Some 2,000 works,
for the most part published between 1945 and 1963, are briefly
annotated in French and in English, and classified in nine sections.
Carol A. Cosgrove's *Reader's Guide to Britain and the European
Communities* (1970) (9) is a small, annotated bibliography of
books, pamphlets, articles, and speeches on the preceding twenty
years of European cooperation. The work is arranged in six sections: West European integration; first steps in integration; the
European communities; the first British application, 1961–63; the
current situation; and possible alternatives for Britain.

Numerous bibliographical reference works are available for
study of the British Isles. Only general works are cited here.
British National Bibliography (1950–) (10) serves a function
similar to the *National Union Catalog* (A.1.b:26). The Library
of Congress issued *Works in the Humanities Published in Great
Britain, 1939–1946: A Selective List* (1950) (11). Scotland is
covered in Hancock's two-volume *Bibliography of Works Relating
to Scotland, 1916–1950* (1959–60) (12), which supplements
Mitchell and Cork's two-volume *Contribution to the Bibliography
of Scottish Topography* (1917) (13); Ireland is covered by A. R.
Eager's *Guide to Irish Bibliographical Material* (1964) (14), an
annotated listing of 4,000 items.

Equally detailed works are available on many European countries; for descriptions of these works, see Walford (A.1.b:12) and

Winchell (A.1.b:13). A number of useful bibliographies in English on European countries are also available. J. E. Pemberton's *How to Find Out about France: A Guide to Sources of Information* (1966) (15) provides a reasonably comprehensive listing of important works on France and the French. A similar work is E. S. Stych's *How to Find Out about Italy: A Guide to Sources of Information* (1970) (16). Probably the most comprehensive and important English-language bibliography on any European region is Sven Groenning's *Scandinavia in Social Science Literature* (1970) (17). This work lists virtually all English-language works in this area, including unpublished theses and dissertations, on Denmark (including Greenland), Finland, Iceland, Norway, and Sweden. About 8,000 items are classified by academic discipline and thereafter by common subheadings under each country.

L.I.c Biographical Dictionaries and Directories

Biographical reference works on European personages drawn from virtually every social class and from all eras from classical Greece to the present day are available. Access to these is provided by Slocum (A.1.d:9).

One of the most comprehensive biographical dictionaries ever compiled is the 45-volume *Biographie universelle ancienne et moderne* (1843–65) (1). Though superseded in large part by more recent and more detailed national biographical dictionaries, the work still holds an honored place in historical scholarship. The biographical dictionary by Avril Pedley and Grant Uden, *They Lived Like This* (1967) (2), attempts to provide "an assembly of authentic word-portraits of men and women in Europe in history, art, and literature over 1900 years."

Biographical information on major figures of the ancient world is most readily and often most authoritatively provided in Pauly's *Realencyclopädie der Classischen Alterumswissenschaft* (L.1.d:6) and the *Oxford Classical Dictionary* (1970) (3). Betty Radice's *Who's Who in the Ancient World* (1967) (4) is a pleasing, well-written, and well-illustrated work with short entries on most of the main figures of antiquity. Volume 1 of what is likely to become a model for all such reference works, *The Prosopography of the Later Roman Empire* (1971–) (5), covers A.D. 260–395. Volumes 2 and 3 are in preparation.

Sketches of the lives of about 100 prominent persons are given in John Fine's *Who's Who in the Middle Ages* (1970) (6), which also provides an assessment of biographical and critical studies of most of the individuals covered.

Later periods are, for the most part, best covered in publications dealing with a single country or an individual group of persons.

The multivolume *Dictionary of National Biography* (1885–1903, reissued in revised form in 1908–9) (7) is the outstanding biographical reference work on the British Isles, and also includes materials on the British colonies, countries of the Commonwealth, and colonial America. In Professor Lawrence Stone's words, it is "the supreme achievement of . . . [a] century-long English movement for collective biography . . . [and] an enduring monument to the drive and dedication of the Victorians in the pursuit of information about the individual dead."[1] Six supplementary volumes issued since the original edition bring the coverage up to 1950. More popular in treatment and more highly selective than the *Dictionary of National Biography,* the four-volume *Who's Who in History* (1960–69) (8) provides short sketches of some 200 representative men and women of the period covered. Frederick Boase's six-volume *Modern English Biography* (1965) (9) contains brief memoirs of some thousands of notable persons who died between the years 1851 and 1900. A continuing series is Dod's *Parliamentary Companion* (1832–) (10), an annual handbook giving biographical information on members of Parliament, as well as other factual information. Members of Parliament who sat during the latter part of the eighteenth century are treated in Namier and Brooke's *The House of Commons, 1754–1790* (1964) (11), the first volumes issued of the government-sponsored History of Parliament series. Volumes 2 and 3 of the three-volume work form a biographical dictionary.

Crone's *Concise Dictionary of Irish Biography* (1937) (12) and the Cymmrodorion Society's *Dictionary of Welsh Biography Down to 1940* (1959) (13) are important reference works on major personages associated with these countries.

Standard biographical dictionaries for the other European countries include, for Austria, the 60-volume *Biographisches Lexikon der Kaiserthums Österreich* (1854–91) (14); for Belgium, the 28-volume *Biographie nationale* (1866–1944) (15); for Denmark, the 27-volume *Dansk Biografisk Leksikon grundlagt af C. F. Bricka* (1933–44) (16); for France, the *Dictionnaire de la biographie française* (1929–) (17) and two single-volume works: *Dictionnaire des personages historiques française* (1962) (18) and *Dictionnaire biographie française contemporaine* (1950) (19); for Germany, the 56-volume *Allgemeine Deutsche Biographie* (1875–1912) (20); for Italy, P. Litta's *Famiglie celebri d'Italia* (1819–23) (21) and the 24-volume *Enciclopedia italiana di scienze, letteri ed arti* (L.1.d:2); for the Netherlands, the 21-volume *Biographisch Woordenboek der Nederlanden* (1852–78) (22) and the 10-volume *Nieuw Nederlandsch Biografisch Woordenboek* (1911–37) (23); for Spain, M. F. Almagro's *Diccion-*

ario de historia de España (1952) (24); and for Sweden, the as yet uncompleted *Svensk Biografiskt Lexikon* (1918–) (25).

For the royal and princely families of Europe, the major reference work has long been the *Almanach de Gotha* (1763–1944) (26), since 1871 published in both German and French. Burke's *Genealogical and Heraldic Dictionary of the Peerage and Baronetage of the United Kingdom* (1847–) (27) and Burke's *Landed Gentry* (1847–1952) (28) are other standard works.

Contemporary leaders of Europe and its individual countries are reasonably well covered, though not always very accurately treated, in a number of "Who's Who" volumes. For Europe as a whole, the most comprehensive general reference work is *Who's Who in Europe* (1964–) (29), which includes short biographical notices on more than 30,000 individuals from some 27 countries. A much more venerable publication of the same kind is the British *Who's Who* (1849–) (30). An accompanying series, *Who Was Who* (1929–) (31), provides short biographical sketches of persons who died during the specific period covered by each volume. Other "Who's Who" volumes are available for a number of countries of Western Europe, though none of these is, as yet, an annual publication, as the British work is. Included among them are *Who's Who in Austria* (1954–) (32), *Who's Who in Belgium and the Grand Duchy of Luxembourg* (1957/58–) (33), *Who's Who in France* (1953–) (34), *Who's Who in Germany* (1955–) (35), *Who's Who in Italy* (1958–) (36), *Who's Who in the Netherlands* (1962–) (37), and *Who's Who in Switzerland* (1952–) (38).

Directories of organizations and associations are further sources of biographical information. Among the more useful are G. P. Henderson's *Current European Directories* (1969) (39), which is a comprehensive listing of major European organizations; the *Directory of European Associations* (1971–) (40); and the *Directory of British Associations* (1965–) (41).

Such works as *Biography Index* (A.1.d:10) should not be overlooked.

L.1.d   Encyclopedias and Dictionaries

Although no current encyclopedia deals specifically with Western Europe, or indeed with Europe as a whole, numerous national encyclopedias—among them Dutch, English, French, German, Italian, and Spanish works—provide varied coverage of many aspects of the Western European scene. However, these are outside the scope of this volume. Rather, specific mention will be made here to a few general English-language encyclopedias. *Chamber's*

Encyclopedia (1967) (1) is the leading British encyclopedia, with concise and reliable survey articles on all countries of Western Europe, as well as more detailed articles on special aspects of most of them. The foremost among foreign-language encyclopedias is the 24-volume *Enciclopedia italiana di scienze, letteri ed arti* (1929–37) (2). Encyclopedic coverage of a single country is provided in the *Encyclopedia of Ireland* (1968) (3). Bibliographies appear at the end of each of the topical sections of what can well be described as an excellently produced, written, and illustrated volume.

The classical world is especially well covered in a number of encyclopedias and dictionaries. The *Oxford Classical Dictionary* (L.1.c:3) is the standard English-language reference on virtually all easily definable aspects of the classical world. Many hundreds of brief, signed articles cover biography, literature, mythology, philosophy, religion, and science, among other topics, and for a large proportion of these, excellent short bibliographies are provided. The *Oxford Companion to Classical Literature* (1937) (4) is a somewhat similar but briefer work. Another venerable work is *A Companion to Greek Studies* (1931) (5). For intensive needs, there are two major foreign-language sources: the Pauly-Wissowa multivolume *Realencyclopädie der Classischen Alterumswissenschaft* (1893–1967) (6), on classical literature, history, archaeology, and culture; and Charles Daremberg and Edmond Saglio's five-volume *Dictionnaire des antiquités grecques et romaines* (1893–1919) (7). Articles of both sets include many detailed bibliographies.

L.1.e Handbooks and Yearbooks

Perhaps the most useful and comprehensive single work is *Western Europe: A Handbook* (I.1.e:7). *The European Yearbook* (1955–) (1) deals with the Council of Europe and most major Western European regional political and economic organizations. A notable feature is the annual bibliography of materials on European integration. The two-volume *Europa Yearbook* (I.1.e:1) is less a European than a world-affairs yearbook. Only the second part of volume 1 is devoted exclusively to Europe. Palmer and Lambert's *Handbook of European Organizations* (1968) (2) is a guide to such organizations as the European Economic Community, the European Free Trade Association, and the Council of Europe, as well as to organizations such as NATO in which Western European countries are involved. Gordon L. Weil's *Handbook to the European Economic Community* (1965) (3) provides basic information on the organization, its membership, and its activities.

In the Geographical Handbook series (E.1.e:5) are volumes on many countries of Western Europe, including Belgium, Denmark, France (four volumes), Germany (four volumes), Greece (three volumes), Iceland, Italy (four volumes), Luxembourg, the Netherlands, Norway (two volumes), and Spain and Portugal (four volumes). In addition, separate volumes are devoted to Corsica and the Dodecanese Islands. Though issued in the 1940s, they provide much valuable basic material on history, topography, and other matters for the individual countries covered. Only one of the U.S. Army's Area Handbooks (I.1.e:12) deals with a European country: volume 29 covers Germany. The American University Field Staff's Reports (I.1.e:14) include two series on Europe: one on Southeast Europe and one on Western Europe.

Numerous travel guides provide an assortment of general information on virtually every Western European country, as well as on Europe as a whole. Many of these volumes form part of some series, and are regularly updated. Among general guides are Fodor's *Europe* (1952–) (4), *Fielding's Travel Guide to Europe* (1948–) (5), *Newman's European Travel Guide* (1950–) (6), and Steffensen and Handel's *Europe This Way* (1968) (7). The French series of Guides Bleus (1918–) (8), the British Blue Guides series (1918–) (9), and the German Baedeker series (1839–) (10) cover many of the countries of Europe, as well as major tourist areas of individual countries, as for instance the fifteen post-1945 Baedeker guides on areas of West Germany. More details on the three preceding items are available in Walford (A.1. b:12).

More academic and scholarly are the volumes of Methuen's Companion series, which provide introductions to the history, literature, and culture of a number of European countries. These include Jethro Bithell's *Germany: A Companion to German Studies* (1955) (11), R. L. G. Ritchie's *France: A Companion to French Studies* (1950) (12), Edmund G. Gardner's *Italy: A Companion to Italian Studies* (1934) (13), and E. Alison Peer's *Spain: A Companion to Spanish Studies* (1963) (14). Two volumes of Oxford's Legacy series, *The Legacy of Greece* (1921) (15) and *The Legacy of Rome* (1936) (16), should not be overlooked.

Official handbooks providing factual and statistical information on most aspects of national life are available for most countries of Western Europe; many of them are English-language publications. For example, *Britain: An Official Handbook* (1946–) (17) is a handsome, annual volume with individual chapters on such topics as government and administration, defense, social welfare, housing and planning, the arts and sciences, the national economy, industry, transportation and communications, and finance and trade. One of its most valuable features is its extensive, well-organized bibliography of recent official and nonofficial works. The *Ulster Yearbook* (1926–) (18) is a triennial publication which provides a somewhat similar coverage of Northern Ireland. For Eire, the *Irish Free State Official Handbook* (1932) (19) remains one of the best and most comprehensive surveys of Irish life, though statistically its value is historical only. *Facts about Germany* (1966) (20) is a compendium of facts covering many aspects of political, economic, social, and cultural affairs of West Germany. *Denmark* (1924–) (21), an official handbook to Danish affairs, is issued at irregular intervals. A classified bibliography on Denmark appeared in the 1961 English-language issue of the work.

Various nonofficial yearbooks are also available. Among these should be noted *The Statesman's Yearbook* (E.1.e:1), a major part of which deals with Britain and the British Commonwealth, but with a chapter on each country of Western Europe; *Whitaker's Almanac* (A.1.f:1), perhaps the most valuable annual compilation of miscellaneous facts on the British Isles; and *The British Commonwealth Yearbook* (L.2.g:20).

L.l.f   Newspapers and News Digests

The most valuable index is that of the *Times* of London (A.1.g:3). The *New York Times* (A.1.g:1) should also be consulted. These newspapers have the widest coverage of Europe and its individual countries. Among news digests, *Keesing's Contemporary Archives* (A.1.g:5) has the most comprehensive coverage of European events. The *Annual Register* (A.1.g:4) is the oldest annual review of events. For more intensive needs see A.1.g.

L.l.g   Statistics Sources

Bibliographical information on Western European statistical publications is provided in Joan Harvey's *Sources of Statistics* (1971) (1), but her *Statistics Europe: Sources for Market Research* (1968) (2) is more comprehensive and more sharply focused. *Statistics Sources* (A.1.h:1) and the *Encyclopedia of Business Information Sources* (A.1.b:7) are also recommended.

Apart from the international sources—in particular, those of the U.N. and its agencies (see A.1.h)—a number of statistical sources specifically concerned with Europe are available. The most valuable are the annual volumes of the United Nations Economic Commission for Europe's *Economic Survey of Europe* (1947–) (3) and its accompanying quarterly, *Economic Bulletin for Europe* (1947–) (4). Statistics on every significant aspect of the European economy are provided for each country on the continent.

Statistics on the European Economic Community are provided in a number of volumes. The annual *Basic Statistics of the Community* (1959–) (5) is supplemented by two monthlies: *General Statistical Bulletin* (1961–) (6) and *Graphs and Notes on the Economic Situation of the Community* (1962–) (7). More detailed statistics are provided in the *Yearbook of Agricultural Statistics: 1970* (1971) (8) and the *Statistiques des transports: 1969* (1971) (9). The U.S. Department of Agriculture's *Agricultural Trade of the European Economic Community, 1959–1964: A Statistical Reference* (1966) (10) and *European Economic Community: Agricultural Trade Statistics, 1961–1967* (1969) (11) cover agriculture. *EFTA Trade, 1959–1964* (1967) (12) and annual volumes of *EFTA Trade* (1964–) (13) give comprehensive statistics of activities within the European Free Trade Association. The Economic Research Service's *European Free Trade Association: Agricultural Trade Statistics, 1961–1967* (1969) (14) is a large and detailed statistical survey of the subject. Other officially derived statistics on European countries are provided in the *OEEC Statistical Bulletin* (1950–) (15) and the OECD Economic Surveys [by country] series (1959–) (16). *Main Economic Indicators* (1962–) (17) and its predecessor, the *Bulletin of General Statistics* (1950–) (18) are issued monthly.

Volume 1 of the *International Guide to Electoral Statistics* (G.2.e:4) provides statistical information on recent national elections in Western Europe.

Claimed to be "the most comprehensive, penetrating survey ever published of 320 million Europeans as consumers and members of a major politico-economic group," the Reader's Digest Association's *Survey of Europe Today* (1970) (19) provides a variety of statistical information based on the findings of 17,500 personal interviews conducted in 16 countries of Western Europe. Statistical tables—covering such topics as people's homes and possessions, the housewife's world, food and drink, the leisure hours, transport and tourism, fashions, attitudes to Europe, and cultural attitudes—contain comparable data for each of the countries sampled. Detailed commentaries accompany each table. Although much of the information is attractively presented and unavailable elsewhere, it is based on what appears to be a totally inadequate sample—17,500 adults out of a total population of more than 320 million. A more orthodox statistical handbook is Mueller's *Statistical Handbook of the North Atlantic Area* (I.1.g:19), which presents comparative statistics on the same European countries, together with Canada and the United States. Useful also for statistical information is J. Frederic Dewhurst's massive handbook,

Europe's Needs, Resources, Trends, and Prospects in Eighteen Countries (1961) (20).

Detailed statistics for individual countries are provided in the various national yearbooks such as those cited in section L.1.e. above, as well as in more specialized volumes such as the *Annual Abstract of Statistics* (1832–) (21), issued by the British government, and the equivalent publications of other European countries. Historical statistics for European countries can be obtained in *Cross-Polity Time-Series Data* (I.1.g:7).

Section 2

L.2.a   Anthropology

Collections of Data.   Data for a few Western European cultures are deposited in HRAF (I.3:1): Europe (as a whole), the imperial Romans, Austria, Finland, the Lapps, the rural Irish, and Malta.

The most comprehensive bibliography is Robert J. Theodoratus's *Europe: A Selected Ethnographic Bibliography* (1969) (1). Its 8,000 entries are arranged by ethnic groups, and these cover all of Europe except the Caucasus Mountains region and the Finno-Ugric and Turkic peoples of the eastern and northeastern regions of the European part of the Soviet Union. Because different policies of selection were required for the groups represented, it is advisable to read the preface before using the book. Coverage is almost entirely limited to modern times, primarily the nineteenth and twentieth centuries. Narrower in its focus is Sweet and O'Leary's *Circum-Mediterranean Peasantry: Introductory Bibliography* (J.2.a:7).

Two volumes of the projected twelve-volume *International Dictionary of Regional European Ethnology and Folklore* (1961–) (2) have been accepted as major reference works. Volume 1 is *General Ethnological Concepts* (B.1.d:2). Volume 2, *Folk Literature (Germanic)*, covering the English, German, Dutch, and Scandinavian languages, is a dictionary of short articles which effectively cover the main terms of folk literature. A system of cross-referencing helps to identify parallel terms. Bibliographical references are given. The myths of ancient Greece are treated in Robert Graves's *The Greek Myths* (1959) (3).

A valuable tool for archaeological research is the *Archaeological Bibliography for Great Britain and Ireland* (1949–) (4), which since 1954 has appeared in annual volumes. Sections 1–8 of *COWA* (B.2.a:1) are concerned with Europe.

L.2.b Demography

In addition to the *Demographic Yearbook* (C.1.g:1) and the *European Demographic Information Bulletin* (C.1.e:1) and other reference works cited in part C, consult Blake and Donovan's *Western European Censuses: 1960* (1971) (1), an English-language guide to the census returns of some twenty Western European nations for the years around 1960. It also includes a glossary of technical terms used in the original languages of the censuses and bibliographical data (including Library of Congress citations) for each census.

L.2.c Economics and Economic History

No detailed economic bibliographies dealing specifically with Europe are presently available. However, a considerable amount of bibliographical information can be gleaned from such general economics reference works as the *International Bibliography of Economics* (D.1.b:12), Melnyk's *Economics: Bibliographical Guide to Reference Books and Information Sources* (D.1.b:1), the *Encyclopedia of Business Information Sources* (A.1.b:7), and Maltby's *Economics and Commerce* (D.1.b:2). The last of these, produced with the British student specifically in mind, is perhaps the best one to start with. The *Index of Economic Journals* (D.1. b:10) should also be consulted.

One of the most valuable sources for detailed information on economic conditions in European countries is the continuing series of Economic Surveys (L.1.g:16) put out by the Organization for Economic Cooperation and Development. Recent surveys are available for Austria, Belgium and Luxembourg, Denmark, Greece, Iceland, Ireland, Italy, the Netherlands, Norway, Portugal, Spain, Sweden, Switzerland, the United Kingdom, and West Germany. New editions are regularly provided and volumes for other countries added to the list. An older work which remains a standard source is *Europe's Needs, Resources, Trends, and Prospects* (L.1. g:20). More detailed statistical information is provided in the *Economic Survey of Europe* (L.1.g:3). A good introduction to two major economic groups of Europe is provided in Walsh and Paxton's *Trade and Industrial Resources of the Common Market and EFTA Countries: A Comparative Statistical Analysis* (1970) (1); British Commonwealth economics is the subject of Hamilton's *Regional Economic Analysis in Great Britain and the Commonwealth: A Bibliographical Guide* (1970) (2).

Many of the more valuable listings of sources for the study of European economic history are found in the general bibliographies of history cited in section L.2.e. The bibliographies provided in the individual volumes of *The Cambridge Economic History of Europe* (1941–) (3) are excellent compilations of important works—books, monographs, and articles—in the major European languages. (For example, the bibliographies for volume 3, *Economic Organization and Policies in the Middle Ages* [1963], fill some 70 pages.) The "Essays in Bibliography and Criticism" which are a regular feature of the quarterly *Economic History Review* (1927–) (4) have included in recent years "Scottish Economic History, 1963–1970" (August 1971) and "The Classical Tradition in West European Farming: The Sixteenth Century" (December 1969). In addition, a "List of Publications on the Economic History of Great Britain and Ireland" is published annually.

Historical statistical data for all European countries is available in *Cross-Polity Time-Series Data* (I.1.g:7). The *Abstract of British Historical Statistics* (1970) (5), by Mitchell and Deane, provides the most useful general survey, while Elizabeth B. Schumpeter's *English Overseas Trade Statistics, 1697–1808* (1960) (6); *Prices and Wages in England from the Twelfth to the Nineteenth Century,* volume 1, *Price Tables: Mercantile Era* (1939) (7), by Sir William Beveridge and others; and J. E. Thorald Rogers's seven-volume *History of Agriculture and Prices in England* (1886–1902) (8) give more detailed historical statistics on specific matters and periods.

L.2.d Geography

No comprehensive bibliography on European geography is available. However, attention should be directed to the AGS *Research Catalog* (E.1.b:4), in which several thousand items on the geography of Europe are listed. Edelman and Eeuwens's *Bibliography on Land and Water Utilization and Conservation in Europe* (1955) (1) is a listing of a wide range of geographical and other literature on land and water utilization and conservation in all parts of the continent. G. Plaisance's *Les Formations végétales et paysages ruraux: Lexique et guide bibliographique* (1959) (2) is an equally valuable work which covers a number of overlapping themes of biogeography, agricultural geography, and settlement.

J. M. Houston's *The Western Mediterranean World* (1964) (3) includes a bibliography of almost 70 pages on all aspects of the region's geography.

The major achievements of French and German geography are considered in separate chapters of *Geography in the Twentieth Century* (E.1.f:12). British geography is reviewed by R. W. Steel in a chapter entitled "British Geographers and the Geography of Britain" in *The British Isles: A Systematic Geography* (1964)

(4), edited by Watson and Sissons. A more recent work, *Trends in Geography* (E.1.f:16), reviews the advances made in each branch of British geography and includes short reading lists. The travel literature pertaining to Europe is covered in Edward G. Cox's *Reference Guide to the Literature of Travel* (E.2.a:8). Two scholarly and extremely valuable bibliographical works on early British geography are E. G. R. Taylor's *Tudor Geography, 1485–1583* (1930) (5) and the same author's *Late Tudor and Early Stuart Geography, 1583–1650* (1934) (6). Another bibliographical work, *Regional Economic Analysis in Great Britain and the Commonwealth: A Bibliographic Guide* (L.2.c:2), should not be overlooked on topics of economic geography.

The most important encyclopedic reference work is the *Larousse Encyclopedia of Geography: Europe* (1961) (7). More than 60 French geographers participated in the preparation of this comprehensive and well-illustrated volume, which has brief articles on the places and topics of greatest significance in European geography.

L.2.e History

Reference works on the history of Europe are so numerous that the items reviewed here can be regarded as no more than a somewhat arbitrary selection.

Some good historical atlases are available for Europe in general and for each major era. In addition to such general historical atlases as Shepherd (F.1.a:1), Muir (F.1.a:2), and Palmer (F.1.a:3), which devote much space to European affairs, there are many others which focus full attention on the European scene. One of the widest in its scope is Fox's *Atlas of European History* (1957) (1), in which 64 pages of six-color maps cover the main stages in Europe's evolution. J. H. Breasted's *European History Atlas* (1954) (2) is an older but still quite useful reference work, as is J. F. Horrabin's collection of black-and-white sketch maps with accompanying text, *An Atlas of European History from the Second to the Twentieth Century* (1935) (3). Perhaps the finest and most authoritative of the general atlases is E. Dahmann's *Historisch-geographisches Kartenwerk* (1958–) (4), which is solidly based on modern archaeological and historical research. This work provides coverage of Europe from the Bronze Age to modern times. Close to 200 maps, an extensive text, diagrams and other illustrations, and bibliographies complete the volume.

Atlases devoted to the main periods of European history are also available. The *Atlas of the Classical World* (1960) (5) provides excellent coverage of the history and heritage of Greece and

Rome with more than 70 maps, accompanying text, and many photographs. Colin McEvedy's *Penguin Atlas of Ancient History* (1967) (6), with close to 100 two-color maps and accompanying text, gives effective treatment of Europe, North Africa, and the Near East from the dawn of civilization to the fourth century A.D. A companion volume is the *Penguin Atlas of Medieval History* (1961) (7).

Modern European history is not especially well served with atlases. Probably the most valuable one for college students is *The New Cambridge Modern History Atlas* (1970) (8), which forms the final volume of the *New Cambridge Modern History* (1957–) (9). It is not devoted solely to Europe, though understandably it has a heavy European emphasis. Close to 300 pages of full-color maps explore the social and economic history of Europe, as well as, more intensively, the political evolution of the continent from the thirteenth century to the close of World War II. Other atlases on modern European history include R. L. Poole's venerable, but still quite useful, *Oxford Historical Atlas of Modern Europe* (1902) (10) and E. A. Freeman's even more venerable atlas in the *Historical Geography of Europe* (1920) (11). A more specialized atlas, which is the first volume of the project series Historical Atlas of Town Plans for Western Europe is *Historic Towns: Maps and Plans of Towns and Cities in the British Isles* (1969) (12).

For materials on different periods of European history, consult such standard sources as the *International Bibliography of Historical Sciences* (F.1.b:4), the *Annual Bulletin of Historical Literature* (F.1.b:3), and the *International Bibliography of Urban History* (1960–) (13), in addition to the many items listed below.

For the ancient world, the bibliographies provided in *The Cambridge Ancient History* (1923–39) (14) will be found invaluable. An excellent brief introduction to the medieval period is provided in R. H. C. Davis's *Medieval European History: A Select Bibliography* (1963) (15), which lists, classifies, and evaluates some 600 items. Recent literature on the Middle Ages is reviewed in Lyon's *The Middle Ages in Recent Historical Thought* in the Service Center for Teachers of History series (O.2.e:8). L. J. Paetow's *Guide to the Study of Medieval History* (1931) (16) provides valuable information on bibliographies, printed source materials, and secondary works on medieval Europe and the Near East. Also useful for this period is Louis Halphen's *Initiation aux études d'histoire du Moyen Age* (1952) (17). A much more detailed bibliography on the medieval period is A. S. Atiya's *The Crusades: Historiography and Bibliography* (1962) (18), which describes about 1,500 items from Middle Eastern as well as European sources. *The Cambridge Mediaeval History* (1966–) (19) is another important source.

The bibliographies in the individual volumes of *The Cambridge Modern History* (1907–24) (20) are extensive and invaluable as surveys of the literature available up to the twentieth century. Unfortunately, no equivalent bibliographies are provided in *The New Cambridge Modern History,* but John Roach has compiled a one-volume *Bibliography of Modern History* (1968) (21) to supplement the set. A useful introductory bibliography that will be of particular value to the undergraduate student is A. Davies's *Modern European History, 1494–1788: A Select Bibliography* (1966) (22). Crane Brinton surveys the literature on *European Intellectual History* in a volume of the Service Center for Teachers of History series (O.2.e:8). Other issues in this series are Bouwsma's *The Interpretation of Renaissance Humanism* and Grimm's *The Reformation in Recent Historical Thought.* William N. Medlicott's *Modern European History, 1789–1945: A Select Bibliography* (1960) (23) is a companion volume to Davies's on the earlier period. Somewhat comparable, unannotated volumes are *A Select List of Works on Europe and Europe Overseas, 1715–1815* (1956) (24) and *A Select List of Books on European History, 1815–1914* (1957) (25).

Eric Lampard's *The Industrial Revolution,* in the Service Center for Teachers of History series (O.2.e:8), is an excellent introductory bibliography for a major topic of European economic history. Much more ambitious and comprehensive is Lowell J. Ragatz's *Bibliography for the Study of European History, 1815–1939* (1942) (26), together with its three supplements, which appeared in 1943, 1945, and 1956. Part 1 treats Europe as whole; part 2, the individual countries in alphabetical order; and part 3, international relations.

In Heath's Problems in European Civilization series are 70 volumes concerned with enduring issues of European historiography. The complete list can be examined in the Heath catalog in *PTLA* (A.1.b:30). [See the discussion of the Problems in American Civilization series (O.2.e:10) for a more detailed description of the purpose of this useful series.]

Among the over 30 titles in Holt's European Problem Studies (M.2.e:9) are *Age of Justinian, Athenian Democracy, Decline of the West, Frederick the Great and the Making of Prussia, Industrial Revolution, Renaissance Debate,* and *The Scientific Revolution.* Other titles are listed in the Holt catalog in *PTLA* (A.1.b:30). [See the discussion of the American Problem Studies series (O.2.e:9) for a more detailed description of this series.]

A major bibliographical source for the study of British history is the annual *Writings on British History* (1934–) (27), a comprehensive listing of books, articles, and other materials. Books and articles on the British Isles are classified and listed in the five-volume *Writings on British History, 1901–1933* (1968–) (28). The Bibliography of British History series, issued jointly by the American Historical Society and the Royal Historical Society, includes three comprehensive standard works: *Bibliography of British History: Tudor Period, 1485–1603* (1959) (29); *Bibliography of British History: Stuart Period, 1603–1714* (1928) (30); and *Bibliography of British History: The Eighteenth Century, 1714–1789* (1951) (31). These are widely regarded as the most important general bibliographies on their respective periods. The Conference on British Studies has inaugurated a series of bibliographical handbooks, more selective in coverage and perhaps better suited to undergraduate research. The series includes Michael Altschul's *Anglo-Norman England, 1066–1154* (1969) (32); Mortimer Levine's *Tudor England, 1485–1603* (1968) (33); William L. Sachse's *Restoration England, 1660–1689* (1971) (34); and Josef L. Altholz's *Victorian England, 1837–1901* (1971) (35). Further volumes on *Angevin England, 1154–1377; Late Medieval England, 1377–1485; The Seventeenth Century, 1603–1660;* and *Twentieth Century England* are in preparation. All volumes contain some 2,000 or more items, which are well organized and briefly annotated. The Historical Association's series Helps to Students of History includes Miller and Newman's *Early Modern British History, 1485–1760: A Select Bibliography* (1970) (36) and Ian R. Christie's *British History since 1760: A Select Bibliography* (1970) (37), both of which can be highly recommended for undergraduate students. Other bibliographical reference works of note on British history include Wilfred Bonser's two-volume *Anglo-Saxon and Celtic Bibliography, 450–1087* (1957) (38); Charles Gross's *The Sources and Literature of English History from the Earliest Times to about 1485* (1915) (39); Clyde L. Grose's *Select Bibliography of British History, 1660–1760* (1939) (40); and Judith B. Williams's two-volume *Guide to the Printed Materials for English Social and Economic History, 1750–1850* (1926) (41).

British public records are best approached through V. H. Galbraith's *Introduction to the Use of the Public Records* (1952) (42). M. S. Giuseppi's two-volume *Guide to the Manuscripts Preserved in the Public Record Office* (1923–24) (43) has been superseded by the two-volume *Guide to the Contents of the Public Record Office* (1963) (44). Two sectional lists issued by Her Majesty's Stationery Office (H.M.S.O.) are helpful for details on published source materials: *British National Archives* (1968) (45) and *Publications of the Royal Commission on Historical*

Manuscripts (1967) (46). A list of record repositories is provided in the Historical Manuscripts Commission's *Record Repositories in Great Britain* (1966) (47). Eleanor S. Upton's *Guide to Sources of English History from 1603 to 1660 in Early Reports of the Royal Commission on Historical Manuscripts* (1964) (48) is an invaluable aid to the use of reports issued by the commission, supplementing for one period the commission's two-volume *Guide to the Reports on the Collections of Manuscripts of Private Families* (1914–38) (49). W. E. Tate's *The Parish Chest* (1951) (50) is the best guide to the many legal and other documents housed in English parish vestries, while John West's *Village Records* (1962) (51) and L. J. Redstone and F. W. Steers's *Local Records: Their Nature and Care* (1953) (52) are other useful handbooks. Two short bibliographies issued by the Historical Association should also be noted: F. G. Emmison and Irvine Gray's *County Records* (1967) (53) and *English Local History Handlist* (1952) (54).

S. H. Steinberg's *New Dictionary of British History* (1963) (55) provides accurate and comprehensive coverage of important events in the history of England, the British Empire, and the Commonwealth. The 7-volume *Dictionnaire historique et biographique de la Suisse* (1931–34) (56) is an excellent example of a more ambitious reference work covering one of the smaller European countries. British chronology is best handled by Maurice Powicke's *Handbook of British Chronology* (1961) (57), while S. H. Steinberg's *New Dictionary of British History* covers chronology and many other aspects of British history. G. R. Elton's *Modern Historians on British History, 1485–1945* (1970) (58) is a critical bibliography of historical writing published between 1945 and 1969. More than 1,300 individual works are discussed; thus it is both a bibliographical and a historiographical work of some significance. Another more specialized work of a similar sort is F. Smith Fussner's *Tudor History and the Historians* (1970) (59).

The irregularly issued bibliography, "Writings on Irish History" (1936–) (60), in *Irish Historical Studies* since 1938, is the most useful work specifically on Irish history. Welsh history is treated in the Board of Celtic Studies' *Bibliography of the History of Wales* (1962) (61), which classifies and briefly annotates some 3,500 separate items.

French history is comprehensively treated in the current *Bibliographie annuelle de l'histoire de France du cinquième siècle à 1939* (1956–) (62). A retrospective bibliography covering the years 1932–54 was issued in 1964. The standard bibliography is Caron and Stein's six-volume *Répertoire bibliographique de l'histoire de France* (1923–38) (63), which covers the subject to

1714. Exhaustive treatment of French local history is provided in
R. Gandilhon and C. Samaran's *Bibliographie générale des travaux
et archéologiques* (1944–) (64). There are four short bibliographies in the Service Center for Teachers of History series (O.2.
e:8) on periods of French history: *The Background of the French
Revolution; The French Revolution: Some Trends in Historical
Writing, 1945–1965; France in the Nineteenth Century, 1815–
1914;* and *France in the Twentieth Century.* Other, more detailed
bibliographies for French history include the 18-volume *Les
Sources de l'histoire de France depuis les origines jusqu'au 1815*
(1901–35) (65) [which, in fact, takes the coverage only to 1715]
and André Mongland's *La France révolutionnaire et impériale*
(1930–) (66).

The projected tenth edition (in 8 volumes) of *Quellenkunde
der Deutschen Geschichte* (1965–) (67) edited by H. Heimpel
and H. Geuss, is a standard bibliography of German history to the
end of World War II. Included in the Service Center for Teachers of History series (O.2.e:8) are *Five Images of Germany*
and *Germany, 1815–1914;* in the same series is Charles F. Del-
zell's *Italy in Modern Times: An Introduction to the Historical
Literature in English.*

An introduction to the archives of Western European countries
is provided in Daniel H. Thomas and Lynn M. Case's *Guide to the
Diplomatic Archives of Western Europe* (1959) (68).

L.2.f   Literature

Three sections of the *Penguin Companion to World Literature*
(1971) (1) are concerned with the literature of Europe; however,
the authors consider *Cassell's Encyclopedia of Literature* (1953)
(2) the best brief encyclopedic source for European literature. It
is in two volumes: the first contains histories of the literatures of
the world, general literary topics, and biographies of authors who
died before 1914; the second includes biographies of authors living
in 1914 or born after that date. Articles, including biographies,
are written by authorities, and bibliographies are included. Other
important reference works associated with European literature are
given in Altick (O.2.f:2), Walford (A.1.b:12), and Winchell
(A.1.b:13).

L.2.g   Political Science

No comprehensive bibliography of European politics and political systems is available, though individual, more specialized bibliographies exist on numerous topics. Many of the general bibliographies noted in section G.1.b, however, will provide ample coverage

of most major topics of European political life. Collections of documents are discussed in section G.2.c.

Stephen Holt's *Six European States: The Countries of the European Community and Their Political Systems* (1970) (1) provides a comparative analysis of the governments of France, Germany, Italy, and the Benelux countries. Political parties, elections, government organization, and judicial systems are among the items considered in this informative handbook. *European Political Parties: A Handbook* (1970) (2), edited by Stanley Henig for Political and Economic Planning (PEP), is a more detailed work on the parties of the Western European countries. Individual chapters deal with Austria, Belgium and Luxembourg, France, Ireland, Italy, the Netherlands, the Scandinavian countries, Switzerland, the United Kingdom, and West Germany. Statistical information, flow charts, and a good bibliography are other notable features. *A Handbook of European Organizations* (L.1.e:2) provides information on the internal and external political aspects of such organizations as the Council of Europe and NATO. Archival materials related to government operations in Western Europe are best approached by means of Thomas and Case's *Guide to the Diplomatic Archives of Western Europe* (L.2.e:68).

A wide range of materials is available for the study of British politics and government. John Palmer's *Government and Parliament in Britain: A Bibliography* (1964) (3) is a short introduction to such subjects as the constitution, Parliament, political parties, and government departments. The *Encyclopedia of Parliament* (1968) (4), by Norman Wilding, is in part a dictionary of terms and phrases, and also a collection of concise articles on the history and working of Parliament. Butler and Freeman's *British Political Facts, 1900–1968* (1969) (5) is the third edition of a veritable encyclopedia of political information. The tracing of British laws and statutes, court cases, and so on is outlined in Price and Bitner's *Effective Legal Research* (O.2.g:19). James G. Olle's *Introduction to British Government Publications* (1965) (6) provides information on Hansard and other parliamentary records, as well as publications issued by the Stationery Office for the various departments of state. *British Government Publications: An Index to Chairmen and Authors, 1941–1966* (1969) (7) is a guide to almost 2,000 special reports prepared by Royal Commissions or issued by Parliament or one of the government departments. Arthur H. Cole's *Finding-List of Royal Commission Reports on the British Dominions* (1939) (8) is a similar but older work covering a wide spectrum of activities. A shorter and more specialized volume is Rodgers and Phelp's *Guide to British Parliamentary Papers* (1967) (9). Serial publications are covered in Frank Rodgers's *Serial Publications in the British Parliamentary*

Papers, 1900–1968: A Bibliography (1971) (10) and the *Check-list of British Official Serial Publications to June 1968* (1968) (11). The most ambitious work on British parliamentary papers is the multivolume series by Percy and Grace Ford. This includes *A Breviate of Parliamentary Papers, 1900–1916: The Foundation of the Welfare State* (1957) (12); *A Breviate of Parliamentary Papers, 1917–1939* (1951) (13); and *A Breviate of Parliamentary Papers, 1940–1954: War and Reconstruction* (1961) (14). The *Select List of Parliamentary Papers, 1833–1899* (1953) (15) is a companion volume. Each work begins with a subject classification of the papers, followed by a subject list. The main part of each volume is taken up by the "breviate," or collection of short notes on each of the papers listed. The Fords have also prepared an excellent general guide to the papers: *A Guide to Parliamentary Papers: What They Are, How to Find Them, How to Use Them* (1956) (16). The debates of the House of Commons are dealt with in an official reference work, *A Bibliography of Parliamentary Debates on Great Britain* (1959) (17), and election statistics by F. W. S. Craig's *British Parliamentary Statistics, 1918–1968* (1968) (18), which contains over 100 tables and appendixes covering fourteen general elections and 800 by-elections held during the period. A recommended reference work on local government is Wilfred H. Snape's *How to Find Out about Local Government* (1970) (19).

General bibliographical reference works on Britain and the Commonwealth are numerous. Among them are *The British Commonwealth Yearbook* (1952–) (20); J. E. Flint's *Books on the British Empire and Commonwealth: A Guide for Students* (1968) (21), which lists some 1,500 items; and *Commonwealth Reference Books: A Bibliographical Guide* (1965) (22), which annotates some 700 items arranged under general and then regional headings. A similar number of works, but excluding any specifically on Britain, is covered in A. J. Horne's *The Commonwealth Today: A Select Bibilography on the Commonwealth and Its Constituent Countries* (1965) (23). For earlier publications on the Empire and Commonwealth the most comprehensive listing is that of the *Subject Catalogue of the Library of the Royal Empire Society* (1930–37) (24), the four volumes of which cover, in turn, the British Commonwealth and Empire and their various constituent parts.

Henry Coston's *Dictionnaire de la politique française* (1967) (25) provides a good introduction to terms and topics of the French political scene. Two brief bibliographies, prepared by the Cultural Center of the French Embassy, New York, are helpful guides. Jean Meyriat's *Political Science, 1950–1958* (1960) (26) and Bernard Gouray's *Public Administration* (1963) (27) survey

French political literature on their respective topics published since World War II. Annotations are in English.

German political affairs are treated in a number of works. Andrew R. Carlson's *German Foreign Policy, 1890–1914, and Colonial Policy to 1914: A Handbook and Annotated Bibliography* (1970) (28) provides not only a survey of German foreign policy, but also much basic information on the structure and organization of German federal and local government, as well as an extensive bibliography of some 3,000 books and articles on the subjects covered. *After Hitler: Germany, 1945–1963* (1963) (29) is an extensive, unannotated listing of some 2,600 items—mainly books and pamphlets—on German politics since World War II. *Source Materials on the Government and Politics of Germany* (1964) (30), by Lane and Pollock, provides translated source materials on the Federal Republic and its constituent parts, political parties, pressure groups, and related matters.

A Catalog of Files and Microfilms of the German Foreign Ministry Archive, 1867–1920 (1959) (31) was prepared by the American Historical Association's Committee for the Study of War Documents. A companion work, *A Catalog of Files and Microfilm of the German Foreign Ministry Archive, 1920–1945* (1962–) (32), prepared by the Historical Office of the Department of State, brings the coverage down through World War II. *A Guide to German Records Microfilmed at Alexandria, Virginia* (1958–65) (33) appeared in 47 parts. An earlier collection of translated German diplomatic documents has been reissued: *German Diplomatic Documents, 1871–1914* (1928–) (34), edited and translated by E. T. S. Dugdale.

A yearbook prepared by the political-science associations of the four Scandinavian countries, *Scandinavian Studies* (1966–) (35), provides articles on political affairs, digests of recent political events, summaries of current political research, and a bibliography of recent works on politics in the four countries. For Finland there is also *A Select List of Books and Articles in English, French, and German on Finnish Politics in the Nineteenth and Twentieth Century* (1967) (36), by Martii Julkunen and Anja Lehikoinen. *European and Atlantic Affairs* (1971) (37) is a briefly annotated list of 139 items concerned with the development of the European and Atlantic communities.

Communist affairs in Europe can be traced in Hammond (M.2.g:3) and the *Yearbook of Communist Affairs* (M.2.g:4).

L.2.h Sociology

Europe: A Selected Ethnographic Bibliography (L.2.a:1), along with the *International Bibliography of Sociology* (H.1.b:2) and *Sociological Abstracts* (H.1.b:1) are recommended.

Part M

Central Europe and the Soviet Union

Section 1

M.1.a   Atlases

Surveys of Soviet maps and atlases are in Maichel's *Guide to Russian Reference Books* (M.1.b:1) and Lock (A.1.a:11). The *World Atlas* (A.1.a:3), *The U.S.S.R. and Eastern Europe* (I.1.a:1), the *Atlas of Central Europe* (L.1.a:6), the *Atlas Östliches Mitteleuropa* (L.1.a:4), and *An Atlas of Soviet Affairs* (I.1.a:13) are widely available.

M.I.b Bibliographies

Bibliographies of Bibliographies.   In addition to Maichel's *Guide to Russian Reference Books* (1), which includes bibliographies, Laurence H. Miller's article in Down and Jenkins's *Bibliography: Current State and Future Trends* (B.1.b:1) is a good survey for researchers requiring intensive knowledge of bibliographies of Eastern European history. Western and indigenous sources are discussed, and Miller approaches the area with a broad interpretation of the scope of history.

Reference Works.   Appropriate sections of Walford (A.1.b:12) and Winchell (A.1.b:13) are worth consulting. Karol Maichel's *Guide to Russian Reference Books* (1962–67) (1) is a 6-volume work of about 3,500 entries that include bibliographies as well as dictionaries, encyclopedias, atlases, and biographical dictionaries, mostly in Russian. A volume is devoted to each of the following topics: general bibliographies and reference books; history, ethnography, and geography; social sciences, religion, and philosophy; humanities; and science, technology, and medicine. Volume 6 is a cumulative index.

General Bibliographies.   We suggest that, because of the unique features of some of the items discussed below, the whole section be perused by anyone requiring an intensive coverage of the English-language materials on Russia. Materials in languages other than English are also covered but not in so great detail; researchers requiring Russian or other Eastern European items should consult Maichel (M.1.b:1) for appropriate bibliographies. The purpose of Paul E. Vesenyi's *European Periodical Literature in the Social Sciences and the Humanities* (L.1.b:1) is "to assist researchers to locate periodical articles published in Europe in the field of the social sciences and humanities"; Gray (A.1.b:3) serves a similar function.

Together, the four bibliographies on Eastern Europe and the Soviet Union edited by Paul Horecky consist of approximately 9,800 entries selected from the vast quantity of materials published in indigenous and Western languages. The expert contributors compiled and annotated the titles included in the chapters for which they were responsible. The extensive annotations contain such extraordinary amounts of information about events, individuals, and issues as to make them valuable sources of information as well as keys to further research. Any research undertaken in connection with Eastern Europe or the Soviet Union should include consultation of all or some of the volumes. *Russia and the Soviet Union* (1965) (2), a guide to almost 2,000 Western-language publications (mostly in English), is a "conspectus of those Western language writings which are considered to be particularly relevant to the study of the political, socio-economic and intellectual life in the Russian Empire and the Soviet Union." *Basic Russian Publications* (1962) (3) describes over 1,800 titles in 1,396 entries relating to the political and social sciences and the humanities published in the Russian language in Czarist Russia, the Soviet Union, and other countries. Non-Western and Western sources are combined in *East Central Europe* (1969) (4) and *Southeastern Europe* (1969) (5). In both volumes, books, periodicals, and significant articles on the political, socioeconomic, and intellectual life, and the organization of scientific-research activities, are described. *East Central Europe* covers Czechoslovakia, East Germany (the Lusatians and Polabians are treated in a separate section), Hungary, and Poland. *Southeastern Europe* covers Albania, Bulgaria, Greece, Rumania, and Yugoslavia. In general, materials in each volume are arranged as follows: general reference aids and bibliographies; general and descriptive works; the land; the people (ethnic and demographic features); history; the state (politics and government, foreign relations, military affairs); economic and social structure; and intellectual and cultural life. In each volume annotations often refer to additional or supplemental related readings, and cross-references connect principal entries, but there are no interconnections between volumes.

Robert Byrnes's *Bibliography of American Publications on East Central Europe, 1945–1957* (1958) (6) and the annual *American Bibliography of Russian and East European Studies* (1956–) (7) list English-language materials. The retrospective volume is limited to U.S. and Canadian publications, but the annual volumes attempt to list materials in English published anywhere outside the Soviet Union and Eastern Europe. The retrospective volume is arranged similarly to Horecky's *Southeastern Europe* (M.1.b:5), except that material on Greece is not included. Annual volumes are arranged by subject, then by country. They are useful for supplementing the Horecky volumes described above.

A section of the AUFS *Select Bibliography* (I.1.b:3) is devoted to Eastern Europe, with divisions for Russia and East Central Europe. Horak's *Junior Slavica* (1968) (8) is an annotated bibliography of over 600 recent reference works, bibliographies, and books on Poland, Czechoslovakia, Hungary, Rumania, Yugoslavia, Albania, Bulgaria, and the USSR (including Estonia, Latvia, Lithuania, Belorussia, Ukraine, Moldavia, Azerbaidzhan, Armenia, and Georgia). Less attention is given the republics of Central Asia. In addition to history, subjects included are philosophy, sociology, education, politics and government, geography, and economics. There are separate chapters on the Jews in Eastern Europe and Russia, on Austria-Hungary, and on communism. Most citations include references to reviews. There are author and "short-title" indexes.

The U.S. Army's *USSR: Strategic Survey* (I.1.b:9) and *Communist Eastern Europe* (I.1.b:10) are useful.

The *Arctic Bibliography* (O.2.a:4) contains references to useful information on activities of the Russians in the Arctic as well as material on native peoples in the North. Although the publications are in Russian, the extensive annotations in English often give enough information to eliminate the necessity of consulting the original work.

Volumes 5–7 of *The Ukrainian Republic in the Great East European Revolution* (1971–) (9) comprise a bibliography of about 25,000 items in Ukrainian, Russian, English, German, French, Polish, Yiddish, Byelorussian, Bulgarian, Serbian, Czech, Swedish, Finnish, Slovak, Rumanian, and other languages. Volume 1 is in two parts: general sources on Ukraine in the Great East European Revolution; and Ukraine in the Prerevolutionary Era, 1907 to March 1917. The second volume consists of six chapters of materials on "the autonomous Ukrainian land, March, 1917–November, 1917 to the republican insurgency and the aftermath, November, 1920–1923." The final volume will be in four parts: Gubernias and lands of the Ukrainian republic in the Great East European revolution, serials, a bibliography of bibliographies, and indexes for the three volumes.

Similar in intent but narrower in scope are four bibliographies issued by the Library of Congress on *Rumania* (1963) (10), *Bulgaria* (1965) (11), *Czechoslovakia* (1967) (12), and *East Germany* (1967) (13). In each volume a specialist presents a brief description (in narrative format) of books in all languages. Bibliographies and reference works are listed first, followed by such categories as land and people; language and literature; and politics, government, and law.

ABSEES (1968–) (14) first appeared as an "Information Supplement" to *Soviet Studies*. Scholars abstracted selected articles from Soviet periodicals and newspapers on the arts; education; foreign relations; government; intellectualism and ideology; law; politics; sociology; administrative structure; agriculture; costing, prices, and incentives; economic theory; finance; foreign trade; industrial planning and internal trade; labor and wages; standard of living; statistics; and transport. Sources are indicated. A few books are also abstracted. In 1970 more subjects (e.g., military affairs and religion) and titles were added, and there was a more elaborate classification scheme, with two broad categories ("Social" and

"Economic") and another category arranged by countries, including Yugoslavia. A special topical bibliographical section was also introduced. Topics in the bibliographies include "Soviet Books on the Sociology of the USSR"; "Siberia and the Far East: A Short Bibliography of Soviet Publications, 1959–1969"; "Budget and Finance in the USSR"; and "A Profile of Soviet Military Publications, 1968–1970." About 1,200 items are abstracted in each issue, but no indexes are given.

Periodicals. Horecky and Carlton's *USSR and Eastern Europe: Periodicals in Western Languages* (1967) (15) comprises an annotated list of 769 titles. The volume is arranged by country, with an index of titles and issuing organizations and a subject guide.

M.I.c Biographical Dictionaries and Directories

Prominent Personalities in the USSR (1968–) (1) is the fourth biographical dictionary issued by the Institute for the Study of the USSR in Munich. It contains over 6,000 biographies, and according to the editors is to be supplemented by a quarterly supplement, *Portraits of Prominent USSR Personalities* (1968–) (2). The same organization published *Party and Government Officials of the Soviet Union, 1917–1967* (1969) (3), arranged in two chapters, supplements, and general and name indexes. "The chapter entitled 'Party Officials' begins its coverage back in 1898, when the Russian Social Democratic Worker's Party (RSDWP) was founded. The chapter thus offers a more comprehensive view of the makeup of the leading party organs, tracing them from the moment of the Party's inception. . . . The chapter entitled 'Government Officials' is arranged by groups of departments and offices as these were set up, dissolved or reorganized" (from the preface). Among the tables in the supplements are dates of CPSU congresses and conferences, CP membership in the Union Republics, organizational diagrams of the RSDRP in 1902 and 1969, and the national state structure of the USSR. Earlier publications of the Institute for the Study of the USSR in Munich are still useful because they contain information deleted from later volumes. The *Biographic Directory of the USSR* (1958) (4) contains about 3,800 entries. The second edition, called *Who's Who in the USSR* (1966) (5), includes almost 5,000 entries, but 573 that had appeared in the first edition were omitted; it contains many bibliographies deleted from *Prominent Personalities in the USSR* (1). *Who Was Who in the USSR* (1972) (6) contains biographies of over 5,000 deceased Soviet citizens who made major contributions to the political, scientific, social, and economic life of the USSR between 1917 and 1967.

M.1.d Encyclopedias and Dictionaries

The *McGraw-Hill Encyclopedia of Russia and the Soviet Union* (1961) (1), edited by Michael T. Florinsky, with over 100 contributors, is a reliable single-volume work for general information. There are about 100 principal entries, interspersed with many minor ones. Coverage includes biographical sketches, historical terms, and institutions. Some articles have brief bibliographies, and there are small black-and-white drawings, tables, and maps.

Still reliable, Roucek's *Slavonic Encyclopedia* (1949) (2) is a work of many contributors. Using material current "as of 1946," the volume covers the most important developments of the history of the Slavic peoples, "including those living outside the territorial limits of the Slavic states as well as those who have joined the stream of America's civilization as the 'new' immigrants, and of the various ramifications of their contemporary life and problems." Many cross-references to topics of related interest are provided.

Marxism, Communism, and Western Society (1972–) (3) promises to be an important source of information on the "ideological, political, economic, social and cultural features of the Communist world, and to assess their relative difference from or similarity to their counterparts in democratic societies." In eight volumes, with contributions from over 700 specialists, "it offers a broad spectrum of comparative data and nonpartisan analysis in conformity with the highest standards of scholarly research and evaluation." Considerable attention is given to biology, economics, education, ethnology, history, law, literature, philosophy, physics, politics, psychology, sociology, and religion.

Information USSR (1962) (4), edited by Robert Maxwell, is essentially an English-language version, with some revision, of volume 50 of the Russian encyclopedia *Bol'shaya sovyetskaya Entsiklopedia.* "The articles are concerned with all the major aspects of life in the Soviet Union today. It is the fruit of the collective labor of many Soviet historians, economists, geographers, scientists and engineers, philosophers, statisticians, lawyers, literary and art critics, and other scholars and experts." Appendixes are also provided on the following topics: statistical data up to 1960 relating to the national economy of the USSR; a directory of institutions of higher learning; an uneven select bibliography of English-language books on the USSR; and a résumé of the Third Program adopted at the 22d Congress of the Communist Party of the Soviet Union, giving the plan, program, and aspirations of the Party for the following twenty years.

A two-volume encyclopedia, *Ukraine* (1963–1970) (5), edited by Volodymyr Kubyovyc, with many expert contributors, is arranged under such broad subjects as general information; physical geography and natural history; population; ethnography; Ukrainian language, literature, and history; Ukrainian culture; economics; law; politics and government; and religion. Articles are accompanied by bibliographies. *Encyclopedia Lituanica* (1970) (6) is an abridgment in six volumes of a thirty-six-volume set, but contains editorial material that did not appear in the original. Jelavich (M.2.e:7) describes *Croatia: Land, People, Culture* (1970) (7) as "a collection of essays, some of which are scholarly, others overly nationalistic in tone."

M.l.e   Handbooks and Yearbooks

The Soviet Union and Eastern Europe (I.1.e:9) is one of the Praeger handbooks. Among the chapters (each written by an authority) in Leonid I. Strakhovsky's *Handbook of Slavic Studies* (1949) (1) are examinations of such topics as "Slavic Origins and Migrations," "Primitive Slavic Culture," "Medieval Poland," and "The Conflict of Slav and German." The bibliographies that accompany each contribution list works in English published up to 1949. A "comparative chronology" and an index are given at the end. Together, Strakhovsky and Schöpfin give brief coverage of historical as well as current matters. The Europa Yearbooks (I.1.e:1) have much valuable data.

There are three U.S. Army Area Handbooks (I.1.e:12) devoted to Eastern Europe and the Soviet Union: *Albania, Mongolia,* and *The Soviet Union.* The AUFS *Reports* (I.1.e:14) include a section entitled "Southeastern Europe."

M.l.f   Newspapers and News Digests

Eastern European and Soviet newspapers and related matters are reviewed in Merrill's *The Foreign Press* (I.1.f:1). The weekly *Current Digest of the Soviet Press* (1949–) (1) provides coverage of *Izvestia* and *Pravda* (the leading Soviet dailies), as well as selected items from about sixty other Soviet publications. Listed weekly are the contents of the dailies, as well as selected articles from them and other Soviet periodicals. Texts of all major public documents, speeches, and laws are provided. Sources are given, including dates, names, and pages, along with number of words and whether the articles are complete or abridged. Arrangement is by subject, with quarterly indexes; however, all material is indexed in *PAIS* (A.1.b:15).

Complete texts of articles from Soviet newspapers and periodicals are contained in the twice-monthly *Reprints from the Soviet Press* (1966–) (2). Subjects covered include economics, politics, foreign affairs, agriculture, industry, labor, science, and law.

ABSEES (M.1.b:14) contains abstracts in English of articles in Soviet newspapers and periodicals.

Many Soviet and Eastern European periodicals are translated by the U.S. and other Western governments. Researchers requiring information on the translation services available and the scope of the titles covered should consult Brock (G.1.b:1) or Mason (G.2.c:2).

M.I.g Statistics Sources

Perhaps the most easily accessible source of statistics is the UN Statistical Office's *Statistical Yearbook* (I.1.g:3), supplemented regularly in its *Monthly Bulletin of Statistics* (I.1.g:5). Harvey's *Statistics Europe* (L.1.g:2) provides recent information on the availability of published statistics for the whole of Europe. Neither the *Encyclopedia of Business Information Sources* (A.1.b:7) nor *Statistics Sources* (A.1.h:1) should be overlooked, though they are limited to English-language sources. *Cross-Polity Time-Series Data* (I.1.g:7) provides historical statistics.

Section 2

M.2.a Anthropology

Collections of Data.   Information on a number of Central European and Russian cultures exist in the Human Relations Area Files (I.3:1). They are arranged below according to *Outline of World Cultures* (B.1.e:3).

CENTRAL EUROPE

Europe	Yugoslavia
Slavic peoples	Serbs
Poland	Albania
Czechoslovakia	Greece
Hungary	Sarakatsani
Rumania	Bulgaria

RUSSIA

Soviet Union	Turkestan
Baltic Countries	Turkic Peoples
Lithuanians	Kazak
Belorussia	Siberia
Ukraine	Samoyed (Nganasan.
Great Russia	Nenets, Kamas)
Estonians (Votes,	Yakut (Dolgan)
Vepsians, Livonians)	Gilyak
Caucasia	Chukchee
Georgia	Kanchadal
Abkhaz	Koryak

Bibliographies. The coverage of *Europe: A Selected Ethnographic Bibliography* (L.2.a:1) includes Central Europe and Russia. *Paleosiberian Peoples and Languages* (1957) (1), by Roman Jakobson et al., provides bibliographic coverage of the ethnographic and linguistic literature of the Chukchi, Kamchada, Koryak, Yukager, Gilyak, Ket, Kat, Arin, and Asan peoples, as well as general Siberian ethnology and linguistics. References include published works and unpublished materials. An appendix contains a sketch of peoples and languages. Halpern (M.2.h:1) lists material in English. A partial list of anthropological studies by American cultural ethnologists of East Central and Southeastern Europe is given by Conrad M. Arensburg in Jelavich's *Language and Area Studies* (M.2.e:7). Lawrence Krader notes 123 works in "Recent Trends in Soviet Anthropology" in the 1959 *Biennial Review of Anthropology* (B.1.b:7).

Ethnomusicology and Folklore. Albert Lord and David Bynum review books and articles published in the United States on East Central and Southeastern European folklore and ethnomusicology in Jelavich's *Language and Area Studies* (M.2.e:7). About 80 studies are discussed. A bibliography of Indo-European folklore has appeared annually since 1950 in the East European section of *MLA Bibliography* (B.2.e:1).

Linguistics. Currently about 300 studies on linguistics appear annually in the *MLA Bibliography* (B.2.e:1), and a much larger number in sections on Baltic and Slavic, Caucasian, Eurasian, and Northern Asian and Altaic languages in the annual *Bibliographie linguistique* (B.2.e:2). Edward Stankiewicz discusses over 200 contributions by American linguists and foreign scholars permanently residing in the United States on East Central and Southeastern European languages in Jelavich (M.2.e:7).

M.2.b   Demography

In Jelavich's *Language and Area Studies* (M.2.e:7), Paul Demeny surveys over 30 non-Western and Western language sources. Demeny states that *Population Index* (C.1.b:1), with its thorough geographical indexes, offers the easiest approach to works concerning the demography of Eastern Europe. *Statistics Sources* (A.1.h:1) and the *Encyclopedia of Business Information Sources* (A.1.b:7) suggest English-language sources for research on the population of East Central Europe and the Soviet Union.

M.2.c   Economics

In Jelavich's *Language and Area Studies* (M.2.e:7), Nicolas Spulber notes that although "a relatively limited amount of noteworthy books and articles on the economics of [East Central and Southeastern Europe] were published in the Western languages during the interwar years . . . a vast increase in books, monographs and articles in the last two decades since World War II was registered." Almost 100 individual works are discussed.

The *Oxford Regional Economic Atlas: The USSR and Eastern Europe* (I.1.a:1) is an authoritative source of information on such subjects as natural resources, agriculture, manufacturing, trade, and communications. Also worth consulting is George Kish's *Economic Atlas of the Soviet Union* (1971) (1). In addition to general maps on physical features, vegetation zones, administrative divisions, and air transportation and population distribution, it includes maps on agriculture and land use, mining and minerals, industry, and transportation and cities, and brief headnotes for each of the fifteen "major component" regions into which the Soviet Union is divided. There is a list of Russian- and Western-language bibliographic sources and an index of regional maps.

M.2.d Geography

The chapter entitled "The Land" by Chauncy D. Harris in Horecky's *Russia and the Soviet Union* (M.1.b:2) is an authoritative, annotated listing of studies up to 1965. *Soviet Geography: A Bibliography* (1951) (1), a two-volume work issued by the U.S. Library of Congress's Reference Department, is a comprehensive bibliography through 1950. There are volumes on Albania and Yugoslavia (three volumes) in the Geographical Handbooks series (E.1.e:5). In Jelavich's *Language and Area Studies* (M.2.e:7), George W. Hoffman's "Geography" surveys Western-language sources, concluding that "the 'state of the art' of geography in East Central and Southeast Europe studies leaves a great deal to be desired." He discusses sixty-odd publications by American geographers that had appeared on the subject in the postwar period, as well as the contributions of East European and West European geographers in the same period.

M.2.e History

Peter Crowther's *Bibliography of Works in English on Early Russian History to 1800* (1969) (1) is designed as a companion to David M. Shapiro's *Select Bibliography of Works in English on Russian History* (1962) (2), which is restricted to 1801–1917. Crowther's work consists of over 2,100 entries of both separately published material and articles in periodicals and collective works. He aims at comprehensiveness in material most pertinent to central Russian history (e.g., general and chronological history, for-

eign relations, and social and economic history). He is more
selective in those sections dealing with the history of Russia's bor-
derlands, while the language section does not pretend to include
more than a selection of those works most relevant to the historian. Materials issued to the end of July 1967 appear in the main
text, and there is an addendum covering materials issued to the
end of 1968. Brief headnotes for each section direct attention to
arrangement, topics included, and significant works. Bibliographies
and historiographical studies appear at the beginning of each section. Occasionally, items are annotated, and the existence of reviews is noted. The index combines names and subjects. Shapiro's
Select Bibliography of Works in English on Russian History (2)
consists of over 1,000 citations of books and articles concerned
with Russian history from 1801 to 1917. Horecky (M.1.b:2) suggests that the coverage is much wider than the title implies, including political, economic, social, and intellectual aspects. As in
the Crowther work, items are arranged in broad chapters with appropriate subdivisions. Headnotes at the beginnings of chapters or
subdivisions point out the arrangement within chapters, significant
books, and so on. As well as references to reviews of books "that
are important or misleading," there are occasional annotations.
The index refers to authors and persons mentioned in titles.

Pushkarev's *Dictionary of Russian Historical Terms from the
Eleventh Century to 1917* (1970) (3) includes approximately
2,400 definitions of political, ecclesiastical, social, economic, and
historical terms. Biographical data and geographical names are
excluded. Pushkarev notes that "the most important terms referring to social categories and political, military, educational and
other institutions are supplied with brief historical sketches," with
occasional references to authorities. Works of Russian, Soviet, and
American historians consulted are listed at the end of the volume.
A useful "Instructions for Users" is given. *An Atlas of Russian
and East European History* (1966) (4), by Arthur E. Adams and
others, consists of 101 small black-and-white maps and descriptions of ethnic, political, social, and economic history for over
1,000 years. A brief list of sources and an index are also provided.
The second edition of Chew's *Atlas of Russian History* (1970)
(5) contains 38 black-and-white maps on Russian history from
the ninth century A.D. to recent times. Each map is accompanied
by a brief description. An appendix gives a list of name changes
of selected Russian cities and towns.

For the first time, in *History in the USSR* (1967) (6), a work
on the history of historical scholarship edited and compiled by
Marin Pundeff, it is possible to examine, in English, documents
and writings on "basic Marxist-Leninist doctrine, views on po-

litical leaders and influential historians, and official decrees and directives governing the writing and teaching of history" by such writers as Marx, Engels, Plekhanov, Lenin, Stalin, Pokronsky, Khrushchev, A. M. Pankratova, and N. L. Rubenstein. Two bibliographies of studies containing Russian and Western titles are appended. Charles and Barbara Jelavich give brief assessments of over 400 works, mostly in English, on Eastern Europe, including individual countries, in *Language and Area Studies: East Central and Southeastern Europe: A Survey* (1969) (7). George Barr Carson's *Russia Since 1917* (1962), in the Service Center for Teachers of History series (O.2.e:8), is a good brief introduction. He begins with "some of the works that created the picture of Soviet Russia before World War II" and traces developments to 1961, examining 28 titles. Among the titles in Heath's Problems in European Civilization (1958–) (8) are *Imperial Russia after 1861: Peaceful Modernization or Revolution; The Russian Revolution and Bolshevik Victory: Why and How;* and *The Stalin Revolution: Fulfillment or Betrayal of Communism?* Other titles in the series are listed in the Heath catalog in *PTLA* (A.1.b:30). In Holt's European Problem Studies (1963–) (9) is T. Emmons's *Emancipation of the Russian Serfs;* other titles in the series are listed in the Holt catalog in *PTLA* (A.1.b:30).

M.2.f   Literature

Slavic literature receives attention in Strakhovsky's *Handbook of Slavic Studies* (M.1.e:1) and *The Penguin Companion to World Literature* (L.2.f:1); but the *MLA Bibliography* (B.2.e:1), Winchell (A.1.b:13), Walford (A.1.b:12), and the Horecky volumes (M.1.b:2–5) are suggested for intensive needs.

M.2.g   Political Science

Articles by John C. Campbell and Paul E. Zinner in Jelavich's *Language and Area Studies: East Central and Southeastern Europe* (M.2.e:7) note the paucity of studies in international relations and political science. Campbell briefly notes 42 titles, and Zinner, over 30.

Richard F. Staar's *Communist Regimes in Eastern Europe* (1967) (1) is a useful source of information on Communist regimes, as well as military and economic integration through the Warsaw Treaty Organization, the Council for Mutual Economic Assistance, and polycentric trends. Sources are indicated, and there is an index and an unannotated bibliography of pamphlets and books. Titles of newspapers and periodicals in many languages are provided. Jan Triska's *Constitutions of the Communist Party-*

States (1968) (2) is a collection of past and present texts of constitutions and amendments of the USSR, the People's Republic of China, the People's Republic of Albania, the People's Republic of Bulgaria, the Democratic Republic of Vietnam, the German Democratic Republic, the People's Republic of Korea, the Hervic People of Cuba, the Mongolian People's Republic, the Polish People's Republic, the Socialist Republic of Rumania, the Czechoslovak Socialist Republic, and the Socialist Federal Republic of Yugoslavia. If Triska's volume is unavailable, Peaslee's *Constitutions of the Nations* (I.2.f:2) is another source.

Over 100 experts have contributed to Hammond's *Soviet Foreign Relations and World Communism* (1965) (3), an annotated bibliography of 7,000 books, doctoral dissertations, a few significant journal articles and pamphlets, and the main newspapers and periodicals concerned with communism in thirty languages. It is acknowledged as the most authoritative treatment of the subject. The work is in three main sections. "Soviet Foreign Relations by Chronological Periods" lists works that discuss Soviet dealings with more than one country. "Soviet Foreign Relations and Communism by Regions and Countries," the largest section, consists of works focusing primarily on one area or country. "Special Topics" consists of works which examine such topics as Communist ideology, strategy, and tactics; propaganda; the Comintern; and Soviet military power. "In some instances a fraudulent book has been listed and annotated for the purpose of warning prospective readers—for example, the so-called memoirs of Maxim Litvinow, Colonel Kalinow, and Captain Krylow. In other cases an inferior work has been included so that readers could be informed of distortions, errors, bias, or other deficiencies" (p. ix). In each category, the best books (approximately 10 percent) are indicated with an "A," and another 20 percent, with a "B." Of particular usefulness are the two last chapters. "Collections of Documents on Soviet Foreign Relations and Treaties" describes 57 items; "Bibliographies" is a highly selective list of the most useful titles in Soviet foreign relations and world communism. Specialized bibliographies dealing with particular countries or subjects are listed in the appropriate sections, and many additional bibliographies of a more general nature are included in the list of sources consulted. The index includes entries for authors, editors, compilers, and anonymous titles. Hammond can be partially supplemented by the *Yearbook on International Communist Affairs* (4), the *International Bibliography of Political Science* (G.1.b:4), and the *Peace Research Abstracts Journal* (G.2.d:12). The *Yearbook on International Communist Affairs* (1966–) (4) provides "a comprehensive annual survey describing the organizational structures, internal developments, and domestic and foreign policies and activities of all the Communist parties in the world. . . . Primary sources are from Communist publications of a broad variety, ranging from regular periodicals . . . to ephemeral pamphlets and newssheets. . . . [Yearbooks contain] data concerning the individual Communist parties and their activities, together with material pertaining to the international Communist movement and its problems. This means that policies of the individual Communist states, and particularly their diplomacy, are not treated systematically; rather, policies are mentioned essentially in illustration of the positions and activities of the Communist parties of these countries. The selection is made with the intention of offering a global picture of the international Communist movement in action, thereby displaying the internal and external elements of strength and vulnerability in the movement as a whole and in its component parties and fronts" (from the preface).

Each *Yearbook* is in seven sections. First, there are "profiles of individual Communist parties" in countries where they exist, giving the date of the founding of the party, a description of its legal status and membership, an indication of its strength and influence, its organization (especially leading administrative bodies and personalities and its role in other organizations), programs, relationships with the international Communist movement, and so on. Section 2 is concerned with international Communist-front organizations, while section 3 examines international Communist conferences and events. Section 4 consists of documentary materials "which illustrate Communist attitudes on basic international issues or reflect local problems of international importance." Section 5 is a chronology of the year's most important facts related to the world Communist movement. Section 6 lists selected books in English, Russian, French, and German published during the year and pertaining to ruling and nonruling Communist parties. This feature supplements Hammond (M.2.g:3). The final section is an index.

Jane T. Degras has edited two volumes of translated documents and statements of the Comintern (an abbreviation of "Communist International," the name given to the Third International, founded in Moscow in 1919) entitled *The Communist International, 1919–1943: Documents* (1956–) (5).

An earlier three-volume set edited by Jane Degras is *Soviet Documents on Foreign Policy* (1951–53) (6), containing translations of government and party statements, diplomatic notes, speeches, and Tass statements, selected from a comprehensive list of documents in *Calendar of Soviet Documents on Foreign Policy*

(1948) (7). Treaties and agreements registered with the League of Nations and published in its Treaty Series (G.2.c:13) have been omitted, as have the speeches and proposals of the Soviet delegation to the League of Nations disarmament conference.

A noted collection of translations of public proceedings since 1952 of the Communist Party Congress is in *Current Soviet Policies* (1952–) (8). Originally they appeared in the *Current Digest of the Soviet Press* (M.1.f:1). For example, Alexander Dallin states in Horecky (M.1.b:2) that Xenia Eudin's *Soviet Russia and the East, 1920–1927* (1957) (9) and *Soviet Russia and the West, 1920–1927* (1957) (10) are "two useful, though necessarily incomplete collections of documents regarding Soviet views on diplomacy and revolution and the actual conduct of foreign policy in the New Economic Policy era, with helpful annotations and comments." The first volume in particular contains some hard-to-find materials and a most useful bibliography. Eudin continues coverage up to 1934 in *Soviet Foreign Policy, 1928–1934* (1967) (11). The latter consists of a brief description and seventy documents examining "the most important points of the Soviet communists' own evaluation of their foreign policies and their general interpretation of the world situation in the period 1928–1934."

Walter C. Clemens's *Soviet Disarmament Policy, 1917–1963* (1965) (12) is a bibliography of over 800 items under two main headings which combine chronological and topical arrangements: part 1, "From the Bolshevik Revolution to World War II: 1917 to 1941"; and part 2, "From World War II to the 'Nth Country Problem': 1941 to 1963." Primary and secondary materials are described. Access to further research is provided in a list of Communist and Western bibliographies, including earlier editions of *USSR: Strategic Survey* (I.1.b:9).

John Gittings's *Survey of the Sino-Soviet Dispute: A Commentary and Extracts from the Recent Polemics, 1963–1967* (1968) (13) is a useful introduction to the development of this dispute. "The extracts chosen for inclusion in this volume come entirely from documents published by both sides from 1963 onwards, and, with two exceptions, from the onset of open polemics in July 1963. Documents published before 1963 are of course equally revealing, although couched in more esoteric language. Twenty-two of the major historical documents relating to Sino-Soviet relations between the years 1950 and 1962 are reproduced in full or in part in the appendices." A checklist containing "the principal polemical documents and interparty or interstate communications for the period January 1963 to June 1967 . . . [and] all other documents from which extracts have been reproduced in the main part" are also in the appendixes.

M.2.h Sociology

In Jelavich's *Language and Area Studies* (M.2.e:7), Irwin T. Sanders evaluates some twenty studies of Eastern Europe by U.S. sociologists. Joel Halpern et al. have compiled a *Bibliography of Anthropological and Sociological Publications on Eastern Europe and the USSR* (1961) (1), an unindexed list of books and articles in English, arranged in geographical divisions, then according to subject. Categories include "the Slavs" (in general); and "Rumania, Yugoslavia, and the USSR."

Part N

Latin America and the Caribbean

Section 1

N.1.a   Atlases

Latin America and the Caribbean are rather poorly provided with good atlases. The best general coverage is afforded by volume 5 of the *Times Atlas of the World* (A.1.a:1), which is devoted to North and South America. Kingsbury and Schneider's *Atlas of Latin American Affairs* (I.1.a:11) is a handy and quite useful compilation of some 60 black-and-white maps, with accompanying text. On similar lines is A. Curtis Wilgus's *Latin America in Maps: Historic, Geographic, Economic* (1951) (1). Ferriday's

Map Book of Africa and South America (1967) (2) comprises 27 sheets at various scales, each covering an individual country or region. The American Geographical Society's *Map of Hispanic America* (1922–45) (3) consists of 107 sheets, compiled and reproduced to conform to the International "One Million" map of the world. An index map to the individual sheets is available.

Official national and other country atlases are available for many countries, though they vary greatly in their quality and comprehensiveness. Among them are atlases of Argentina (1965–) (4), Bolivia (1958) (5), Brazil (1966) (6), British Honduras (1939) (7), Chile (1966) (8), Colombia (1959–) (9), Costa Rica (1952–) (10), Cuba (1949) (11), El Salvador (1955) (12), Mexico (1962) (13), and Venezuela (1969) (14).

There are two extensive lists of maps of Latin America: the four-volume *Catalog of Maps of Hispanic America* (1930–32) (15) and Palmyra V. M. Monteiro's two-volume *Catalog of Latin-American Flat Maps, 1926–1964* (1967–69) (16), which updates the earlier publication. Aerial photographs and topographic maps of South and Central America are inventoried in the Pan American Union's country-by-country *Annotated Index of Aerial Photographic Coverage and Mapping of Topography and Natural Resources* (1964–66) (17). Lock (A.1.a:11) should also be consulted.

N.1.b   Bibliographies

A considerable range of bibliographical material is available for the study of Latin America.

Bibliographies of Bibliographies.   The only bibliography of bibliographies of general significance is the one compiled by Arthur E. Gropp, *A Bibliography of Latin American Bibliographies* (1968) (1), which lists approximately 7,000 bibliographies, covering virtually all aspects of Latin America. The arrangement is first by subject, then by country. A detailed index of names, corporate bodies, government offices, series titles, and subjects is provided.

Guides to Reference Works.   Martin H. Sable's two-volume *Guide to Latin American Studies* (1967) (2) is an extensive compilation of annotated entries on reference works, monographs, periodical articles, and government publications in the social sciences, the humanities, and the natural and applied sciences. The entries are arranged alphabetically in broad subjects, and there are author and subject indexes. Abel Rodolfo Geoghegan's *Obras de referencia de América Latina* (1965) (3) is a selected, annotated listing of encyclopedias, dictionaries, bibliographies, biographical dictionaries and directories, catalogs, guides, yearbooks, and other reference works.

General Bibliographies. The *Handbook of Latin American Studies* (1935–) (4) is the most important bibliographical reference work on Latin America for the social sciences, as well as the humanities. Annual volumes include sections on anthropology, economics, education, geography, history, and sociology; each has an author and subject index. Each section and subsection begins with an introduction by the scholar responsible for its compilation, evaluating many of the works annotated. Unfortunately, the system of listing and abbreviating periodicals is confusing. However, students should not allow this drawback to be an obstacle to effective use of this indispensable source. A cumulative author index has been published for the years 1936–66. The *British Bulletin of Publications on Latin America, the West Indies, Portugal, and Spain* (1949–) (5) appears twice yearly and provides annotated listings of selected articles, books, monographs, and reports published in the United Kingdom on these geographical areas. Each issue contains about 150 items. The Pan American Union's quarterly *Inter-American Review of Bibliography* (1951–) (6) lists, among other items, all current publications of the Organization of American States. *Current Caribbean Bibliography* (1951–) (7) is a useful regional bibliography.

Of wide coverage are *Latin America, Hemispheric Partner: A Bibliographic Survey* (I.1.b:6) and *Latin America and the Caribbean: Analytical Survey of Literature* (I.1.b:5). *Latin America, Spain, and Portugal: An Annotated Bibliography of Paperback Books* (1971) (8) issued by the Library of Congress, includes brief annotations on more than 1,500 items, about two-thirds dealing with Latin America. *Latin America: An Introduction to Modern Books in England Covering the Countries of Latin America* (1966) (9) is a brief but useful British bibliography. The American Universities Field Staff's *Select Bibliography: Asia, Africa, Eastern Europe, Latin America* (I.1.b:3) should not be overlooked. S. A. Bayitch's *Latin America: A Bibliographical Guide to Economic History, Law, Politics, and Society* (1961) (10) and the same author's *Latin America and the Caribbean: A Bibliographical Guide to Works in English* (1967) (11) are standard reference works. More than 10,000 unannotated items are cited in the earlier work. *Latin America in Soviet Writings, 1945–1958: A Bibliography* (1959) (12) lists some 2,200 items by Russian authors or Russian translations of works from other languages relating to Latin America. Titles are printed in English and in transliterated Russian. Grieder and Berry's *Bibliography of Latin Amer-*

ican Philosophy and Art since Independence (1964) (13), though concerned more with the humanities than the social sciences, may also be useful. The Pan American Union's *Guide for the Study of Culture in Central America: Humanities and Social Sciences* (1968) (14) lists and briefly annotates close to 1,000 items on many aspects of the region. Rogers and Haberly's *Brazil, Portugal, and Other Portuguese-Speaking Lands: A List of Books Primarily in English* (1968) (15) covers only works published after World War II. Comita's *Caribbeana, 1900–1965: A Topical Bibliography* (1968) (16) lists more than 7,000 items—including monographs, articles, reports, theses, and dissertations—on the non-Hispanic parts of the Caribbean.

The most useful and comprehensive index is the Pan American Union's quarterly *Indice general de publicaciones periódicas latinoamericanas: humanidades y ciencias sociales* (1961–) (17). Some 330 periodicals are regularly indexed, with materials arranged by subject. Annual cumulations are made. An eight-volume set, *Index to Latin American Periodical Literature, 1929–1960* (1962) (18), has also been issued by the Pan American Union, and a further two volumes covering the years 1961–65 appeared in 1967. Irene Zimmerman's *Guide to Current Latin American Periodicals: Humanities and Social Sciences* (1961) (19) and Tamara Brunnschweiler's *Current Periodicals: A Select Bibliography in the Area of Latin American Studies* (1968) (20), which is concerned largely with agriculture and the natural and applied sciences, are invaluable. Also of importance is *Latin American Economic and Social Serials* (1969) (21), issued by the Committee on Latin America. The most complete listing of serials when completed will be the set *Latin American Serial Documents* (1968–) (22). One volume is devoted to each of the twenty countries of Latin America, except for the Dominican Republic and Haiti, which are treated together in volume 13.

Reviews of Research. Regular reviews of research on Latin American topics, with extensive bibliographical lists, are published in the *Latin American Research Review* (1966–) (23), issued thrice yearly. Recent reviews include "Trends and Issues in Latin American Urban Research, 1965–70," by Richard M. Morse, and "Current Research and Prospects in Andean Ethnohistory." *Social Science Research on Latin America* (1964) (24), edited by Charles Wagley, is an important reference work in which eight distinguished Latin Americanists review the state of Latin American studies in the early 1960s. Anthropology, economics, geography, history, law, political science, and sociology are the disciplines covered. Each chapter has a selected bibliography. Roberto Esquenazi-Mayo and Michael C. Meyer's *Latin American Scholar-*

ship since World War II: Trends in History, Political Science, Literature, Geography, Economics (1971) (25) is arranged in four sections: "Historical Scholarship since World War II," "Research in Political Science," "Literary Currents since World War II," and "Geographic and Economic Scholarship." Each of the noted specialists examines twenty-five years of scholarship and research trends in his field. Close to 1,600 items are cited. More narrowly focused, volume 1 of *Latin American Urban Research* (1970–) (26), edited by Rabinovitz and Trueblood, covers research completed and in progress, trends in research, and bibliographical materials. An introduction, "Latin American Research, 1970," is followed by a bibliography covering the years 1968–69. Ten evaluative essays by experts in various fields such as migration, urban culture, government institutions, and the consequences of urbanization are each provided with extensive bibliographical references.

N.1.c Biographical Dictionaries and Directories

Many of the sources mentioned in section A.1.d are useful, notably *Biography Index* (A.1.d:10), Hyamson (A.1.d:11), the *New York Times Obituaries Index* (A.1.d:12), the *New York Times Biographical Edition* (A.1.d:13), and Slocum (A.1.d:9).

The most comprehensive biographical dictionary of Latin America is, unfortunately, almost a generation out of date. Nonetheless, *Who's Who in Latin America: A Biographical Dictionary of Notable Living Men and Women in Latin America* (1945–51) (1), edited by Ronald Hilton, is a monumental reference that will be found indispensable for a variety of research purposes. More than 8,000 short biographies are included in the seven volumes, which deal, in turn, with Mexico; Central America and Panama; Colombia, Ecuador, and Venezuela; Bolivia, Chile, and Peru; Argentina, Paraguay, and Uruguay; Brazil; and Cuba, the Dominican Republic, and Haiti. A more recent and more specialized work of great value is Marvin Alisky's *Who's Who in Mexican Government* (1969) (2).

The Hispanic Foundation's *National Directory of Latin Americanists* (1971) (3) provides brief bio-bibliographies of more than 1,800 specialists from many fields of academic life and government. A more specialized work, *Historians of Latin America in the United States* (1966) (4), compiled by Howard F. Cline, includes close to 700 short bio-bibliographies.

N.1.d Encyclopedias and Dictionaries

The most extensive encyclopedic coverage of Latin American topics is provided in the seventy-volume *Enciclopedia universal illustrada europea-americana* (1907–30) (1). A ten-volume appendix for the years 1930–33 has been followed by annual supplements. The one-volume *Diccionario enciclopédico de las Américas* (1947) (2) covers the whole of the Americas but with greatest emphasis on Latin America. Most entries are confined to a few lines. Much more elaborate national encyclopedias and dictionaries of various sorts are also available. Two noteworthy national encyclopedias are the eight-volume *Gran enciclopedia argentina* (1956–64) (3) and the *Enciclopedia de México* (1966–) (4), to be completed in ten volumes. Another useful work, though in some respects much out of date, is the two-volume *Diccionario historico, geográphico e etnográphico do Brasil* (1922) (5).

N.1.e   Handbooks and Yearbooks

Perhaps the most valuable single reference work on Latin America of this kind is *Latin America and the Caribbean: A Handbook* (I.1.e:5), a massive compilation of information and comment provided by some eighty experts and edited by Claudio Veliz.

Long the main standby of businessmen, tourists, and scholars for accurate, concise, and up-to-date information on the individual countries of South and Central America, *The South American Handbook* (1924–) (1) is revised annually. Each country is treated in terms of its terrain, climate, and vegetation; history and settlement; education and cultural life; agriculture and industry; and trade and transportation. The main cities of each country are particularly well covered, with a number of useful sketch-maps of downtown areas. Also available in many college libraries are *The New World Guides to the Latin American Republics* (1950) (2), edited by Earl Parker Hanson. In three volumes, these guides may still be found useful for historical and other material on the individual countries. Volume 1 covers Mexico and Central America; volume 2, Bolivia, Chile, Colombia, Ecuador, and Peru; and volume 3, the remaining countries of South America.

Skinner's *Yearbook of the West Indies and the Countries of the Caribbean* (1969–) (3) includes much valuable miscellaneous information on the economy, geography, history, political organization, and social aspects of individual countries. Similar material, aimed particularly at the tourist, is provided in Fodor's *Guide to the Caribbean* (1960–) (4), which is regularly updated and revised. Two dozen regional maps are a useful feature of the guide. *The Caribbean: Who, What, Why* (1965) (5) provides information on most aspects of the region. A notable feature is the arrangement of biographical sketches in professional categories, as, for example, banking, commerce, and industry.

The most detailed encyclopedic information, however, is provided in the Area Handbooks (I.1.e:12), compiled by The American University for the U.S. Army. Volumes are available currently for Argentina, Brazil, Colombia, the Dominican Republic, Ecuador, and Peru. *Background Notes on the Countries of the World* (I.1.e:13), issued by the U.S. Department of State, provide brief factual information on each country of Latin America and a number of other territories, but the Europa Yearbooks (I.1.e:1) contain more extensive information.

O. C. Stoetzer's *The Organization of American States: An Introduction* (1965) (6) provides a variety of information on the OAS, as well as the texts of some important documents connected with its operation. The Pan American Union's *Yearbook of Educational, Scientific, and Cultural Development in Latin America* (1966–) (7) is another general reference work that will be helpful for a number of research problems. The *Master Directory for Latin America* (1965) (8) aims to cover "organizations, associations and institutions in the fields of agriculture, business-industry-finance, communications, education, research, government, international cooperation, labor-cooperatives, publishing and religion, and professional, social and social service organizations and associations."

There are a number of official, semiofficial, and nonofficial handbooks to individual countries. These include C. B. R. Wrzoz's *Brazilian Information Handbook* (1956–) (9), which is regularly updated; *Quick Colombian Facts* (1955–) (10), issued by the Colombian Institute of Public Opinion; the official, annual *Handbook of Jamaica* (1881–) (11); *Mexico: Facts, Figures, and Trends* (1960–) (12), issued by the Banco Nacional de Commercio Exterior; and the official *Trinidad and Tobago Yearbook* (1865–) (13).

N.1.f Newspapers and News Digests

Latin American Newspapers in United States Libraries (1969) (1), a Union List, provides basic information on some 5,500 newspapers, including bibliographical information, as well as coded lists of the libraries which hold the individual newspapers.

Latin America (1967–) (2) is a British weekly newsletter, edited in London by journalists with considerable field experience in Latin America. Each issue contains about half a dozen fairly lengthy reports on issues of topical importance, while the sections "Business Briefs" and "News in Brief" present a wide variety of up-to-the-minute factual information. An index is provided. Unfortunately discontinued, the monthly *Air Mail News from Latin*

America (1967–1971) (3) aimed to provide periodic reviews of the Latin American press. Articles were selected for their focus on scientific discoveries and on sociopolitical and economic development. Photocopied clippings of articles from Latin American newspapers were accompanied by typed translations. There is no index, but each issue has a detailed table of contents. *Latin American Digest* (1966–) (4) includes articles on economic, political, social, and other topical matters, condensed from a wide range of Latin American periodicals.

N.1.g   Statistics Sources

The main sources of statistical information on the economies of the countries of Latin America are two serials issued by the United Nations Commission for Latin America—*The Economic Survey of Latin America* (1957–) (1) and the *Boletín estadístico de América Latina/Statistical Bulletin for Latin America* (1964–) (2), which supplements the *Economic Survey,* providing biannual statistical information on such matters as production, national income and accounts, finance and investment, prices, and foreign trade.

Wider in scope, the annual *Statistical Abstract of Latin America* (1955–) (3) gives statistics on area, population size, census returns and estimates, population density, life expectancy, birth and death rates, ethnic and linguistic composition of population, literacy, religion, and health matters, as well as a variety of economic statistics on such matters as production, investment, and trade. The series of annual reports of the Inter-American Development Bank entitled *Socio-Economic Progress in Latin America* (1961–) (4) provides a variety of statistical information on the region as a whole and on each of the Latin American member countries of the bank. Other publications of the bank, such as *The Process of Industrialization in Latin America* (1969) (5), have much detailed statistical information and should not be overlooked.

Statistical material is provided also in the serial publications of two private British banks. The monthly *BOLSA Review* (1936–) (6), formerly known as the *Fortnightly Review,* includes accurate statistical information, as well as commentary on economic and political affairs of current significance. *Barclays International Review* (J.2.c:4) includes Guyana, British Honduras, and many of the islands of the West Indies.

Statistics Sources (A.1.h:1) and the *Encyclopedia of Business Information Sources* (A.1.b:7) are useful, and historical statistics are in *Cross-Polity Times-Series Data* (I.1.g:7).

Section 2

N.2.a   Anthropology

Collections of Data.   Information on over fifty cultures is deposited in HRAF (I.3:1). Arrangement below is according to the *Outline of World Cultures* (B.1.e:3).

SOUTH AMERICA

Mosquito (Sumu)	Bush Negroes
Talamanca (Bribri,	(Saramacca, Boni)
Boruca)	Tehuelche
Cuna	Yahgan
Cagaba	Abipon
Goajiro	Mataco
Paez	Choroti
Cayapa	Guana (Terena)
Jivaro	Caingain (Aweikoma)
Inca	Guarani (Cayua)
Aymara	Timbira (Ramcocamecra)
Chiriguano	Tupinamba
Siriono	Bahia Brazilians
Uru (Chipaya)	Bacairi
Nambicuara	Bororo
Tapirape	Carib
Trumai	Pemon (Camaracoto)
Mundurucu	Warao
Yanoama (Sanema, Waica,	Yaruro
Surara, Pakidai)	Callinago
Tucano (Cubeo)	Puerto Rico
Tucuna	Haiti
	Jamaica

Gordon D. Gibson's article "A Bibliography of Anthropological Bibliographies: The Americas" (1960) (1) is a compilation of the most significant bibliographies published prior to 1955. The arrangement is by geographical area, then alphabetical by author. The *International Bibliography of Social and Cultural Anthropology* (B.1.b:4) brings the lists up to date. Timothy J. O'Leary's *Ethnographic Bibliography of South America* (1963) (2) deals with the literature on the native tribes of South America. The primary arrangement is by area and then by tribal group. A tribal index is provided. No such bibliographical reference work is available as yet for Central America or the Caribbean. There are, however, two excellent, multivolume handbooks on the Indian tribes of both South and Middle America. The *Handbook of South American Indians* (1946–59) (3), edited by Julian Haynes Steward, provides detailed ethnographic, linguistic, cultural, and other miscellaneous information on each of the tribal groups of the continent. Volumes are entitled *The Marginal Tribes, The Andean Civilizations, The Tropical Forest Tribes, The Circum-Caribbean Tribes, The Comparative Ethnology of South American Indians,* and *Physical Anthropology, Linguistics, and Cultural Geography of South American Indians.* Volume 7 is an index.

The *Handbook of Middle American Indians* (1964–) (4) is nearing completion. With Robert Wauchope as general editor and other specialists as editors of individual volumes, this handbook is a landmark in cooperative scholarship at the highest level. Each volume is profusely illustrated and equipped with both an index and a bibliography. The titles of the individual volumes indicate the wide scope of the work: volume 1, *Natural Environment and Early Cultures;* volumes 2 and 3, *Archaeology of Southern Mesoamerica;* volume 4, *Archaeological Frontiers and External Connections;* volume 5, *Linguistics;* volume 6, *Social Anthropology;* volumes 7 and 8, *Ethnology;* volume 9, *Physical Anthropology;* and volumes 10 and 11, *Archaeology of Northern Mesoamerica.* Volumes 12–15 will be entitled *Guide to Ethnohistorical Sources.* Volume 12 will cover *Geography and Ethnogeography;* volume 13, *Sources in the European Tradition: Printed Collections, Secular and Religious Chronicles, Bio-Bibliographies;* volume 14, *Sources in the Native Tradition: Prose and Pictorial Materials;* and volume 15, *Checklist of Repositories: Index of Authors, Titles, and Synonyms; Annotated References.* Volume 16 will contain a master bibliography for the entire handbook.

N.2.b   Demography

In *Latin American Population Studies* (1960) (1), T. Lynn Smith provides demographic data for Latin America as a whole, together with basic bibliographical information. Far more detailed is the information on vital statistics provided in Eduardo E. Arriaga's *New Life Tables for Latin American Populations in the Nineteenth and Twentieth Centuries* (1968) (2).

Denton R. Vaughn's *Urbanization in Twentieth-Century Latin America: A Working Bibliography* (1970) (3) is an introduction to much of the most useful demographic literature on the Latin American region. *Latin American Urban Research* (N.1.b:26), already noted, has a section on urban migration. International migration during recent decades is treated in Fernando Bastos do Avila's *Immigration in Latin America: A Study Made With the Cooperation of the Intergovernmental Committee for European Migration* (1964) (4). Carl Solberg's brief monograph *Immigration and Nationalism: Argentina and Chile, 1890–1914* (1970) (5) contains a thirty-page bibliography.

N.2.c Economics

The Economic Literature of Latin America: A Tentative Bibliography (1935–36) (1) is a two-volume work covering the main fields of economics and economic history. It lists more than 12,000 individual items. Jerry L. Weaver's *Latin American Development: A Selected Bibliography, 1950–1967* (1969) (2) goes some way towards updating the earlier work. Close to 2,000 items on economic, political, and social development are classified by region or country. Though John R. Wish's *Economic Development in Latin America: An Annotated Bibliography* (1965) (3) includes many general works, it is primarily focused on food marketing. *A Bibliography of South American Economic Affairs* (1955) (4), by Tom B. Jones and others, covers articles that appeared on economic topics in nineteenth-century periodicals.

A detailed regional bibliography is the Bank of Mexico's quarterly *Bibliografía económica de México* (1955–) (5), and a bibliography focused on part of one sector of the Latin American economy is Robert C. Mings's *Bibliography of the Tourist Industry of Latin America* (1971) (6).

Latin American Scholarship since World War II (N.1.b:25) has a section on economics.

N.2.d Geography

No adequate general bibliography of Latin American geography has yet appeared. However, the Pan American Institute of Geography and History's *Bibliografía de geografía urbana de América* (1961) (1) provides an extensive listing of the published literature on urban geography. The geographical journals and other serial publications of Latin America are treated in a pamphlet by Chauncy D. Harris called "Geographical Serials of Latin America" (1966) (2).

The International Geographical Union's *Select Annotated Bibliography of the Humid Tropics* (E.2.c:7) lists many hundreds of items on a variety of aspects of most South American and all Central American and Caribbean countries. A more narrowly focused but quite valuable listing of items on Latin America may be found in the three-volume set, *Fire in Relation to Primitive Agriculture and Grazing in the Tropics: Annotated Bibliography* (1955–57) (3), by Harley H. Bartlett. Other aspects of agriculture are covered in the *Inventory of Information Basic to the Planning of Agricultural Development in Latin America: Selected Bibliography* (1963–) (4), by the Inter-American Committee for Agricultural Development (CIDA) of the Pan American Union. *Latin American Scholarship since World War II* (N.1.b:25) should be consulted for its comments and short bibliography on Latin American geographical studies dealing with the development process.

Certain individual countries, notably Brazil and Mexico, have fine geographical bibliographies. The Brazilian Institute of Geography and Statistics issues a continuing series, *Bibliografia geográfica do Brasil* (1956–) (5). This bibliography is well indexed and cross-referenced. Angel Bassols Batalla's *Bibliografia geoggráfica de Mexico* (1955) (6) is a systematic bibliography covering all aspects of Mexico's geography.

N.2.e History

The bibliographical literature dealing with the history of Latin America is both extensive and comprehensive. Easily the most significant is the recent historical bibliography *Latin America: A Guide to the Historical Literature* (1971) (1). Although intended as an introductory bibliography, its extensive, though selective, listings and its critical annotations make it of great use also to the more advanced scholar and the expert. The items, nearly all published prior to 1966, have been selected from those available in many languages—in particular, English, Spanish, Portuguese, and French. They cover the whole field of Latin American history, including prehistory, archaeology, and ethnohistory. Three main sections deal with the colonial period, the period of independence, and the postindependence period. The listings in each are subdivided according to geographical region. Other sections cover reference works; general works dealing with more than one country or period; "background" studies in precolonial history, archaeology, and ethnohistory; and international (including inter-Hispanic American) relations since 1830. The third of these latter sections warrants additional comment, as both archaeology and ethnohistory have been encompassed within the purview of history, thus making the bibliography a uniquely comprehensive reference work. The section on archaeology is devoted entirely to American prehistory and preconquest archaeology, while the section on ethnohistory covers many aspects of Indian history since the conquest.

More generally useful for undergraduates is Robin A. Humphrey's annotated *Latin American History: A Guide to the Literature in English* (1958) (2), which includes more than 2,000 items. *Latin American History* (1967) (3), edited by Howard F. Cline, is a two-volume collection of writings in English on the development of Latin American historiography in the United States from the late nineteenth century to the present day. A. Curtis Wilgus's *Histories and Historians of Hispanic America* (1942) (4) covers a similar but wider field not confined to United States sources.

A more detailed bibliographical reference is *A Bibliography of United States-Latin American Relations since 1810* (1968) (5), edited by Trask, Meyer, and Trask. Approximately 11,000 items are included. The beginning chapters deal with bibliographies and handbooks; the remainder of the work is divided into two sections: a chronological survey of United States-Latin American relations and a country-by-country survey.

Michael R. Martin's *Encyclopedia of Latin American History* (1968) (6) treats the major pre-Columbian civilizations; the founding and growth of European colonies; the political, social, and economic development of Latin America since independence; and Latin American international relations. Religion, the arts, major cities, and notable Latin Americans are among the other subjects treated.

Because of its extensive coverage of Latin American history in all its main periods, *Latin American Scholarship since World War II* (N.1.b:25) should not be overlooked.

N.2.f Literature

Along with the *Penguin Companion to World Literature* (L.2. f:1), Maxim Newmark's *Dictionary of Spanish Literature* (1963) (1) provides brief information on Spanish and Latin American authors and their works, literary terms, and important currents in Spanish literature. For more intensive needs, the *Handbook of Latin American Studies* (N.1.b:4) and the MLA *Bibliography* (B.2.e:1) are excellent sources. A selected list of additional works is described in Winchell (A.1.b:13).

N.2.g Political Science

Harry Kantor's *Latin American Political Parties: A Bibliography* (1968) (1), is an excellent starting point. More than 2,200 items cover the most important political parties of each Latin American country. A more specialized bibliography is *Latin American Political Systems in an Urban Setting: A Preliminary Bibliography* (1967) (2), by Francine F. Rabinovitz and others. Well over 400 books and articles are listed. The rural scene is considered in its political context in *The Political Dimensions of Rural Development in Latin America: A Selected Bibliography, 1950–1967* (1968) (3), by Jerry L. Weaver, listing some 1,500 items.

Ronald H. Chilcote's two-volume *Revolution and Structural Change in Latin America: A Bibliography on Ideology, Development, and the Radical Left (1930–1965)* (1971) (4) is organized into a series of general and country sections, each indicating the usefulness and the availability of sources. Books and pamphlets, articles, and periodicals are grouped separately in each section, and many items are briefly annotated. The subject index reorganizes the works cited into sixteen topics, including anarchism and anarcho-syndicalism, anticommunism, the democratic left, and Fidelismo. There are also author and periodical indexes.

Latin American Political Guide (1957–) (5) provides brief country-by-country descriptions of conditions in Latin America. *The Yearbook on Latin American Communist Affairs* (1971–) (6), an outgrowth of the Hoover Institution's *Yearbook on International Communist Affairs* (M.2.g:4), includes a wealth of information on the Communist parties of the individual countries, as well as various other Marxist-Leninist organizations, and on events in the Communist world of significance to Latin America. Hammond (M.2.g:3) is useful for pre-1965 studies of communism in Latin America.

Four chapters in *Latin American Scholarship since World War II* (N.1.b:25) cover aspects of Latin American political science, including organized labor, the military, and inter-American relations.

N.2.h Sociology

The best available bibliography of Latin American sociology is the *"bibliografia sistemática"* compiled by Orlando Sepulveda and Francisco Fernández, and published as volume 1 of the three-volume *Anuario de sociología de los pueblos ibéricos* (1966–) (1). Sugiyama Intaka's article, "Social Stratification Research in Latin America," in the 1966 volume of *Latin American Research Review* (N.1.b:23), is a valuable bibliographical essay on a major branch of the field.

Two older bibliographies may still be found helpful. These are Sylvia P. Bernstein's *Bibliography on Labor and Social Welfare in Latin America* (1944) (2) and Donald Pierson's *Survey of the Literature in Brazil of Sociological Significance* (1945) (3).

South American Sociologists: A Directory (1970) (4), is another work that will be helpful to the researcher.

Part O

American Studies

Introduction

Most aspects of American civilization have been intensively researched, resulting in a large body of literature. It would be almost impossible and of questionable utility to provide a comprehensive list of reference works associated with American studies. Instead, a selected number of what are considered the most useful sources of information on the United States are described in this part. These titles are included because experience has demonstrated that they suit the needs of students and teachers confronted with the demands of research. We have attempted to provide a balanced selection, while suggesting other sources for further investigation if the items mentioned fail to contain what is required. For example, as usually understood, "ethnic studies" embraces elements of political science, history, anthropology, and sociology; because of the format of the present volume, however, the authors have arbitrarily placed ethnic studies in section O.2.g:2 (sociology), where it seems most appropriate. At the same time, it must be acknowledged that certain aspects of ethnic studies are evident in other subdivisions, including economics. Therefore it is suggested that the complete part be read, along with other parts in section 1, rather than only a particular subdivision.

Section I

O.I.a   Atlases

Several fine atlases are devoted to the United States. One of the most attractive, and perhaps the most useful, is *The National Atlas of the United States* (1970) (1). It consists of 765 colored maps illustrating physical features, historical evolution, economic activities, sociocultural conditions, administrative subdivisions, and involvement in world affairs, as well as indicating locations of over 41,000 places. There are individual maps of 27 major cities. Transparent plastic overlays are provided to indicate physical features, boundaries and names of the 3,049 U.S. counties, and so on. Among the thematic maps are maps showing more than 60 current types of administrative divisions such as counties, judicial districts, civil-defense areas, and postal zones. There is an index. The *Rand McNally Commercial Atlas and Marketing Guide* (1869–) (2), issued annually, is an important source of information on the population, business and industry, and agriculture of the states. As well as a map (with index) for each state, some 50 maps illustrate aspects of agriculture, communications, manufacturing, population, retail trade, and transportation as they concern the whole country. There is a gazetteer of over 127,000 places. Somewhat different in format, the Reader's Digest's *These United States: Our Nation's Geography, History, and People* (1968) (3) is an authoritative and attractive volume of over 500 maps and illustrations. There are maps and brief descriptions of the states and their largest cities, and brief illustrated chapters on such topics as archaeological findings, explorations, Indians, wars, demography, and education, as well as geological features, agriculture, natural resources, transportation, and communications. There are indexes of 46,000 place names and subjects. The *United States and Canada* (I.1.a:5) is also recommended.

Of more limited use, but with unique features, *An Atlas of North American Affairs* (I.1.a:14) is a brief compilation of miscellaneous information and small black-and-white maps of 56 topics such as soils, vegetation, Indian linguistic families, agriculture, petroleum, population, and civil rights. Other atlases concerned with the United States are described in Lock (A.1.a:11).

O.1.b Bibliographies

Bibliographies of Bibliographies. Besterman (A.1.b:1) provides bibliographical coverage up to 1965. The Library of Congress has issued many bibliographies, including lists of works on ethnic groups and social problems. The *Bibliographic Index* (A.1.b:2) is useful for minor topics, and many of the periodicals in Gray's *Serial Bibliographies in the Humanities and Social Sciences* (A.1.b:3) are in academic libraries in the United States.

Reference Works. The *Encyclopedia of Business Information Sources* (A.1.b:7) brings a new dimension to bibliographies of reference works, since its analytical approach allows researchers with limited knowledge of reference works to determine quickly which ones to consult for information on a topic. Such well-established titles as Winchell (A.1.b:13) and Walford (A.1.b:12) should not be overlooked, since their approach often uncovers features in reference works not evident in the *Encyclopedia of Business Information Sources*. Sally Wynkoop's *Government Reference Books* (1970–) (1) is a biennial publication describing the wide range of reference works published by the U.S. government. Items listed include bibliographies, directories, indexes, dictionaries, statistical works, handbooks and guides, almanacs, catalogs of collections, and biographical directories. Each citation provides the Superintendent of Documents' classification number, as well as a descriptive annotation indicating purpose, scope, arrangement, and special features. There is an author-title-subject index.

General Bibliographies. For a decade the Library of Congress's *Guide to the Study of the U.S.* (1960) (2) has been an indispensable source for books reflecting the development of American life and thought. It consists of 6,487 critically annotated titles published before 1958 and considered significant contributions to an understanding of the United States. In addition, chapters on literature, biography, travel and travelers, and philosophy and psychology have extensive headnotes. There is an index of authors, subjects, and titles. A supplement is to be issued, bringing coverage up to 1970.

Less well known is the *American Quarterly* (1949–) (3). Since 1955, a selected, briefly annotated bibliography of about 700 articles has appeared in the summer issue. The "criterion for listing an article is the extent to which it manifests a relationship between two or more aspects of American civilization." Articles are arranged under the following subjects: art and architecture, economics, education, folklore, history, language, law, literature and drama, mass culture, music, political science, psychiatry and psychology, public address, religion, science and technology, and sociology and anthropology. Interdisciplinary relevance is further indicated with letter symbols. There are no author indexes. Although considerable attention has been given to *PAIS* (A.1.b:15) in other sections of this handbook, *PAIS's* prime concern is with U.S. public affairs. Similar attention should be given to the *Reader's Guide* (A.1.b:20). The coverage of *Writings on American History* (O.2.e:7) and *America: History and Life* (O.2.e:6) is comprehensive.

Oscar Winther's *Classified Bibliography of the Periodical Literature of the Trans-Mississippi West* (*1811–1967*) (1961–71) (4) is often overlooked as a source for material on many topics other than history. It lists over 9,000 articles from 70 historical and related journals arranged by subject. In addition to chapters on each of the 23 states west of the Mississippi River, there are chapters on agriculture, the frontier, Hispanic America, immigrant groups, Indians, the "inland empire," the Lewis and Clark expedition, the military, the Mormons, national parks and monuments, the Pacific Northwest, reclamation and conservation, and utopian communities, as well as British Columbia, Canada, and Mexico. Each chapter is arranged under such subdivisions as bibliography, general, geography, economics, and politics.

The *Alternative Press Index* (1969–) (5) is a quarterly subject index to over 70 left-of-center magazines (including such titles as *Dissent, The Progressive,* the defunct *I. F. Stone's Bi-Weekly,* and the *New York Review of Books*) and underground newspapers. According to the editors, this index is "one answer to the need to provide access to the mountains of facts, thoughts, and theories which are being turned out by the revolutionary movement of this country and of the world." As well as radical politics, subjects include American Indians, blacks, Chicanos, "gay" liberation, women's liberation, and "the Third World." The index has several frustrating features. The subject headings often present difficulties to those accustomed to traditional bibliographies, but of more concern is the difficulty of obtaining complete runs of particular titles. Some of the periodicals indexed in the *Alternative Press Index* are in the microfilmed *Underground Newspaper Collection* (1965–) (6). About 180 underground newspapers, mostly from the United States, but including titles from Canada, Great Britain, and other countries are microfilmed annually.

O.I.c   Biographical Dictionaries and Directories

Many of the sources mentioned in section A.1.d are useful, most
notably *Biography Index* (A.1.d:10), Hyamson (A.1.d:11), the
New York Times Obituaries Index (A.1.d:12), the *New York
Times Biographical Edition* (A.1.d:13), *Current Biography* (A.1.
d:14), *American Men and Women of Science* (A.1.d:15), and
Slocum (A.1.d:9). *American Men and Women of Science* (A.1.
d:15) and the *Directory of American Scholars* (F.1.c:1) are useful for directory information on scholars in the humanities and
social sciences. Currently about 60,000 brief sketches of prominent
persons are included in *Who's Who in America* (1899–) (1),
issued biennially. The same firm publishes biennial regional directories: *Who's Who in the East* (1943–) (2), *Who's Who in the
Midwest* (1950–) (3), *Who's Who in the South and Southwest*
(1950–) (4), and *Who's Who in the West* (1949–) (5), as well
as the retrospective volumes *Who Was Who in America: Historical Volume, 1607–1896* (1963) (6) and (from 1897) *Who
Was Who in America* (1942–) (7).

The *Dictionary of American Biography* (1928–58) (8) is an
authoritative work in twenty-two volumes, with over 14,000 extensive articles on persons now deceased who made significant contributions to American life and culture. Volume 21, supplement 1,
brings coverage to 1933, and volume 22, supplement 2, to 1940.
The *Concise Dictionary of American Biography* (1964) (9) provides briefer treatment of each article in the larger work, but entries from supplementary volumes have been integrated with the
main alphabet and annotated for reference to the larger set.

Brief information on U.S. political figures of the past and the
present can be found in the *Biographical Directory of the American
Congress, 1774–1971* (1971) (10), the *Official Congressional
Directory* (1809–) (11), Nathan Kane's *Facts about the Presi-
dents* (1968) (12), and *Who's Who in American Politics* (1967/
68–) (13). The *Biographical Directory* has brief information on
U.S. representatives and senators, delegates of the Continental
Congress, territorial delegates, and vice-presidents. The *Official
Congressional Directory,* issued for each Congress, includes biographical sketches of congressmen and their committee assign-
ments, lists of foreign diplomatic representatives in the United
States, and a directory of members of the press accredited to
Congress. *Facts about the Presidents* has biographical and historical
data. *Who's Who in American Politics* is a directory of information on 12,500 political figures and public servants. Included are
federal and state elected officials and cabinet members; key presidential appointees; state and county officials of both major parties;
delegates to national conventions; mayors and council members of

major cities; and leaders of the Liberal, Progressive-Socialist, So-
cialist-Labor, and other minority parties. It is updated every two
years.

O.I.d Encyclopedias and Dictionaries

Although there is no encyclopedia devoted exclusively to the
United States, there is a substantial amount of material in such
general encyclopedias as the *Americana* (A.1.e:6), the *Britannica*
(A.1.e:5), *Colliers,* and *The Columbia Encyclopedia* (A.1.e:7).
Filler's *Dictionary of American Social Reform* (1963) (1) includes
over 3,000 brief definitions of terms and biographical sketches, as
well as abbreviations, court decisions, and related items associated
either directly or indirectly with U.S. social reform. Entries often
include suggestions for obtaining additional information.

The purpose of the *Dictionary of Americanisms* (1951) (2), by
Mitford M. Mathews, is "to treat historically as many as possible
of those words and meanings of words which have been added to
the English language in the United States." Attention is given
etymology and pronunciation; definitions and illustrative quotations
are arranged chronologically; and there is a bibliography. According to the *Dictionary of American Slang* (1960) (3), an extremely
useful reference work for primary research, "American slang is the
body of words and expressions frequently used by or intelligible
to a large portion of the general American public [including taboo
or derogatory words] but not accepted as good, formal usage by
the majority." In addition to a large and representative body of
American slang, there are colloquialisms, cant, jargon, argot, and
idioms common in popular novels and movies. Entries come from
every period of American history, but the emphasis is on modern
slang. Along with definitions are quotations illustrating usage, with
full citations.

O.I.e Handbooks and Yearbooks

Unfortunately, no yearbook gives coverage of the annual events
of the United States over its entire history, although in some respects the *Annual Register* (A.1.g:4) provides brief information.
Two series covering limited periods, however, are worth consulting. Appleton's *Annual Cyclopedia* (1861–1902) (1) was published as an annual supplement to the *American Cyclopedia*
(1878–83). The *Annual Cyclopedia* "is uniform with the *American
Cyclopedia,* and will supplement the latter work so far as relates
to the events of history, the records of religious movements, science, politics, literature, biography, etc."[1] Each volume is indexed.
Volumes of the *American Yearbook* (1911–50) (2) are arranged

in such broad categories as political (national and international), government functions, economics and business, and social conditions. Although the events of the year are of primary concern, coverage includes a brief survey of antecedent events and policies. Often lists of periodicals and organizations associated with various aspects of American society are given, along with statistical charts and selected bibliographies. For example, the volume for 1947 contains a survey by William Anthony Aery on "Negro Education," focusing on economics, enrollment, problems of equalization, favorable trends, the problem of discrimination, professional level, segregated education, college-education enrollment, teachers' salaries, faculty shortages, graduate education, professional education, Negro physicians, a test case in Oklahoma, and a South Carolina decision. There is a list of important publications. Each volume is indexed.

The *Encyclopedia of American Facts and Dates* (1966) (3) provides chronological treatment from A.D. 986 to 1965 in columnar format of the following topics: politics and government, war, disasters, vital statistics; books, painting, drama, architecture, sculpture; science, industry, economics, education, religion, philosophy; and sports, fashions, popular entertainment, folklore, and society. There is a detailed index.

O.1.f Newspapers and News Digests

Suggestions for using newspapers in research, along with a selected bibliography concerned with various aspects of research with newspapers, appears in the *Harvard Guide* (O.2.e:5). *Newspapers on Microfilm* (1967) (1) indicates the locations of over 16,000 newspapers in libraries in the United States and Canada. The *New York Times* (A.1.g:1) is especially useful for research on U.S. topics of the last 120 years. A "Subject Index" of the *Christian Science Monitor* (1908–) (2) was begun in 1960. The *Monitor* excels at covering events with considerably more thoroughness than is usual in newspaper reporting. The *Wall Street Journal* (1899–) (3) is selectively indexed in *PAIS* (A.1.b:15), as well as having its own index. Access to underground newspapers is provided by the *Underground Newspaper Collection* (O.1.b:6). *Facts on File* (A.1.g:6) is useful for verifying dates, events, and so on; as a source of texts of speeches and documents; and as a summary of news events.

Newsbank Urban Affairs Library (1970–) (4) provides, on microfiche, reports on urban political, economic, and social conditions in the United States from over 150 newspapers of 103 cities in 45 states. The reports are clipped from the newspapers, microfilmed, and arranged according to the following categories: education, employment, environment, government structure, health, housing and urban renewal, law and order, minority economic development, political development, race relations, transportation, and welfare and poverty. All varieties of the press are represented, including black, underground, and conservative, as well as the large-circulation daily newspapers. Up to 70,000 reports are filmed annually. Indexes are provided for each category, with annual cumulations. Currently, only cities are identified in the indexes by a letter code, but a *Newsbank* official indicated that in the future, newspapers are to be so identified. Unfortunately, the subject entries are quite general, and since indexing is done monthly it is often difficult to identify a specific event. This problem is partially overcome by having items from a given month arranged according to narrow topics within the broad categories on each microfiche card; by examining the whole microfiche card, one is able to find a report or a number of reports on the desired event.

O.1.g   Statistics Sources

American Statistics Index (1973–) (1), an annual with monthly and quarterly supplements, promises to be a descriptive guide to statistical publications issued by the U.S. government. In addition to a bibliographical citation, each entry includes a description of the publication's contents, references to related publications, technical notes, lists of tables, and notes of illustrative material. There are indexes of names and subjects, and one arranged by categories. The initial volume includes publications of the last decade. At first, coverage is to be limited to social statistics (from the Departments of Justice, HEW, and Labor, and the Census Bureau, including results of the 1970 censuses of population and housing), with expansion projected to include statistics published on commerce, agriculture, and natural resources.

Considerable attention has already been given Wasserman's *Statistics Sources* (A.1.h:1) and the *Encyclopedia of Business Information Sources* (A.1.b:7). Often, however, the annual *Statistical Abstract of the U.S.* (1878–) (2) will provide the statistical information required. The statistics are from many sources—private as well as public—on social, political, and economic conditions in the United States. Other valuable features are the descriptive headnotes and indications of sources, the former explaining the method of obtaining the statistics, calculations, and so on, the latter a guide to more detailed information. A useful companion to the *Statistical Abstract* is the *Historical Statistics of the United States: Colonial Times to 1962* (1965) (3). Along with headnotes and indications of sources, it includes over 8,000 statistical time series showing U.S. economic and social development from 1610 to 1962. (*Cross-*

Polity Time-Series Data [I.1.g:7] also contains historical statistical data on the United States.) The *County and City Data Book* (1949–) (4) provides statistical information selected from government and private sources; it covers the four geographic regions and nine divisions into which the Bureau of the Census divides the nation, as well as the states, counties, standard metropolitan statistical areas, urbanized areas, cities, and unincorporated urban places. A description of the statistics produced by the U.S. government is found in the *Statistical Services of the United States Government* (1968) (5).

Section 2

O.2.a   Anthropology

Gordon Gibson's "Bibliography of Anthropological Bibliographies: The Americas" (N.2.a:1) is a compilation of the bibliographies published before 1955. Arrangement is by geographical area, then alphabetically by author. The *International Bibliography of Social and Cultural Anthropology* (B.1.b:4) brings this list up to date. The best single-volume bibliography is Murdock's *Ethnographic Bibliography of North America* (1960) (1), a listing of over 17,000 selected items on primitive and historical cultures, arranged by geographical area, then by tribal group. There is an index of tribes. *America: History and Life* (O.2.e:6) regularly features a section on Indians.

Hodge's *Handbook of American Indians North of Mexico* (1907–10) (2) remains a valuable source. It treats all the tribes north of Mexico, including the Eskimo, and those tribes south of the boundary more or less affiliated with those of the United States. It aims to give a brief description of every linguistic stock, confederacy, tribe, subtribe or tribal division, and settlement known to history or even tradition, as well as the origin and derivation of every name treated, whenever such is known, and to record every form of the name and every other appellation that could be learned. These names, in alphabetical order, are assembled as cross-references in part 2. Each tribal entry has a brief account of the ethnic relations of the tribe, its history, its location at various periods, statistics of population, and so on. Accompanying each entry is an authoritative bibliography.

John R. Swanton's *The Indian Tribes of North America* (1952) (3) contains extensive information on Indian tribes, including location, history, and population, and has a detailed index. The *Arctic Bibliography* (1953–) (4) provides access to works on native peoples of the Arctic and sub-Arctic areas. It is an extensive, annotated bibliography with about 100,000 entries, including works on administration and government, Eskimos, archaeology, economic and social conditions, expeditions, mapping, population, communication, colonization, transportation, and ethnographic material.

The Human Relations Area Files (I.3.1) contain data on forty-two North American tribes and historical groups, as follows:

Aleut	Crow	Yurok
Tlinglit	Dhegiha (Omaha,	Eastern Apache
Copper Eskimo	Kansa, Ponca,	Navaho
Nahane	Osage)	Plateau Yumans
Bellacoola	Gros Ventre	Walapai,
Nootka (Makah,	Mandau	Havasupai)
Nootka)	Pawnee	River Yumans
Ojibwa (Chippewa,	Plateau Indians	(Maricopa)
Ojibwa)	Northern Paiute	Tewa
Montagnais	Southeast Salish	Washo
(Naskapi)	(Sanpoil,	Zuni
Micmac	Nespelem,	Aztec
Historical	Sinkaietk,	Papago
Massachusetts	Couer d'Alene,	Seri
Delaware	Okanogan,	Tarahumara
Iroquois	Flathead)	Tarasco
Creek	Pomo	Tepoztlan
Comanche	Tubatulabal	Tzeltal
Winnebago	Yokuts	Yucatec Maya

Charles Haywood's two-volume *Bibliography of North American Folklore and Folksong* (1961) (5) lists over 40,000 books, articles, and recordings, some accompanied by descriptions. Entries in volume 1, *American People North of Mexico,* are arranged by subject, under regional, ethnic, and occupational headings. Volume 2, *American Indians North of Mexico,* is classified by cultural areas, with subsections on folklore and music. The Library of Congress's *Folklore of the North American Indians* (1969) (6) is a selective, annotated bibliography of recorded folklore. Within each of the eleven culture areas (including Eskimos) are listed source books, followed by children's editions. Folklore studies, anthologies, bibliographies, and indexes are listed in a final section. There are indexes of subjects, authors, and titles. Robert Wildhaber, a well-known European folklorist, in his "Bibliographical Introduction to American Folklife" (1964) (7), discusses the works he considers useful and important in several areas of American folklore. Marjorie Tallman's *Dictionary of American Folklore* (1959) (8) contains brief definitions of works and phrases related to folk-

lore originating or popular in North America, but critics say it is
unreliable and uneven.

O.2.b   Demography

Along with *ASI* (O.1.g:1), the *Statistical Abstract* (O.1.g:2)
and related publications, the *Encyclopedia of Business Information Sources* (A.1.b:7) and *Statistics Sources* (A.1.h:1) are
the most useful sources for demographic data. For intensive needs
see part C.

O.2.c   Economics and Economic History

Many of the items mentioned in part D, especially in the second
section, are concerned with U.S. economics. For example, the Mc-
Graw-Hill *Dictionary of Modern Economics* (D.1.d:1) and Horton's *Dictionary of Modern Economics* (D.1.d:3) are primarily
directed to aspects of U.S. economics, while the Gale Research
Company's Management Information Guide series is almost exclusively concerned with the United States. *F and S Index to Corporations and Industries* (1965–) (1) is a weekly index (with
monthly, quarterly, and annual cumulations) to articles from about
100 periodicals, to such other sources as financial and corporation
report findings on industries, to individual corporations' report
findings on industries, and to individual corporations in the United
States. It is arranged by SIC (Standard Industrial Classification)
number or product, by region, and by company. International coverage is provided by *F and S International* (I.2.c:1). Wasserman's
Encyclopedia of Business Information Sources (A.1.b:7) and *Statistics Sources* (A.1.h:1) should not be overlooked. *United States
and Canada* (I.1.a:5) is an authoritative atlas. Many bibliographies in the Council of Planning Librarians' *Exchange Bibliography* (E.2.d:9) are concerned with economics, including problems
of public finance and social economics. Parts of *Metropolitan
Communities* (O.2.g:28) cover urban economics. Dorothy Tompkins's *Poverty in the U.S. during the Sixties* (O.2.h:2) should not
be overlooked. Andrew Brimmer and Harriet Harper's "Economists' Perception of Minority Economic Problems: A View of
Emerging Literature" (1970) (2) directs attention to about 500
recent books and articles on minority problems in the United
States. Topics include poverty, labor, and manpower; the economics of discrimination; the economics of race; black capitalism; the
income of nonwhites; economic aspects of education; and economic aspects of crime and social organization.

American Economic and Business History Information Sources
(1971) (3), edited by Robert W. Lovett, is a large, well-annotated bibliography of books and information sources on all phases

of economic history. George Roger Taylor's *American Economic History before 1860* (O.2.c:8) and Edward C. Kirkland's *American Economic History since 1860* (O.2.c:9), briefer, selective compilations designed for undergraduates, are also useful, although they lack annotation. Lovett's volume contains chapters on economic history, business history, agricultural history, labor history, the history of science and technology, and general reference works. Four appendixes list and very briefly describe articles and books on the historiography and methodology of economic and business history, as well as organizations and journals concerned with those disciplines. Chapters begin with a section devoted to reference works and bibliographies, arranged in the following categories: organizations and journals, source collections, bibliographies, and surveys. Where sufficient material exists, further groupings are made for texts, readings, series reprints, and specialized aids. Chapter 1, "Economic History," lists general titles. Most of chapter 2, "Business History," is devoted to firms, biographies of businessmen, and industry studies, as well as "what might be called business in history" (i.e., studies of individual firms and of the entrepreneur and his place in history). Special consideration is given Lorna Daniells's bibliography *Studies in Enterprise* (1957) (4); bibliographical supplements in the *Business History Review;* the model bibliography by Henrietta Larson, *Guide to Business History* (1948) (5), a critical and annotated bibliography of over 4,900 entries; and the historiographical surveys by Thomas C. Cochran, "Economic History, Old and New" (1969) and Arthur H. Cole, "Economic History in the U.S.: Formative Years of a Discipline" (1968). In chapter 3, "Agricultural History," selected titles bearing on the relation of agricultural history to economic history are listed; such additional bibliographies as John T. Schlebecker's *Bibliography of Books and Pamphlets on the History of Agriculture in the U.S., 1609–1967* (1969) (6), Pursell and Rogers's *Preliminary List of References for the History of Agriculture, Science, and Technology in the U.S.* (1966) (7), and the "History" entries in the *Biological and Agricultural Index* (E.2.c:4) are noted. As well as general accounts, there are such special topics as cooperatives, selected commodities, and land policy. In chapter 4, "Labor History," only those topics closely related to economic history are described. Special topics considered separately include unions (subdivided into several parts), population, immigration, the blacks and slavery, and wages. Chapter 5, "History of Science and Technology," and chapter 6, "General Reference Works," emphasize works of special interest to business and economic historians. The index combines names, titles, and subjects.

Taylor's *American Economic History before 1860* (1969) (8) and Edward C. Kirkland's *American Economic History since 1860* (1971) (9) can be used most effectively if more information on the unannotated entries is obtained from Lovett's *American Economic and Business History* (3), Larson's *Guide to Business History* (O.2.c:5), or such other recommended titles as *Guide to the Study of the U.S.* (O.1.b:2), Schlebecker (O.2.c:6), and Egbert (O.2.e:32).

O.2.d Geography

In addition to the bibliographical coverage given the United States among the items discussed in part E, especially the *Research Catalog* (E.1.b:4) and *Current Geographical Publications* (E.1.b:5), B. J. L. Berry's *Bibliographic Guide to the Economic Regions of the U.S.* (1963) (1) lists 378 items, most of them annotated. Perhaps of greater use to geographical research, particularly research concerned with narrow aspects of the United States, is the Council of Planning Librarians' *Exchange Bibliography* (E.2.d:9).

Douglas R. McManis's *Historical Geography of the U.S.* (1965) (2) is a selection of over 3,500 scholarly books and articles, published up to 1964, covering prehistoric times to 1900 (but excluding Alaska and Hawaii). Agricultural history is well covered by Schlebecker (O.2.c:6). Paullin (O.2.e:1) and the *American Heritage Pictorial Atlas* (O.2.e:3) are recommended atlases of historical geography.

O.2.e History

Selecting from the numerous sources available for the study of U.S. history and maintaining a balanced coverage is a difficult task. The volumes described here have proven their usefulness for all levels of research, from the simplest to the most intensive, for undergraduate students and for doctoral candidates, for those seeking a list of titles to read for a particular topic, and as sources of suggested works for obtaining more detailed investigation. Effective use of bibliographies and reference works—it cannot be stressed too much—requires some familiarity with their contents, and time spent becoming experienced in using them will be richly rewarded.

Atlases.   Charles O. Paullin's *Atlas of the Historical Geography of the U.S.* (1932) (1) contains 688 maps and descriptive text of excellent detail covering such topics as natural environment; cartography, 1492–1867; Indians, 1567–1930; explorations; settlements; populations and towns, 1650–1790; states, territories, and cities, 1790–1930; and many narrower topics. Lord's *Historical Atlas of the U.S.* (1953) (2), intended for students, is especially useful for its maps showing economic development and distribution of population. The *American Heritage Pictorial Atlas of United States History* (1966) (3) is an attractive volume consisting of 210 newly commissioned maps in color, 150 historical illustrations and maps, and a substantial text. Coverage ranges from the Ice Age to the 1960s. Some material included is not available in Paullin (1) or Lord (2), and Winchell (A.1.b:13) notes there is a particularly good section on U.S. operations in World War I. James Truslow Adams's *Atlas of American History* (1943) (4) is designed as a companion for his *Dictionary of American History* (O.2.e:11).

Bibliographies. Along with the *Guide to the Study of the U.S.* (O.1.b:2), the *Harvard Guide to American History* (1955) (5) is a standard source, but it is important that its scope, arrangement, and format are understood. Chapters 1–5, the first of two main divisions, consist of 66 essays dealing with the methods, resources, and materials of American history, including a list of suggested works for further investigation. Chapters 6–30 consist of detailed reading lists arranged according to historical periods or topics. Usually each chapter comprises five parts: a summary outlining topics treated, general treatments, special studies, documentary sources, and bibliographies. The 40,000-odd works cited are given full entries only once, generally where first mentioned. If an incomplete citation is encountered, use the index to locate the complete entry.

Similar in format to *Historical Abstracts* (F.1.b:10), *America: History and Life* (1964–) (6) annually abstracts about 3,000 articles on North American history and culture from over 2,000 periodicals. There are 6 sections: North America; Canada; U.S. history to 1945; U.S. history since 1945; regional, state, and local history; and "history, the humanities, and social sciences." There is a combined index (including cumulative volumes every five years) of author, biographical, geographical, and subject entries.

One of the most neglected bibliographies in U.S. history is *Writings on American History* (1902–3, 1906–40, 1948–[59?]) (7). All books and articles, wherever published, containing material on the history of the United States and Canada (national, regional, and local), and books published in the United States and Europe on Latin America and the Philippines were included up to 1935. Coverage was reduced in 1936 to cover only the United States and its outlying possessions. History is broadly interpreted, to include diplomatic history, military and naval history, social and economic history (anthropology, fine arts, education, music, religion, science, and technology), and biography. Although the organization has been adjusted over the years, a subject arrangement is used, and each volume has an author and subject index. Volumes to 1935 include analysis of the contents of books and brief annotations, and note the existence of reviews. No volumes were published for 1941–47. Compilation of annual volumes continued in 1948, but at present 1959 is the most recent year covered. Reviews are no longer noted, but most entries are briefly annotated. In 1956 a cumulative index covering 1902–40 was issued; according to the foreword, indexing was slightly expanded, so that it contains entries not found in the separate indexes. White (A.1. b:10), however, claims it is not always reliable. From 1948, indexing was "expanded to aid in the pursuit of a single topic through all regions and periods" (Winchell [A.1.b:13]).

Published by the American Historical Association, the Service Center for Teachers of History (1956–70) (8) is a series of excellent, brief bibliographical essays in which specialists discuss various interpretations of major issues. Among titles are *Civil War and Reconstruction, The American Frontier, The New Deal in Historical Perspective, The Far West in American History, Emigration and Immigration, American Intellectual History,* and *American Religious History.* Since this is a numbered series, in most cases there is a series entry card in a library's card catalog, indicating which numbers are held by that library.[2] Another series, American Problem Studies (1962–) (9), comprises studies of crucial questions in U.S. history, utilizing readings in the historiography of the period. Items in this series are not numbered, and it is unlikely that the series card in the card catalog will indicate anything beyond the fact that titles are listed only by author, title, and subject. A complete list is available in the Holt, Rinehart & Winston catalog in *PTLA* (A.1.b:30). Among titles issued are *The Atomic Bomb, The Frontier Thesis, The Abolitionists, The Progressive Era, Populism,* and *Reconstruction.* Oldest and best-known among these types of anthologies is Problems in American Civilization (1949–) (10), sometimes referred to as the Amherst series. Each volume consists of a collection of primary and secondary sources on a particular issue as interpreted by various authorities. A brief bibliography of suggested reading is included. A complete list is available in the D. C. Heath catalog in *PTLA* (A.1.b:30). Among the volumes are *Franklin D. Roosevelt and the Supreme Court, Lincoln and the Coming of the Civil War, Evolution and Religion: The Conflict between Science and Theology in Modern America, The Declaration of Independence and the Constitution, The Causes of the*

American Civil War, The Meaning of Jacksonian Democracy, The New Deal: Revolution or Evolution?, Reconstruction in the South, Slavery as a Cause of the Civil War, Jackson vs. Biddle: Struggle over the Second Bank of the United States, The Causes of the American Revolution, and *Pearl Harbor: Roosevelt and the Coming of the War.* The Berkeley Series in American History (22) has similar usefulness.

Encyclopedias and Dictionaries. Consisting of six volumes and an index, the *Dictionary of American History* (1940–63) (11), edited by James Truslow Adams, contains more than 6,000 articles by specialists, with brief bibliographies for most entries. The work covers political, economic, social, industrial, and cultural history; biography is excluded. Among the entries are popular names for congressional legislation, court cases, and brief descriptions of the presidential campaigns to 1960. The 1963 index includes the five main volumes and the first supplement. The *Concise Dictionary of American History* (1962) (12) is a regrouping and digesting of articles from the original work and its supplement. Another set edited by James Truslow Adams, the *Album of American History* (1960) (13), consists of six volumes of photographs, pictures, drawings, and text illustrating and describing the social history of the United States from colonial times to 1953.

The *Encyclopedia of American History* (1970) (14) combines a chronological and topical approach to U.S. history with a biographical dictionary of 400 prominent Americans, living and dead. Part 1 presents major political and military issues, along with accounts of explorations, settlements, and colonial and Revolutionary problems. Part 2 examines nonpolitical aspects, with discussions of constitutional development and demographic, economic, scientific, and cultural trends. The years 1965–69 are covered in a supplementary section. "Dates, events and achievements, and persons stand out, but the text is designed to be read as a narrative" (from introduction). Maps and charts are included. There are no bibliographies, but books by people in the biographical section are noted. There is a separate index for the supplementary section.

Webster's *Guide to American History* (1971) (15) is a chronology of the important events annually to 1969, with brief quotations from the writings of noted Americans, some illustrations, historical maps in color, and biographical sketches of over 1,000 historically prominent Americans. The *Oxford Companion to American History* (1966) (16) and Kull and Kull's *Chronological Encyclopedia of American History* (1969)(17) are similar. The *Oxford Companion,* with over 4,000 topical articles and 1,800 biographical sketches, gives attention to social, political, and labor movements; the observations of travelers, both foreign and domestic; and art, science, commerce, literature, education, law, sports, and entertainment. The *Chronological Encyclopedia of American History* briefly describes more than 10,000 events in American political, social, economic, and cultural history.

The formats of the *Encyclopedia of the American Revolution* (1966) (18) and *The Civil War Dictionary* (1966) (19) are very similar. Each consists of over 1,500 brief articles, including about 600 biographical sketches. The emphasis is on military events and issues, with maps. Many passages are quoted from other sources. As well as suggested sources of additional information for most articles, each volume has a partially annotated bibliography and indexes of maps.

Both *Makers of America* (O.2.h:3) and *The Annals of America* (1969) (20) have sparked controversy among historians as to their worth. *Annals of America* combines the elements of a "documentary" history and the principles of a detailed index. The set consists of 18 volumes of more than 2,000 selected, chronologically arranged writings dating from 1493 to 1968, of over 1,100 authors; a two-volume "conspectus" containing 25 chapters of topics (or issues) in American history; an index with a chronological listing of all selections; and name, author, and source indexes. Among the chapters are "National Character," "Frontier," "Constitutionalism," "Pluralism," "Individualism," "Minorities," "Standard of Living," "Family," and "Education." Each chapter includes a lengthy essay tracing the development of the issue throughout U.S. history, with reference to passages among the selections bearing on the issue. It is well illustrated with contemporary pictures, cartoons, and so on.

Collections of Documents. Commager's single-volume *Documents of American History* (1963) (21) is the best-known collection of historical documents, but the *Harvard Guide* (O.2.e:5), *Annals of America* (O.2.e:20), and *Makers of America* (O.2.h:3) should not be overlooked. ("Documentary Sources" is the fourth section of chapters devoted to historical periods or topics in the *Harvard Guide.*) Commager's volume consists of over 600 basic sources arranged chronologically from the Age of Discovery to 1962. Often overlooked as a source of documents, volumes of the Berkeley Series in American History (1963–) (22) are studies using annotated primary sources with chronologies and bibliographies. Consult the Rand-McNally catalog in *PTLA* (A.1.b:30) for a complete list. Among titles issued are *Labor and the New Deal, Spoilmen and Reformers, Adams and Jefferson: "Posterity Must Judge," The Puritan in the Enlightenment: Franklin and Edwards, Reconstruction and the Freedman, The War with*

Mexico: Why Did It Happen?, The Cold War: Containment and Its Critics, and *Populism: Nostalgic or Progressive?*

Special Topics. This section is intended to suggest some of the many bibliographies of particular topics or periods. Perhaps the most useful are the Goldentree Bibliographies in American History. They are inexpensive and designed for undergraduate research, and although they lack annotation, they are highly recommended. In general they are arranged with bibliographical sources listed first, followed by lists of articles and books on various aspects of the subject. *American Social History since 1860* (1969) (23), by Robert H. Bremner et al., is one of the most useful because it covers a relatively neglected area. According to the editors, "social history is not a precisely delimited field of study, but a way of looking at the past which seeks to recognize and reveal relationships among aspects of human experience." Thus, besides "everyday events" and "the life of the common man," it is concerned with "the structure of society, social change and mobility, and styles of life in various classes and cultures." Sources include books and articles from many branches of history and related disciplines. Among chapter topics are the following: bibliographical guides, selected reference and historiographical works; general surveys; the nation and its sections; the rise of the city; the American people (population, social classes, immigration, Negroes, Indians, women, the family, children and youth); work; the American and his attitude toward other Americans; religious life; social and political thought; social problems and reform movements; cultural life; education and intellectual trends; communications; and science. There is an author index. Other Goldentree Bibliographies are Green's *The American Colonies in the Eighteenth Century, 1689–1783* (1969) (24); Grob's *American Social History before 1860* (1970) (25); Donald's *The Nation in Crisis, 1861–1877* (1969) (26); Link's *The Progressive Era and the Great War* (1969) (27); and Burr's *Religion in American Life* (1971) (28). Other titles in the series are listed in the AHM catalog in *PTLA* (A.1.b:30).

Colonization and Settlement in the Americas (1960) (29) lists articles, books, and maps published up to the mid-1950s concerning the history of colonization and settlement.

Guide to the Diplomatic History of the U.S., 1775–1921 (1935) (30), by Samuel Flagg Bemis, is a substantial bibliography in narrative format arranged by historical period, with a system of numbering citations somewhat similar to that of this handbook. Included in three parts are over 5,000 books and articles in many languages, printed and manuscript sources, and indexes of collections of personal papers and authors.

Two specialized bibliographies accompany James Ward Smith's *Religion in American Life* (1961–) (31) and Donald Drew Egbert's *Socialism and American Life* (1952) (32). Volumes 1–3 of *Religion in American Life* are devoted to the history of religion in the United States, and volume 4, parts 1 and 2, is a comprehensive critical bibliography of religion in the United States, edited by Nelson Burr. (Burr's *Religion in American Life* [28] is more recent.) Volume 2, by T. D. Seymour Bassett, of *Socialism and American Life,* is entitled *Bibliography, Descriptive and Critical.* The *Guide to the Study of the U.S.* (O.1.b:2) notes that "in one of the most elaborate contributions to American intellectual history thus far made, various hands present the European background, Christian Communitarianism, secular Utopianism, the development of American Marxism, and the relations of American socialism to philosophy, economics, political theory, sociology, psychology, literature and art. The bibliography, which runs to 510 pages, is interlaced with so elaborate a commentary as to constitute an independent work in its own right."

Regional and Local History.   Ramon F. Adams's *The Rampaging Herd* (1959) (33) and *Burs under the Saddle* (1964) (34) are examples of bibliographies of regional history. The former is subtitled "A Bibliography of Books and Pamphlets on Men and Events in the Cattle Industry" and the latter "A Second Look at Books and Histories of the West." Both are crammed with discussions of historical inaccuracies and legends. Many other regional bibliographies are unavailable in published form, but often exist in the form of card catalogs for special regional collections. The publishing firm of G. K. Hall has published many of the larger, more well-known regional bibliographies. The Hall catalog can be examined in *PTLA* (A.1.b:30).

Clifford L. Lord is the general editor of the Localized History series (1965–) (35), with almost fifty inexpensive paperback volumes devoted to individual states, regions, cities, or ethnic groups. Written by specialists, each is designed to provide a guide to the published and manuscript sources of what had been a neglected area. Titles include *Tennessee* (1965), *The Ohio Valley* (1967), *Georgia* (1965), *Montana* (1970), *Kentucky* (1965), *The Wisconsin Valley* (1969), *New Mexico* (1970), *Illinois* (1968), *Houston* (1969), *Minnesota* (1966), *Oklahoma* (1965), *The Canadian River Valley* (1970), *The Norwegians in America* (1967), *The Upper Mississippi Valley* (1966), *Wyoming* (1966), *Hawaii* (1966), *The Finns in America* (1968), *The Sacramento Valley* (1968), *The Mexicans in America* (1968), *Raleigh-Durham-Chapel Hill* (1968), *New York* (1968), *Los Angeles* (1965), *The Greeks in America* (1967), *The Irish in America* (1968), and *The Germans in America* (1967). A complete list is available in the Teachers College catalog in *PTLA* (A.1.b:30).

O.2.f Literature and Fine Arts

Although the primary concern of this book is the social sciences, often in doing research on these subjects it is necessary to consult works associated with literature or art. A few of the most useful items are given here, with suggested titles for further investigation, if necessary. Spiller's *Literary History of the U.S.* (1963) (1) is the best survey and is accompanied by an extensive bibliography. Richard Altick's *Selective Bibliography for the Study of English and American Literature* (1971) (2) provides a convenient and authoritative guide to other more specialized research aids such as literary encyclopedias, dictionaries, handbooks, general histories, and bibliographies. Walford (A.1.b:12) and Winchell (A.1.b:13) describe reference works in art criticism and art history. The *McGraw-Hill Encyclopedia of Art* (B.2.b:1) is especially worth consulting.

O.2.g Political Science

Brock (G.1.b:1) and the Library of Congress's *Guide to the Study of the U.S.* (O.1.b:2) are good single-volume sources for selected studies on all levels of politics and government in the United States. In the latter work, items are arranged in the following sequence: federal politics (executive, legislative, judicial); elections; state politics; local government; political parties and political groups; foreign affairs; and special topics. Plano and Greenberg's *American Political Dictionary* (1967) (1) is similar in intent and format to their *International Relations Dictionary* (G.2.c:5). The *American Political Dictionary* consists of 1,100-odd terms, agencies, court cases, and statutes "which are most relevant for a basic comprehension of American governmental institutions, practices, and problems." Each term is briefly defined; its significance in the governmental process is then described. Since terms are listed alphabetically in broad subject categories, it is often necessary to use the index; the editors note, however, that a "complete reading of a chapter will provide a useful, basic understanding of an entire subject area." Among the categories are the U.S. Constitution (background, principles, development); federal union; immigration and citizenship; civil liberties; political parties and pressure groups; congressional and state-level legislative processes; office and powers of the president; the judicial process; government, business, and labor; health, education, and welfare; and foreign policy, international affairs, and national defense.

Federal Politics.   A large amount of published material concerning
the U.S. government (executive, legislative, and judicial branches)
—much of it interrelated and requiring a certain amount of familiarity and sophistication to use effectively—is available. Brock
(G.1.b:1) reproduces typical pages and gives descriptions of how
to use many of the publications discussed below.

Among the reference works on Congress, the most useful is the
Congressional Quarterly Almanac (1943–) (2) and its related
publications, *Congressional Quarterly Weekly Report* (1943–)
(3), *Congress and the Nation* (1965–) (4), and *Guide to the
Congress of the United States* (1972) (5). The latter provides an
examination of the origins and development of Congress, its functioning, its powers, pressures upon it, prospects for change, and ethics. Each chapter is appropriately subdivided and accompanied by
a bibliography of sources. The *Weekly Report* provides an impar-
tial summary and interpretation of activities in Congress, as well as
activities of the president and his cabinet, the Supreme Court, and
lobbying activities of many groups. Each issue has information on
the status of pending legislation (i.e., whether it has been sent to
committee, whether there have been roll-call votes on the floor,
and so on); there are quarterly and annual cumulative indexes.
The *Almanac* appears annually, providing briefer treatment of the
material that has appeared in the *Weekly Reports,* but it does not
entirely supersede them. At present, *Congress and the Nation* is
in two volumes and is a "distillation and elaboration" of information contained in the Almanacs of activities of Congress from 1945
to 1968. Volume 1 reviews legislative and political aspects of such
topics as foreign policy, civil rights, and natural resources; there
is a directory of persons and events. Volume 2 covers similar topics, but lacks a directory of persons and events. Subsequent volumes are planned. A somewhat similar intent is found in the
Congressional Index (1937–) (6), a weekly loose-leaf publication
that indexes by subject, author, and bill number all congressional
bills and resolutions of general interest. Bills are traced from introduction to passage or defeat. Although primarily useful as a
key to pending legislation, it provides information on members of
Congress (voting records, political affiliations, committee appointments, and so on) and indicates bill numbers of companion bills
in the House or Senate. Combining statistical data, descriptive,
and interpretive comment, the biennial *Almanac of American Politics* (1972–) (7) promises to be a reliable single-volume source
of biographical sketches, voting records, and ratings of senators
and representatives, along with brief descriptions of the political,
economic, and demographic situations in states and individual
districts.

Presidential activities, speeches, executive orders, and so on, can be traced in the *U.S. Federal Register* (1936–) (8) and the *Weekly Compilation of Presidential Documents* (1965–) (9). The *Federal Register* is a daily compilation of executive orders, administrative regulations and rules, and a mass of regulatory decrees from executive offices, commissions, and other groups. The *Weekly Compilation of Presidential Documents* contains transcripts of presidential news conferences, messages to Congress, speeches, and other items. Both have weekly indexes, with quarterly and annual cumulations.

Coming shortly after the establishment of the *Federal Register* was the establishment of the *Code of Federal Regulations* (1938–) (10), which provides codification of all existing presidential orders and administrative regulations such as treaties and executive agreements, reorganization plans, proclamations, and executive orders. The *CFR* comprises 50 titles (or categories) which frequently correspond to those of the *U.S. Code* (O.2.g:15). Volumes are revised annually (with three exceptions, for which supplements have been issued), and there is a general index, revised as of 1955; another index is expected. In addition, each title has an index.

The *U.S. Government Organization Manual* (1937–) (11), revised annually, gives information about the functions, administrative structure, and principal officers of the agencies and subdivisions of the legislative, judicial, and executive branches. A supplemental section lists quasi-official agencies, organization charts, abbreviations, and acronyms, as well as abolished and transferred agencies. There are indexes of names, agencies, and departments.

The *Congressional Record* (1789–) (12) is the official record of debates in Congress. (Its title has been changed from time to time.) Several features of the *Record* are confusing, especially materials appended by congressmen. The following are included in the *Record:* the introduction of all bills, resolutions, and amendments; debates in both houses; the texts of many bills and resolutions; simple and concurrent resolutions, printed as passed; presidential messages; and treaties, when debated. In addition, there is an appendix in which may be printed communications from government departments concerned with pending legislation; extensions of the remarks of representatives or senators, inserted in the *Record* rather than expressed on the floor; and much miscellaneous material inserted by congressmen. Unfortunately, some matter inserted in the appendix is deleted from the cumulations that appear as bound volumes of the *Congressional Record;* tracing fugitive material such as this is often impossible. Consult Schmeckebier (O.3:1) or Brock (G.1.b:1) for procedures for using this source. (Brock includes examples of typical indexes and pages.)

At the end of each session of Congress the texts of all laws passed are printed in *U.S. Statutes at Large* (1789–) (13). A summary of the content and purpose of bills and resolutions passed by Congress is contained in the Library of Congress's *Digest of Public General Bills and Selected General Bills* (1936–) (14). The *United States Code* (1926–) (15), a subject arrangement of all federal laws presently in force, is kept up to date by periodic supplements and revisions.

Students may discover that finding Supreme Court decisions is complicated, often requiring the assistance of a reference librarian. Once the principles of identifying cases are understood, however, finding individual cases is not difficult. According to Schmeckebier (O.3:1), "the publication of the decisions of the Supreme Court of the U.S. has run the gamut from entirely commercial publishing, through commercial publishing with official sanction, to complete government publishing." Currently decisions are published annually in volumes entitled *United States Reports* (1875–) (16). Several other commercially published services, some having annotations, are available in many academic libraries. Titles of preceding cumulations of decisions are described by Schmeckebier; the crazy-quilt pattern he depicts is what students will encounter in college libraries, but fortunately a method of identifying individual cases (a combination of the volume number of *United States Reports* and the case number) has been devised (outlined in Schmeckebier), and once this method is understood, cases are not difficult to find, particularly if Corwin's *Constitution of the United States Annotated* (1964) (17) or a commercially published service such as the *United States Supreme Court Digest* (1943–) (18) is used. In Corwin, for each clause of the Constitution and its amendments, there are listed citations to leading cases of the Supreme Court, an abstract of the ruling of the court, and in some cases a brief quotation from the decision. At the end of the volume are lists of cases cited, and acts of Congress, as well as state and local legislation, that have been declared unconstitutional, with citations of the cases. Included with the cases cited are their identifying numbers. By consulting Corwin to determine the identifying number of a particular case or cases, one can readily discover in which volume of the *United States Reports* texts of decisions of the required case are contained; the volume number is marked prominently on the spine of each volume. Note, however, that Corwin goes up to June 1964 only; decisions handed down since that date or not included in Corwin will have to be located in the individual indexes of *United States Reports*. Another difficulty often encountered for recent cases is the different methods of referring to cases. The Supreme Court term is from October to June, but a term is identified as the "October term" of a given year. Thus the term beginning October 1959, but ending in June of 1960 is the October term, 1959, and decisions appear in the volumes of that term, even though handed down in 1960. However, decisions are usually disclosed in the spring, and some receive considerable attention from the press, which identifies them with the current year. The *United States Supreme Court Digest* (1943–) (18) comprises a more comprehensive approach to information about individual cases. Its cost, however, precludes its purchase by many college libraries. Excellent descriptions of the *Digest of the United States Supreme Court Reports* and other similar services are contained in Price and Bitner's *Effective Legal Research* (1969) (19). Another source—probably more widely available—is *United States Law Week* (1933–) (20), a weekly loose-leaf service providing information on and digests of statutes, federal and state court decisions, and federal agency rulings; a journal of proceedings of the Supreme Court, summary orders of the Court, cases docketed and summaries of cases recently filed, a calendar of hearings scheduled and special articles on Supreme Court work, including summaries of arguments in important cases, and reports on cases argued and awaiting decision; and full texts of opinions (supplemented with headnotes) and a list of opinions for a given term of the Court. Indexes for the general-law sections and for the Supreme Court sections appear at regular intervals.

Elections. *America Votes* (1956–) (21) is a biennial statistical guide from the late 1940s for presidential, senatorial, congressional, and gubernatorial elections. Tables carry data down to the county level (to ward level for some major cities) and give percentage breakdowns of votes by major parties. Accompanying maps show congressional districts, counties, and some ward boundaries.

State Politics. B. Crichton Jones's *State Government* (1970) (23) is a brief, mimeographed bibliography of books and articles focusing primarily on state organization. Items, predominantly from 1965–1969, are arranged in the following categories: general, governors, executive reorganization, and regional studies—followed by items on individual states. The *Book of the States* (1935–) (24), published biennially, is designed to provide an authoritative source of descriptive and statistical information on constitutions and elections, legislation, the judiciary, administrative organization, finance, intergovernmental relations, and state services.

Local Government. The *Municipal Yearbook* (1934–) (25) is "an authoritative résumé of activities and statistical data of American cities." Although the emphasis is on individual city programs, considerable attention is given to developments in urban counties and metropolitan areas. Other features are the bibliographies for most chapters, and directories of officials. Official documents published by city, county, state, and federal governments concerned with social, political, economic, and public-administration matters of urban affairs are listed in the quarterly *Index to Current Urban Documents* (1972–) (26).[3] Listing documents associated with 154 cities of 100,000 or more inhabitants and 24 counties of 1,000,000 or more inhabitants in the United States and Canada is projected. Two approaches are possible: by city, where documents are arranged by level of government, or by subject. Joint use with the *Municipal Yearbook* (25), *PAIS* (A.1.b:15), and *Newsbank* (O.1.f:4) is suggested. Bollens's *American County Government* (1969) (27) is an annotated guide to recent literature, covering such topics as finance and intergovernmental relations, subdivided by material relating to the United States in general, then to individual states. Books, pamphlets, magazines, and federal and state publications are included.

The four volumes of *Metropolitan Communities* (1956–) (28) contain over 16,000 entries arranged in two broad areas of concern in urban studies: (1) government and politics in metropolitan communities, and (2) socioeconomic background (social structure and process, population, metropolitan economy). In volume 1, short headnotes describe the contents of each division and give appropriate cross-references. Most sections include lists of journals, agencies, bibliographies, and other sources of additional information, along with books, articles, and government publications. Unfortunately, both these features are missing from subsequent volumes. Items are often annotated, although the editors stress that the presence of an annotation "should not be interpreted as an evaluation." All items are indexed by names and places, whether in titles or annotations, important because access to individual chapters of books is often provided. Concern is predominantly with the United States, but material on other countries is included.

The Council of Planning Librarians' Exchange Bibliographies (E.2.d:9) are concerned with local government.

Political Parties and Political Groups. Wynar's *American Political Parties* (1969) (29) is "a selective guide to parties and movements of the twentieth century," consisting of over 3,000 occasionally annotated entries, including reference works, government publications, theoretical and behavioristic studies, and publications of individual parties. There are separate chapters on nineteenth-century party development, individual parties and movements (from the various progressive parties through the Communist movement, anarchism, and so on, to George Wallace's American Independent party), and studies of U.S. federal and state government.

Among the numerous directories and guides to right- and left-wing groups are *From Radical Left to Extreme Right* (1970–72) (30), by Robert Muller et al., with descriptions of over 500 "current periodicals of protest, controversy, advocacy, or dissent, with dispassionate content summaries to guide [you] through the polemic fringe." It provides brief information on the content of each periodical, including names of people and issues associated with them. Publications are classified in such categories as radical left, Marxist-Socialist left, underground, anarchist, liberation, Utopian, liberal, civil rights, racial and ethnic pride, sex, peace, servicemen's papers, conservative, anti-Communist, race-supremacist, humanism, atheism, rationalism, UFOs, and miscellaneous. Laird M. Wilcox has compiled directories of left- and right-wing groups in the United States in his *Guide to the American Left* (1970) (31) and *Guide to the American Right* (1970) (32). Bibliographies are included, but the descriptions are not always reliable.

Joel Seidman's *Communism in the United States* (1969) (33), an expanded and updated edition of his 1955 bibliography, consists of 7,000 annotated citations of books and articles on the activities of the Communist movement from 1919 to 1959, with significant later items noted. A preliminary section contains 38 items dealing with antecedent movements, including the Socialist and Anarchist movements, leftist union groups such as the IWW, and labor or third-party political efforts. (See Egbert [O.2.e:32] for a thorough study of the Socialist movement.) An author's political position is given when that information aids in understanding. In the main body, items are arranged alphabetically by author, then in a chronological sequence if there is more than one work, a feature that allows the reader to trace the changes in the political thinking of such writers as John Dos Passos, Max Eastman, and Benjamin Gitlow. Creative writing such as fiction is selectively included. There is a subject index. A companion, the *Digest of the Public Record of Communism in the United States* (1955) (34), is a collection of abstracts of decisions, laws, ordinances, hearings, reports, and other public documents relating to communism in the United States. Together, these books provide a basis for examining the events of the Communist movement in the United States. Hammond (M.2.g:3) and the *Yearbook of International Communist Affairs* (M.2.g:4) are also useful for tracing the course of communism in the United States.

Foreign Affairs. U.S. Treaties and Other International Agreements (G.2.c:19), *Treaties in Force* (G.2.c:18), and the U.S.

Department of State *Bulletin* (G.2.c:21) are important. According to Brock (G.1.b:1), the U.S. Department of State's *Foreign Relations of the United States: Diplomatic Papers* (1861–) (35) is "the primary source for study of U.S. foreign relations. The series, now running to over 180 volumes, contains diplomatic communications between Washington and U.S. embassies abroad, diplomatic notes and memoranda, reports and much other material." A cumulative index covers the volumes to 1918; volumes since then have their own indexes. "Arrangement of the content varies but is generally by geographic area."

The Council on Foreign Relations annually publishes *The U.S. in World Affairs* (1931–) (36) and *Documents on American Foreign Relations* (1953–) (37). The former gives "a concise analytical record of the American International experience." Sources of all quotations are given at the end of each volume; many of them refer to *Documents on American Foreign Relations.* The latter volumes consist of the most important documents concerned with the foreign relations of the United States, including presidential messages, speeches, reports, letters, communiqués, news conferences, comments, official statements, resolutions, and so forth. *Documents on American Foreign Relations* refers to information in *The U.S. in World Affairs.*

Bemis's *Guide to the Diplomatic History of the U.S., 1775–1921* (O.2.e:30) is designed to direct attention to published and unpublished material concerned with U.S. diplomatic history. Part 1 is arranged topically and chronologically, with brief comments about 6,000 items. It indicates the printed sources or how to get at them and gives suggestions for further sources in manuscript and archival collections. Part 2 contains an analysis of printed state papers and manuscript material, with remarks on the nature of the sources.

Special Topics. Selected issues of the *Law and Society Review* (1966–) (38) have annotated bibliographies of articles, books, and documents on such topics as law and the disadvantaged, civil liberties, civil rights, race relations, social conflict and social control, and juveniles and the law.

O.2.h   Sociology (including Ethnic Studies)

Sociology, perhaps more than any other discipline, is predominantly concerned with American society. Supplement what is described below with part H.

Religion is covered by *Religion in American Life* (O.2.e:28), while Gaustad's *Historical Atlas of Religion in America* (1962) (1) illustrates with maps, charts, tables, text, and bibliographies the development of churches and the expansion of membership of various denominations from 1650 to 1960. Dorothy Tompkins's *Poverty in the U.S. during the Sixties* (1970) (2) lists over 8,000 books, articles, government publications, and other publications on a wide range of subjects relating to poverty. Annotations note reprintings and the existence of abstracts, as well as important features in the texts. The index includes authors and subjects, as well as conferences and U.S.- and state-government agencies concerned with poverty. Bibliographies periodically appearing in the *Law and Society Review* (O.2.g:38) are worth noting for other aspects of sociology.

Ethnic Studies.   Combining history, political science, and sociology (and perhaps anthropology), the emergence of "ethnic studies" as a subject indicates the increasing concern for the conditions of minority groups in the United States. Minority groups are included in the *Guide to the Study of the U.S.* (O.1.b:2), the Localized History series (O.2.e:35), and other, similar bibliographies. Blacks, Mexican-Americans, Indians, and Asian-Americans are treated separately below.

The *Encyclopaedia Britannica*'s ten-volume *Makers of America* (1971) (3) is a collection of over 700 documents connected with ethnic groups and ranging over four centuries of U.S. history. It includes items on the pre-Mayflower groups (Indians, blacks, and Mexican-Americans). The set is designed to illustrate issues of ethnic pluralism, immigration, nativism, and race and violence, along with related legal, political, and social matters. Although it suffers from a lack of depth (an inevitable feature when such vast coverage is attempted), it makes many items available for the first time. In general the material is arranged chronologically. *The First Comers, Builders of a New Nation, Seekers of the Freedom, Seekers after Wealth, Natives and Aliens, The New Immigrants, Hyphenated Americans, Children of the Melting Pot, Refugees and Victims,* and *Emergent Minorities* are some titles of volumes. Each volume contains a number of subdivisions with headnotes, and there is a brief description indicating the source and context of each selection. The editors claim that over 80 ethnic groups and over 100 American Indian tribes are mentioned in the text, but some references are fleeting. The selections include letters, speeches, diaries, poems, songs, editorials, articles, congressional debates, presidential addresses and vetoes, petitions, court decisions, sermons, stories, and plays. Access to these groups is provided through the "Ethnic Index" in volume 10, which also includes a "Proper Name Index," with references to persons, places, organizations, and so on; a "Topical Index," which is a guide to issues and subjects; an "Author-Source Index," an alphabetical list of the authors and titles of the 700-odd selections; and an "Illustration Index," which refers by title, ethnic group pictured, and other designations to the more than 1,100 photographs, cartoons, and other illustrations reproduced in the set. The bibliography—fiction, as well as nonfiction—is selective and unannotated, and arranged by ethnic group; it includes recent titles as well as authoritative older works. The *Harvard Guide* (O.2.e:5) and the Library of Congress's *Guide to the Study of the U.S.* (O.1.b:2) should be used to supplement the nonfiction bibliography. Another source for fictional accounts of various ethnic groups is Coan and Lillard's *America in Fiction* (1967) (4). Brief critical annotations accompany each title.

Adams and Burke's *Civil Rights: A Current Guide to the People, Organizations, and Events* (1970) (5) consists of brief articles on individuals and organizations prominent in the U.S. civil-rights movement. The appendixes have congressional voting records on civil-rights bills, lists of states with civil-rights laws, and state agencies with civil-rights responsibilites; a chronology of events having to do with civil rights, 1954–1970; and a list of leading black elected officials. There is a brief glossary of acronyms and a "suggested bibliography."

Brimmer and Harper's "Economists' Perception of Minority Economic Problems" (O.2.c:2) is a survey of 500 recent books and articles.

Black Studies.   Single-volume handbooks on black Americans are John P. Davis's *American Negro Reference Book* (1966) (6), Ebony Magazine's *Negro Handbook* (1966) (7), and Harry A. Ploski's *Negro Almanac* (1971) (8). The *American Negro Reference Book* attempts to provide "a reliable summary of current information on the main aspects of Negro life in America and to present this information in sufficient historical depth to provide the reader with a true perspective." It is arranged in broad subject categories, each the contribution of a scholar; an index and selected bibliographies are included. The *Negro Handbook* covers much the same ground, but its arrangement, together with considerable directory information and statistical tables, makes it a more useful work. Ploski is similar in design.

Although somewhat out of date, Thomas Pettigrew's *Profile of the Negro American* (1964) (9) considers issues of race and racism, Negro health, Negro intelligence, Negro crime, Negro reactions to oppression, the impact of the Negro role on human personality, and Negro protest movements. Reviewing the work in *Scientific American,* Paul Bohannon wrote that "seldom does one see so much research summarized so lucidly with such seemingly simple exposition."[4] A bibliography and index are included. Clarence Major's *Short Dictionary of Afro-American Slang* (1970) (10), an authoritative work of brief definitions of terms that have originated among black people, is a useful supplement to Wentworth's *Dictionary of American Slang* (O.1.d:3).

Several single-volume bibliographies concerning black Americans have appeared recently. The best one, *Blacks in America: Bibliographical Essays* (1971) (11) is "an attempt to combine narrative, interpretation and bibliography in a chronological and topical framework. The history of Black Americans has been arranged in 100 categories, ranging from African origins and the slave trade through abolition to northern migration and the growth of nationalism, as well as examining aspects of Black culture. Each topic is introduced by one or more paragraphs summarizing the factual data and interpretive questions involved in a study of the subject followed by a discussion of the major books, articles, and printed primary sources relevant to research on the topic. Interwoven with the bibliographical portions of the essays in many cases are further narrative or interpretive commentaries on the subject matter of the topic itself" (from introduction). More than 4,000 titles are discussed. "Each topic or subtopic and in some cases each paragraph provides the basic bibliography for a research paper, seminar discussion, or lecture" (from introduction). History and literature predominate, but some material is included on anthropology, economics, folklore, musicology, psychology, political science, sociology, and other disciplines. The index includes authors, historical figures and institutions, and subjects. Another excellent work is Elizabeth Miller's *The Negro in America* (1970) (12), which treats such topics as history, demography, literature and fine arts, economics and employment, education, politics, and Black Nationalism and Black Power. Books and articles are included, and important items are briefly annotated. Section 21, "A Guide to Further Research," is a description of indexes, abstracts, bibliographies, serials, checklists, and other reference works required for additional information or further research. There is an author index. *The Negro in the United States* (1970) (13) is similar to Miller, but more selective. Work's *Bibliography of the Negro in Africa and America* (J.1.b:13) and the *Journal of Negro Education* (J.1.b:14) are valuable retrospective bibliographies. The former includes items on federal-government publications concerning Negroes issued before 1928. *The Negro in Print* (1965–) (14), which appears six times a year, is a bibliography containing "lists, reports, and extensive reviews of current American and foreign publications on the Negro—adult and juvenile, fiction and nonfiction, bound and unbound," and "information (though on a less comprehensive scale) on publications treating minority groups other than the Negro." An attempt was made "to cover publications beginning with the 1960s and to issue special bulletins including materials published prior to that date." Each issue includes extensive annotations of one or two significant articles. A cumulative index covering 1965–70 appeared in 1971. Survey articles concerning blacks in America appear occasionally in *Current Bibliography on African Affairs* (J.1.b:7). *Black History Viewpoints* (J.2.e:6) is arranged under such broad categories as "Afro-American Studies" and "Reflections on the African Diaspora." The *Index of Periodical Articles by and about Negroes* (1950–) (15) is a quarterly subject index to black periodicals.

Mexican-American Studies.   Evidently the only bibliography of bibliographies concerning Mexican-Americans is Joseph A. Clark y Moreno's "Bibliography of Bibliographies Relating to Mexican-American Studies" (1970) (16), a listing by author of 457 bibliographies in books and journals published up to 1971. It covers all subjects but has no annotations. *The Mexican American* (1969) (17) is a guide to materials relating to persons of Mexican-American heritage in the United States compiled by the U.S. Inter-Agency Committee on Mexican-American Affairs. It is arranged alphabetically under the following categories: books, reports, hearings, and proceedings; periodical literature; current periodicals; dissertations; bibliographies; audiovisual materials; and a list of Spanish-language radio and television stations. The results of UCLA's Mexican-American Study Project are in *The Mexican-American People* (1970) (18), by Leo Grebler et al. It employs an interdisciplinary approach, utilizing census data, household-samples surveys, informal interviews, and so on. It deals with the setting, historical perspective, socioeconomic conditions, the individual in the social system, the role of churches, and political interaction. Appendixes contain a 65-page bibliography and lists of tables, charts, maps, and figures.

Indian Studies.   Bernard L. Fontana's *The Indians of North America: Bibliographical Sources* (1970) (19) is a recommended brief list of sources. Current materials on American Indians are to be published annually in the *Index to Literature on the Native Americans* (1971–) (20) in September of each year. Articles in popular and scholarly journals, and books concerned with "native Americans" will be indexed. Special sections containing information on periodicals and newspapers published by Indian tribes and organizations, and a list of Indian organizations will also be given. Prucha's *The Indian in American History* is a recent addition to the American Problem Studies series (O.2.e:9). V. J. Vogel's *The*

Indian in American History (1968) (21) examines the treatment of American Indians in American historical writings. ("Four principal methods have been used to create or perpetuate false impressions: obliteration, defamation, disembodiment, and disparagement.") Indian contributions to American civilization are emphasized. The author suggests specific reading materials for various age levels which reflect accurately these contributions. A bibliography on the American Indian influence on American civilization is appended. Many academic libraries have the U.S. Department of the Interior's *Biographical and Historical Index of American Indians and Persons Involved in Indian Affairs* (1966) (22), an eight-volume bibliography of Indian biography, history, and social conditions during the latter half of the nineteenth century and the first part of the twentieth. There are extensive listings of the names of Indian agents, other BIA personnel, Indian chiefs, and historically prominent Indians, as well as other information related to tribal affairs. Arranged alphabetically under such headings as "names of tribes," "individuals," and "events," it includes articles, books, parts of books, and government publications. "The entries do not always follow standard bibliographical forms, and frequently the alphabetizing is informal within a single letter. For example, such names as Adams and Adam tend to be interfiled, and the various versions of an Indian name are not always brought together under the same person. Thus, it is best to scan an entire name when searching for a particular person. There is no listing by author or title of the works cited, except as these happen to occur as subjects" (from the preface).[5] Arlene Hirschfelder's *American Indian Authors* (1970) (23) is devoted to fiction and nonfiction by American Indians. There are brief annotations. Also included is a list of selected anthologies, oral and written literature, and selected periodicals published by American Indians.

The Klein and Icolori *Reference Encyclopedia of the American Indian* (1967) (24) is unreliable and uneven. It gives brief information on Indian history, art, languages, religions, social life, and customs. There are directories of reservations and tribal councils, government agencies, Indian schools, and biographical sketches of living Indians and non-Indians notable in Indian affairs, as well as an annotated bibliography of 2,000 items. A more authoritative work will be the projected multivolume *Handbook of North American Indians*. Although in a somewhat awkward format and available only in libraries designated depositories of U.S.-government publications or those having purchased microfilmed versions of the Serial Set of U.S.-government documents, *Materials Relating to the Indians of the U.S. and the Territory of Alaska* (1953–) (25) provides updating of much material appearing in Hodge's

Handbook of North American Indians (O.2.a:2).⁶ *Materials Relating to the Indians of the U.S.* combines a "directory of tribes and bands with short summaries or statistics regarding histories, populations, descriptions of locations, tribal governments, hospitals, full bloods, illiterates, those unable to speak English, school attendance and types of schools, maps locating the tribes, a listing of tribal claims cases and selected references and treaties, laws and important executive ordinances applying to specific tribes or other groups of Indians." Briefly, information (if available) on each tribe includes history to 1907, population in 1930, reservations, government, hospitals as of 1950, statistics to 1930, school attendance in 1947, culture and economics in 1944, claims to the U.S. Court of Claims and the Indian Claims Commission, selected bibliographies, lists of government hearings and tribal documents, tribal funds, and tribal laws. For example, the entry "Apache" has extensive quotes from Hodge (O.2.a:2); a population study for 1930; a summary of data on Apache cultural, economic, and social conditions; a list of claims filed with the Indian Claims Commission; a table of Apache tribal funds; selected references on the Apache, the Chiricahua, the Coyotero, the Jicarilla, the Lipan, and the Mescalero; and a list of Apache tribal documents. The third of the volume's four addenda contains material on the development of federal-Indian relations from 1755 to 1952, including a chronological list of the ratified treaties, establishment of reservations, and tribal claims filed in the U.S. Court of Claims for each tribe.

Tracing Laws Affecting American Indians. Felix Cohen's *Handbook of Federal Indian Law* (1942) (26) is the key volume among a number of interrelated government publications. Unfortunately, it is somewhat confusing to use. The first part, concerned with federal-Indian relationships, describes in twenty-three chapters the "functioning of legal rules and concepts and the actual consequences of statutes and decisions" (Schmeckebier [O.3:1], p. 238). Chapter topics include the field of Indian law (Indians and the Indian country); the Office of Indian Affairs, Indian treaties, legislation; the scope of federal and state powers over Indian affairs; tribal self-government, personal rights and liberties of the Indians; individual rights in tribal property; rights of the Indian in his personalty, individual rights in real property; federal services for Indians; taxation; legal status of the tribes; tribal property; Indian trade; liquor laws; criminal jurisdiction; and special conditions appertaining to the Pueblos of New Mexico, Alaskan natives, New York Indians, and Oklahoma Indians. The second part consists of indexes and tables of U.S. statutes and treaties, the decisions of federal courts (including territorial courts), the administrative rulings of the Attorney General and the Department of the Interior, and a bibliography. An index to materials on Indian law lists for each tribe statutes (special, private, and appropriation), federal cases, Interior Department rulings and regulations, tribal constitutions and charters, hearings, text references, and treaties. (The need for such an approach results from the practice of dealing with tribes and reservations individually; thus there has developed for each tribe a special body of law which supplements or modifies general legislation on Indian affairs.) The index on statutes and treaties contains descriptions of each act of Congress, treaty, and joint or concurrent resolution, along with references to earlier and later related statutes, treaties, federal cases, or opinions of attorneys general; the *U.S. Code* (O.2.g:15), the *U.S. Code Annotated* (an annotated, commercially published version of the *Code*); decisions and memoranda (published and unpublished) of the Interior Department; unpublished memoranda of the Lands Division of the Department of Justice; legal texts and periodicals; and congressional and other government documents. Volume, page, date, and title of each opinion are given in the table of opinions of attorneys general. Only unpublished memoranda of the Lands Division of the Department of Justice collected between 1929 and 1939 are cited. The bibliography is in four parts: compilations of federal Indian laws, treaties, and regulations; significant books and articles on Indian law; background materials, including works on Indian policy and administration; and such documents as the *American Archives, American State Papers,* and *Journals of the Continental Congress* (these are described in the *Harvard Guide* [O.2.e:5] and Schmeckebier [O.3:1]) pertaining to Indian affairs. The index refers to selected topics. In *Federal Indian Law* (1958) (27) part 1 of Cohen's original volume has been condensed. The tribal index, annotated table of statutes and treaties, table of Interior Department rulings, and table of Attorney General's opinions have been omitted, and the table of cases at the end is limited to those cited in the text; page references are furnished. Note, however, that features of *Material Relating to the Indians of the U.S.* (O.2.h:25) update Cohen.

Indian Affairs, Laws, and Treaties (1903–41) (28), compiled by Charles J. Kappler, consists of texts of the laws, executive orders, proclamations, and treaties relating to Indian affairs up to June 1938. It is used jointly with Cohen (above). Volumes 1–2 cover to 1902; volume 3, to 1913; volume 4, to 1927 (along with the texts of unratified treaties), as well as discussions of the power of Congress over Indian tribes and treaties; of federal jurisdiction over Indian lands, allotments, alienation and inheritance; of Indian citizenship; and of the doctrine of Indian right of occupance and possession of land. Volume 4 also has an addenda to volumes 1 and 3 and separate indexes to volumes 1–4. Volume 5 brings the coverage to 1938. Title 25 of the *U.S. Code* (O.2.g:15) contains the codes of laws in force in the United States, while the commercially published *U.S. Code Annotated* refers to the cases associated with individual laws. Title 25 of the *Code of Federal Regulations* (O.2.g:10) contains regulations of the executive branch of the U.S. government dealing with matters concerned in carrying out federal legislation.

The *American Indian Law Newsletter* (1969–) (29) reports on materials concerned with Indians in the *Congressional Record* (O.2.g:12), administrative decisions from the *Federal Register* (O.2.g:8), and Indian Claims Commission decisions. In February 1971, coverage of Indian cases which reach the state supreme courts, federal district courts, federal courts of appeals, or U.S. Supreme Court levels was begun. Special issues have dealt with such topics as the Alaskan Native Land Claims Settlement Act and federal Indian programs. Among the almost 200 articles listed in bibliographies in special issues of the *American Indian Law Newsletter* are Warren H. Cohen and Philip I. Mause's "The Indian: The Forgotten American," in *Harvard Law Review* 81 (1968): 1818–58; Richard Schifter's "Trends in Federal Indian Administration" in *South Dakota Law Review* 15 (Winter 1970): 1–21; and Robert W. Oliver's "The Legal Status of American Indian Tribes" in *Oregon Law Review* 38 (1959): 193–245. Numerous other materials on legal problems of American Indians can be found in *PAIS* (A.1.b:15) and the *Index to Legal Periodicals* (G.1.b:8).

Asian Americans. *Asians in America: A Selected Annotated Bibliography* (1971) (30), edited by Isao Fujimoto, includes sections on Chinese, Japanese, Filipino, East Indian, Korean, and Thai affairs; Asian Americans in general; and bibliographies. Works are indexed by author and subject. A list of current publications and ethnic newspapers with addresses is provided. Although the bibliography excludes newspaper accounts, popular periodicals prior to 1960, and Asian-language sources, it is the most useful survey of the resources in Asian-American studies.

O.3   U.S. Government Publications

The importance of government publications has been pointed out in part A.

Among the most useful reference works devoted to U.S.-government publications is Schmeckebier and Easton's *Government Pub-*

lications and Their Use (1969) (1). Although selective in the items it discusses, it is considered a classic source for information on little-known aspects of important government publications, past and present. It covers the essential catalogs, indexes, and bibliographies which provide access to almost the total published output of the U.S. government since 1774; publications issued in connection with the activities of Congress, such as the *Congressional Record* (O.2.g:12) and its predecessors; committee hearings, bills, and resolutions; federal and state constitutions, especially Corwin (O.2.g:17); federal laws; federal court decisions; presidential papers, including messages and speeches as well as the purposes of the *Federal Register* (O.2.g:8) and the *Weekly Compilation of Presidential Documents* (O.2.g:9); foreign affairs; organization and personnel of the three branches of government; maps; and periodicals. The appendix gives a list of depository libraries. The index contains only names of government agencies, subjects, and titles; names of individuals are not included. Brock (G.1.b:1) has reproductions of typical pages and suggestions for using many of the important titles described by Schmeckebier.

Jackson's *Subject Guide to Major U.S. Government Publications* (1968) (2) lists and describes some of the government publications of permanent value that appeared over the previous 25 years. A list of "Guides, Catalogs, and Indexes" is appended. Sally Wynkoop's *Government Reference Books* (O.1.b:1) promises to be of continuing usefulness.

John L. Andriot's *Guide to U.S. Government Serials and Periodicals* (1962–) (3) provides organization to the great number of periodicals issued by U.S.-government agencies. At present there are four volumes, with supplements and revised editions published at intervals. Bibliographical information (frequency of publication, classification number, and so on) is given for all entries, and most are annotated. There are indexes of titles, subjects, and agencies. Over 700 bibliographies on a wide range of subjects published between 1958 and 1969 by the U.S. government are described by Alexander Body in his *Annotated Bibliography of Bibliographies on Selected Government Publications* (1967–) (4), in the original volume and supplements. In addition, there is a list of abbreviations, symbols, and acronyms of government agencies; an index of issuing agencies; and an agency, author, title, and subject index.

The appearance of the *CIS Index to Publications of the U.S. Congress* (1970–) (5) provides easier access to what was formerly a confusing area of research, congressional hearings. This service is not retrospective, however, and the procedures for tracing hearings, reports, committee prints, and official documents of the House and Senate published before 1970 have not changed. Schmeckebier

(O.3.1) and Brock (G.1.b:1) have extensive descriptions for tracing hearings published before 1970, but because of local idiosyncrasies in treating these publications, a documents librarian should be consulted as well. The *CIS Index* is a monthly loose-leaf service that abstracts and indexes publications of Congress, with each issue covering the hearings, reports, committee prints, and official documents of that particular month. Reports and hearings on private bills and ceremonial publications are excluded. Citations are arranged by issuing committee with an elaborate code (described in the introduction) used as a numbering system. Entries in the main index include the following: subjects of documents and hearings; subjects discussed by witnesses; names and affiliations of witnesses; and popular names of laws, reports, and bills. There are indexes of bill, report, and document numbers, and names of committee and subcommittee chairmen. Indexes are cumulated quarterly and annually.

In *Popular Names of U.S. Government Reports* (1971) (6), a selection of 753 significant reports published since 1821 that have become identified with personal names are matched with the Library of Congress entry used by academic libraries.

Part P

Canadian Studies

Section 1

P.1.a Atlases

Although out of date in many respects, the *Atlas of Canada* (1957–) (1) covers all aspects of the country, with special emphasis on economic factors; there is an outline of the physical background and the economic development of the nation at mid-century, showing how these factors contributed to the characteristics of Canadian life. The basic scale is 1 to 10 million. The fourth edition (1970–) (2) is being issued in loose-leaf format. Adams and Rodgers's *Atlas of North American Affairs* (I.1.a:14) is a brief compilation of miscellaneous information and small black-and-white maps on 56 topics. The coverage of D. G. G. Kerr's

Historical Atlas of Canada (1966) (3) is broad enough to war-
rant including it among the general atlases. There are six parts:
"Environment and Prehistory"; "Exploration and Development to
1763"; "British North America, 1763–1867"; "Founding a Nation, 1867–1914"; "Wars and Expansion since 1914"; and "Main
Economic and Political Trends since 1867." About 150 books are
listed at the end of the volume. There is an index to maps and
text. The volume is attractive, consisting of colored maps, descriptive text, statistical diagrams, political charts, and drawings of
early ships, fortifications, and so on. Consult Lock (A.1.a:11) for
descriptions of other Canadian atlases.

P.1.b   Bibliographies

Douglas Lochead's *Bibliography of Canadian Bibliographies*
(1972) (1) lists bibliographies of works (books, periodicals,
maps, newspapers, and so on) concerned with Canada. There is
an index of names and subjects. Only bibliographies published
separately are included. Bibliographies in books or in periodical
articles have to be traced in such sources as *Bibliographic Index*
(A.1.b:2) and *Canadian Periodical Index* (P.1.b:4). *Canadiana*
(1951–) (2) attempts to lists all books relating to Canada, including publications of provincial governments and such series as
Canadian Historical Association Historical Booklets (P.2.e:3) and
Problems in Canadian History (P.2.e:4). *The Encyclopedia of
Business Information Sources* (A.1.b:7), Walford (A.1.b:12),
and Winchell (A.1.b:13) are worth consulting for reference works
concerned with Canada.

How to Find Out about Canada (1967) (3), edited by H. C.
Campbell, is a descriptive bibliography in narrative format of selected reference works and general titles on most aspects of Canadian culture. Some important items are accompanied by reproductions of typical pages. The first chapter examines bibliographies
and catalogs, encyclopedias, museums, libraries and archives, and
newspapers and periodicals. Chapters 2, 4, and 6–12 focus on
Canadian intellectuals, education, language, science, technology,
medicine, art, sports and recreation, and literature. The other chapters examine subjects in the social sciences, including history and
biography. There is an index of subjects, authors, and titles. Unfortunately omitted are such important items as *America: History
and Life* (O.2.e:6), *Writings on American History* (O.2.e:7),
Canadian News Facts (P.1.f:1), *Canadian News Index* (P.1.f:2),
Colonization and Settlement in the Americas (O.2.e:29), Haywood's *Bibliography of North American Folklore and Folksong*
(O.2.a:5), and *Arctic Bibliography* (O.2.a:4). Certain features of
Beaulieu's *Guide d'histoire du Canada* (P.2.e:1) make it worth

consulting as a general bibliography, and—curiously—the *Dictionary of Canadian Biography* (P.1.c:1) makes a unique contribution.

The *Canadian Periodical Index* (1928–) (4) was issued from 1928 to 1932 in mimeographed format, then suspended until 1938, when a Carnegie grant ensured that it would be compiled on a permanent basis. At present there are cumulated volumes covering 1938–1959 and annual volumes from 1960, with monthly issues available since the most recent annual cumulation. The cumulated annual volumes for 1938–1947, issued by the Public Libraries Branch of the Ontario Department of Education, were reprinted in three volumes in 1966. Articles are arranged under author and subject in a single index. Each entry gives the title of the article; an indication of illustrations, tables, and so on; and the name of the magazine, volume number, pages, and date. Subject headings are in English, with references from equivalent French terms. Entries such as "Book Reviews," "Moving Pictures Produced in Canada," and "Reproductions of Paintings and Sculpture" (listed under artists' names) are among the special features which make this index very useful. *America: History and Life* (O.2.e:6) contains abstracts of historical and related articles covering Canada. A source often overlooked, the *Arctic Bibliography* (O.2.a:4), is an extensive bibliography on arctic and subarctic areas of Canada, including administration and government, Eskimos, archaeology, and economic and social conditions. Finally, a number of Canadian "underground" periodicals are indexed in the *Alternative Press Index* (O.1.b:5).

P.1.c   Biographical Dictionaries and Directories

It is projected that the definitive *Dictionary of Canadian Biography* (1966–) (1) will consist of twenty volumes. Volume 1 covers people who died between A.D. 1000 and 1700, and volume 2 covers 1701–40. Articles range between 300 and 1,000 words. Persons who had a hand in shaping Canada and those born in Canada who achieved prominence abroad are to be included. Bibliographies for articles are in three categories: manuscript sources, printed sources, and secondary works. Citations are abbreviated, but full information is given in the general bibliography at the end of the volume. The general bibliography contains descriptions of manuscript deposits, series of books, dictionaries, reference guides, and periodicals important for the study of Canadian history to 1700, making the set a valuable bibliography as well as a dictionary of biography. An attempt has been made to make each volume self-contained. For example, volume 1 contains four essays: "The Indians of Northeastern North America," "The Northern

Approaches to Canada," "The Atlantic Region," and "New France, 1524–1713." Sketches of 65 Indians are included in this volume.

The *Macmillan Dictionary of Canadian Biography* (1963) (2) includes about 1,700 brief sketches of deceased Canadians. Besides vital statistics, each entry records achievements of the subject and suggests sources for further information. The *Canadian Who's Who* (1910–) (3) is similar to other "Who's Who" volumes, having brief directory information about the vital statistics, education, profession, publications, and addresses of prominent Canadian men and women. It is published every three years and supplemented by booklets. *Who's Who in Canada* (1914–) (4) is a directory of Canadian businessmen. The *Oxford Companion to Canadian History and Literature* (P.2.e:1) is a source of biographical sketches.

P.l.d   Encyclopedias and Dictionaries

The work of many contributors, the *Encyclopedia Canadiana* (1966–68) (1) is an excellent source of information on historical and contemporary aspects of Canada. Included among its articles are descriptions of Canadian flora, fauna, minerals, population, religion, health, education, and welfare. There are about 3,500 biographical sketches of prominent Canadians, and over 2,700 geographical entries. Most articles have brief bibliographies. There is an index.

The *Dictionary of Canadianisms on Historical Principles* (1967) (2) provides a historical record of words and expressions characteristic of the various spheres of life during the almost four centuries that English has been used in Canada. Along with definitions are dated examples of usage and a bibliography.

P.l.e   Handbooks and Yearbooks

The *Canadian Annual Review* (1960–) (1) is concerned with the internal and external politics and economic conditions of the country, as well as its education, health, welfare, science, mass media, drama, music, art, and sport. Each volume is the work of about 25 contributors. Several articles examine in detail features of federal political issues, including federal-provincial relations; an article is devoted to each of the provinces and one to the Yukon and Northwest Territories. Various aspects of foreign and defense policies are analyzed in separate chapters. Additional articles focus on such economic matters as inflation, employment, and trade policy. Occasionally, bibliographies accompany articles. Each volume is indexed. As the set becomes larger it becomes more valuable for tracing developments in various sectors of Canadian society over an extended period. The titles of the *Canadian Almanac and Directory* (1960–) (2) and *The McGraw-Hill Directory and Almanac of Canada* (1966) (3) are somewhat misleading. They are directories of public and private institutions, associations, and individuals, with little attention given to statistics. Each contains information not found in the other. A more useful source is the *Canada Year Book* (P.1.g:1).

If the Praeger publishing firm's *The United States and Canada* (I.1.e:11), edited by Richard Fisher, is at the level of the other handbooks in the series, it will be useful for years. Although Glen Taplin's *Canadian Chronology* (1970) (4) is somewhat confusing to use and contains a few inaccuracies, it is a useful source of information on historical events and persons. Arrangement of most chapters is according to province or territory, but others are concerned with such topics as European monarchs, the Royal Canadian Mounted Police, and distribution of Indians. There is an index of names, places, and subjects.

P.I.f   Newspapers and News Digests

Canadian News Facts (1967–) (1) digests news of Canada from eighteen Canadian newspapers, the *New York Times* (A.1. g:1), and The Canadian Press (the national news-gathering agency). For the most part, it is concerned with developments in Ottawa and the provincial capitals and news of business and labor, science and the arts, religion and education, and international relations. Occasionally, texts of dominion-provincial agreements are included, but only summaries of international agreements. [If texts of agreements between Canada and other nations are required, consult such sources as *International Legal Materials: Current Documents* (G.2.c:17), *PAIS* (A.1.b:15), or other titles discussed in section G.2.c.] *Canadian News Facts* is useful for news of dominion and provincial election returns, including lists of elected officials, cabinet appointments, and so on. Sources are not indicated. There are indexes of names and subjects. The *Canadian News Index* (1967–) (2) is a computer-produced index from 13 newspapers in 10 provinces. Canadian underground newspapers are included in the *Underground Newspaper Collection* (O.1.b:6).

P.I.g   Statistics Sources

The *Canada Year Book* (1905–) (1) is packed with statistical data and other information on such "measurable phases" of Canada's development as physiography and related sciences, constitution and government, population and vital statistics, crime and delinquency, natural resources and industry, and transportation.

Sources are indicated, and often additional readings are listed at the end of each table. Perhaps the most useful feature, however, is the separate chapter on sources of information and miscellaneous data, most of which consists of a bibliography arranged by subject of government publications, books, and monographs. Also provided is a directory of sources of official information, giving, in columnar format, addresses for federal and provincial agencies, arranged by subject, as follows: agriculture, arctic, bilingualism, broadcasting, economic planning, Eskimos, Indians, elections, parks, resource development, urban renewal, and water resources. Finally, there is a subject listing of selected significant articles and descriptive text from previous Year Books.[1] Other sections list, chronologically, parliamentary legislation and important events. There are about twenty-five pages of index.

Excellent coverage of Canadian statistics is provided in *Statistics Sources* (A.1.h:1) and the *Encyclopedia of Business Information Sources* (A.1.b:7).

Historical Statistics of Canada (1965) (2) covers the period from 1865 to 1969. "The text accompanying tables is an integral part of each section. In addition to giving the sources of the data, it is designed to give a sufficient description of the content of the individual time series that the general user may be able to use them without reference to the basic sources" (Introduction). Most of the data are from published sources such as government publications. Sources are indicated. Section titles are "Population and Migration"; "Vital Statistics, Health, and Welfare"; "Labor Force"; "Wages and Working Conditions"; "National Income and Capital Stock"; "Balance of International Payments, International Indebtedness, and Foreign Trade"; "Government Finance"; "Banking and Finance"; "Price Indexes"; "Lands and Forests"; "Agriculture"; "Fisheries"; "Minerals and Fuel"; "Electric Power"; "Manufactures"; "Construction and Housing"; "Transportation and Communication"; "Internal Trade and Service"; "Education"; "Politics and Government"; and "Justice." For example, "Justice" consists of statistics on crime, delinquency, penal institutions, suicides, and bankruptcies and insolvencies. Often *Cross-Polity Times-Series Data* (I.1.g:7) is satisfactory as a source of historical data.

Section 2

P.2.a   Anthropology

Gibson (N.2.a:1) notes that about 180 annotated entries per year have been listed in the *Annual Report* (1928–) (1) of Can-

ada's Museum of Man. This continues "Recent Publications Relating to Canada: Ethnology, Anthropology, and Archaeology,"
which appeared annually in the *Canadian Historical Review*
(1921–) (2) from 1920 to 1955. Gibson can be supplemented by
the *International Bibliography of Social and Cultural Anthropology* (B.1.b:4), Haywood's *Bibliography of North American Folklore* (O.2.a:5), Hodge's *Handbook of Indians of Canada* (P.2.
h:1), Swanton's *Indian Tribes of North America* (O.2.a:3), and
Arctic Bibliography (O.2.a:4). Recent material by and about
Canadian Indians is in Hirschfelder (O.2.h:23) and *OCCHL* (P.2.
e:1). Haywood is updated by the U.S. Library of Congress's *Folklore of the North American Indians* (O.2.a:6). The third edition of
·Murdock's *Ethnographic Bibliography of North America* (O.2.
a:1) covers material up to 1960. Culture groups in Canada with
data deposited in HRAF (I.3.1) are listed in section O.2.a.

P.2.b Economics

Outside of the two discontinued annual bibliographies of articles and books noted in Melnyk (D.1.b:1) and the odd survey
article (e.g., "Recent Contributions to Economic History: Canada," in the *Journal of Economic History* 19, 1 [March 1959]:
75–102), research concerning the economics or economic history
of Canada requires examining items discussed in part D. A number of bibliographies in the Council of Planning Librarians' *Exchange Bibliography* (E.2.d:9) are concerned with Canadian economic issues. The *United States and Canada* (I.1.a:5) is an
authoritative atlas of economic affairs. Lorna Daniells's *Studies in
Enterprise* (O.2.c:4) and supplements in issues of the *Business
History Review* cover Canadian company histories.

P.2.c Demography

If more detailed information on population is required than is
available in the *Canada Year Book* (P.1.g:1), consult part C.

P.2.d Geography

As part of Canada's annual contribution to the *Bibliographie
géographique internationale* (E.1.b:6) and other international
bodies, the Geographical Branch of the Canadian Department of
Mines and Technical Surveys has issued several excellent bibliographies of geography. A cumulative *Bibliography of Periodical
Literature on Canadian Geography* (1960) (1) is issued in six
parts: Canada—general, Atlantic provinces, Quebec and Ontario,
prairie provinces, British Columbia, and Northern Canada. In general, articles are arranged under such headings as bibliography;

biogeography; description and travel; economic; historical-human; mathematical, physical, and political geography; and place names. There are appropriate subdivisions. This is continued, with books and pamphlets added, in the annual *Selected Bibliography of Canadian Geography* (1950–) (2). *Canadian Urban Geography* (1957) (3) includes theses and dissertations as well as articles and books, but perhaps the most useful feature is the list of materials on individual cities, towns, and settlements arranged alphabetically under place name. The Council of Planning Librarians' *Exchange Bibliography* (E.2.d:9) should not be overlooked as a source for material on specialized topics.

P.2.e   History

The *Oxford Companion to Canadian History and Literature* (1967) (1) is a commendable summary. Perhaps the most valuable feature is the critical bibliography which accompanies most historical articles. Often longer than the article, it can save time in obtaining authoritative bibliographies on a broad range of topics, some of them minor. Historical entries include political and constitutional issues, forts, important places, and such special topics as Indian tribes, exploration, the fur trade, and political parties. Among the article topics are Acadia, the Klondike gold rush, the Fraser River gold rush, halfbreeds (preferred by the author to the term *métis*), folklore, the Orange order, Oriental immigration (unfortunately lacking a bibliography), Mennonites, North West Rebellion, the Royal Canadian Mounted Police, Ukrainians, and Doukhobors. Regrettably, there is little concern with economic history.

The *Guide d'histoire du Canada* (1969) (2), by André Beaulieu et al., is the best recent bibliography on the history of Canada. (Two unfortunate features are the fact that the title fails to imply that its broad coverage of Canadian culture makes it useful as a bibliography for disciplines other than history, and that the descriptive text is in French.) Chapters survey historiography, bibliography and reference works, universal histories which include Canadian history, primary sources and archives (including map collections), and general and specialized treatments. The chapter on reference works is perhaps the best available. Each chapter consists of descriptive headnotes for each division, and where appropriate, individual citations are annotated. Cross-references are liberally provided. There is an index of names, subjects, and titles. Chapter 12 is a highly selective listing of important sources of information on such "auxiliary sciences" as geography, demography, statistics, economics, political science, sociology, social psychology, and the history of science and technology. Both reference items and general works are included. The unique contribution to a bibliography of historical research of the *Dictionary of Canadian Biography* (P.1.c:1) should not be overlooked.

Books and articles on Canadian history appear in *Writings in American History* (O.2.e:7) (up to 1935); *America: History and Life* (O.2.e:6); *Colonization and Settlement in the Americas: A Selected Bibliography* (O.2.e:29); and Winther's *Classified Bibliography of the Periodical Literature of the Trans-Mississippi West* (O.1.b:4).

Although limited to books, Robin Winks's *Recent Trends and New Literature in Canadian History* (1959), one of the AHA's Service Center for Teachers of History series (O.2.e:8), is an authoritative survey covering early historiography, changing interpretations, and prospects and problems, along with a survey of studies published since 1939.

Canadian Historical Association Historical Booklets (n.d.) (3) provide the general reader, the teacher, and the historical specialist with concise accounts of special problems in Canadian history and politics. A complete list is available inside the back cover of issues of the *Canadian Historical Review* (P.2.a:2). Among the titles of the twenty-odd booklets are *Louis Riel: Patriot or Rebel, The West and Confederation, Papineau,* and *The Clergy Reserves.* A similar series is Problems in Canadian History (1966–68) (4); topics covered include confederation, the Northwest Rebellion, the Winnipeg general strike, the social structures of New France, and the Loyalists. Issues in Canadian History (1969–) (5) (in paperback) is a series of collections of contemporary documents and related material, as well as critical studies by modern historians of controversial problems in Canadian history. Titles include *The French Canadians, 1759–1766; The United Empire Loyalists; The King-Byng Affair, 1926; Racism or Responsible Government: The French Canadian Dilemma of the 1840's; The Family Compact; Joseph Howe; The Manitoba School Question; The Bennett New Deal; Canadian Foreign Policy since 1945 (Middle Power or Satellite?); The Acadian Deportation; Quebec in the Duplessis Era: 1935–1959; The 1917 Election;* and *The Frontier Thesis in the Canadas.* Sources of quotations and a list of suggested readings are included. For other titles consult the annual index volumes of *Canadiana* (P.1.b:2), under the entry "Issues in Canadian History."

P.2.f Literature

The *Oxford Companion to Canadian Literature* (P.2.e:1) is an excellent source, and the *Penguin Companion to World Literature* (L.2.f:1), Winchell (A.1.b:13), Walford (A.1.b:12), and the *MLA Bibliography* (B.2.e:1) should not be overlooked.

P.2.g   Political Science

It is necessary to consult appropriate sections of this part and part G for material on Canadian politics. The following are among the specialized sources available. Some of the Canadian Historical Association Historical Booklets (P.2.e:3) are concerned with Canadian politics. Procedures for tracing Canadian federal and provincial laws and statutes, court cases, and so on, are outlined in Price and Bitner's *Effective Legal Research* (O.2.g:19). In *Canadian Party Platforms* (1969) (1), D. Owen Carrigan has compiled "the platforms and policy statements issued by Canadian political parties or their leaders for federal elections from 1867 to 1968, with a breakdown of the election results for each province included." Brief headnotes describe each campaign. "Provincial-Municipal Relations in Canada" is one of the bibliographies (no. 12) on Canada in the Council of Planning Librarians' *Exchange Bibliography* (E.2.d:9). Hammond (M.2.g:3) and the *Yearbook of International Communist Affairs* (M.2.g:4) are useful for tracing Communist activities.

P.2.h   Sociology

Because of the lack of bibliographies concerned specifically with the sociology of Canada, researchers on this subject are referred to part H. Meg Richeson's "Canadian Rural Sociology Bibliography," issued in November 1971, number 238 of the Council of Planning Librarians' *Exchange Bibliography* (E.2.d:9), is an example in that source of the type of bibliography relating to Canada. Monographs, articles, bibliographies, and films are included among the over fifty typed pages. For material concerning current conditions of the Indians of Canada see section P.2.a. The *Handbook of Indians of Canada* (1913) (1) consists largely of material from Hodge's *Handbook of American Indians North of Mexico* (O.2.a:2). Notable exceptions are the articles concerned with "Treaties," "Department of Indian Affairs," and "Indian Reserves." Bibliographies in the *American Indian Law Newsletter* (O.2.h:29) include articles concerned with laws affecting Canadian Indians. Access to publications of governmental agencies on Canadian urban affairs is available in *Index to Current Urban Documents* (O.2.g:26).

Part Q

Australasia, Oceania, and Antarctica

Section 1

Q.1.a   Atlases

A variety of general and specialized atlases provide good to excellent coverage of Australasia, Oceania, and Antarctica, or parts
of these regions. T. F. Kennedy's *Descriptive Atlas of the Pacific
Islands* (1966) (1) is a reasonably comprehensive atlas of Australia, New Zealand, and many island groups of the Pacific, including the Philippines, Melanesia, Micronesia, and Polynesia. A
series of two-tone black-and-grey maps is accompanied by short,
descriptive commentaries on each.

A major official atlas is the *Atlas of Australian Resources*
(1953–60; 1962–) (2). Comprising the first series, 30 large colored maps on a scale of 1 to 6 million, and accompanied by pertinent commentary, provide authoritative information on most aspects of the country. A second series, begun in 1962, includes a
number of maps revised since their appearance in the first series,
together with additional maps on such topics as electricity and
soils. A. Ferriday's *Map Book of Australasia* (1966) (3) is a useful little atlas comprising about two dozen maps. Among detailed
regional atlases of Australia are *A Regional Atlas of New South
Wales* (1966–) (4), *An Atlas of Population and Production for
New South Wales* (1932) (5), and a *Regional Planning Atlas of
Tasmania* (1965) (6). Topical atlases include *Australian Rural
Industries* (1948) (7), subtitled "A Graphic Representation."

New Zealand is equally well provided with good, reliable atlases. *A Descriptive Atlas of New Zealand* (1959) (8) is an excellent systematic atlas of that dominion. The settlement and history of New Zealand, as well as physical, political, economic, and
regional aspects of the country's geography are covered. Linge and
Frazer's *Atlas of New Zealand Geography* (1968) (9), with some
30 black-and-white maps and brief accompanying commentary,
has been prepared primarily for school use. It is, nonetheless, a
valuable research aid, for it includes a variety of reference materials and numerous short bibliographies. *The Oxford Atlas of New
Zealand* (1966) (10), like *The Oxford Australian Atlas* (1966)
(11), is based on the 1951 *Oxford Atlas* (A.1.a:4). Both atlases
provide a series of good general purpose physical/political maps
of the respective countries, in addition to maps covering other regions of the world.

The most important atlas dealing with the Antarctic continent
and the surrounding oceanic waters is the Russian *Atlas antarktiki*
(1966–67) (12). The maps appear in the first volume, and detailed commentaries on them comprise volume 2. Of great significance also is the projected 18-volume *Antarctic Map Folio Series*
(1964–) (13), jointly sponsored by the American Geographical
Society and the National Science Foundation. All but three of the
folios have now been issued. The volumes include detailed maps,
diagrams, and commentaries on such subjects as the characteristics
of the ice sheets and glaciers of Antarctica, the terrestrial life of
the continent, the Antarctic atmosphere, the structure and productivity of the surrounding seas, bedrock geology, marine inverte-
brates, and birds and fishes. Volume 1 of the *Oceanographic Atlas
of the Polar Seas* (1957–) (14), issued by the Hydrographical
Office of the United States Navy, is an older work which provides

good coverage of many aspects of the continent and its adjacent water bodies.

Other atlases on the above areas are discussed in Lock (A.1. a:11).

Q.1.b Bibliographies

As in other regional parts, it is necessary to distinguish between the type of bibliographies available.

Bibliographies of Bibliographies. Ida Leeson's *Bibliography of Bibliographies of the South Pacific* (1954) (1) is one of the few such reference works available. General bibliographies, bibliographies of specific areas, and subject bibliographies, which have been published separately or in books and periodicals, are arranged first by geographical area and then by subject. The New Zealand Library Association has issued *A Bibliography of New Zealand Bibliographies* (1967) (2), which includes more than 300 different items covering most aspects of New Zealand life. Other bibliographies are listed in *Bibliographic Index* (A.1.b:2).

Reference Works. One of the few bibliographical guides to any of the regions covered in this chapter is the *Guide to New Zealand Reference Materials* (1950–57) (3). This is an annotated listing of more than 100 sources, both general and specific. Supplements issued in 1951 and 1957 provide numerous additional items. D. H. Borchardt has prepared a somewhat similar volume for Australia, *Australian Bibliography: A Guide to Printed Sources of Information* (1963) (4).

General Bibliographies. The *Australian National Bibliography* (1961–) (5), issued annually by the National Library of Australia, claims to list all "books published in Australia and books dealing wholly or substantially with an Australian subject or written by authors believed to be Australian." Pamphlets, sheet music, first issues of serials and newspapers, and commonwealth- and state-government documents and publications are included, as well as books. *Antarctic Bibliography* (1965–) (6) is a continuing series of compilations presenting abstracts and indexes of current Antarctic literature. In volume 2 more than half the entries are in English, and more than one quarter are Russian. The remaining items are in Japanese and about a dozen European languages. The abstracts throughout are in English, and translations of each of the titles of books, monographs, articles, documents, and films are provided. There are author, subject, and geographical indexes.

One of the most extensive general bibliographies of English-language sources covering the Southwest Pacific region is the *Annotated Bibliography of the Southwest Pacific and Adjacent Areas* (1944) (7). Volume 1 covers the Netherlands and British East Indies and the Philippines; volume 2, the Mandated Territories of New Guinea, Papua, the British Solomon Islands, the New Hebrides, and Micronesia; and volume 3, Malaya, Thailand, Indochina, the China coast, and the Japanese Empire. Volume 4 is a close to 700-page supplement to the first three volumes. *Pacific Islands and Trust Territories: A Select Bibliography* (I.1.b:11) is published by the U.S. Army. *Island Bibliographies* (1965) (8), compiled by Sachet and Fosberg, contains three quite separate bibliographies, each with its own index and list of addenda. The bibliographies are on Micronesian botany, the land environment and ecology of atolls, and the vegetation of tropical Pacific Islands. More generally useful to the undergraduate student is A. G. Day's *Pacific Island Literature: One Hundred Basic Books* (1971) (9).

Australia is provided with a variety of general bibliographies. John Alexander Ferguson's monumental *Bibliography of Australia, 1784–1900* (1941–) (10) is the standard bibliography of the literature of Australia. The entries are grouped by year of publication, and then listed alphabetically by author. The *Annotated Bibliography of Select Government Publications on Australian Territories, 1951–1964* (1965) (11) is an annotated listing of more than 700 official publications which deal with the Northern Territory, Papua and New Guinea, and various South Pacific islands administered by Australia. The contributions of Dutch, French, and German authors to the literature on Australia are dealt with in three brief bibliographies by Ludwig L. Politzer: *Bibliography of Dutch Literature on Australia* (1953) (12), *Bibliography of French Literature on Australia, 1595–1946* (1952) (13), and *Bibliography of German Literature on Australia, 1770–1947* (1952) (14).

Thomas Morland Hocken's *Bibliography to the Literature Relating to New Zealand* (1909) (15) is the standard bibliography of nineteenth-century literature on New Zealand. Most of the 4,000 items are annotated. A number of early colonial newspapers are included. A supplement, compiled by A. H. Johnstone in 1927, includes some 500 additional items. Leonard J. B. Chapple's *Biblio-Brochure Containing Addenda and Corrigenda to Extant Bibliographies of New Zealand* (1938) (16) contains 116 further items not listed in either Hocken or its supplement.

Philip A. Snow's *Bibliography of Fiji, Tonga, and Rotuma* (1969) (17) lists more than 10,000 items in four parts, with subdivisions.

S. A. Spence's *Antarctica: Its Books and Papers from the Ear-*

liest to the Present Time (1966) (18) contains items primarily on discovery and exploration. The entries are grouped alphabetically in two sections: books, and magazines and periodicals. *National Interests in Antarctica: An Annotated Bibliography* (1960) (19) provides an extensive compilation of close to 1,200 items on the political and other activities of twenty-seven individual countries, the United Nations, and other international agencies, as they have been concerned with, or have affected, Antarctica. The arrangement is by country or agency.

The Australian Public Affairs Information Service's *Subject Index to Current Literature* (1945–) (20) is very similar in its arrangement and content to *PAIS* (A.1.b:15).

Reviews of research on Australian, New Zealand, Pacific, and Antarctic topics are undertaken, though not on any regular basis, in such journals as the *Australian Geographer* (1928–), *Pacific Viewpoint* (1960–), and the *Antarctic Journal of the United States* (1966–). Monograph-length works include Felix M. Keesing's *Social Anthropology in Polynesia: A Review of Research* (1953) (21) and *Antarctic Research: A Review of British Scientific Achievement in Antarctica* (1964) (22), edited by Raymond Priestley and others. Much bibliographical detail is provided in these works.

Q.1.c   Biographical Dictionaries and Directories

About 1,500 short biographical sketches of important men and women in the Pacific world are included in the *Pacific Islands Yearbook and Who's Who* (1932–) (1).

Two major biographical dictionaries covering Australia are P. Serle's two-volume *Dictionary of Australian Biography* (1949) (2), which contains more than 1,000 entries, and the *Australian Dictionary of Biography* (1966–) (3). Volumes 1 and 2 cover the years 1788 to 1850. The years 1851 to 1890 will be completed in four volumes, and the years from 1891 to 1938, probably in six volumes. Nearly 2,000 individual contributors will provide the material on about 6,000 Australians from the time of the first settlements to the immediate pre-Second World War period. In addition to the biographical sketches, a "biographical register" will provide a listing of other names significant in the settlement and development of Australia.

Who's Who in Australia (1906–) (4) is a "biographical dictionary and register of titled persons; with which is incorporated John's 'Notable Australians.'" More than 8,500 persons are included in the work, which, in addition, lists Australian baronets, knights, and recipients of the Victoria Cross. *Who's Who in New*

Zealand (1908–) (5) has some 2,500 entries, as well as a variety of miscellaneous information.

Q.I.d   Encyclopedias and Dictionaries

The one-volume *Modern Encyclopaedia of Australia and New Zealand* (1964) (1) carries brief articles on a wide range of topics about Australia, New Zealand, and New Guinea.

The outstanding encyclopedia of Australia is the ten-volume *Australian Encyclopaedia* (1958) (2). Articles by around 4,500 contributors are considered both authoritative and up-to-the-minute for the year in which the encyclopedia appeared. Some of these are lengthy and unusually comprehensive, as for example the hundred-page article on the Aborigines. A great deal of detailed biographical, geographical, historical, and other material is included, and the volumes as a whole are magnificently illustrated with colored and monochrome photographs, maps, and diagrams. The aim of the one-volume *Encyclopaedia of Australia* (1968) (3), compiled and written by Andrew and Nancy Learmonth, was to provide a valuable "family reference work" on selected topics. Brief bibliographical detail is provided for further reading.

For New Zealand there is the three-volume *Encyclopaedia of New Zealand* (1966) (4). About 350 contributors have provided articles on a wide spectrum of topics, and among the notable features of the work are its excellent illustrations—close to 500 maps and many hundreds of photographs grouped in almost 100 plates. The articles vary in length; most are brief, but a few are of great length, as for example the article on the Maoris, which runs to more than 75 pages. The *Oxford New Zealand Encyclopaedia* (1965) (5), is a one-volume reference work.

The three-volume *Encyclopaedia of Papua and New Guinea* (1972) (6) is another major reference work, to which contributions have been made on a wide variety of topics by leading international authorities. Bibliographies are provided at the end of most articles, and a detailed index, a place-name gazetteer, and copious cartographic and photographic illustrations are other features of the work.

A useful place-name dictionary is Aldo Massola's *Aboriginal Place Names of Southeast Australia and Their Meanings* (1968) (7). The aboriginal names of towns, shires, homesteads, rivers, mountains, and other physical features are among those included and explained.

Q.I.e   Handbooks and Yearbooks

A large number of handbooks, yearbooks, and other such reference items are available for the study of Australia and Oceania;

few exist for Antarctica. In *Australia, New Zealand, and the South Pacific: A Handbook* (I.1.e:10), a wide variety of cultural, economic, political, and social material, as well as historical and geographical items, is presented in a well-organized and authoritative manner. *The Far East and Australasia* (K.1.e:2) provides surveys of geography, history, and education, and concise information about constitutions and government, as well as directories or organizations and prominent people, while Hinton's *The Far East and South Pacific* (K.1.e:3) presents a range of statistical data and brief historical and socioeconomic information on 19 independent countries and other small territories and dependencies. The *Pacific Islands Yearbook and Who's Who* (Q.1.c:1), after dealing with the region as a whole, covers each of the individual islands, or island groups, in greater detail. More than 80 maps are a notable feature of the work, which is provided with both general and geographical indexes. *Pacific Islands and Trust Territories* (I.1.b:11) has some 26 appendixes, which cover many aspects of the trust territories and other islands, including administration and political organization, population, and government revenues and expenditures. The *Handbook of the Trust Territories of the Pacific Islands* (1948) (1) is, despite its age, a valuable source book of information on a great many aspects of those islands of the Pacific administered by the United States as Trust Territories of the United Nations. Much more exhaustive is the four-volume set of British Naval Intelligence Division *Geographical Handbooks* (E.1.e:5) on the Pacific Islands. A large number of photographs and many detailed maps of seaports and other towns are especially valuable features of the work. Other older, but still quite useful, reference works include Hawthorne Daniel's *Islands of the Pacific* (1943) (2) and John Wesley Coulter's *The Pacific Dependencies of the United States* (1957) (3).

Among the tourist guidebooks that provide a variety of reliable, up-to-date information on the Pacific are P. F. Kluge and Bob Boeberitz's *Micronesian Guide Book: Official Visitors' Guide Book to the Trust Territories of the Pacific Islands* (1968) (4), with information on the Marianas and the Marshall Islands, and Robert S. Kane's *South Pacific A to Z: Australia, New Zealand, the Tropic Isle of Fiji, New Caledonia, the Samoas, Tahiti, Tonga, and Hawaii* (1966) (5). The U.S. Department of State's *Background Notes* (I.1.e:13) are available for Australia, New Zealand, and Western Samoa.

Among the handbooks on particular territories, the *Handbook of Fiji* (1968) (6) and the *Handbook of Papua and New Guinea* (1966) (7) cover a wide range of information on general and specialized topics concerning their respective areas, and both include statistical data. For Australia the most useful source of information is the annual *Official Year Book of the Commonwealth of Australia* (1908–) (8). Though primarily a statistical work, it includes chapters on virtually every aspect of the country's life. Noteworthy features include a statistical summary of the Australian economy since the beginning of the century, a chronological table of important events since 1788, and a list of special articles that appeared in earlier issues of the yearbook. Osmar White's *Guide to Australia* (1968) (9) is another valuable, comprehensive handbook. The *New Zealand Official Yearbook* (1892–) (10) provides a detailed survey, together with statistical data, on every significant aspect of the New Zealand scene. A statistical summary of the New Zealand economy since 1913 and useful bibliographical lists are also provided. The yearbook can be supplemented with information derived from the *New Zealand Guide* (1969) (11). Included in the guide is an alphabetical gazetteer of every place in New Zealand.

Trevor Hatherton's *Antarctica* (1965) (12) is a comprehensive and systematic handbook to the continent, with authoritative articles written by some twenty authors. The physical and biological aspects of Antarctica are particularly well handled. A more detailed treatment of some of these subjects, including climatology, flora and fauna, and human adaptation is provided in *Biogeography and Ecology in Antarctica* (1965) (13), edited by Jacques van Mieghem and P. van Oye.

Q.l.f Newspapers and News Digests

For Australasia and Oceania the best sources of news items will likely be the indexes of the *New York Times* (A.1.g:1) and the *Times* of London (A.1.g:3). *Keesing's Contemporary Archives* (A.1.g:5) and *Facts on File* (A.1.g:6) should be consulted also. These sources will be found of value also for Antarctica, although more specific sources of such information are on hand. *Polar Record* (1931–) (1) provides news of fieldwork, scientific research, and other matters of concern in both the Arctic and the Antarctic. The *Antarctic Journal of the United States* (1966–) (2) is another source of news on current activities in Antarctica. The Russian bimonthly *Information Bulletins* (1964–) (3), which is available in an English translation, provides information on current Russian scientific activities in Antarctica.

Q.l.g Statistics Sources

Brief statistical information on a few aspects of the Pacific Islands is provided in *Pacific Islands and Trust Territories* (I.1. b:11). The *Official Year Book of the Commonwealth of Australia*

(Q.1.e:8) and *Australia in Facts and Figures* (n.d.) (1) are the best sources of information on Australia and its dependencies. The *New Zealand Official Yearbook* (Q.1.e:10) will provide statistical information sufficient for most undergraduate research; in addition it cites sources of statistics for detailed inquiry. *Statistics Sources* (A.1.h:1), the *Encyclopedia of Business Information Sources* (A.1.b:7), and *Cross-Polity Times-Series Data* (I.1.g:7) are also useful.

Section 2

Q.2.a   Anthropology

Collections of Data.   Information on over forty cultures is deposited in HRAF (I.3:1). The arrangement below is according to the *Outline of World Cultures* (B.1.e:3).

OCEANIA

Philippines (Subanun, Bontoc, Magahat)	Wogeo
	Kapauku
Apayao	Trobriands
Cental Sisayan	Manus
Ifugao	New Ireland (Lesu)
Indonesia	Buka
Iban	Santa Cruz
Alor	Malekula (Atchin and
Bali	Vao)
Flores	Lau
Makassar	Marshalls
Toradja	Truk
Ambon	Woleai
Aranda	Yap
Murngin	Tikopia'
Tasmanians	Samoa
Tiwi	Marquesas
Kwoma	Easter Islanders
Orokaiva	Maori
	Pukapuka

More than for any other discipline in this area, reference materials on anthropological aspects of Australia and Oceania are abundant and unusually comprehensive. C. R. H. Taylor's *Pacific Bibliography: Printed Materials Relating to the Native Peoples of Polynesia, Melanesia, and Micronesia* (1965) (1) is an extensive bibliography of 16,000 books and periodical articles in a number of languages dealing with the peoples and cultures of the Pacific.

The arrangement is by island group, and then by subject. Cammack and Saito's *Pacific Island Bibliography* (1962) (2), which was planned to supplement Taylor's work, is based on a selection of materials in the Pacific collection of the University of Hawaii's Gregg M. Sinclair Library. Most of the 1,700-odd items, which deal mainly with the social sciences, have been published since 1948. A useful, but more selective, bibliography is provided in A. P. Vayda's *Peoples and Cultures of the Pacific* (1968) (3).

Greenway's *Bibliography of the Australian Aborigines and the Native Peoples of Torres Strait to 1959* (1963) (4), is an alphabetical listing of more than 10,000 books, documents, and periodical articles, primarily in English. The items are indexed both by subject and aboriginal tribe. Four bibliographies published by the Australian Institute of Aboriginal Studies are other invaluable sources of information: *Arnhem Land Peninsular Region* (1966) (5), *Cape York* (1967) (6), *Kimberley Region* (1968) (7), and *Central Australia and Western Desert Regions* (1969) (8).

The *Ethnographic Bibliography of New Guinea* (1968) (9) is a three-volume work which attempts a complete bibliographic coverage through 1964 of the fields of material culture and social organization. It also includes some items on physical environment, prehistory, physical anthropology, and language. The arrangement is alphabetical by author. Volume 2 is an index by administrative district, and volume 3, by subject (as, for example, languages, social groups, and physical features).

More specialized bibliographies of interest to anthropologists will be H. L. Klieneberger's *Bibliography of Oceanic Linguistics* (1957) (10) and Douglas Fraser's *Bibliography of Torres Straits Art* (1963) (11).

Two encyclopedias are also worthy of note. Alexander W. Reed's *Illustrated Encyclopaedia of Aboriginal Life* (1969) (12) features brief articles, alphabetically arranged, on topics relating to the Australian Aborigines. Appendixes include a reading list and a list of tribes and tribal locations. Alan McCulloch's *Encyclopedia of Australian Art* (1968) (13), though primarily concerned with modern art, has some information on aboriginal art and artists.

Q.2.b Demography

Norma McArthur's *Island Populations of the Pacific* (1968) (1) is the most useful single work on the subject. Past and present populations of Fiji, Tonga, Samoa, the Cook Islands, and French Polynesia are covered, with a variety of statistical data. Robert C. Schmitt's *Demographic Statistics of Hawaii, 1779–1965* (1968)

(2) considers four main themes: the depopulation of the native Hawaiians, the immigration of foreign laborers, intermarriage among groups, and exchange with the mainland. Detailed statistics, including United States census materials from 1900 through 1960, are provided, as well as source references.

Q.2.c Economics and Economic History

No bibliographies, and only a few reference works, dealing specifically with the economics and economic history of these regions, have yet appeared. Numerous items covering economic and economic historical matters, however, are listed in the various bibliographies cited in section 1.b of this part, while statistical material is provided in many of the handbooks cited in sections Q.1.e and Q.1.g. Palmer's *Guide to Australian Economic Statistics* (1966) (1) and *Publications of the Commonwealth Bureau of Census and Statistics* (n.d.) (2) are two items to be consulted for detailed work on Australia.

ReQua and Statham's *The Developing Nations* (I.1.b:1) should be consulted. Historical statistics are available in *Cross-Polity Time-Series Data* (I.1.g:7), while Finlayson's *Historical Statistics of Australia* (1970) (3) is concerned with one country.

Q.2.d Geography

No detailed bibliography of Australian, Pacific, or Antarctic geography has been published as yet. The *Australian Geographer,* however, has regular book reviews and lists of books received. Also valuable is the International Geographical Union's *Selected Annotated Bibliography of the Humid Tropics* (E.2.c:7). For Antarctica, many items of geographical importance are cited in the *Antarctic Bibliography* (Q.1.b:6) and Hayton's *National Interests in Antarctica* (Q.1.b:19).

Q.2.e History

Three essays in Robin W. Winks's *The Historiography of the British Empire-Commonwealth* (J.2.e:11) provide critical assessments of recent literature on Australia, New Zealand, and the British Territories of the Pacific. *Historical Studies: Australia and New Zealand* (1940–) (1) includes an annual record of monographic and periodical literature in the sections "Writings in New Zealand History" and "Writings in Australian History."

Jennifer Finlayson's *Historical Statistics of Australia: A Select List of Official Sources* (Q.2.c:3) is a monograph designed as one of a series of publications dealing with Australian statistical source materials. The serials selected for coverage in the work include mainly those issued by the Commonwealth Bureau of Census and Statistics, the State Offices of Statistics prior to their amalgamation with the Commonwealth Bureau, and the colonial predecessor whose serials were continued by the State Statistical Offices.

Q.2.f   Literature

In addition to the appropriate volumes in the *Penguin Companion to World Literature* (L.2.f:1) and the *MLA Bibliography* (B.2.e:1), several useful treatments of Australian and New Zealand literature are discussed in the third volume of Walford (A.1. b:12).

Q.2.g   Political Science

The only bibliography which specifically pertains to political science for any of the regions covered in this chapter is Robert D. Hayton's *National Interests in Antarctica* (Q.1.b:19). Official publications, books and pamphlets, signed articles, and miscellaneous materials concerning Antarctic administration and control are the classes of printed works included in the volume. Some 1,168 items are arranged alphabetically in these four groups for each of 26 countries and the United Nations and other international agencies. Many are briefly annotated.

For other regions covered in this chapter, the student is advised to consult the *International Bibliography of Political Science* (G.1. b.4) and *International Political Science Abstracts* (G.1.b:5). A useful guide to Australian federal politics is *Inside Canberra: A Guide to Australian Federal Politics* (1971) (1).

Q.2.h   Sociology

No specific bibliographies of sociological studies on Australasia or the Pacific have yet appeared. Numerous items of sociological significance are listed in certain of the bibliographies listed in section 1.b of this part. The student is recommended also to consult the appropriate sections of the *International Bibliography of Sociology* (H.1.b:2).

Notes

Introduction

1. A more extensive treatment is given these ideas—especially the structure and function of intermediary sources (i.e., reference works) in providing access to the bibliographic structure of literature networks —in "Integrating Classroom Instruction and Library Research: An Essay-Review" by Raymond McInnis in *Studies in History and Society* 6 (Fall 1974).

Part A

1. Melvin Weinstock's "Citation Indexes," *Encyclopedia of Library and Information Science,* vol. 5, pp. 16–40 (New York: Dekker, 1971) is an extensive discussion of the principles and uses of citation indexes.

2. Late in 1973 a revised and expanded second edition of White's book was published. It is reviewed by R. G. McInnis in "Integrating Classroom Instruction and Library Research."

3. Incidentally, Melnyk (D.1.b:1) and Walford (A.1.b:12) cite a *Statistical Sources Review* as a quarterly publication of the Gale Research Company of Detroit; however, plans for publication were announced but never undertaken, according to the publisher.

Part B

1. In 1972 *BRA* was discontinued and replaced by the *Annual Review of Anthropology* (beginning October 1972).

2. In *Behavior Science Notes* (vol. 2, 1969, p. 167) is a list of supplements to the *Ethnographic Atlas* that have appeared in *Ethnology*.

Part F

1. Ironic evidence of the latter point was discovered by Dr. Harvey Einbinder, who revealed in his book *The Myth of the Britannica* that no less than 666 articles (of at least one-half page in length) were being used unchanged from the ninth, eleventh, or thirteenth editions in current editions of *Encyclopaedia Britannica* as late as 1963. The *Encyclopaedia* quietly took advantage of Einbinder's research and had these articles revised.

2. "The Relations between History and History of Science," *Daedalus* 99 (Spring 1971):273.

Part G

1. *American Political Science Review* 61 (1967):562.

Part I

1. *College and Research Libraries* 19 (1958):111–17.

Part J

1. *Journal of Modern African Studies* 5 (1967):567. More detail about the project, including W. E. B. DuBois's attempts throughout his life to produce an encyclopedia for Africa and Africans, is given in Clarence G. Contee's "The *Encyclopedia Africana* project of W. E. B. DuBois," *African Historical Studies* 4 (1967): 77–91.

Part L

1. *Daedalus* 100 (1):49.

Part O

1. Robert Collison, *Encyclopedias* (New York: Hafner, 1964), p. 187. According to Collison, *The American Cyclopedia* was an authoritative work of over 300 contributors.

2. According to the American Historical Association, the Service Center for Teachers of History series is being discontinued. In its place are two new series. The first, to be known as AHA Pamphlets, will abandon the essentially bibliographical approach of most of the earlier series. Instead, it will offer "concise, readable, and stimulating essays, narrative and critical," summarizing recent interpretations, and select bibliographies. Some pamphlets will be revisions of items in the old series. Others, though by the same authors, will be entirely rewritten to conform to the new program, and new pamphlets will be added. The series on records, Discussions on Teaching, will be devoted to problems of particular interest to teachers in the schools. It will cover questions of interpretation, method, and approaches suitable to the modern classroom.

3. Microfiche versions of most documents published by city and county governments are available from the publisher.

4. *Scientific American* 212 (June 1965):137.

5. According to the *Indian Historian* 4 (4), the American Indian Historical Society will publish a biographical dictionary of living and deceased Indian leaders, traditionalists, historians, educators, and scholars.

6. See Schmeckebier (O.3.1) for a discussion of the availability of U.S.-government publications, including a list of depository libraries.

Part P

1. For example, in the 1970–71 volume, attention is directed to G. S. H. Barton's "Historical Background of Canadian Agriculture" (1939), R. H. Tarr's "Wartime Control under the Foreign Exchange Control Board" (1941 and 1942), J. Douglas Gibson's "Commercial Banking in Canada" (1961), an article on "Early Naturalization Procedure and Events Leading up to the Canadian Citizenship Act" (1951), Augustin Frigon's "History and Development of the Canadian Broadcasting Corporation" (1947), an examination of the "Terms of Union of Newfoundland with Canada, 1949," (1950), a survey of "Historical and Current Administration of Yukon Territory and Northwest Territories" (1968), R. E. Watt's "Historical Sketch of Criminal Law and Procedure" (1932), S. T. Wood's "The Influence of the Royal Canadian Mounted Police in the Building of Canada" (1950), C. A. Morell's "Federal Food and Drug Legislation in Canada" (1961), Eugene Foresey's "History of the Labor Movement in Canada" (1967), A. H. Le Neveu's "Use of the English and French Languages in Canada" (1965), and Pierre Camu's "The First Decade of the St. Lawrence Seaway" (1969).

Bibliography

Part A

A.I.a

1. Bartholomew (John) and Sons. *Times Atlas of the World.* London: Times Publishing Co., 1971. 272 pp.
2. Touring Club Italiano. *Atlante internazionale.* 8th ed. Milan, 1968. Milan: Indice dei romi, 1965. 1,032 pp.
3. USSR. Glavnoe upravlenie geodezii i kartografii. *The World Atlas.* 2d ed. Moscow, 1967. 250 pp.
4. Lewis, Clinton, and Campbell, J. D., eds. *Oxford Atlas.* Rev. reprint. London: Oxford University Press, 1966. 186 pp.
5. *McGraw-Hill International Atlas.* Under the direction of W. Bormann. New York: McGraw-Hill, 1964. 552 pp.
6. Bartholomew, John. *The Advanced Atlas of Modern Geography.* 7th ed. New York: McGraw-Hill, 1963. 159 pp.
7. *Hammond Medallion World Atlas.* Maplewood, N.J.: Hammond, 1969. 656 pp.
8. National Geographic Society, Cartographic Division. *National Geographic Atlas of the World.* Rev. 3d ed. Washington, 1970. 331 pp.
9. Espenshade, Edward B., ed. *Goode's World Atlas.* 13th ed. Chicago: Rand McNally, 1970. 288 pp.
10. Philip (George) and Son. *Aldine University Atlas.* 1st ed. Chicago: Aldine, 1969. 309 pp.
11. Lock, Clara Beatrice Muriel. *Modern Maps and Atlases.* Hamden, Conn.: Archon Books, 1969. 619 pp.
12. U.S. Library of Congress. *A List of Geographical Atlases in the Library of Congress, with Bibliographical Notes.* Washington: Library of Congress, 1909–.
13. British Museum. *Catalog of Printed Maps in the British Museum: Accessions.* London: Trustees of the British Museum, 1884–.
14. American Geographical Society, Map Department. *Index to Maps in Books and Periodicals.* 10 vols. Boston: G. K. Hall, 1967.

A.I.b

1. Besterman, Theodore. *A World Bibliography of Bibliographies.* 5 vols. 4th ed. Geneva: Societas Bibliographica, 1965.
2. *Bibliographic Index.* New York: Wilson, 1938–.

3. Gray, Richard A., comp. *Serial Bibliographies in the Humanities and Social Sciences.* Ann Arbor: Pierian Press, 1969. 345 pp.
4. Arnim, Max. *Internationale Personalbibliographies, 1800–1959.* 3 vols. Leipzig: K. W. Hiersemann, 1944–63.
5. *London Bibliography of the Social Sciences.* 18 vols. London: London School of Political and Economic Sciences, 1931–.
6. *Social Sciences Citation Index.* Philadelphia: Institute for Scientific Information, 1973–.
7. Wasserman, Paul, ed. *Encyclopedia of Business Information Sources.* 2 vols. Detroit: Gale Research Co., 1970.
8. The American Behavioral Scientist. *The A.B.S. Guide to Recent Publications in the Social and Behavioral Sciences.* New York, 1965–.
9. Hoselitz, Berthold F., ed. *A Reader's Guide to the Social Sciences.* 2d ed. New York: Free Press, 1970. 435 pp.
10. White, Carl M. *Sources of Information in the Social Sciences.* Totowa, N.J.: Bedminster Press, 1964. 498 pp.
11. Lewis, Peter R. *Literature of the Social Sciences.* London: Library Association, 1960. 222 pp.
12. Walford, A. J., ed. *Guide to Reference Material.* 3 vols. 2d ed. London: Library Association, 1968–70.
13. Winchell, Constance M., ed. *Guide to Reference Books.* Chicago: A.L.A., 1967–.
14. Harris, Chauncy D. *Bibliographies and Reference Works for Research in Geography.* 2d ed. Chicago: University of Chicago, forthcoming.
15. Public Affairs Information Service. *Bulletin.* New York, 1913–.
16. ———. *Foreign Language Index.* New York, 1971–.
17. *Social Sciences and Humanities Index.* New York: Wilson, 1907–.
18. *British Humanities Index.* London: Library Association, 1915–.
19. *Internationale Bibliographie der Zeitschriftenliteratur.* Osnabrück: Felix Dietrich, 1897–.
20. *Readers' Guide to Periodical Literature.* New York: Wilson, 1900–.
21. *Poole's Index to Periodical Literature.* Boston: Houghton Mifflin, 1802–1907.
22. *Ulrich's International Periodicals Directory.* New York: Bowker, 1932–.
23. *Indexed Periodicals.* Ann Arbor: Pierian Press, 1970–.
24. U.S. Library of Congress. *Catalog of Books. . . .* 167 vols. Ann Arbor: Edwards, 1942–46.
25. U.S. Library of Congress. *Library of Congress Author Catalog.* 24 vols. Ann Arbor: Edwards, 1948–52.
26. *National Union Catalog.* Washington, D.C.: Library of Congress, Card Division, 1953–.
27. *National Union Catalog: Pre-1956 Imprints.* London: Mansell, 1968–.
28. U.S. Library of Congress. *Library of Congress Catalog. Books: Subjects.* Ann Arbor: Edwards, 1955–.
29. *Cumulative Book Index.* New York: Wilson, 1898–.
30. *Publishers' Trade List Annual.* New York: Bowker, 1873–.

31. The Publishers' Trade List Annual. *Books in Print*. New York: Bowker, 1948–.
32. *Subject Guide to Books in Print*. New York: Bowker, 1957–.
33. *Paperbound Books in Print*. New York: Bowker, 1955–.

A.l.c

1. *The Book Review Digest*. New York: Wilson, 1906–.
2. *Book Review Index*. Detroit: Gale Research Co., 1965–.
3. *Mental Health Book Review Index*. New York: Council on Research in Bibliography, 1956–.
4. *Social Science Book Review Index*. Ann Arbor: Pierian Press, 1971–.
5. *Index to Book Reviews in the Humanities*. Detroit: P. Thomson, 1960–.
6. *Internationale Bibliographie der Rezensionen wissenschaftlicher Literatur*. Osnabrück: Dietrich, 1900–43, 1971–.
7. Gray, Richard A., comp. *A Guide to Book Review Citations*. Columbus: Ohio State University Press, 1969. 221 pp.

A.l.d

1. Thorne, J. O., ed. *Chambers's Bibliographical Dictionary*. Rev. ed. Edinburgh: Chambers, 1968. 1,432 pp.
2. Barnhart, Clarence L., ed. *New Century Cyclopedia of Names*. 3 vols. New York: Appleton, 1954.
3. *Webster's Biographical Dictionary*. Springfield, Mass.: Merriam, 1963. 1,697 pp.
4. Thomas, Joseph. *Universal Pronouncing Dictionary of Biography and Mythology*. 5th ed. Philadelphia: Lippincott, 1930. 2,550 pp.
5. Payton, Geoffrey. *Webster's Dictionary of Proper Names*. Springfield, Mass.: Merriam, 1970. 752 pp.
6. *International Who's Who*. London: Europa Publications, 1935–.
7. *Who's Who in the World*. Chicago: Marquis, 1971–.
8. *McGraw-Hill Encyclopedia of World Biography*. 12 vols. New York: McGraw-Hill, 1972.
9. Slocum, Robert B. *Biographical Dictionaries and Related Works*. Detroit, Gale Research Co., 1967. 1,056 pp. (Supplement, 1972).
10. *Biography Index*. New York: Wilson, 1937–.
11. Hyamson, Albert M. *Dictionary of Universal Biography*. 2d ed. New York: Dutton, 1951. 679 pp.
12. *New York Times Obituaries Index, 1858–1968*. New York: New York Times Co., 1970. 1,136 pp.
13. *New York Times Biographical Edition*. New York: New York Times Co., 1970–.
14. *Current Biography*. New York: Wilson, 1940–.
15. *American Men and Women of Science*. Lancaster, Pa.: Science Press, 1906–.

A.1.e

1. Seligman, Edwin R. A., and Johnson, Alvin, eds. *Encyclopedia of the Social Sciences*. 15 vols. New York: Macmillan, 1930–35.
2. Sills, David L., ed. *International Encyclopedia of the Social Sciences*. 17 vols. New York: Macmillan, 1968.
3. Zadrozny, John Thomas. *Dictionary of Social Science*. Washington: Public Affairs, 1959. 369 pp.
4. Gould, Julius, and Kolb, William L., eds. *Dictionary of the Social Sciences*. New York: Free Press, 1964. 761 pp.
5. *Encyclopaedia Britannica*. Chicago, London, Toronto, in continuous revision.
6. *Encyclopedia Americana*. New York: Americana, in continuous revision.
7. Bridgwater, W., and Kurtz, S., eds. *The Columbia Encyclopedia*. 3d ed. New York: Columbia University Press, 1963. 2,388 pp.
8. Edwards, Paul, ed. *Encyclopedia of Philosophy*. 8 vols. New York: Macmillan, 1967.
9. Hastings, James, ed. *Encyclopedia of Religion and Ethics*. 13 vols. New York: Scribner, 1908–26.
10. Schaff-Herzog Encyclopedia. *The New Encyclopedia of Religious Knowledge*. 13 vols. New York and London: Funk & Wagnalls, 1908–14.
11. *New Catholic Encyclopedia*. 15 vols. New York: McGraw-Hill, 1967.
12. *Encyclopaedia Judaica*. 16 vols. Jerusalem: Encyclopaedia Judaica, 1972.
13. Ruffner, Frederick G., ed. *Code Names Dictionary*. Detroit: Gale Research Co., 1963. 555 pp.
14. *Acronyms and Initialisms Dictionary*. 3d ed. Detroit: Gale Research Co., 1970. 484 pp.
15. *Reverse Acronyms and Initalisms Dictionary*. Detroit: Gale Research Co., 1972–.

A.1.f

1. *Whitaker's Almanack*. London, 1869–.
2. *The World Almanac and Book of Facts*. New York: World-Telegram, 1893–.
3. *Information Please Almanac*. New York: Simon & Schuster, 1947–.
4. *Reader's Digest Almanac*. New York: Reader's Digest Association, 1966–.
5. *New York Times Almanac*. New York, 1970–.

A.1.g

1. *New York Times,* 1851–.
2. *New York Times Newspaper Index*. 1851–.
3. *Times* (London). London, 1785–.
4. *Annual Register of World Events*. London, 1758–.

5. *Keesing's Contemporary Archives.* Keynsham, Bristol, England: Keesing's Publications, 1931–.
6. *Facts on File.* New York: Facts on File, 1941–.

A.I.h

1. Wasserman, Paul, ed. *Statistics Sources.* 3d ed. Detroit: Gale Research Co., 1971. 647 pp.

A.I.i

1. Vinge, C. L. *United States Government Publications for Teaching and Research in Geography.* Totowa, N.J.: Littlefield, Adams, 1967. 360 pp.

Part B

B.I.a

1. Spencer, Robert F. *Atlas for Anthropology.* 2d ed. Dubuque: Brown, 1968. 61 leaves.

B.I.b

1. Downs, R. B., and Jenkins, F. B., eds. *Bibliography: Current State and Future Trends.* Urbana: University of Illinois Press, 1967. 611 pp.
2. Harvard University. Peabody Museum of Archaeology and Ethnology. *Catalog: Author and Subject.* 53 vols. Boston: G. K. Hall, 1963.
3. Mandelbaum, David Goodman, ed. *Resources for the Teaching of Anthropology.* Berkeley: University of California Press, 1963. 316 pp.
4. *International Bibliography of Social and Cultural Anthropology.* Chicago: Aldine, 1959–.
5. Royal Anthropological Institute of Great Britain and Ireland Library. *Anthropological Index to Current Periodicals.* London, 1963–.
6. *Abstracts in Anthropology.* Westport, Conn.: Greenwood Press, 1970–.
7. *Biennial Review of Anthropology.* Stanford, Calif.: Stanford University Press, 1959–71.

B.I.c

1. *Current Anthropology,* vol. 8, no. 5 (December 1967), pt. 2 ("Directories Issue"); vol. 2, no. 3 (June 1970).

B.I.d

1. International Symposium on Anthropology, New York, 1952. *An-*

thropology Today: An Encyclopedic Inventory. Chicago: University of Chicago Press, 1953. 377 pp.

2. Hultkrantz, Ake, ed. *International Dictionary of Regional European Ethnology and Folklore.* Vol. 1, *General Ethnological Concepts.* Copenhagen: Rosenkilkde & Bagger, 1960. 282 pp.

3. Winick, Charles. *Dictionary of Anthropology.* New York: Philosophical Library, 1956. 579 pp.

B.1.e

1. Murdock, George Peter. *Ethnographic Atlas.* Pittsburgh: University of Pittsburgh Press, 1967. 128 pp.

2. *Ethnology.* New Haven: HRAF Press, 1962–.

3. Murdock, George Peter, *Outline of World Cultures.* 3d ed. rev. New Haven: HRAF Press, 1963. 222 pp.

4. O'Leary, Timothy J. "Concordance of the *Ethnographic Atlas* with the *Outline of World Cultures." Behavior Science Notes,* vol. 4, no. 2, 1969, pp. 165–207.

5. Murdock, George P. et al. *Outline of Cultural Materials* 4th ed. rev. New Haven: HRAF Press, 1967. 164 pp.

6. *HRAF Source Bibliography.* New Haven: HRAF Press, 1969–.

7. Textor, Robert B. *A Cross-Cultural Summary.* New Haven: HRAF Press, 1967.

B.1.f

1. Royal Anthropological Institute of Great Britain and Ireland. *Notes and Queries on Anthropology.* London: Routledge & Kegan Paul, 1951. 403 pp.

2. Adams, Richard N. *Human Organization Research: Field Relations and Techniques.* Homewood, Ill.: Dorsey Press for the Society for Applied Anthropology, 1960. 456 pp.

3. Glock, Charles Y., ed. *Survey Research in the Social Sciences.* New York: Russell Sage Foundation, 1967. 543 pp.

4. Jongmans, D. G. *Anthropologists in the Field.* Assen, Netherlands: Van Gorcum & Co., 1967. 277 pp.

5. *Social Science Information.* Paris: Mouton, 1962–.

B.2.a

1. *COWA Surveys and Bibliographies.* Cambridge, Mass.: Council For Old World Archaeology, 1957–.

2. Cottrell, Leonard, ed. *Concise Encyclopedia of Archaeology.* 2d ed. New York: Hawthorn, 1971. 430 pp.

3. Bray, Warwick, and Trump, David. *The American Heritage Guide to Archaeology.* New York: American Heritage Press, 1970. 269 pp.

4. Heizer, Robert F. *A Guide to Field Methods in Archaeology.* Palo Alto, Calif.: National Press, 1967. 274 pp.

B.2.b

1. *Encyclopedia of World Art.* 15 vols. New York: McGraw-Hill, 1959–68.

B.2.c

1. Nettl, Bruno. *Reference Materials in Ethnomusicology.* Detroit: Information Coordinators, 1967. 40 pp.
2. Duckles, Vincent, comp. *Music Reference and Research Materials.* 2d ed. New York: Free Press, 1967. 385 pp.

B.2.d

1. *Internationale Volkskundliche Bibliographie.* Rédigé . . . par R. Wildhaber. Basel: Krebs, 1939–.
2. *Abstracts of Folklore Studies.* Philadelphia: American Folklore Society, 1963–.
3. *Journal of American Folklore.* Boston: American Folklore Society, 1954–62.
4. *Southern Folklore Quarterly.* Gainesville: University of Florida Press, 1938–.
5. Thompson, Stith, ed. *Motif-Index of Folk-Literature.* 6 vols. Rev. ed. Bloomington: Indiana University Press, 1955–1958.
6. Leach, Marie, ed. *Funk and Wagnalls Dictionary of Folklore, Mythology, and Legend.* 2 vols. New York: Funk & Wagnalls, 1949.
7. Diehl, Katherine Smith. *Religions, Mythologies, Folklores: An Annotated Bibliography.* 2d ed. Metuchen, N.J.: Scarecrow Press, 1962. 573 pp.
8. Cavendish, Richard, ed. *Man, Myth, and Magic.* 7 vols. Maple Plain, Minn.: Purnell, 1970.
9. *Larousse Encyclopedia of Mythology.* New York: Prometheus Press, 1959. 500 pp.
10. Grey, Louis H., MacCulloch, John A. et al., eds. *Mythology of All Races.* 13 vols. Boston: Marshall Jones, 1916–32.
11. Bulfinch, Thomas. *Bulfinch's Mythology.* New York: Crowell, 1970. 957 pp.
12. Watts, Harold Holliday. *The Modern Reader's Guide to Religions.* New York: Barnes & Noble, 1964. 620 pp.
13. Adams, Charles J., ed. *A Reader's Guide to the Great Religions.* New York: Free Press, 1965. 364 pp.
14. Frazer, Sir James George. *The Golden Bough.* 12 vols. New York: Macmillan, 1907–1935.
15. Gaster, Theodore, ed. *New Golden Bough.* New York: Criterion, 1959. 738 pp.

B.2.e

1. Modern Language Association of America. *MLA International Bibliography of Books and Articles on the Modern Languages and Literatures.* New York: New York University Press, 1922–.

2. Permanent International Committee of Linguists. *Bibliographie linguistique.* Utrecht: Spectrum, 1939–.

B.2.f

1. Krogman, Wilton Marion. *A Bibliography of Human Morphology, 1914–1939.* Chicago: University of Chicago Press, 1941. 385 pp.
2. *Biological Abstracts* (Section H, *Abstracts of Human Biology*). Philadelphia, 1926–.

B.2.g

1. Naroll, Raoul. *A Handbook of Method in Cultural Anthropology.* Garden City, N.Y.: Natural History Press, 1970. 1,017 pp.
2. Keesing, Felix M. *Culture Change.* Stanford: Stanford University Press, 1953. 242 pp.
3. Albert, Ethel M., *A Selected Bibliography on Values, Ethics, and Aesthetics in the Behavioral Sciences and Philosophy, 1920–1958.* Glencoe, Ill.: Free Press, 1959. 342 pp.

Part C

C.I.a

1. USSR. Glavnoe upravlenie geodezii i kartografii. *Atlas narodov mira* [Atlas of the peoples of the world]. Moscow, 1964. 184 pp. Translation of titles and legends of the maps by V. G. Telberg. 1 vol. unpaged. New York: Telberg Book Corp., 1965.
2. Burgdörfer, Friedrich. *World Atlas of Population.* Hamburg: Falk-Verlag, 1956–.
3. May, Jacques M. "Atlas of Diseases." *Geographical Review,* 1950–55.
4. Rodenwaldt, Ernst. *Welt-Seuchen Atlas* [World atlas of epidemic diseases]. 3 vols. Hamburg: Falk-Verlag, 1952–56.
5. Howe, George Melvyn. *National Atlas of Disease Mortality in the United Kingdom.* Rev. and enl. ed. New York: Nelson, 1963. 197 pp.

C.I.b

1. *Population Index.* Princeton, Office of Population Research, Princeton University, and the Population Association of America. Princeton, 1935–.
2. *Current Publications in Population/Family Planning.* New York: Population Council, 1969–.
3. Eldridge, Hope Tisdale. *The Materials of Demography.* New York: International Union for the Scientific Study of Population, 1959. 222 pp.
4. Zelinsky, Wibur. *A Bibliographic Guide to Population Geography* (Chicago University Department of Geography Research Paper

no. 80). Chicago: University of Chicago, Department of Geography, 1962. 257 pp.

5. *Population Bulletin*. Washington, D.C.: Population Reference Bureau, 1945–.

C.l.c

1. Hutchinson, Edward Prince. *The Population Debate*. Boston: Houghton Mifflin, 1967. 466 pp.
2. Bonar, James. *Theories of Population from Raleigh to Arthur Young*. London: Allen & Unwin, 1931. (Reprinted, 1966.) 253 pp.

C.l.d

1. Hyrenius, Hannes. *Demographic Dictionary in Interlingua, English, and French*. Gothenburg, Sweden: Demographic Institute, University of Gothenburg, 1969. 96 leaves.

C.l.e

1. *European Demographic Information Bulletin*. The Hague: Nijhoff, for Centre Europeen d'etudes de population, 1970–.
2. Woytinsky, Wladimir W. *World Population and Production: Trends and Outlook*. New York: Twentieth Century Fund, 1953. 1,268 pp.

C.l.f

1. Hauser, Philip Morris, ed. *The Study of Population*. Chicago: University of Chicago Press, 1959. 864 pp.
2. Glass, David Victor, ed. *Introduction to Malthus*. London: Watts, 1953. 205 pp.
3. Coontz, Sydney H. *Population Theories and the Economic Interpretation*. New York: Humanities, 1957. 200 pp.
4. U.S. Bureau of the Census. *Methods and Materials of Demography*. 2 vols. Washington, 1971.

C.l.g

1. United Nations, Statistical Office. *Demographic Yearbook*. New York: 1949–.
2. United Nations, Statistical Office. *Population and Vital Statistics Report*. Statistical Papers, Series A. New York, 1953–.
3. *World Health Statistics Annual*. Geneva: World Health Organization, 1950–.
4. Population Reference Bureau. *World Population Data Sheet*. Washington, 1962–.
5. University of Texas, Population Research Center. *International Population Census Bibliography*. Austin: Bureau of Business Research, University of Texas, 1965–68. 7 vols.
6. International Labor Office. Library. *Census Publications, 1945–54*. Geneva, 1955.

7. United Nations, Statistical Office. *Handbook of Population Census Methods*. 3 vols. New York, 1958.
8. United Nations, Statistical Office. *Handbook of Vital Statistics Methods*. New York, 1958–59. 258 pp.
9. Keyfitz, Nathan. *World Population: An Analysis of Vital Data*. Chicago: University of Chicago Press, 1968. 672 pp.
10. Davis, Kingsley, ed. *World Urbanization, 1950–1970*. Vol. 1., *Basic Data for Cities, Countries, and Regions;* Vol. 2, *Analysis of Trends, Relationships, and Development*. Population Monograph series, nos. 4 and 9. Berkeley: University of California Press, 1969–72.
11. Deldycke, Tilo. *La Population active et sa structure* [The working population and its structure]. International Historical Statistics, vol. 1. Brussels: Centre d'économie politique (de l') Université libre de Bruxelles, 1968.

C.2.a

1. Pearl, Raymond. *The Natural History of Population*. London: Oxford University Press, 1939. 416 pp.
2. Freedman, Ronald. "The Sociology of Human Fertility: A Trend Report and Bibliography." *Current Sociology,* vol. 10/11, no. 2, 1961–62, pp. 82–119.
3. Milbank Memorial Fund. *Papers Presented at the 1958 Annual Conference. . . . Part 2, Thirty Years of Research in Human Fertility*. New York, 1959.
4. Milbank Memorial Fund. *Trends and Differentials in Mortality*. New York, 1956. 165 pp.

C.2.b

1. Mangalam, J. J. *Human Migration: A Guide to Migration Literature in English, 1955–1962*. Lexington: University of Kentucky Press, 1968. 194 pp.
2. George Washington University. *A Report on World Population Migrations*. Washington: George Washington University, 1956. 449 pp.
3. Thomas, Brinley. *International Migration and Economic Development: A Trend Report and Bibliography*. Paris: UNESCO, 1961. 85 pp.
4. Larimore, Ann Evans. *World Urbanization and Urban Migration: An Annotated Bibliography*. 1 vol. Ann Arbor, 1969.
5. Willcox, Walter Francis. *International Migration*. Demographic Monographs, 7–8. 2 vols. New York: Gordon & Breach, 1929–31.
6. *International Migration*. The Hague, 1961–.
7. *International Migration Review*. New York: Center for Migration Studies, 1964–.

C.2.c

1. Stanford Research Institute. International Development Center.

Human Resources and Economic Growth: An Annotated Bibliography on the Role of Education and Training in Economic and Social Development. Menlo Park, Calif.: 1963. 398 pp.

2. Hazelwood, Arthur. *The Economics of Underdeveloped Areas: An Annotated Reading List of Books, Articles, and Official Publications.* 2d enl. ed. London: Oxford University Press, 1959. 156 pp.

3. ————. *The Economics of Development: An Annotated List of Books and Articles Published 1958–1962.* London: Oxford University Press, 1964. 104 pp.

C.2.d

1. Kasdon, David L. *International Family Planning, 1966–1968: A Bibliography.* Public Health Service publication no. 1917. Chevy Chase, Md.: National Institute of Mental Health, 1969. 62 pp.

2. United Nations, Economic and Social Council. *Family Planning, International Migration, and Urbanization in ECAFE Countries.* Asian Population series, no. 2. New York, 1968.

3. Tietze, Christopher. *Selected Bibliography of Contraception, 1940–1960.* New York: National Committee on Maternal Health, 1960. Supplement, 1963.

4. Tietze, Christopher, ed. *Bibliography of Fertility Control, 1950–65.* New York: National Committee on Maternal Health, 1965. 198 pp.

5. Geijerstam, Gunnar af, ed. *An Annotated Bibliography of Induced Abortion.* Ann Arbor: Center for Population Planning, University of Michigan, 1969. 359 pp.

6. Dollen, Charles. *Abortion in Context: A Select Bibliography.* Metuchen, N.J.: Scarecrow, 1970. 150 pp.

Part D

D.1.a

1. The Economist Intelligence Unit. *Oxford Economic Atlas of the World.* 4th ed. London: Oxford University Press, 1972. 239 pp.

D.1.b

1. Melnyk, Peter. *Economics: Bibliographic Guide to Reference Books and Information Resources.* Littleton, Colo.: Libraries Unlimited, 1971. 263 pp.

2. Maltby, Arthur. *Economics and Commerce.* Hamden, Conn.: Archon Books, 1968. 239 pp.

3. Fletcher, John, ed. *The Use of Economics Literature.* Hamden, Conn.: Archon Books, 1971. 310 pp.

4. Fundaburk, Emma Lila. *Reference Materials and Periodicals in Economics.* 5 vols. Metuchen, N.J.: Scarecrow Press, 1971–.

5. Harvard University, Graduate School of Business Administration, Baker Library. *CORE Collection.* Cambridge, 1970–.

6. *Business Periodicals Index.* New York: Wilson, 1958–.
7. *Economics Selections: An International Bibliography.* Series 1. New York: Gordon and Breach, 1953–.
8. *Cumulative Bibliography of Economic Books, 1954/62–.* New York: Gordon and Breach, 1965–.
9. American Economic Association. *Journal of Economic Literature.* 1963–.
10. American Economic Association. *Index of Economic Journals.* Homewood, Ill.: Irwin, 1886–.
11. American Economic Association. *Index of Economic Articles in Collective Volumes.* Homewood, Ill.: Irwin, 1964–.
12. *International Bibliography of Economics.* Chicago: Aldine, 1955–.
13. American Economic Association. *Surveys of Economic Theory.* 3 vols. London: Macmillan, 1965–66.

D.l.c

1. American Economic Association. *Handbook.* Menasha, Wis.: American Economic Assn., 1938–.

D.l.d

1. Greenwald, Douglas, ed. *McGraw-Hill Dictionary of Modern Economics.* New York: McGraw-Hill, 1973. 697 pp.
2. Taylor, Philip A. S. *A New Dictionary of Economics.* London: Routledge & Kegan Paul, 1966. 304 pp.
3. Horton, Byrne J., Ripley, J., and Schapper. *Dictionary of Modern Economics.* Washington: Public Affairs, 1948. 365 pp.

D.l.e

1. *Financial Times Yearbook: Business Information.* New York: St. Martin, 1969–.
2. Andreano, Ralph L., Farler, E. I., and Reynolds, S. *The Student Economist's Handbook.* Cambridge, Mass.: Schenckman Publishing Co., 1967. 169 pp.

D.2.a

1. Palgrave, Sir Robert Hally Inglis. *Palgrave's Dictionary of Political Economy.* Rev. ed., 1925–26. Reprint. New York: Kelley, 1963.
2. Schleiffer, E., and Crandall, R., eds. *Index to Economic History Essays in Festschriften, 1900–1950.* Cambridge, Mass.: Harvard University Press, 1953. 68 pp.
3. Mulhall, Michael G. *The Dictionary of Statistics.* 4th ed. London: Routledge & Kegan Paul, 1899. Reprint. Detroit: Gale Research Co., 1969. 853 pp.
4. Webb, A. D., comp. *New Dictionary of Statistics.* London: Routledge & Kegan Paul, 1911. 682 pp.

D.2.b

1. Popescu, Oreste. "On the Historiography of Economic Thought: A Bibliographical Survey." *Cahiers d'histoire mondiale* [Journal of world history] 64, no. 8 (1964): 168–209.
2. Batson, Harold E., comp. *A Select Bibliography of Modern Economic Theory, 1870–1929.* New York: Dutton, 1930. 224 pp.
3. *Economics Library Selections.* Series 2. Baltimore: Johns Hopkins University, Department of Political Economy, 1954–61.

D.2.c

1. Demarest, Rosemary R. *Accounting: Information Sources.* Management Information Guide, no. 18. Detroit: Gale Research Co., 1970. 420 pp.
2. Woy, James B. *Business Trends and Forecasting.* Management Information Guide, no. 9. Detroit: Gale Research Co., 1965. 152 pp.
3. Jones, Gwendolyn. *Packaging Information Sources.* Management Information Guide, no. 10. Detroit: Gale Research Co., 1967. 285 pp.
4. Randle, Gretchen R. *Electronic Industries: Information Sources.* Management Information Guide, no. 13. Detroit: Gale Research Co., 1968. 227 pp.
5. Vara, Albert C. *Food and Beverage Industries: A Bibliography and Guidebook.* Management Information Guide, no. 16. Detroit: Gale Research Co., 1970. 215 pp.
6. Metcalf, Kenneth N. *Transportation: Information Sources.* Management Information Guide, no. 8. Detroit: Gale Research Co., 1965. 307 pp.
7. Flood, Kenneth U. *Research in Transportation: Legal/Legislative and Economic Sources and Procedure.* Management Information Guide, no. 20. Detroit: Gale Research Co., 1970. 126 pp.
8. McDermott, Beatrice S. *Government Regulation of Business Including Antitrust.* Management Information Guide, no. 11. Detroit: Gale Research Co., 1967. 229 pp.

D.2.e

1. Woy, James B., ed. *Investment Information.* Management Information Guide, no. 19. Detroit: Gale Research Co., 1970. 231 pp.
2. Christian, Portia. *Ethics in Business Conduct: Selected References from the Record-Problems, Attempted Solutions, Ethics, in Business Education.* Management Information Guide, no. 21. Detroit: Gale Research Co., 1970. 156 pp.
3. Knox, Vera H. *Public Finance Information Sources.* Management Information Guide, no. 3. Detroit: Gale Research Co., 1964. 142 pp.

D.2.f

1. Wheeler, Lora Jeanne. *International Business and Foreign Trade.* Management Information Guide, no. 14. Detroit: Gale Research Co., 1968. 221 pp.
2. International Monetary Fund. *International Financial Statistics.* Washington: International Monetary Fund, 1948–.

D.2.g

1. Allen, Victor Leonard. *International Bibliography of Trade Unionism.* London: Merlin Press, 1968. 180 pp.
2. International Labor Office. *Yearbook of Labor Statistics.* Geneva: International Labor Office, 1936–.
3. International Labor Office. *Bulletin of Labor Statistics.* Geneva: International Labor Office, 1965–.
4. International Labor Office. *Bulletin of Labor Statistics: Supplement.* Geneva: International Labor Office, 1965–.

Part E

E.1.a

1. *Bibliographie cartographique internationale.* Paris: Colin, 1938–.
2. *Times Index-Gazetteer of the World.* London: Times Publishing Co., 1965. 964 pp.
3. U.S. Board on Geographic Names of the Department of the Interior. *Gazetteer . . . Official Standard Names* (series). Washington: GPO, 1955–.
4. Seltzer, Leon, ed. *The Columbia-Lippincott Gazetteer of the World.* New York: Columbia University Press, 1962. 2,170 pp.
5. *Webster's Geographical Dictionary.* Rev. ed. Springfield, Mass.: Merriam, 1969. 1,293 pp.

E.1.b

1. Wright, John Kirtland, and Platt, E. T. *Aids to Geographical Research.* American Geographical Society Research series, no. 22. 2d ed. New York: Columbia University Press, 1947. 331 pp.
2. Minto, C. S. *How to Find Out in Geography.* Elmsford, N.Y.: Pergamon, 1966. 99 pp.
3. Lewthwaite, Gordon Rowland, ed. *A Geographical Bibliography for American College Libraries.* Washington: Association of American Geographers, Commission on College Geography, 1970. 214 pp.
4. American Geographical Society. *Research Catalog of the American Geographical Society.* 15 vols. Boston: G. K. Hall, 1962.
5. *Current Geographical Publications.* New York: American Geographical Society, 1938–.

6. Association des Géographes Français. *Bibliographie géographique internationale*. Paris, 1891–.
7. *New Geographical Literature and Maps*. London: The Royal Geographical Society, 1951–.
8. London School of Economics, Department of Geography. *Geographical Abstracts*. London, 1966–.
9. *Progress in Geography*. London: Edward Arnold, 1969–.
10. Harris, Chauncy Dennison, and Fellmann, Jerome D., comps. *International List of Geographical Serials*. University of Chicago, Department of Geography, Research paper, no. 138. 2d ed. Chicago: University of Chicago Press, 1971. 267 pp.
11. Harris, Chauncy Dennison. *Annotated World List of Selected Current Geographical Serials in English*. Research paper, no. 96. 2d ed. Chicago: University of Chicago Press, 1964. 32 pp. (3d ed. forthcoming)

E.I.c

1. Freeman, Thomas Walter. *A Hundred Years of Geography*. Chicago: Aldine, 1962. 335 pp.
2. Association of American Geographers. *Directory*. Washington, 1970.
3. Schwendeman, Joseph R., ed. *Directory of College Geography of the United States*. Lexington: University of Kentucky Press, 1949–.
4. Association of American Geographers. *Guide to Graduate Departments of Geography in the United States and Canada*. Washington, 1968. 171 pp.
5. *Orbis Geographicus: World Directory of Geography*. Wiesbaden: Steiner, 1952–.

E.I.d

1. Deffontaines, Pierre, ed. *Larousse Encyclopedia of World Geography*. New York: Odyssey, 1965. 736 pp.
2. Bertin, Leon. *Larousse Encyclopedia of the Earth*. New York: Prometheus Press, 1961. 419 pp.
3. Gresswell, R. Kay, ed. *Standard Encyclopedia of the World's Rivers and Lakes*. New York: Putnam, 1965. 384 pp.
4. Fairbridge, Rhodes Whitmore, ed. *The Encyclopedia of Oceanography*. Encyclopedia of Earth Sciences, vol. 1. New York: Reinhold, 1966. 1,021 pp.
5. ———. *The Encyclopedia of Atmospheric Sciences and Astrogeology*. Encyclopedia of Earth Sciences, vol. 2. New York: Reinhold, 1967. 1,200 pp.
6. ———. *The Encyclopedia of Geomorphology*. Encyclopedia of Earth Sciences, vol. 3. New York: Reinhold, 1968. 1,295 pp.
7. Tietze, Wolf, ed. *Westermann Lexikon der Geographie*. Braunschweig, Germany: Westermann, 1968–.
8. Stamp, Laurence Dudley, ed. *A Glossary of Geographical Terms*. 2d ed. London: Longmans; New York: Wiley, 1966. 539 pp.

9. ———. *Dictionary of Geography*. New York: Wiley, 1966. 492 pp.
10. Monkhouse, Francis John. *A Dictionary of Geography*. 2d ed. London: Edward Arnold, 1970. 378 pp.
11. Moore, Wilfred George. *A Dictionary of Geography*. New York: Praeger, 1967. 246 pp.
12. Swayne, J. C. *A Concise Glossary of Geographical Terms*. 2d ed. London: Philip, 1959. 164 pp.
13. Schmieder, Allen A., Griffith, Paul F., Chatham, Ronald L., and Natoli, Salvatore J. *A Dictionary of Basic Geography*. Boston: Allyn & Bacon, 1970. 299 pp.
14. Knox, Alexander. *Glossary of Geographical and Topographical Terms*. London: Edward Stanford, 1904. Reprint. Detroit: Gale Research Co., 1968. 432 pp.
15. Lana, Gabriella. *The Glossary of Geographical Names in Six Languages*. Amsterdam: Elsevier, 1967. 184 pp.
16. Fischer, Eric, and Elliot, Francis E. *A German and English Glossary of Geographical Terms*. New York: American Geographical Society, 1950. 118 pp.

E.I.e

1. *The Statesman's Yearbook*. London: Macmillan, 1864–.
2. *Geographical Digest*. London: Philip, 1963–.
3. *New Geography*. New York: Abelard-Schuman, 1966–.
4. Lock, Clara Beatrice Muriel. *Geography: A Reference Handbook*. 2d ed. Hamden, Conn.: Archon Books, 1972. 179 pp.
5. Great Britain, Admiralty, Naval Intelligence Division. Geographical Handbook series. 58 vols. London: 1941–46.

E.I.f

1. Hartshorne, Richard. *The Nature of Geography*. Lancaster, Pa.: Association of American Geographers, 1939. 495 pp.
2. ———. *Perspective on the Nature of Geography*. Association of American Geographers Monograph series, no. 1. Chicago: Rand McNally, 1959. 201 pp.
3. Harvey, David W. *Explanation in Geography*. London: Edward Arnold, 1969. 521 pp.
4. Chorley, Richard J. and Haggett, Peter. *Models in Geography*. London: Methuen, 1967. 816 pp.
5. Bowman, Isaiah. *Geography in Relation to the Social Sciences*. New York: Scribner, 1934. 382 pp.
6. Ackerman, Edward Augustus. *Geography as a Fundamental Research Discipline*. University of Chicago, Department of Geography, Research Paper no. 53. Chicago, 1958. 37 pp.
7. National Academy of Sciences, National Research Council, Ad Hoc Committee on Geography. *The Science of Geography*. Washington, 1965. 80 pp.
8. Behavioral and Social Sciences Survey Committee, Geography

Panel. *Geography*. Edited by E. J. Taaffe. Englewood Cliffs, N.J.: Prentice-Hall, 1970. 143 pp.

9. Broek, Jan Otto Marius. *Compass of Geography*. Columbus, Ohio: Merrill, 1966. 82 pp.
10. Wooldridge, Sidney William, and East, W. G. *The Spirit and Purpose of Geography*. 3d rev. ed. London: Hutchinson's University Library, 1967. 168 pp.
11. Durrenberger, Robert W. *Geographical Research and Writing*. New York: Crowell Collier Macmillan, 1971. 246 pp.
12. Taylor, Thomas Griffith, ed. *Geography in the Twentieth Century: A Study of Growth, Fields, Techniques, Aims, and Trends*. 3d ed. New York: Philosophical Library, 1957. 674 pp.
13. James, Preston Everett, and Jones, Clarence F., eds. *American Geography: Inventory and Prospect*. Syracuse, N.Y.: Syracuse University Press, 1954.
14. Chorley, Richard J., and Haggett, Peter, eds. *Frontiers in Geographical Teaching*. 2d ed. London: Methuen, 1970. 384 pp.
15. Cohen, Saul B., ed. *Problems and Trends in American Geography*. New York: Basic Books, 1967. 298 pp.
16. Cooke, Ronald U., ed. *Trends in Geography: An Introductory Survey*. Oxford: Pergamon, 1969. 287 pp.

E.1.g

1. Chisholm, C. C. *Handbook of Commercial Geography*. Edited by Dudley Stamp and S. Carter Gilmour. 18th ed. London: Longmans, 1966. 918 pp.
2. Warren, Harry V., and Wilks, E. F. *World Resource Production: Fifty Years of Change*. Vancouver: Tantalus Research, 1966. 96 pp.

E.2.a

1. Debenham. Frank. *Discovery and Exploration: An Atlas-History of Man's Journeys into the Unknown*. 2d ed. London: Hamlyn, 1968. 272 pp.
2. USSR, Glavnoe upravlenie geodezii i kartografii. *Atlas istorii geograficheskikh otkrytii i issledovanii* [An atlas of the history of geographical discoveries and explorations]. Moscow, 1959. 108 pp.
3. Skelton, Raleigh Ashlin. *Explorers' Maps: Chapters in the Cartographic Record of Geographical Discovery*. New York: Praeger, 1958. 337 pp.
4. Riverain, Jean. *Concise Encyclopedia of Explorations*. Glasgow: Collins, 1969. 279 pp.
5. Langnas, Izaak Abram. *Dictionary of Discoveries*. New York: Philosophical Library, 1959. 201 pp.
6. Lemosof, Paul. *Le livre d'or de la géographie*. Paris: Delagrave, 1902.
7. Hakluyt Society. *Prospectus, with List of Publications and Maps*. London: 1956. 53 pp.

8. Cox, Edward Godfrey. *A Reference Guide to the Literature of Travel.* Publications in Language and Literature, vols. 9, 10, and 12. Seattle: The University of Washington, 1935–49.

E.2.b

1. Bell, Gwendolyn. *Annotated Bibliography of the Patterns and Dynamics of Rural Settlements.* University Graduate School of Public and International Affairs. Publication series in Public and International Affairs. Pittsburgh, 1968. 70 pp.
2. *Ekistics Index.* Athens: Athens Center of Ekistics, 1955–.
3. Kasperson, Roger E., and Minghi, Julian V. *The Structure of Political Geography.* Chicago: Aldine, 1969. 527 pp.
4. Goodey, Brian R. *The Geography of Elections: An Introductory Bibliography.* North Dakota University Center for the Study of Cultural and Social Change. Monograph no. 3. Grand Forks: Center for the study of Cultural and Social Change, Department of Sociology and Anthropology, University of North Dakota, 1968. 65 pp.
5. Peltier, Louis C., comp. *Bibliography of Military Geography.* Washington: Military Geography Committee, Association of American Geographers, 1962. 76 ll.

E.2.c

1. Ginsburg, Norton Sydney. *Atlas of Economic Development.* Department of Geography. Research paper no. 68. Chicago: University of Chicago Press, 1961. 119 pp.
2. Van Royen, William. *Atlas of the World's Resources.* 2 vols. New York: Prentice-Hall, 1952–54.
3. International Association of Agricultural Economists. *World Atlas of Agriculture.* 4 vols. Novara, Italy: Istituto Geografico De Agostini, 1969–.
4. *Biological and Agricultural Index.* New York: Wilson, 1916–.
5. Blanchard, Joy R., and Ostvold, H. *Literature of Agricultural Research.* University of California Bibliographic Guides, 1. Berkeley: University of California Press, 1958. 231 pp.
6. Thompson, Edgar T. *The Plantation: A Bibliography.* Washington: Social Science Section, Department of Cultural Affairs, Pan American Union, 1957. 93 pp.
7. Hills, Theo L., comp. International Geographical Union. Special Commission on the Humid Tropics. *A Selected Bibliography of the Humid Tropics.* Montreal: Geography Department, McGill University, 1960. 238 pp.
8. *Tropical Abstracts.* Amsterdam: Royal Tropical Institute, 1946–.
9. Jackson, Nora, and Penn, P. *A Dictionary of Natural Resources.* . . . 2d ed. Oxford, New York: Pergamon, 1969. 151 pp.
10. Kaplan, R. Stuart, ed. *A Guide to Information Sources in Mining,*

Minerals, and Geosciences. Guides to Information Sources in Science and Technology, vol 2. New York: Interscience, 1965. 599 pp.

11. Firth, Frank E., ed. *The Encyclopedia of Marine Resources.* New York: Reinhold, 1969. 740 pp.

12. Harris, Chauncy. *A Bibliography of the Geography of Manufacturing.* Chicago: Department of Geography, University of Chicago, 1952. 26 leaves.

13. Stevens, Benjamin H., and Brackett, Carolyn A. *Industrial Location: A Review and Annotated Bibliography of Theoretical, Empirical, and Case Studies.* Philadelphia: Regional Science Research Institute, 1967. 199 pp.

14. Wolfe, Roy I. *An Annotated Bibliography of the Geography of Transportation.* Institute of Transportation and Traffic Engineering, University of California, Information Circular no. 29. Berkeley: University of California Press, 1961. 61 leaves.

15. Olsson, Gunnar. *Distance and Human Interaction: A Review and Bibliography.* The Institute Bibliography series, no. 2. Philadelphia: Regional Science Research Institute, 1965. 112 pp.

16. Siddall, William R., comp. *Transportation Geography: A Bibliography.* Kansas State University Library series, 1. 3d ed. Manhattan: Kansas State University Library, 1969. 94 pp.

17. Black, William R. *A Bibliography of Selected Research on Networks and Urban Transportation Relevant to Current Transportation Geography Research.* Studies in Geography no. 16. Evanston, Ill.: Northwestern University, Department of Geography, 1968. 47 pp.

18. *Current Literature in Transportation.* Evanston, Ill.: Library of the Transportation Center, Northwestern University, 1958–.

19. Grotewold, Andreas. *A Selective Annotated Bibliography of Publications Relevant to the Geographic Study of International Trade.* Washington, 1960.

E.2.d

1. Sommer, John W. *Bibliography of Urban Geography.* Hanover, N.H.: Dartmouth Department of Geography, 1966. 94 pp.

2. Berry, Brian Joe Lobley. *Central Place Studies: A Bibliography of Theory and Application.* Philadelphia: Regional Science Research Institute, 1961. 153 pp. (Supplement, 1965. 50 pp.)

3. Hauser, Philip Morris, ed. *The Study of Urbanization.* New York: Wiley, 1965. 554 pp.

4. Shillaber, Caroline. *References on City and Regional Planning.* Cambridge: MIT Press, 1960. 41 pp.

5. Chapin, Francis Stuart, Jr. *Selected References on Urban Planning Methods and Techniques.* Chapel Hill: University of North Carolina, Department of City and Regional Planning, 1963. 58 leaves.

6. Bestor, George C., and Jones, H. R. *City Planning: A Basic Bibliography of Sources and Trends.* Sacramento, Calif.: Council of Civil Engineers and Land Surveyors, 1962. 195 pp.

7. International Union of Local Authorities. *Metropolis: A Select*

Bibliography of Administrative and Other Problems in Metro-politan Areas throughout the World. Compiled and edited by D. Halasz. 2d ed. The Hague: M. Nijhoff, 1967. 267 pp.

8. Branch, Melville Campbell. *Comprehensive Urban Planning.* Beverly Hills, Calif.: Sage Publications, 1970. 477 pp.

9. Council of Planning Librarians. Exchange Bibliography (series). Monticello, Ill.: Council of Planning Librarians, 1958–.

10. Boston College, Institute of Human Sciences. *Urban and Social Change Review.* Boston, Mass.: 1967–.

11. American Institute of Planners. *Journal.* Washington, 1925–.

E.2.e

1. "The Environmental Crisis." In *Paperbound Books in Print,* March 1970.

2. Moore, John Alexander. *Science for Society: A Bibliography.* AAAS misc. publication 70–6. Washington: American Association for the Advancement of Science, 1970. 42 pp.

3. Durrenberger, Robert W. *Environment and Man: A Bibliography.* Palo Alto, Calif.: National Press Books, 1970. 118 pp.

4. *Environment Information Access.* New York: Ecology Forum, 1971–.

5. *The Environment Index.* New York: Ecology Forum, 1971–.

6. *Environment Reporter.* Washington: Bureau of National Affairs, 1970–.

7. *Annual Review of Ecology and Systematics.* Palo Alto, Calif.: Annual Reviews, 1970–.

8. *Advances in Environmental Sciences and Technology.* New York: Interscience, 1969–.

9. Mitchell, John G., ed. *Ecotactics: The Sierra Club Handbook for Environmental Activists.* New York: Pocket Books, 1970. 288 pp.

10. Swatek, Paul. *The User's Guide to the Protection of the Environment.* New York, Friends of the Earth/Ballantine, 1970. 312 pp.

11. U.S. Bureau of Sport Fisheries and Wildlife. *Handbook of Toxicity of Pesticides to Wildlife.* Washington: GPO, 1970.

12. *Conservation Directory.* Washington: National Wildlife Federation, 1956–.

13. Wolfe, Roy I. "Perspective on Outdoor Recreation: A Bibliographic Survey." *Geographical Review* 54 (1964):203–38.

14. U.S. Outdoor Recreation Resources Review Commission. *Outdoor Recreation Literature: A Survey.* Study Report no. 27. Washington: 1962. 137 pp.

15. Pinkerton, James R., and Pinkerton, Marjorie J. *Outdoor Recreation and Leisure.* Columbia: Research Center, School of Business and Public Administration, University of Missouri, 1969. 332 pp.

16. *Pollution Abstracts.* La Jolla, Calif., 1970–.

17. McCrone, Walter C. *The Particle Atlas: A Photomicrographic Reference for the Microscopical Identification of Particulate Substances.* Ann Arbor: Ann Arbor Science Publishers, 1970. 220 pp.

18. U.S. National Air Pollution Control Administration. *Guide to Research in Air Pollution.* 7th ed. Washington: GPO, 1970. 193 pp.
19. Burd, Patricia A. *An Index to Air Pollution Research: A Guide to Current Government and Industry Supported Research.* University Park: Center for Air Environment Studies, Pennsylvania State University, 1968. 164 leaves.
20. *Air Pollution Abstracts.* Stevenage, England: Department of Trade and Industry, Warren Springs Laboratory, 1969–.
21. *Water Pollution Abstracts.* London, 1927–.
22. Stewart, R. Keith. *Water Pollution Control.* Washington: Department of the Interior, Federal Water Pollution Control, 1966. 126 pp.
23. Sinha, Evelyn. *Coastal/Estuarine Pollution: An Annotated Bibliography.* Ocean Engineering Information series, vol. 3. La Jolla, Calif.: Ocean Engineering Information Service, 1970. 87 pp.
24. U.S. Office of Water Resources Research. *Water Resources Research Catalog.* Washington: GPO, 1965–.
25. Lund, Herbert F., ed. *Industrial Pollution Control Handbook.* New York: McGraw-Hill, 1971.

Part F

F.I.a

1. Shepherd, William R. *Shepherd's Historical Atlas.* 9th ed. New York: Barnes & Noble, 1965. 341 pp.
2. Muir, R. *Muir's Historical Atlas: Ancient, Medieval, and Modern.* 10th ed. Edited by R. F. Treherne and H. Fullard. London: Philip, 1964. 96 pp.
3. Palmer, Robert R., ed. *Atlas of World History.* Chicago: Rand McNally, 1965. 216 pp.
4. Stier, Hans-Erich. *Westermanns Grosser Atlas zur Weltgeschichte: Vorzeit, Altertum, Mittelalter, Neuzeit.* Braunschweig: Westermann Verlag, 1968. 171 pp.
5. Gilbert, Martin. *Recent History Atlas: 1870 to the Present Day.* Cartography by John R. Flower. New York: Macmillan, 1969. 121 pp.
6. ———. *First World War Atlas.* New York: Macmillan, 1970. 159 pp.

F.I.b

1. Poulton, Helen S., ed. *The Historian's Handbook.* Norman: University of Oklahoma Press, 1972. 304 pp.
2. American Historical Association. *Guide to Historical Literature.* New York: Macmillan, 1961. 962 pp.
3. Historical Association (London). *Annual Bulletin of Historical Literature.* London, 1912–.

4. *International Bibliography of Historical Sciences*. Paris, 1926–1939, 1947–.

5. Irwin, Leonard B., comp. *A Guide to Historical Reading: Non-Fiction*. McKinley Bibliographies, vol. 2. 9th rev. ed. Brooklawn, New Jersey: McKinley Publishing Co., 1970.

6. Frewer, Louis Benson. *Bibliography of Historical Writings Published in Great Britain and the Empire, 1940–1945*. Oxford: Blackwell, 1947. 346 pp.

7. Lancaster, Joan Cadogan, comp. *Bibliography of Historical Works Issued in the United Kingdom, 1946–56*. London: University of London, Institute of Historical Research, 1957. 388 pp.

8. Kellaway, W., comp. *Bibliography of Historical Works Issued in the United Kingdom, 1957–60*. London: University of London, Institute of Historical Research, 1962. 236 pp.

9. Kellaway, William. *Bibliography of Historical Works Issued in the United Kingdom, 1961–1965*. London: University of London, Institute of Historical Research, 1967. 298 pp.

10. *Historical Abstracts, 1775–1970*. New York, 1955–.

11. Ziegler, Janet. *World War II: Books in English, 1945–1965*. Stanford, Calif.: Hoover Institution Press, 1971. 194 pp.

12. *Revue d'histoire de la deuxième guerre mondiale*. Paris, 1950–.

F.I.c

1. *Directory of American Scholars*. New York: Bowker, 1942–.

F.I.d

1. Langer, William Leonard, ed. *An Encyclopedia of World History*. 4th ed. rev, and enl. Boston: Houghton Mifflin, 1968. 1,504 pp.

2. Dunner, Joseph, ed. *Handbook of World History: Concepts and Issues*. New York: Philosophical Library, 1967. 1,011 pp.

3. Larned, Josephus N. *New Larned History for Ready Reference, Reading, and Research*. . . . 12 vols. Rev. ed. Springfield, Mass.: Nichols, 1922–24.

4. *Encyclopaedia Britannica*. 25 vols. 9th ed. Edinburgh, 1875–89.

5. *Encyclopaedia Britannica*. 32 vols. 11th ed. New York, 1910–1911.

6. Morris, Richard B., and Irwin, Graham W., eds. *Harper Encyclopedia of the Modern World*. New York: Harper & Row, 1970. 1,271 pp.

7. Palmer, A. W. *A Dictionary of Modern History, 1789–1945*. London: Cresset, 1962. 314 pp.

8. Dupuy, Richard Ernest, and Dupuy, Trevor. *The Encyclopedia of Military History*. New York: Harper & Row, 1970. 1,406 pp.

9. *Ten Eventful Years*. 4 vols. Chicago: Encyclopaedia Britannica, 1947.

10. Haydn, J. *Dictionary of Dates and Universal Information Relating to All Ages and Nations*. 25th ed. London: Ward, Lock, 1910. 1,614 pp.

F.l.e

1. Steinberg, Sigfrid H. *Historical Tables, 58* B.C.–A.D. *1963.* 7th ed. London: Macmillan, 1964. 259 pp.
2. Collison, R. L. W. *Newnes' Dictionary of Dates.* 2d rev. ed. London: Newnes, 1966. 428 pp.
3. DeFord, Miriam Allen. *Who Was When?* 2d ed. New York: Wilson, 1950.
4. Williams, Neville, comp. *Chronology of the Modern World.* New York: McKay, 1967. 923 pp.
5. ———. *Chronology of the Expanding World, 1492–1762.* New York: McKay, 1969. 710 pp.

F.l.f

1. Barzun, Jacques, and Graff, Henry F. *The Modern Researcher.* Rev. ed. New York: Harcourt Brace Jovanovich, 1970. 430 pp.
2. Finberg, H. P. R., ed. *Approaches to History.* Toronto: University of Toronto Press, 1962. 221 pp.
3. Gilbert, Felix, ed. *Historical Studies Today.* New York: Norton, 1972. 469 pp.
4. Thompson, James Westfall. *A History of Historical Writing.* 2 vols. New York: Macmillan, 1942.
5. Barnes, Harry Elmer. *A History of Historical Writing.* 2d rev. ed. New York: Dover, 1962. 440 pp.
6. Shafer, Robert J., et al. *Guide to Historical Method.* Homewood, Ill.: Dorsey Press, 1969. 235 pp.
7. Kitson-Clark, George Sidney Roberts. *Guide for Research Students Working on Historical Subjects.* 2d ed. London: Cambridge University Press, 1968. 63 pp.
8. Nugent, Walter T. K. *Creative History: An Introduction to Historical Study.* Philadelphia: Lippincott, 1967. 204 pp.
9. Dollar, Charles M., and Jensen, Richard J. *Historian's Guide to Statistics.* New York: Holt, Rinehart & Winston, 1971. 332 pp.

F.l.g

1. Singer, J. David. *The Wages of War, 1816–1965: A Statistical Handbook.* New York: Wiley, 1972. 419 pp.

F.2

1. *Isis.* Baltimore: Johns Hopkins Press, 1913–.
2. Sarton, George. *Introduction to the History of Science.* 3 vols. in 4. Carnegie Institute publication no. 376. Baltimore: Williams & Wilkins, 1927–48.
3. *History of Science.* Cambridge: Heffer, 1962–.
4. *Technology and Culture.* Detroit: Society for the History of Technology, 1959–.
5. Ferguson, Eugene S., ed. *Bibliography of the History of Technol-*

ogy. Cambridge, Mass.: Society for the History of Technology,
1968. 347 pp.
6. Rider, K. J. *History of Science and Technology: A Select Bibliography for Students*. 2d ed. London: Library Association, 1970.
75 pp.
7. Singer, Charles, et al. *A History of Technology*. 5 vols. Oxford:
Clarendon, 1956–64.

Part G

G.1.b

1. Brock, Clifton. *The Literature of Political Science: A Guide for Students, Librarians, and Teachers*. New York: Bowker, 1969. 232 pp.
2. Harmon, Robert B. *Political Science: A Bibliographical Guide to the Literature*. Metuchen, N.J.: Scarecrow, 1965. 388 pp. (with supplements)
3. Wynar, Lubomyr. *Guide to Reference Materials in Political Science*. 2 vols. Rochester, N.Y.: Libraries Unlimited, 1966–68.
4. *International Bibliography of Political Science*. Paris: UNESCO, 1953–.
5. *International Political Science Abstracts*. Paris: UNESCO, 1951–.
6. *ABC POL SCI*. Santa Barbara: ABC Clio, 1969–.
7. *Universal Reference System*. New York: Metron, 1967–.
8. *Index to Legal Periodicals*. New York: Wilson, 1908–.
9. *Index to Periodical Articles Related to Law*. Stanford: Stanford University, Law Library, 1959–.
10. James A. Robinson, ed. *Political Science Annual*. Indianapolis: Bobbs-Merrill, 1966–.
11. "A Current Appraisal of the Behavioral Sciences," section 4. "Political Science, Jurisprudence." In *American Behavioral Scientist*, vol 7, no. 4 (December 1963): Supplement. Great Barrington, Mass.: Behavioral Research Council, 1963.
12. Problems in Political Science (series). Neal Reiner, general ed. Lexington, Mass.: Heath, 1967–.

G.1.c

1. American Political Science Association. *Biographical Directory*. Evanston, Ill., 1945–.
2. *Almanac of Current World Leaders*. Pasadena, Calif.: 1957–.

G.1.d

1. Dunner, Joseph, ed. *Dictionary of Political Science*. New York: Philosophical Library, 1964. 585 pp.
2. Theimer, Walter. *An Encyclopedia of Modern World Politics*. New York: Rinehart, 1950. 471 pp.

3. Cranston, Maurice, ed. *A Glossary of Political Ideas.* New York: Basic Books, 1968. 180 pp.
4. Heimanson, Rudolph. *Dictionary of Political Science and Law.* Dobbs Ferry, N.Y.: Oceana, 1967. 188 pp.

G.I.f

1. *Deadline Data on Foreign Affairs.* New York, 1965–.
2. *On Record.* Greenwich, Conn.: DMS, 1963–.

G.I.g

1. Behavioral and Social Sciences Survey Committee, Political Science Panel. *Political Science.* Edited by Heinz Eulau and James G. March. Englewood Cliffs, N.J.: Prentice-Hall, 1969. 148 pp.

G.I.h

1. Banks, Arthur. *Cross-Polity Survey.* Cambridge: MIT Press, 1963. 1,476 pp.
2. Taylor, Charles L. *World Handbook of Political and Social Indicators.* 2d ed. New Haven: Yale University Press, 1972.

G.2.b

1. Speeckaert, George Patrick, comp. *Select Bibliography on International Organization, 1885–1964.* Brussels: Union des associations internationales, 1965. 150 pp.
2. *International Organization.* Boston, 1947–.
3. Johnson, Harold S., and Singh, B., comps. *International Organization: A Classified Bibliography.* Asian Studies Center, South Asia series, occasional paper no. 11. East Lansing: Michigan State University, 1969. 261 pp.
4. Field, Norman S., ed. *League of Nations and United Nations Monthly List Selected Articles: Cumulative, 1920–1970.* Dobbs Ferry, N.Y.: Oceana 1971–.
5. U.N., Dag Hammarskjold Library. *Current Bibliographical Information.* New York, 1971–.
6. Robinson, Jacob. *International Law and Organizations.* Leiden: A. W. Sijthoff, 1967. 560 pp.
7. Peaslee, Amos J., ed. *International Governmental Organizations: Constitutional Documents.* 4 vols. 3d ed. The Hague: Martinus Nihoff, 1965–68.
8. *Yearbook of International Organizations.* Brussels: Union of International Organizations, 1948–.
9. *International Associations.* Brussels: Union of International Associations, 1949–.
10. *Who's Who in International Organizations.* Brussels: Union of International Organizations, 1962–.
11. Flynn, Alice H., ed. *World Understanding: A Selected Bibliog-*

raphy. Dobbs Ferry, N.Y.: Published for the United Nations Association of the United States by Oceana Publications, 1965. 263 pp.

12. *Monthly List of Books Cataloged in the Library of the United Nations.* New York: United Nations, 1946–.

13. Douma, J. *Bibliography on the International Court of Justice, 1918–1964, Including the Permanent Court of Justice: A Consolidated Bibliography. The Case Law of the International Court,* vol. 4-c. Leiden, 1966. 387 pp.

14. *United Nations Document Index.* New York, 1950–.

15. League of Nations, Library. *Publications Issued by the League of Nations.* Geneva, 1935. (Supplements, 1936 and 1937.)

16. United Nations. *Publications Catalog.* New York, 1967. (Supplement, 1968–69.)

17. Aufricht, Hans. *Guide to League of Nations Publications.* New York: Columbia University Press, 1951. (Reprinted 1966.) 682 pp.

18. Breycha-Vauthier, A. C. von. *Sources of Information: A Handbook on the Publications of the League of Nations.* New York: Columbia University Press, 1939. 118 pp.

19. Winton, H. N. M., comp. and ed. *Publications of the United Nations System.* New York: Bowker, 1972. 202 pp.

20. *Everyman's United Nations.* New York: UN Department of Public Information, 1948–. 634 pp.

21. United Nations, Department of Public Information. *Yearbook.* New York: United Nations, 1947–.

22. *Annual Review of United Nations Affairs.* New York: New York University Press, 1949–.

23. Hall, H. Duncan. *Commonwealth: A History of the British Commonwealth of Nations.* New York: Van Nostrand, 1971. 1,015 pp.

G.2.c

1. Zawodny, Janusa K. *Guide to the Study of International Relations.* San Francisco: Chandler, 1966. 150 pp.

2. Mason, John Brown. *Research Resources: Annotated Guide to the Social Sciences.* 2 vols. Santa Barbara, Calif.: ABC Clio Press, 1968–1971.

3. Dexter, Byron, ed. *The Foreign Affairs Fifty-Year Bibliography.* New York: Bowker, 1972. 936 pp.

4. *Yearbook of World Affairs.* London: Stevens, 1947–.

5. Plano, Jack C., and Olton, Ray. *The International Relations Dictionary.* New York: Holt, Rinehart & Winston, 1969. 337 pp.

6. Hyamson, A. M. *Dictionary of International Affairs.* Washington: Public Affairs, 1947. 353 pp.

7. Haensch, Gunther. *Dictionary of International Relations and Politics.* Amsterdam and New York: Elsevier, 1965. 638 pp.

8. *Survey of International Affairs.* London: Oxford University Press, 1925–.

9. Royal Institute of International Affairs. *Documents on International Affairs.* London: Oxford University Press, 1929–.

10. *International Review Service.* New York: International Review Service, 1954–.
11. *Treaties and Alliances of the World.* New York: Scribner, 1968. 214 pp.
12. Harvard University, Law School, Library. *Index to Multilateral Treaties: A Chronological List of Multiparty International Agreements from the Sixteenth Century to 1963.* Cambridge, Mass., 1965. 301 pp.
13. League of Nations. *Treaty Series.* New York: United Nations, 1920–45.
14. *United Nations Treaty Series.* New York: United Nations, 1946–.
15. Israel, Fred L., ed. *Major Peace Treaties of Modern History, 1648–1967.* 4 vols. New York: McGraw-Hill, 1967.
16. Parry, Clive, comp. and ed. *The Consolidated Treaty Series.* New York: Oceana, 1969–.
17. *International Legal Materials: Current Documents.* Washington: American Society of International Law, 1962–.
18. *Treaties in Force.* Washington: GPO, 1929–.
19. U.S. Department of State. *United States Treaties and Other International Agreements.* Washington: GPO, 1950–.
20. U.S. Department of State. *United States Treaties and Other International Agreements of the United States of America, 1776–1949.* Washington: Department of State, 1968–.
21. U.S. Department of State. *Bulletin.* Washington: GPO, 1939–.
22. Great Britain. Foreign Office. *British and Foreign State Papers.* London, 1841–.
23. Great Britain. Foreign Office. *Documents on British Foreign Policy, 1919–1939.* 32 vols. London: H.M.S.O., 1947–.
24. U.S. Department of State. *Documents on German Foreign Policy, 1918–1945: From the Archives of the German Foreign Ministry.* Washington: GPO, 1957–.
25. Toscano, Mario. *History of Treaties and International Politics.* Baltimore: Johns Hopkins University Press, 1966. 686 pp.

G.2.d

1. *Brassey's Annual.* London, 1886–.
2. *Reference Handbook of the Armed Forces of the World.* Washington: Robert C. Sellers & Associates, 1966–.
3. *The Military Balance.* London: Institute of Strategic Studies, 1958–.
4. Riddleburger, Peter B. *Military Roles in Developing Countries: An Inventory of Past Research and Analysis.* Washington: Special Operations Research Office, American University, 1965. 182 pp.
5. American University, Cultural Information Analysis Center. *CINFAC Bibliographic Review: Supplement.* Washington 1966–.
6. American University, Special Operations Research Office. *Psychological Operations: Bibliography.* Washington, 1960. 174 pp.
7. Condit, D. M., Reese, H. C., and Feder, C. A. American Uni-

versity, Special Operations Research Office. *A Counterinsurgency Bibliography*. Washington, 1963.

8. Miller, Hope, Lybrand, W. A., and Brohheim, H. *A Selected Bibliography on Unconventional Warfare*. Washington: Special Operations Research Office, American University, 1961. 137 pp.

9. Lang, Kurt. *Military Institutions and the Sociology of War*. Beverly Hills: Sage Publications, 1972. 337 pp.

10. Crawford, Elizabeth T. *The Social Sciences in International and Military Policy: An Analytic Bibliography*. Washington: Bureau of Social Science Research, 1965. 671 pp.

11. Williams, Stillman P. *Toward a Genuine World Security System*. Washington: United World Federalists, 1964. 65 pp.

12. *Peace Research Abstracts Journal*. Clarkson, Ont.: Canadian Peace Research Institute, 1964–.

13. *Peace Research Review*. Clarkson, Ont.: Canadian Peace Research Institute, 1967–.

14. *Arms Control and Disarmament*. Washington: GPO, 1965–.

15. Legault, Albert. *Peacekeeping Operations*. Paris: International Information Center on Peacekeeping Operations, 1967. 204 pp.

16. Carter, April, ed. *Nonviolent Action: A Selected Bibliography*. Rev. and enl. ed. Haverford, Pa.: Center for Nonviolent Conflict Resolution, Haverford College, 1970. 83 pp.

17. Schwarz, Urs, and Hadik, L. *Strategic Terminology: A Trilingual Glossary*. New York: Praeger, 1966. 159 pp.

G.2.e

1. Smith, Bruce L. *International Communication and Political Opinion: A Guide to the Literature*. Princeton: Princeton University Press, 1956. 325 pp.

2. *Journalism Quarterly*. Urbana, Ill., 1930–.

3. Beck, Carl, and McKechnie, Thomas. *Political Elites: A Select Computerized Bibliography*. Cambridge, Mass.: M.I.T. Press, 1968. 661 pp.

4. Rokkan, Stein, ed. *International Guide to Electoral Statistics*. Mouton: The Hague Press, 1969–.

G.2.g

1. University of Michigan, Institute of Public Administration. *Comparative Public Administration: A Selective Annotated Bibliography*. 2d ed. Ann Arbor, 1960. 98 pp.

2. Great Britain. Ministry of Overseas Development. *Public Administration: A Select Bibliography*. London: H.M.S.O., 1967. 101 pp.

3. *International Review of Administrative Sciences*. Brussels, Institut Internationale des Sciences Administratives, 1928–.

4. *Public Administration Abstracts and Index of Articles*. New Delhi: Indian Institute of Public Administration, 1957–.

5. American Society for Public Administration. *Society Directory*. Chicago, 1955–.

6. Government Research Association. *Directory of Organizations and Individuals Professionally Engaged in Governmental Research and Related Activities.* New York, 1935–.

Part H

H.I.b

1. *Sociological Abstracts.* New York, 1952–.
2. *International Bibliography of Sociology.* Paris: UNESCO, 1959–.
3. *Humanitas.* Boston, 1965–.
4. Faris, Robert, ed. *Handbook of Modern Sociology.* Chicago: Rand McNally, 1964. 1,088 pp.

H.I.c

1. American Sociological Association. *Directory of Members.* New York, 1950–.

H.I.d

1. Mitchell, Geoffrey Duncan. *Dictionary of Sociology.* Chicago: Aldine, 1968. 224 pp.
2. Theodorson, George A. *Modern Dictionary of Sociology.* New York: Crowell Collier Macmillan, 1969. 469 pp.
3. Lindzey, Gardner, and Aronson, Elliot, eds. *The Handbook of Social Psychology.* 5 vols. Reading, Mass.: Addison-Wesley, 1968–70.
4. Freedman, Alfred M., and Kaplan, H. I., eds. *Comprehensive Textbook of Psychiatry.* Baltimore: Williams & Wilkins, 1967. 1,666 pp.
5. Ellis, Albert, and Abarbanel, Albert, eds. *The Encyclopedia of Sexual Behavior.* New and rev. 2d ed. New York: Hawthorn, 1967. 1,072 pp.
6. Berelson, Bernard, ed. *Human Behavior.* New York, Harcourt Brace Jovanovich, 1964. 712 pp.

H.I.e

1. Hauser, Philip M., ed. *Handbook for Social Research in Urban Areas.* Paris: UNESCO, 1964. 214 pp.
2. Behavioral and Social Science Survey Committee, Sociology Panel. *Sociology.* Edited by Neil J. Smelser and James A. Davis. Englewood Cliffs, N.J.: Prentice-Hall, 1969. 178 pp.

H.I.f

1. Bonjean, Charles, et al. *Sociological Measurement: An Inventory of Scales and Indices.* San Francisco: Chandler, 1967. 580 pp.
2. Holland, Janet. *Mathematical Sociology.* New York: Schocken Books, 1970. 109 pp.
3. *Sociological Methodology.* San Francisco: Jossey-Bass, 1969–.

H.2.a

1. Aldous, Joan. *International Bibliography of Research in Marriage and the Family, 1900–1964*. Minneapolis: University of Minnesota Press, 1967. 508 pp.
2. Mogey, John. *Sociology of Marriage and Family Behavior, 1957–1968*. The Hague: Mouton, 1971. 368 pp.
3. Goode, William J. *Social Systems and Family Patterns: A Propositional Inventory*. Indianapolis: Bobbs-Merrill, 1971. 779 pp.
4. Christensen, Harold T., ed. *Handbook of Marriage and the Family*. Chicago: Rand McNally, 1964. 1,028 pp.
5. Straus, Murray A. *Family Measurement Techniques*. Minneapolis: University of Minnesota Press, 1969. 316 pp.
6. *Child Development Abstracts and Bibliography*. Washington: National Research Council, 1927–.
7. Goslin, David A., ed. *Handbook of Socialization Theory and Research*. Chicago: Rand McNally, 1969. 1,182 pp.
8. Glenn, Norval D. *Social Stratification*. Berkeley, Calif.: Glendessary Press, 1970. 466 pp.
9. March, James G. *Handbook of Organizations*. Chicago: Rand McNally, 1965. 1,247 pp.
10. Mendes, Richard H. P. *Bibliography on Community Organization for Citizen Participation in Voluntary Democratic Associations*. Washington: President's Committee on Juvenile Delinquency and Youth Crime, 1965. 98 pp.
11. Berkowitz, Morris I., and Johnson, J. E. *Social Scientific Studies of Religion: A Bibliography*. Pittsburgh: University of Pittsburgh Press, 1967. 258 pp.

H.2.b

1. Knop, Edward, and Aparicio, Kathryn, eds. *Current Sociocultural Change Literature*. Grand Forks: University of North Dakota, 1967. 270 pp.
2. U.S. Department of State, Agency for International Development. *Community Development Abstracts*. New York: Sociological Abstracts, 1964. 281 pp.
3. Jones, Garth, Ali, S., Barber, R., and Chambers, J. F., comps. *Planning, Development, and Change*. Honolulu: East-West Center Press, 1970. 180 pp.
4. Bienen, Henry. *Violence and Social Change*. Chicago: University of Chicago, 1968. 119 pp.
5. Spitz, Allan A. *Developmental Change*. Lexington: University Press of Kentucky, 1969. 316 pp.
6. Frey, Frederick W., ed. *Survey Research in Comparative Social Change: A Bibliography*. 1 vol. (unpaged). Cambridge, Mass.: M.I.T. Press, 1969.

H.2.d

1. Pinson, William M., Jr. *Resource Guide to Current Social Issues*. Waco, Tex.: Word Books, 1968. 272 pp.

2. *IRC Recommends.* New York: Information Resources Center for Mental Health and Family Life Education, 1969–.
3. Deutsch, Albert, and Fisman, Helen, eds. *Encyclopedia of Mental Health.* 6 vols. New York: F. Watts, 1963.
4. *Encyclopedia of Social Work.* New York: National Association of Social Workers, 1929–.
5. Smigel, Erwin O., ed. *Handbook on the Study of Social Problems.* Chicago: Rand McNally, 1971. 734 pp.
6. Social Science Research Council, Committee on Survey of Research on Crime and Criminal Justice. *A Guide to Material on Crime and Criminal Justice.* Prepared by Augustus Frederick Kuhlman. New York: Wilson, 1929. Reprinted, 1969. 633 pp.
7. University of California, Institute of Governmental Studies. *Bibliography of Crime and Criminal Justice, 1932–1937.* Compiled by Dorothy Campbell Culver. New York: Wilson, 1949. 391 pp.
8. ———. *Sources for the Study of Administration of Criminal Justice, 1938–1948.* Prepared by Dorothy Campbell Tompkins. Sacramento: State Board of Corrections, 1949. 294 pp.
9. ———. *Administration of Criminal Justice, 1949–1956: A Selected Bibliography.* Compiled by Dorothy Campbell Tompkins. Sacramento: State Board of Corrections, 1956. 351 pp.
10. ———. *The Offender: A Bibliography.* Compiled by Dorothy Campbell Tompkins. Berkeley, 1963. 268 pp.
11. *Crime and Delinquency Abstracts.* Bethesda, Md.: National Clearinghouse for Mental Health Information, 1961–.
12. *Crime and Delinquency Literature.* New York: National Council on Crime and Delinquency, 1968–.
13. *Excerpta Criminologica.* Amsterdam: Excerpta Criminologica Foundation, 1961–.
14. Chambliss, William J., and Seidman, R. B. *Sociology of the Law: A Research Bibliography.* Berkeley: Glendessary Press, 1970. 113 pp.
15. Keller, Mark, and McCormick, Mairi, eds. *A Dictionary of Words about Alcohol.* New Brunswick, N.J.: Rutgers University Center on Alcohol Studies, 1968. 236 pp.
16. Keller, Mark, ed. *International Bibliography of Studies on Alcohol.* New Brunswick, N.J.: Rutgers Center of Alcohol Studies, 1960–.
17. *Quarterly Journal of Studies on Alcohol.* New Brunswick, N.J.: Rutgers University Press, 1940–.
18. Lingeman, Richard R. *Drugs from A to Z.* New York: McGraw-Hill, 1969. 277 pp.
19. U.S. Department of Health, Education, and Welfare, Public Health Service, National Clearinghouse for Mental Health Information. *Bibliography on Drug Dependence and Abuse, 1928–1966.* Washington: National Clearinghouse for Mental Health Information, 1966. 258 pp.
20. Gamage, James R. *A Comprehensive Guide to the English Language Literature on Cannabis (Marijuana).* STASH Bibliographic Series, no. 1. Beloit, Wisc.: STASH Press, 1969. 265 pp.
21. Menditto, Joseph. *Drugs of Addiction and Nonaddiction: Their Use and Abuse.* Troy, N.Y.: Whitson, 1970. 315 pp.

22. *Drug Abuse Bibliography.* Troy, N.Y.: Whitson, 1970–.
23. *Poverty and Human Resources: Abstracts and Survey of Current Literature.* Ann Arbor, 1966–.
24. Bahr, Howard M., ed. *Disaffiliated Man: Essays and Bibliography on Skid Row, Vagrancy, and Outsiders.* Toronto: University of Toronto Press, 1970. 428 pp.

Part I

I.I.a

1. The Economist. *The USSR and Eastern Europe.* London: Oxford University Press, 1956. 134 pp.
2. *Western Europe.* Oxford: Oxford University Press, 1971.
3. *The Middle East and North Africa.* London: Oxford University Press, 1960. 135 pp.
4. *Africa.* Prepared by P. H. Ady and the Cartographic Department of the Clarendon Press, with the assistance of A. D. Hazelwood. Oxford: Clarendon, 1965. 224 pp.
5. *United States and Canada.* Prepared by the Cartographic Department of the Clarendon Press. Oxford: Clarendon, 1967.
6. *Oxford Economic Atlas for India and Ceylon.* London: Oxford University Press, 1953. 97 pp.
7. *Oxford Economic Atlas for Pakistan.* London: Oxford University Press, 1955. 97 pp.
8. Boyd, Andrew Kirk Henry. *An Atlas of World Affairs.* New York: Praeger, 1965. 133 pp.
9. Pounds, N. J. G. *An Atlas of Middle Eastern Affairs.* New York: Praeger, 1964. 117 pp.
10. Boyd, Andrew Kirk Henry. *An Atlas of African Affairs.* Rev. ed. New York: Praeger, 1965. 133 pp.
11. Schneider, Ronald M. *An Atlas of Latin American Affairs.* New York: Praeger, 1965. 136 pp.
12. Pounds, Norman J. G. *An Atlas of European Affairs.* New York: Praeger, 1964. 135 pp.
13. Taaffe, Robert N. *An Atlas of Soviet Affairs.* New York: Praeger, 1965. 143 pp.
14. Adams, D. K. *An Atlas of North American Affairs.* London: Methuen, 1969.

I.I.b

1. ReQua, Eloise G., and Statham, Jane. *The Developing Nations: A Guide to Information Sources Concerning Their Economic, Political, Technical, and Social Problems.* Management Information Guide no. 5. Detroit: Gale Research Co., 1965. 339 pp.
2. *Journal of Developing Areas.* Macomb: Western Illinois University Press, 1966–.
3. American Universities Field Staff. *A Select Bibliography: Asia, Africa, Eastern Europe, Latin America.* New York, 1960–.

4. U.S. Department of the Army. *Africa, Problems and Prospects: A Bibliographic Survey.* Washington: Department of the Army, 1967. 226 pp.

5. U.S. Department of the Army. *Latin America and the Caribbean: Analytical Survey of Literature.* Washington: GPO, 1969. 319 pp.

6. U.S. Department of the Army. *Latin America, Hemispheric Partner: A Bibliographic Survey.* Washington: GPO, 1964. 128 pp.

7. U.S. Department of the Army. *Middle East, Tricontinental Hub: A Strategic Survey.* 2 vols. Washington: GPO, 1965–68.

8. U.S. Department of the Army. *Communist China: A Strategic Survey and Bibliography.* 2 vols. Washington: GPO, 1966–71.

9. U.S. Department of the Army. *USSR: Strategic Survey: A Bibliography.* Washington: GPO, 1969. 238 pp.

10. U.S. Department of the Army. *Communist Eastern Europe.* Washington: GPO, 1971. 349 pp.

11. U.S. Department of the Army, Office of the Deputy Chief of Staff for Military Operations. *Pacific Islands and Trust Territories: A Select Bibliography.* Washington: GPO, 1971. 171 pp.

12. "Annotated Bibliography of Major U.N. Publications and Documents on Development Planning, 1955–1968." *Journal of Development Planning,* no. 1 (1969):173–208.

I.I.d

1. *Worldmark Encyclopedia of the Nations.* 5 vols. 5th ed. New York: Worldmark Press, 1972.

I.I.e

1. *The Europa Yearbook.* London: Europa Publications, 1959–.

2. Council on Foreign Relations. *Political Handbook of the World: Parliaments, Parties, and Press.* New York, 1927–.

3. *International Yearbook and Statesmen's Who's Who.* London: Burke's Peerage, 1953–.

4. Legum, Colin, ed. *Africa: A Handbook to the Continent.* New York: Praeger, 1966. 558 pp. (A paperback edition was issued in 1969.)

5. Veliz, Claudio, ed. *Latin America and the Caribbean: A Handbook.* New York: Praeger, 1968. 840 pp.

6. Adams, Michael. *The Middle East: A Handbook.* New York: Praeger, 1971. 633 pp.

7. Calmann, John. *Western Europe.* New York: Praeger, 1967. 697 pp.

8. Wint, Guy. *Asia: A Handbook.* New York: Praeger, 1966. 856 pp.

9. Schöpflin, George, ed. *The Soviet Union and Eastern Europe: A Handbook.* New York: Praeger, 1970. 614 pp.

10. Osborne, Charles, ed. *Australia, New Zealand, and the South Pacific: A Handbook.* New York: Praeger, 1970. 580 pp.

11. Fisher, Richard, ed. *The United States and Canada.* New York: Praeger, forthcoming.

12. U.S. Department of the Army. Area Handbooks (series). Washington: GPO, 1957–.
13. U.S. Department of State. Background Notes on the Countries of the World (series). Washington: GPO, in continuous revision.
14. American Universities Field Staff. Reports (series). New York, 1952–.

I.I.f

1. Merrill, John C. *The Foreign Press*. Baton Rouge: Louisiana State University Press, 1970. 365 pp.
2. Wilcox, Dennis L. *English Language Dailies Abroad*. Detroit: Gale Research Co., 1967. 243 pp.

I.I.g

1. Ball, Joyce. *Foreign Statistical Documents*. Hoover Institution Bibliographical series, no. 28. Stanford: Hoover Institution, 1967. 173 pp.
2. United Nations. Educational, Scientific, and Cultural Organization. *Statistical Yearbook*. Paris, 1963–.
3. United Nations. Statistical Office. *Statistical Yearbook*. New York, 1949–.
4. League of Nations. *Statistical Yearbook*. New York, 1926–44.
5. United Nations. Statistical Office. *Monthly Bulletin of Statistics*. New York, 1947–.
6. United Nations. Statistical Office. *Compendium of Social Statistics*. New York, 1967. 662 pp.
7. Banks, Arthur S. *Cross-Polity Time-Series Data*. Cambridge, Mass.: MIT Press, 1971. 299 pp.
8. *World Trade Annual*. Prepared by the Statistical Office of the United Nations. 4 vols. New York: Walker & Co., 1964–.
9. *Commodity Yearbook*. New York: Commodity Research Bureau, 1939–.
10. *Quarterly Economic Review*. London: Economist Intelligence Unit, 1956–.
11. United Nations. Statistical Office. *Yearbook of International Trade Statistics*. 1950–.
12. United Nations. Food and Agriculture Organization. *Trade Yearbook*. Rome, 1947–.
13. ———. *Production Yearbook*. Rome, 1948–.
14. ———. *State of Food and Agriculture*. Rome, 1947–.
15. ———. *World Crop Statistics: Area, Production, and Yield, 1948–64*. Rome, 1966. 458 pp.
16. U.S. Bureau of Mines. *Minerals Yearbook*. Washington: GPO, 1933–.
17. Great Britain. Overseas Geological Surveys. Mineral Resources Division. *Statistical Summary of the Mineral Industry: World Production, Exports and Imports*. London: H.M.S.O., 1913/20–.

18. Woytinsky, Wladimir S. *World Commerce and Governments*. New York: Twentieth Century Fund, 1955. 907 pp.
19. Mueller, Bernard. *A Statistical Handbook of the North Atlantic Area: Western Europe, Canada, United States*. New York: Twentieth Century Fund, 1965. 239 pp.

I.2.c

1. *F and 'S Index International*. Cleveland: Predicasts, 1967–.
2. Business International Corporation. *I.L. & T.: Investing, Licensing, and Trading Conditions Abroad*. New York, 1965–.

I.2.f

1. *Comparative Political Studies*. Beverly Hills: Sage Publications, 1968–.
2. Peaslee, Amos J. *Constitutions of Nations*. 3 vols. Rev. 3d ed. The Hague: Nijhoff, 1965–68.
3. Bwy, Douglas. *Social Conflict*. Evanston, Ill.: Northwestern University Council of Intersocial Studies, 1966. 87 pp.

I.2.g

1. Marsh, Robert M. *Comparative Sociology*. New York: Harcourt Brace Jovanovich, 1967. 528 pp.
2. *World Agricultural Economics and Rural Sociology Abstracts*. Farnham Royal, Buckinghamshire: Commonwealth Agricultural Bureaus, 1959–.
3. University of Minnesota, Department of Political Science. Center for Comparative Political Analysis. *Bibliography on Planned Social Change*. 3 vols. Minneapolis: University of Minnesota, 1967.

I.3.

1. Human Relations Area Files. New Haven, 1949–.

Part J

J.1.a

1. Horrabin, J. F. *An Atlas of Africa*. London: Gollancz, 1960. 126 pp.
2. Martin, Geoffrey J. *Africa in Maps*. 1 vol. Dubuque: Brown, 1962.
3. *Atlas of the Arab World and the Middle East*. New York: St. Martin's Press, 1960. 72 pp.
4. *Atlas of the Middle East*. Tel Aviv: Yavneh Publishing House, 1964. 40 pp.
5. Israel. Mahleket ha-medidot. *Atlas of Israel*. 1 vol. 2d ed. Jerusalem: Survey of Israel, Ministry of Labor, 1970.

6. Kenya Colony and Protectorate. Survey of Kenya. *Atlas of Kenya.* Nairobi: Survey of Kenya, 1962. 46 leaves.
7. Comité de géographie du Maroc. *Atlas du Maroc.* Rabat, 1954–.
8. Tanganyika. Department of Lands and Surveys. *Atlas of Tanganyika, East Africa.* Dar es Salaam, 1956. 29 pp.
9. Institut fondamental d'Afrique noire. *West African International Atlas.* Dakar, 1968–.

J.1.b

1. Garling, Althea, comp. *Bibliography of African Bibliographies.* Cambridge: African Studies Centre, 1968. 138 pp.
2. Pearson, James Douglas. *Oriental and Asian Bibliography: An Introduction with Some Reference to Africa.* Hamden, Conn.: Archon Books, 1966. 261 pp.
3. Molnos, Angela. *Sources for the Study of East African Cultures Development.* EARIC Information Circular no. 1. Nairobi: East African Research Information Centre, 1968. 54 pp.
4. Duignan, Peter, ed. *Guide to African Research and Reference Works.* Stanford: Hoover Institution Press, 1971. 1,000 pp.
5. Paden, John N., and Soja, Edward W., eds. *The African Experience.* 3 vols. in 4. Evanston: Northwestern University Press, 1970.
6. Gutkind, Peter Claus Wolfgang and Webster, John B., comps. *A Select Bibliography on Traditional and Modern Africa.* Occasional Bibliography no. 8. Syracuse, N.Y.: Syracuse University, Program on Eastern African Studies, 1968. 323 pp.
7. *Current Bibliography on African Affairs.* New York: Greenwood Periodicals, 1962–.
8. African Bibliographic Center. *African Affairs for the General Reader.* New York: African-American Institute, 1967. 210 pp.
9. International African Institute. *West Africa.* London, 1958. 116 leaves.
10. ———. *Northeast Africa.* London, 1959. 51 leaves.
11. ———. *East Africa.* London, 1960. 62 leaves.
12. ———. *Southeast Central Africa and Madagascar.* London, 1961. 53 leaves.
13. Work, Monroe N., comp. *A Bibliography of the Negro in Africa and America.* New York: Wilson, 1928. Reprinted, 1965. 698 pp.
14. *Journal of Negro Education.* Washington: Howard University, 1932–.
15. Lystad, Robert A., ed. *The African World.* New York: Praeger, 1965. 575 pp.
16. Carter, Gwendolyn M., and Paden, Ann, eds. *Expanding Horizons in African Studies.* Program of African Studies, Northwestern University, Proceedings of the 20th Anniversary Conference, 1968. Evanston, Ill.: Northwestern University Press, 1969. 364 pp.
17. U.S. Library of Congress. African Section. *Sub-Saharan Africa: A Guide to Serials.* Washington: Library of Congress, 1970. 409 pp.
18. Maison des sciences de l'homme, Paris. Service d'échange d'infor-

mation scientifiques. *African Studies: World List of Specialized Periodicals*. The Hague: Mouton, 1970. 214 pp.

19. Pearson, J. D., comp. *Index Islamicus, 1906–1955*. Cambridge: Heffer, 1958. Supplements, 1961 and 1965.

20. Ettinghausen, Richard, ed. *A Selected and Annotated Bibliography of Books and Periodicals in Western Languages Dealing with the Near and Middle East, with Special Emphasis on Medieval and Modern Times*. Washington: Middle East Institute, 1954. 137 pp.

21. *Middle East Journal*. Washington: Middle East Institute, 1947–.

22. International African Institute. *Selected Annotated Bibliography of Tropical Africa*. Compiled under the direction of Daryll Forde. New York: Twentieth Century Fund, 1956. About 490 mimeographed pp.

23. *U.S. and Canadian Publications on Africa*. Stanford: Stanford University Press, Hoover Institution on War, Revolution, and Peace, 1960–.

24. *Africa*. London: International Institute of African Languages and Cultures, 1928–.

25. *International African Bibliography*. London: International African Institute, 1971–.

26. *African Abstracts*. London: International African Institute, 1950–.

27. *African Affairs*. London: Royal African Society, 1901–.

J.l.c

1. Taylor, Sidney, ed. *The New Africans*. New York: Putnam, 1967. 504 pp.

2. Segal, Ronald. *African Profiles*. Rev. ed. Magnolia, Mass.: Peter Smith, 1962. 406 pp.

3. Segal, Ronald. *Political Africa*. New York: Praeger, 1961. 475 pp.

4. Italiaander, Rolf. *The New Leaders of Africa*. Englewood Cliffs, N.J.: Prentice-Hall, 1961. 306 pp.

5. *Who's Who in East Africa*. New York: International Publications Service, 1963–64–.

6. *Who's Who of Southern Africa*. Johannesburg: Wootton & Gibson, 1907–64; Combined Publishers, 1965–.

7. Rosenthal, Eric. *Southern African Dictionary of National Biography*. London: Warne, 1966. 430 pp.

8. deKock, W. J., ed. *Dictionary of South African Biography*. Pretoria: Nasional Boekhandel Bpk, for National Council for Social Research, Department of Higher Education, 1968–.

9. United Nations Educational Scientific and Cultural Organization. Secretariat. *Social Scientists Specializing in African Studies*. École pratique des hautes études, 6 sec. Sciences économiques et sociales: 4. Ser. vol. 5. Bibliographies et instruments de travail. Monde d'outre-mer passé et présent. Paris: École pratique des hautes études, 1963. 375 pp.

J.l.d

1. *Encyclopedia Africana*. Accra, Ghana, forthcoming.

2. Rosenthal, Eric, comp. and ed. *Encyclopedia of Southern Africa.* 3d ed. London and New York: Warne, 1965. 628 pp.
3. Gibb, H. A. R., et al. *Encyclopedia of Islam.* New ed. Leiden: Brill, 1954–.
4. Gibb, H. A. R., ed. *Shorter Encyclopedia of Islam.* Ithaca, N.Y.: Cornell University Press, 1965. 671 pp.
5. Ronart, Stephan, and Ronart, Nandy. *Concise Encyclopedia of Arabic Civilization.* 2 vols. New York: Praeger, 1960–1966.
6. Levine, Evyatar A., and Shimoni, Y., eds. *Political Dictionary of the Middle East in the Twentieth Century.* Jerusalem, Israel: Jerusalem Publishing House, 1972. 434 pp.

J.l.e

1. Legum, Colin, ed. *African Contemporary Record.* London: African Research, 1969–.
2. *Africa.* New York: Africana Publishing Corp., 1969–.
3. Junod, Violaine I., ed. *The Handbook of Africa.* New York: New York University, 1963. 472 pp.
4. Hatch, John Charles. *Africa Today and Tomorrow.* 2d rev. ed. New York: Praeger, 1965. 362 pp.
5. Kitchen, Helen. *Handbook of African Affairs.* New York: Praeger, 1965.
6. Hailey, William Malcolm. *An African Survey.* Rev. ed. Oxford: Oxford University Press, 1957. 1,676 pp.
7. Kimble, George Herbert Tinley. *Tropical Africa.* 2 vols. New York: Twentieth Century Fund, 1960.
8. *The Middle East and North Africa.* London: Europa Publications, 1948–.
9. *Africa South of the Sahara.* London: Europa Publications, 1971–.
10. *West Africa Annual.* Lagos: John West Publications, 1962–.
11. *Yearbook and Guide to East Africa.* London: R. Hale, 1950–65.
12. *Yearbook and Guide to Southern Africa.* London: R. Hale 1901–.

J.l.f

1. Feuereisen, Fritz. *Africa: A Guide to Newspapers and Magazines.* New York: Africana, 1969. 251 pp.
2. *Africa Research Bulletin.* London: Africa Research, 1964–.
3. *Africa Diary.* Delhi: Africa Publications. 1961–.
4. *African Recorder.* New Delhi, 1962–.
5. *Mideast Mirror.* Beirut: Arab News Agency, 1948–.

J.l.g

1. Africa Institute. *Africa at a Glance.* Pretoria: Africa Institute, 1967–.
2. Africa Institute. Africa: Maps and Statistics (series). Johannesburg, 1962–.

3. Harvey, Joan M. *Statistics Africa*. Beckenham, Kent: CBD Research, 1970. 175 pp.

J.2.a

1. Forde, Daryll, ed. Ethnographic Survey of Africa (series). London: International African Institute, 1954–.
2. Gibson, Gordon, comp. "A Bibliography of Anthropological Bibliographies: Africa." *Current Anthropology* 10, no. 5 (1969): 527–66.
3. Hambly, Wilfrid Dyson. *Source Book for African Anthropology*. Anthropological series, Field Museum of Natural History, vol. 26. Publication 394,396. Chicago. 1937. Reprint (2 vols. in 1). New York: Krause Reprint, 1968. 953 pp.
4. "Bibliography of African Anthropology, 1937–1949." *Fieldiana, Anthropology* 37, no. 2: 185–292. Chicago: Field Museum of Natural History, 1952.
5. Wieschhoff, H. A. *Anthropological Bibliography of Negro Africa*. American Oriental series, vol. 23. New Haven: American Oriental Society, 1948. 461 pp.
6. Field, Henry. *Bibliography of Southwestern Asia*. 10 vols. Coral Gables, Fla.: University of Miami Press, 1953–62.
7. Sweet, Louise E. and Timothy J. O'Leary, eds. *Circum-Mediterranean Peasantry: Introductory Bibliographies*. New Haven: HRAF Press; distributed by Taplinger, 1969. 106 pp.
8. Sweet, Louise, ed. *The Central Middle East*. New Haven: HRAF Press, 1971. 373 pp.
9. Clark, John Desmond. *Atlas of African Prehistory*. Chicago: University of Chicago Press, 1967. 62 pp.
10. Murphy, John D., and Godd, Harry, comps. *A Bibliography of African Languages and Linguistics*. Washington: Catholic University of America Press, 1969. 147 pp.
11. Handbook of African Languages (series). London: International African Institute, 1948–.
12. U.S. Library of Congress. Music Division. *African Music*. Compiled by Darius L. Thieme. Washington: Library of Congress, 1964. 55 pp.
13. International African Institute. *A Select Bibliography of Music in Africa*. Compiled at the International African Institute by L. J. P. Gaskin under the direction of K. P. Wachsmann. London, 1965. 83 pp.

J.2.c

1. *Economic Survey of Africa since 1950*. New York, 1959, 248 pp.
2. *Economic Bulletin for Africa*. Addis Ababa: U.N. Economic Commission for Africa, 1961–.
3. U.N. Bureau of Economic Affairs. *Economic Developments in the Middle East*. New York: United Nations, 1949–.
4. *Barclays International Review*. London: Barclays Bank, 1946–.

5. *Standard Bank Review*. Johannesburg, 1919–.
6. Neville-Rolfe, Edmund. *Economic Aspects of Agricultural Development in Africa*. Oxford: Oxford University Press, 1969. 257 pp.
7. Martin, Jane. *Bibliography on African Regionalism*. Boston: African Studies Center, Boston University, 1969. 121 pp.

J.2.d

1. Sommer, John W. *Bibliography of African Geography, 1940–1964*. Hanover, N.H.: Dartmouth College, 1965, 139 pp.
2. Bederman, Sanford Harold. *A Bibliographic Aid to the Study of the Geography of Africa: A Selected Listing of Recent Literature Published in the English Language*. Atlanta: Bureau of Business and Economic Research, Georgia State University, 1970. 212 pp.

J.2.e

1. *Cambridge History of the British Empire*. Edited by J. H. Rose and others. Cambridge: Cambridge University Press, 1929–59.
2. Fage, J. D. *An Atlas of African History*. London: Edward Arnold, 1958. 62 pp.
3. Gailey, Harry A. *The History of Africa in Maps*. Chicago: Denoyer-Geppert, 1967. 96 pp.
4. Hazard, Harry W. *The Atlas of Islamic History*. 3d ed. rev. Princeton: Princeton University Press, 1954. 49 pp.
5. Roolvink, Roelof, et al., comps. *Historical Atlas of the Muslim Peoples*. Amsterdam: Djambatan, 1957. 40 pp.
6. African Bibliographic Center. *Black History Viewpoints: A Selected Bibliographical Guide to Resources for Afro-American and African History: 1968*. New York: Negro Universities Press, 1969. 71 pp.
7. Matthews, Daniel G., ed. *Current Themes in African Historical Studies: A Selected Bibliographical Guide to Resources for Research in African History*. Westford, Conn.: Negro Universities Press, 1970. 389 pp.
8. Collins, Robert O. "African History in the 1960s: Enthusiasm, Vitality, and Revelations," *Choice* 4 (December 1967):1083–86.
9. Sauvaget, Jean. *Introduction to the History of the Muslim East*. Berkeley: University of California Press, 1965. 252 pp.
10. Rosenthal, Franz. *History of Muslim Historiography*. Leiden: Brill, 1952. 558 pp.
11. Winks, Robin W. *The Historiography of the British Empire-Commonwealth*. Durham, N.C.: Duke University Press, 1966. 596 pp.
12. Contee, Clarence G. "Current Problems in African Historiography." *Negro History Bulletin,* April 1967, pp. 5–10.
13. Collins, Robert O. *Problems in African History*. Englewood Cliffs, N.J.: Prentice-Hall, 1968. 374 pp.
14. International Congress of African Historians, University College, Dar es Salaam, 1965. *Emerging Themes of African History: Pro-*

ceedings. Edited by T. O. Ranger. Nairobi: East Africa Publishing House, 1968. 230 pp.

J.2.f

1. Jahn, Janheinz. *Bibliography of Creative African Writing.* Nendeln: Krausthomson, 1971. 446 pp.
2. Abrash, Barbara. *Black African Literature in English since 1952: Works and Criticism.* New York: Johnson Reprint Corp., 1967. 92 pp.
3. Brown, Evelyn S. *Africa's Contemporary Art and Artists.* New York: Harmon Foundation, Division of Social Research and Experimentation, 1966. 136 pp.
4. International African Institute. *A Bibliography of African Art.* Compiled by L. J. P. Gaskin. London: International African Institute, 1965. 120 pp.

J.2.g

1. *Chronology of Arab Politics.* Beirut: Political Studies and Public Administration Department, American University of Beirut, 1963–.
2. *Middle East Record.* Tel Aviv: Israel Oriental Society, Reuven Shiloah Research Center, 1960–.
3. McGowan, Patrick J. *African Politics: A Guide to Research Resources, Methods, and Literature.* Program of Eastern African Studies. Occasional Paper no. 55. Syracuse: Syracuse University, 1970. 85, 45 pp.
4. Hanna, William John, and Hanna, Judith. *Politics in Black Africa.* East Lansing: African Studies Center, Michigan State University, 1964. 139 pp.
5. Spiro, Herbert J. *Politics in Africa: Prospects South of the Sahara.* Englewood Cliffs, N.J.: Prentice-Hall, 1962. 183 pp.
6. Wauthier, Claude. *The Literature and Thought of Modern Africa.* New York: Praeger, 1967. 323 pp.
7. Alderfer, Harold Freed. *A Bibliography of African Government, 1950–1966.* Narberth, Pa.: Lincoln University Press, 1967. 163 pp.
8. African Bibliographic Center. *The Sword and Government: A Preliminary and Selected Bibliographical Guide to African Military Affairs.* Washington, 1967. 5 pp.
9. Matthews, D. G. "Soviet View of Africa: A Select Guide to Current Resources for Study and Analysis," *Current Bibliography of African Affairs* 6, no. 4 (August 1967): 5–12.

J.2.h

1. University of Edinburgh, Department of Social Anthropology. *African Urbanization.* London: International African Institute, 1965. 27 pp.
2. Simms, Ruth P. *Urbanization in West Africa: A Review of Current*

Literature. Evanston: Northwestern University Press, 1965. 109 pp.

3. Deregowska, Eva L. *Some Aspects of Social Change in Africa South of the Sahara: A Bibliography*. Lusaka: University of Zambia, Institute for Social Research, 1967. 93 pp.

Part K

K.I.a

1. *Atlas of Southeast Asia*. London: Macmillan; New York: St. Martin, 1964. 84 pp.

2. Grandidier, Guillaume, ed. *Atlas des colonies françaises, protectorats et territoires sous mandat de la France*. Paris: Société d'éditions géographes, maritimes et coloniales, 1934. 286 pp.

3. Chang Chi-Yun. *National Atlas of China*. 5 vols. Taiwan: National War College, 1959–62.

4. U.S. Central Intelligence Agency. *People's Republic of China: Atlas*. Washington, D.C., 1971. 82 pp.

5. Fullard, Harold, ed. *China in Maps*. London: Philip, 1968. 25 pp.

6. Buck, John Lossing. *Land Utilization in China*. Shanghai: Commercial Press, 1937. Reprinted, 1964. 494 pp.

7. India (Republic) National Atlas Organization. *National Atlas of India*. Edited by S. P. Chatterjee. 1 vol. Calcutta, 1957.

8. *Teikoku's Complete Atlas of Japan*. 3d ed. Tokyo: Teikoku Shoin, 1969. 55 pp.

9 Kokusai Kyoiku Joho Senta. *Atlas of Japan: Physical, Economic, and Social*. Tokyo: International Society for Educational Information, 1970. 64 pp.

10. *Economic Atlas of Japan*. Edited by Koichi Aki. Tokyo: Zenkokukyoikutosho Co., 1954. 165 pp.

11. Saso Chulp ansa. *Standard Atlas of Korea*. Seoul, 1960. 47 pp.

12. Olson, Everett C., and Whitmarsh, A. *Foreign Maps*. New York: Harper & Row, 1944. 237 pp.

13. U.S. Engineer Agency for Resources Inventories. *Atlas of Physical, Economic, and Social Resources of the Lower Mekong Basin*. Paris: United Nations, 1968. 257 leaves.

K.I.b

1. Nunn, G. Raymond. *Asia: A Selected and Annotated Guide to Reference Works*. Cambridge, Mass.: M.I.T. Press, 1971. 233 pp.

2. Patterson, Maureen L. P. "Bibliographical Controls for South Asian Studies." *Library Quarterly* 41, no. 2 (April 1971): 83–105.

3. Johnson, Donald Clay. *A Guide to Reference Materials on Southeast Asia*. Yale Southeast Asia Studies, 6. New Haven: Yale University Press, 1970. 160 pp.

4. *Journal of Asian Studies*. Ann Arbor: Association for Asian Studies, 1941–.

5. Association for Asian Studies. *Cumulative Bibliography, 1941–1965*. 8 vols. Boston: C. K. Hall, 1970.

6. Birnbaum, Eleazar. *Books on Asia from the Near East to the Far East: A Guide for the General Reader*. Toronto: University of Toronto Press, 1971. 341 pp.

7. Embree, Ainslie Thomas. *Asia: A Guide to Basic Books*. New York: Asia Society, 1966. 57 pp.

8. *South Asia: An Introductory Bibliography*. Prepared and edited by Maureen L. P. Patterson and Ronald B. Inden. Chicago: Syllabus Division, University of Chicago Press, 1962. 412 pp.

9. Tregonning, Kennedy G. *Southeast Asia: A Critical Bibliography*. Tucson: University of Arizona Press, 1969. 103 pp.

10. Embree, John Fee. *Books on Southeast Asia: A Select Bibliography*. 4th rev. ed. New York: American Institute of Pacific Relations, 1956. 43 pp.

11. Cordier, Henri. *Bibliotheca Indosinica*. Publication de l'école française d'Extrème-Orient, vols. 15–18. 4 vols. and index. Leiden: Brill, 1912–15.

12. Irikura, James K. *Southeast Asia: Selected Annotated Bibliography of Japanese Publications*. New Haven: Southeast Asia Studies, Yale University in association with HRAF Press, 1956. 544 pp.

13. Wilbur, Donald N. *Annotated Bibliography of Afghanistan*. 2d ed. New Haven: HRAF Press, 1962. 259 pp.

14. University of Chicago, Philippine Studies Program. *Selected Bibliography of the Philippines*. New Haven: HRAF Press, 1956. 138 pp.

15. New York University, Burma Research Project. *Annotated Bibliography of Burma*. New Haven: HRAF Press, 1956. 230 pp.

16. Mahar, J. Michael. *India: A Critical Bibliography*. Tucson: University of Arizona Press, 1964. 119 pp.

17. *Index India*. Jaipur, India: Library, University of Rajasthan, 1967–.

18. Pelzer, Karl Josef. *West Malaysia and Singapore: A Selected Bibliography*. New Haven: HRAF Press, 1971. 394 pp.

19. Ghani, A. R. *Pakistan: A Select Bibliography*. Lahore: Association for the Advancement of Science, University Institute of Chemistry, 1951. 339 pp.

20. National Book Centre of Pakistan. *Books from Pakistan Published during the Decade of Reform, 1958–1968*. 2d ed. Karachi: National Book Center of Pakistan, 1968. 159 pp.

21. Schappert, Linda G. *Sikkim, 1800–1968: An Annotated Bibliography*. Occasional Paper of East-West Center Library, no. 10. Honolulu: East-West Center Library, East-West Center, 1968. 69 pp.

22. Berton, Peter, and Wu, Eugene. *Contemporary China: A Research Guide*. Stanford, Calif.: Hoover Institution on War, Revolution, and Peace, 1967. 695 pp.

23. Hucker, Charles O. *China: A Critical Bibliography*. Tucson: University of Arizona Press, 1962. 125 pp.

24. Fairbank, John King, and Liu, Kwang Chiang. *Modern China: A*

Bibliographical Guide to Chinese Works, 1898–1937. Harvard-Yenching Institute Studies, vol. 1. Cambridge: Harvard University Press, 1950. 608 pp.

25. Stanford University. Hoover Institution on War, Revolution, and Peace. *Library Catalogs: Catalog of the Chinese Collection.* 13 vols. Boston: G. K. Hall, 1969.

26. Cordier, Henri. *Bibliotheca Sinica.* 2d ed. 4 vols. Paris: Guilmoto, 1904–8. (Author Index compiled by East Asiatic Library, Columbia University Libraries, New York, 1953. 84 pp.)

27. Yuan, Tung-li. *China in Western Literature.* New Haven: Far Eastern Publications, Yale University, 1958. 802 pp.

28. Lust, John, comp. *Index Sinicus.* Cambridge: Heffer, 1964. 663 pp.

29. Silberman, Bernard S. *Japan and Korea: A Critical Bibliography.* Tucson: University of Arizona Press, 1962. 120 pp.

30. Cordier, Henri. *Bibliotheca Japonica.* Publication de l'École des Langues Orientales Vivantes. 5. ser., vol. 8. Paris: Leroux, 1912. 762 col.

K.I.c

1. Giles, Herbert Allen. *A Chinese Biographical Dictionary.* London: Quaritch, 1898. (Reprinted 1939.) 1,022 pp.

2. U.S. Library of Congress. Asiatic division. *Eminent Chinese of the Ch'ing Period, 1644–1912.* Edited by Arthur W. Hummel. 2 vols. Washington: GPO, 1943–44.

3. Boorman, Howard L., ed. *Biographical Dictionary of Republican China.* 4 vols. New York: Columbia University Press, 1967–70.

4. *Who's Who in Communist China.* Hong Kong: Union Research Institute, 1966–.

5. *Who's Who in China: Biographies of Chinese Leaders.* Shanghai: China Weekly Review, 1918–.

6. Klein, Donald W., and Clarke, Anne B. *Biographic Dictionary of Chinese Communism, 1921–1965.* Harvard East Asian Series, 57. 2 vols. Cambridge: Harvard University Press, 1971.

7. *Japan Biographical Encyclopedia and Who's Who.* Tokyo: Renzo Press, 1958–.

8. Buckland, Charles Edward. *Dictionary of Indian Biography.* London: Sonnenschein, 1906. Reprinted, 1968. 494 pp.

9. *Times of India Directory and Yearbook.* Bombay: Bennett, Coleman, 1914–.

10. *Who's Who in Malaysia.* Kuala Lumpur, 1956–.

11. *Asia Who's Who.* Hong Kong: Pan-Asia Newspaper Alliance, 1957–.

K.I.d

1. Couling, Samuel. *Encyclopedia Sinica.* Shanghai: Kelly and Walsh, 1917. 633 pp.

2. Mayers, William Frederick. *The Chinese Readers' Manual.* Reprint of original 1874 ed. Taipei: Literature House, 1964. 444 pp.

3. *Gazetteer of India: Indian Union*. Delhi: Publications Division, Ministry of Information and Broadcasting, 1965–.
4. Yule, William. *Hobson-Jobson: A Glossary of Colloquial Anglo-Indian Words and Phrases*. New ed. Delhi: Munshiram Monohartal, 1903. (Reprinted 1968.) 1,021 pp.
5. Chen, Janey. *A Practical English-Chinese Pronouncing Dictionary*. Rutland, Vt.: C. E. Tuttle Co., 1970. 601 pp.

K.I.e

1. *Asian Annual: The "Eastern World" Handbook*. London: Eastern World, 1954–.
2. *Far East and Australasia*. London: Europa Publications, 1969–.
3. Hinton, Harold C. *The Far East and South Pacific*. Washington: Stryker-Post, 1968–.
4. Olson, Harvey Stuart. *Olson's Orient Guide*. Philadelphia: Lippincott, 1962. 1,008 pp.
5. *Fodor's Guide to Japan and East Asia*. New York: McKay, 1962–.
6. *China Year Book, 1912–1939*. London: Routledge & Kegan Paul, 1912–39.
7. *China Yearbook, 1937/43*. Taipeh, Taiwan: China Publishing Co., 1943–.
8. Yu lien yen chiu so, Kowloon. *Communist China*. Kowloon: Union Research Institute, 1955–.
9. *Communist China Yearbook*. Hong Kong: China Research Associates, 1962–.
10. *Contemporary China: Economic and Social Studies, Documents, Bibliography, and Chronology*. Hong Kong: Hong Kong University Press, 1955–.
11. Wagret, Paul, ed. *China*. Geneva: Nagel, 1968. 1,504 pp.
12. *India: A Reference Annual*. Delhi: Ministry of Information and Broadcasting, 1953–.
13. *Hindustan Yearbook and Who's Who*. Calcutta: M. C. Sarkar, 1933–.
14. *Handbook for Travelers in India, Pakistan, Burma, and Ceylon*. London: Murray, 1859–. (20th ed., 1965).
15. *Japan Handbook, 1966*. 2d ed. Toyko: Rengo Press, 1966. 216 pp.
16. Webb, Herschel. *Research in Japanese Sources: A Guide*. New York: Columbia University Press, 1965. 170 pp.
17. Pakistan. Central Statistical Office. *Twenty Years of Pakistan, 1947–1967*. Karachi: Pakistani Central Statistical Office, 1968. 333 pp.
18. *Pakistan Year Book*. Karachi: National Publishing House, 1969–.
19. *Singapore Yearbook*. Singapore: Government Printing Office, 1966–.

K.I.f

1. Feuereisen, Fritz, and Schmacke, Ernst. *Die Presse in Asien und Ozeanien*. München-Pullach: Verlag Dokumentation, 1968. 303 pp.

2. King, Frank H. H., and Clarke, Prescott. *Research Guide to China-Coast Newspapers, 1822–1911*. Harvard East Asian Monographs, 18. Cambridge: Harvard University Press, 1965. 235 pp.
3. *Asian Recorder*. New Delhi: D. B. Samuel, 1955–.
4. *Asia Research Bulletin*. Singapore: Asia Research, 1971–.
5. *Asian Survey*. Berkeley: Institute of International Studies, University of California, 1961–.
6. *Asia Letter*. Hong Kong, 1964–.
7. *SEATO Record*. Bangkok: Southeast Asia Treaty Organization, 1960–.
8. *Survey of China Mainland Press*. Hong Kong: U.S. Consulate General, 1950–.
9. *Selections from China Mainland Magazines*. Hong Kong: U.S. Consulate General, 1965–.

K.I.g

1. United Nations. Economic Commission for Asia and the Far East. *Economic Survey of Asia and the Far East*. Bangkok, 1948–.
2. United Nations. Economic Commission for Asia and the Far East. *Economic Bulletin for Asia and the Far East*. Bangkok: Research and Statistics Division, 1950–.
3. Japan. Prime Minister's Office. Statistics Bureau. *Japan Statistical Yearbook*. Tokyo, 1949–.
4. Pakistan. Central Statistical Office. *Pakistan Statistical Yearbook*. Karachi: Manager of Publications. 1952–.

K.2.a

1. Embree, John Fee, and Dotson, Lillian O. *Bibliography of the Peoples and Cultures of Mainland Southeast Asia*. New Haven: Yale University, Southeast Asia Studies, 1950. 821 pp.
2. LeBar, Frank. "Ethnography of Mainland Southeast Asia: A Bibliographic Survey." *Behavior Science Notes* 1, no. 1 (1966):14–40.
3. Fürer-Haimendorf, Elizabeth von. *An Anthropological Bibliography of South Asia*. École pratique des hautes études. 6 ser. Le Monde d'outre-mer passé et présent. 4. sér: Bibliographies 3, 4, etc. Paris: Mouton, 1958–.
4. Harris, George L. *North Borneo, Brunei, Sarawak (British Borneo)*. New Haven: HRAF Press, 1956. 528 pp.
5. Blanchard, Wendell. *Thailand: Its People, Its Society, Its Culture*. New Haven: HRAF Press, 1966. 528 pp.
6. Steinberg, David J. *Cambodia: Its People, Its Society, Its Culture*. Rev. ed. New Haven: HRAF Press, 1959. 528 pp.
7. Hu, Chang-tu. *China: Its People, Its Society, Its Culture*. New Haven: HRAF Press, 1960. 611 pp.
8. LeBar, Frank M., ed. *Laos: Its People, Its Society, Its Culture*. Rev. ed. New Haven: HRAF Press, 1967. 320 pp.

9. Wilber, Donald N., ed. *Afghanistan: Its People, Its Society, Its Culture.* New Haven: HRAF Press, 1962. 320 pp.
10. McVey, Ruth T., ed. *Indonesia.* 2d ed., rev. New Haven: HRAF Press, 1967. 600 pp.
11. Wilber, Donald N. *Pakistan: Its People, Its Society, Its Culture.* New Haven: HRAF Press, 1964. 487 pp.
12. Kennedy, Raymond. *Bibliography of Indonesian Peoples and Cultures.* 2d rev. ed. New Haven: Southeast Asia Studies, Yale University, 1962. 207 pp.
13. LeBar, Frank M. *Ethnic Groups of Mainland Southeast Asia.* New Haven: HRAF Press, 1964. 288 pp.
14. U.S. Department of the Army. *Minority Groups in Thailand.* Washington: GPO, 1970. 1,135 pp.
15. University of California at Los Angeles. Department of Anthropology and Sociology. *Laos Project Paper.* Los Angeles, 1961–.
16. Calcutta. National Library. *A Bibliography of Indology.* Calcutta: National Library, 1960–.
17. Humphrey, Christmas. *A Popular Dictionary of Buddhism.* London: Arco, 1962. 223 pp.

K.2.b

1. U.N. Bureau of Social Affairs. *The Population of Asia and the Far East, 1950–1960.* New York: United Nations, Department of Economics and Social Affairs, 1959. 110 pp.

K.2.c

1. Chen, Nai-Ruenn. *The Economy of Mainland China, 1949–1963: A Bibliography of Materials in English.* Berkeley: Committee on the Economy of China, Social Science Research Council, 1963. 297 pp.
2. *An Economic Profile of Mainland China.* New York: Praeger, 1968. 684 pp.
3. Eckstein, Alexander, ed. *Economic Trends in Communist China.* Chicago: Aldine, 1968. 757 pp.

K.2.d

1. Pelzer, Karl Josef. *Selected Bibliography on the Geography of Southeast Asia.* 3 vols. New Haven: Yale University, Southeast Asia Studies, 1949.
2. Reiner, Ernst. "Vorderindien, Ceylon, Tibet, 1926–1953." *Geographisches Jahrbuch,* 1954, pp. 1–186.
3. Herman, Theodore. *The Geography of China: A Selected and Annotated Bibliography.* Foreign Area Materials Center, University of the State of New York. Occasional Publication no. 7. New York: State Education Department, 1967. 44 pp.
4. Hall, Robert Burnett, and Noh, Toshio. *Japanese Geography: A Guide to Japanese Reference and Research Materials.* University

of Michigan Center for Japanese Studies. Bibliographical series
no. 6. Ann Arbor: University of Michigan Press, 1956. 128 pp.
5. Huke, Robert. *Bibliography of Philippine Geography, 1940–1963*.
Geography Publications at Dartmouth, no. 1. Hanover, N.H.:
Dartmouth College, 1964. 84 pp.

K.2.e

1. Herrmann, Albert. *An Historical Atlas of China*. Edited by Norton Ginsburg. New ed. Chicago: Aldine, 1966. 88 pp.
2. Beek, Martin A. *Atlas of Mesopotamia: A Survey of the History
and Civilization of Mesopotamia from the Stone Age to the Fall
of Babylon*. New York: Nelson, 1962. 164 pp.
3. University of London. School of Oriental and African Studies.
Handbook of Oriental History. Royal Historical Society, London,
Guides and Handbooks, no. 6. London: Offices of the Royal Historical Society, 1951. 265 pp.
4. Pluvier, Jan M. *Handbook and Chart of Southeast Asian History*.
New York: Oxford University Press, 1967. 58 pp.
5. Bhattacharya, Sachidananda. *A Dictionary of Indian History*.
New York: Oxford University Press, 1967. 58 pp.
6. Goedertier, Joseph M. *A Dictionary of Japanese History*. New
York: Walker, 1968. 415 pp.
7. Tsuchibashi, Yachita. *Japanese Chronological Tables from 601 to
1872 A.D.* Monuments Nipponica monographs, no. 11. Tokyo:
Sophia University Press, 1952. 128 pp.
8. Problems in Asian Civilization (series). Lexington, Mass.: Heath,
1963–.
9. Dawson, Raymond S., ed. *The Legacy of China*. Oxford: Clarendon, 1964. 392 pp.
10. Garratt, Geoffrey Theodore, ed. *The Legacy of India*. Oxford:
Clarendon, 1938. 428 pp.
11. University of London, School of Oriental and African Studies. *Historical Writing on the Peoples of Asia*. 4 vols. London and New
York: Oxford University Press, 1961–62.
12. Hay, Stephen N., and Case, Margaret H. *Southeast Asian History:
A Bibliographic Guide*. New York: Praeger, 1962. 138 pp.
13. Morrison, Gayle. *A Guide to Books on Southeast Asian History,
1961–1966*. Bibliography and Reference Series, no. 8. Santa Barbara, Calif.: American Bibliographical Center, 1969. 105 pp.
14. Case, Margaret H. *South Asian History, 1750–1950: A Guide to
Periodicals, Dissertations, and Newspapers*. Princeton, N.J.:
Princeton University Press, 1968. 561 pp.
15. Varley, H. Paul. *A Syllabus of Japanese Civilization*. New York:
Columbia University Press, 1968. 98 pp.

K.2.g

1. Wilson, Patrick. *Government and Politics of India and Pakistan,
1885–1955*. Modern India Project, Bibliographical Study, no. 2.

Berkeley: University of California, Institute of East Asiatic Studies, South Asian Studies, 1956. 356 pp.
2. Hsueh, Chun-tu. *The Chinese Communist Movement, 1921–1949*. 2 vols. Palo Alto: Hoover Institute on War, Revolution, and Peace, 1960–1962.
3. Congressional Quarterly Service. *China and United States Far East Policy, 1945–1966*. Washington: Congressional Quarterly Service, 1967. 348 pp.

Part L

L.I.a

1. *Collins Road Atlas, Europe*. London: Collins, 1965. 232 pp.
2. *Road and Travel Atlas of Europe*. London: Benn, 1961. 56 pp.
3. *Atlas Sozialökonomischer Regionen Europas* [Atlas of social and economic regions of Europe]. Frankfurt am Main: Sozialgraphiches Institut an der Johann Wolfgang Goethe-Universität im Verlag A. Lutzeyer, Baden-Baden, 1964–.
4. Dollfus, Jean. *Atlas of Western Europe*. Paris: Société européenne d'études et d'information, 1963. 46 pp.
5. Kraus, Theodor, *Atlas Östliches Mitteleuropa*. Bielfield: Velhagen und Klasing, 1959. 308 pp.
6. *Atlas of Central Europe*. London: Murray, 1963. 52 pp.
7. Akademie der Wissenschaften, Vienna. Kommission für Raumforschung und Wiederaufbau. *Atlas der Republic Österreich*. Vienna: Freytag-Berndt und Artaria, 1961–.
8. Belgium. Comité national de géographie. *Atlas de Belgique*. Brussels: Institut géographique militaire, 1950–64.
9. Nielsen, Niels, ed. *Atlas of Denmark*. 2 vols. Copenhagen: Hagerup, 1949–61.
10. Geografiska sällskapet i Finland, Helsingfors. *Atlas of Finland*. Helsinki: Otava, 1960. 12 pp.
11. Comité national français de géographie. *Atlas de France*. 2d ed. Paris: Editions géographique de France, 1951–58.
12. West German Federal Republic. Statistisches Bundesamt. *Die Bundesrepublik Deutschland in Karten*. Mainz: W. Kohlhammer, 1965–.
13. Oxford University Press. *Atlas of Britain and Northern Ireland*. Oxford: Clarendon, 1963. 200 pp.
14. Dainelli, Giotto. *Atlante fisico-economico d'Italia*. Milan: Consociazione Turistica Italiana, 1940.
15. Ortremba, Erich. *Atlas der Deutschen Agrarlandschaft*. Wiesbaden: Steiner Verlag, 1962–65.
16. Coppock, John Terrence. *An Agricultural Atlas of England and Wales*. London: Faber, 1964.
17. Sømme, Axel Christion Zetlitz. *Atlas of Norwegian Agriculture*. 1 vol. Oslo: Norwegian Bureau of Statistics, 1950.
18. Anisensel, F. *Atlas industriel de la France*. Paris: Documentation française, 1960. 201 pp.

19. *Reader's Digest Complete Atlas of the British Isles*. London: Reader's Digest Association, 1966. 230 pp.
20. Selection du Reader's Digest, S.A.R.L., Paris. *Grand Atlas de la France*. Paris, 1969. 244 pp.
21. Association pour l'atlas de la France de l'Est. *Atlas de la France de l'Est*. 1 vol. Strasbourg: Istra, 1959–.
22. Lille. Université. Institut de géographie. *Atlas du Nord de la France*. 1 vol. Paris: Editions Berger-Levroult, 1961.
23. Association pour l'atlas de Normandie. *Atlas de Normandie*. Caen, 1965–70.
24. Jones, Emrys, ed. *Atlas of London and the London Region*. London: Pergamon, 1968–69.
25. *Atlas de Paris et de la région parisienne*. 1967.
26. Akademmie fur Raumforschung und Landesplanung, Hanover. *Deutscher Planungsatlas*. Idee und Leitung: Kurt Brüning. Vol. 9, Berlin. Bremen: W. Dort, 1960–.

L.I.b

1. Vesenyi, Paul E. *European Periodical Literature in the Social Sciences and the Humanities*. Metuchen, N.J.: Scarecrow, 1969. 226 pp.
2. *L'Année philologique*. Paris: Societé d'editions "Les Belles Lettres," 1928–.
3. *Quarterly Checklist of Renaissance Studies*. Darien, Conn.: American Bibliographic Service, 1958–.
4. *Atlantic Studies*. Boulogne-sur-Seine, France: Atlantic Institute, 1964–.
5. U.S. Dept. of State. *External Research: Western Europe, Great Britain, and Canada*. Washington: GPO, 1958–.
6. U.S. Library of Congress. *Introduction to Europe: A Selected Guide to Background Reading*. Washington: Library of Congress, 1950. 201 pp. (Supplement, 1955.)
7. Council for Cultural Cooperation of the Council of Europe. *Books Dealing with Europe*. Strasbourg, 1965. 67 pp.
8. European Cultural Centre. *The European Bibliography*. Edited by Hjalmar Pehrsson. Leiden: A. W. Sijthoff, 1965, 472 pp.
9. Cosgrove, Carol A., *A Reader's Guide to Britain and the European Communities*. London: P.E.P., 1970. 106 pp.
10. *The British National Bibliography*. London: Council of the British National Bibliography. 1950–.
11. U.S. Library of Congress. General Reference and Bibliography Division. *Works in the Humanities Published in Great Britain, 1939–1946: A Selective List*. Washington, 1950. 123 pp.
12. Hancock, Philip D. *A Bibliography of Works Relating to Scotland 1916–1950*. 2 vols. Edinburgh: University Press, 1959–60.
13. Mitchell, A. *A Contribution to the Bibliography of Scottish Topography*. 2 vols. Edinburgh: University Press, 1917.
14. Eager, A. R. *A Guide to Irish Bibliographical Material*. London: Library Association, 1964. 392 pp.

15. Pemberton, John E. *How to Find Out about France*. New York: Pergamon, 1966. 199 pp.
16. Stych, E. S. *How to Find Out about Italy*. New York: Pergamon, 1970. 320 pp.
17. Groenning, Sven. *Scandinavia in Social Science Literature*. Bloomington: Indiana University Press, 1970. 284 pp.

L.I.c

1. *Biographie universelle (Michaud) ancienne et moderne*. 45 vols. New ed. Paris: Mme. C. Deplaces, 1843–65.
2. Pedley, Avril, and Uden, Grant. *They Lived Like This (Europe)*. Oxford: Blackwell, 1967. 265 pp.
3. Hammond, N. G. L. *Oxford Classical Dictionary*. 2d ed. London: Oxford University Press, 1970. 1,189 pp.
4. Radice, Betty. *Who's Who in the Ancient World*. New York: Stein & Day, 1967. 225 pp.
5. Jones, A. H. M. *The Prosopography of the Later Roman Empire*. Cambridge: Cambridge University Press, 1971–.
6. Fines, John. *Who's Who in the Middle Ages*. London: Anthony Blond, 1970. 218 pp.
7. *The Dictionary of National Biography*. London: Oxford University Press, 1921–22. Supplements, 1908–59.
8. *Who's Who in History*. General ed., C. R. N. Routh. Oxford: Blackwell, 1960–69.
9. Boase, Frederick. *Modern English Biography*. 6 vols. London: Cass, 1965.
10. *Dod's Parliamentary Companion*. London: Business Directories, 1832–.
11. Namier, Lewis Bernstein, and Brooke, John. *The House of Commons, 1754–1790*. 3 vols. London: H.M.S.O., 1964.
12. Crone, J. S. *A Concise Dictionary of Irish Biography*. Rev. ed. Dublin: Talbot, 1937. 290 pp.
13. *The Dictionary of Welsh Biography Down to 1940*. Oxford: Blackwell, 1959. 1,157 pp.
14. Wurzback, Constantin. *Biographisches Lexikon der Kaiserthums Österreich*. 60 vols. Vienna: Zamaiski, 1854–91.
15. Académie royale des sciences, des lettres et des beaux-arts de Belgique, Brussels. *Biographie nationale*. 28 vols. 1866–1944. Supplements.
16. *Dansk Biografisk Leksikon grundlagt af C. F. Bricka*. 27 vols. Copenhagen: J. H. Schultz, 1933–44.
17. *Dictionnaire de biographie française*. Under the direction of J. Baltcau. Paris: Letouzey et Ane, 1929–.
18. *Dictionnaire des personnages historiques français*. Paris: Editeurs Seghars, 1962. 131 pp.
19. *Dictionnaire de biographie contemporaine française et étrangère*. 2d ed. Paris: Centre international de documentation, 1950. 708 pp. Supplements.

20. *Allgemeine Deutsche Biographie.* 56 vols. Leipzig: Duncker, 1875–1912.

21. Litta, P. *Famiglie celebri d'Italia.* 13 vols. Milan: Presso l'autore (Tip. della famiglie italiane) 1819–23.

22. Aa, Abraham Jacob Van der. *Biographisch Woordenboek der Nederlanden.* 21 vols. in 17. Haarlem: J. J. Van Brederode, 1852–78.

23. Molhuysen, P. C., ed. *Nieuw Nederlandsch Biografisch Woordenboek.* 10 vols. Leiden: A. W. Sijtholt, 1911–37.

24. *Diccionario de historia de España.* Madrid: Revista de Occidente, 1952.

25. Boethius, B., ed. *Svensk Biografiskt Lexikon.* Stockholm: A. Bonnier, 1918–.

26. *Almanach de Gotha.* Gotha: Perthes, 1763–1944.

27. *Burke's Genealogical and Heraldic Dictionary of the Peerage and Baronetage of the United Kingdom.* London: Burke's Peerage, 1847–.

28. Burke, John Bernard, *Burke's Genealogical and Heraldic History of the Landed Gentry.* London: Burke's Peerage, 1847–1952. 2,840 pp.

29. *Who's Who in Europe.* Brussels: Éditions des Fenks, 1964–.

30. *Who's Who: An Annual Biographical Dictionary.* London, 1849–.

31. *Who Was Who.* London, 1929–.

32. *Who's Who in Austria.* Montreal: Intercontinental Book, 1954–.

33. *Who's Who in Belgium and the Grand Duchy of Luxembourg.* Brussels: Intercontinental Book & Publishing Co., 1957/58–.

34. *Who's Who in France.* Paris: Lafitte, 1953–.

35. *Who's Who in Germany.* Munich: Intercontinental Book & Publishing, 1955–.

36. *Who's Who in Italy.* Milan: Intercontinental Book & Publishing, 1958–.

37. *Who's Who in the Netherlands.* Montreal: Intercontinental Book & Publishing, 1962–.

38. *Who's Who in Switzerland.* Zurich: Central European Times Publishing Co., 1952–.

39. Henderson, G. P. *Current European Directories.* Beckenham, England: CBD Research, 1969. 222 pp.

40. *Directory of European Associations.* Croyden, England: CBD Research, 1971–.

41. *Directory of British Associations.* Croyden, England: CBD Research, 1965–.

L.l.d

1. *Chamber's Encyclopedia.* 15 vols. New rev. ed. New York: Pergamon, 1967.

2. *Enciclopedia italiana di scienze, letteri ed arti.* 35 vols. Roma: Istituto della enciclopedia italiana, 1929–37.

3. *Encyclopedia of Ireland.* New York: McGraw-Hill, 1968. 463 pp.

4. Harvey, Paul. *The Oxford Companion to Classical Literature.* London: Oxford University Press, 1937. 480 pp.

5. Whibley, Leonard, ed. *A Companion to Greek Studies.* 4th ed. Cambridge: Cambridge Univ. Press, 1931. 790 pp.
6. Pauly, August Friedrich von. *Pauly Realencyclopädie der Classischen Altertumswissenschaft.* 33 vols. in 67. Stuttgart: Druckmiller, 1893–1967.
7. Daremberg, Charles, and Saglio, Edmond. *Dictionnaire des antiquités grecques et romaines.* 5 vols. Paris: Hachette, 1893–1919.

L.I.e

1. *The European Yearbook.* Strasbourg: Council of Europe, 1955–.
2. Palmer, Michael, and Lambert, J. *A Handbook of European Organizations.* New York: Praeger, 1968. 519 pp.
3. Weil, Gordon L. *A Handbook to the European Economic Community.* New York: Praeger, 1965. 479 pp.
4. Fodor's Modern Guides (series). London: Neame, 1953–.
5. Fielding, Temple H. *Fielding's Travel Guide to Europe.* New York: Sloane, 1948–.
6. *Newman's European Travel Guide.* New York: Harper & Row, 1950–.
7. Steffensen, James L., and Handel, Lawrence. *Europe This Way.* New York: Atheneum, 1968. 617 pp.
8. *Les Guides Bleus.* Paris: Hachette, 1918–.
9. *Blue Guides.* London: Benn, 1918–.
10. Baedeker, K. Handbook(s) for Travelers (series). London: Allen & Unwin, 1839–.
11. Bithell, Jethro. *Germany: A Companion to German Studies.* London: Methuen, 1955. 578 pp.
12. Ritchie, R. L. Graeme. *France: A Companion to French Studies.* 5th ed. London: Methuen, 1950. 520 pp.
13. Gardner, Edmund G., ed. *Italy: A Companion to Italian Studies.* London: Methuen, 1934. 274 pp.
14. Peers, Edgar Allison, ed. *Spain: A Companion to Spanish Studies.* 5th ed. London: Methuen, 1963. 319 pp.
15. Livingstone, Richard Winn. *The Legacy of Greece.* Oxford: Clarendon, 1921. 424 pp.
16. Bailey, Cyril, ed. *The Legacy of Rome.* Oxford: Clarendon, 1936. 512 pp.
17. Great Britain. Central Office of Information. *Britain: An Official Handbook.* Annual. London: H.M.S.O., 1946–.
18. Northern Ireland. General Register Office. *Ulster Yearbook.* Triennial. Belfast: H.M.S.O., 1926–.
19. *Irish Free State Official Handbook.* Dublin: Progress, 1932. 323 pp.
20. West German Federal Republic. Press and Information Office. *Facts about Germany.* 6th ed. Bonn: German Government Printing Office, 1966.
21. Denmark. Royal Danish Ministry of Foreign Affairs. Press and Information Department. *Denmark.* Copenhagen: Krak, 1924– (irregularly).

L.I.g

1. Harvey, Joan M. *Sources of Statistics*. 2d ed. Hamden, Conn.: Linnet Books, 1971. 126 pp.
2. Harvey, Joan M. *Statistics Europe: Sources for Market Research*. Beckenham, England: CBD, 1968. 177 pp.
3. United Nations. Economic Commission for Europe. *Economic Survey of Europe*. Geneva: United Nations, 1947–.
4. United Nations. Economic Commission for Europe. *Economic Bulletin for Europe*. New York: United Nations, 1947–.
5. Statistical Office of the European Communities. *Basic Statistics of the Community*. Brussels, 1959–.
6. European Economic Community. Statistical Office. *General Statistical Bulletin*. Brussels, 1961–.
7. European Economic Community. Statistical Office. *Graphs and Notes on the Economic Situation of the Community*. Brussels, 1962–.
8. European Economic Community. *Yearbook of Agricultural Statistics*. Brussels, 1971.
9. European Economic Community. *Statistiques des transports: 1969*. Geneva, 1971.
10. U.S. Dept. of Agriculture. *Agricultural Trade of the European Economic Community, 1959–1964: A Statistical Reference*. Washington: GPO, 1966.
11. U.S. Dept. of Agriculture. Economic Research Service. *European Economic Community: Agricultural Trade Statistics. 1961–1967*. Washington: GPO, 1969.
12. European Free Trade Association. *EFTA Trade, 1959–1965*. Geneva, 1967. 96 pp.
13. *EFTA Trade*. Geneva: European Free Trade Association, 1964–.
14. United States Department of Agriculture Economic Research Service. *European Free Trade Association: Agricultural Trade Statistics, 1961–1967*. Washington: GPO, 1969.
15. Organization for European Economic Cooperation. *OEEC Statistical Bulletin*. Paris, 1950–.
16. Organization for Economic Cooperation and Development. *Economic Surveys [by country] (series)*. Paris, 1959–.
17. Organization for Economic Cooperation and Development. *Main Economic Indicators*. Paris, 1962–.
18. Organization for Economic Cooperation and Development. *General Statistics*. Paris, 1950–.
19. Reader's Digest Association. *A Survey of Europe Today*. London: Reader's Digest Association, 1970. 212 pp.
20. Dewhurst, J. F., Coppock, J. O., and Yates, P. L. *Europe's Needs, Resources, Trends, and Prospects in Eighteen Countries*. New York: Twentieth Century Fund, 1961. 1,198 pp.
21. Great Britain. Central Statistical Office. *Annual Abstract of Statistics*. London: H.M.S.O., 1832–.

L.2.a

1. Theodoratus, Robert J. *Europe: A Selected Ethnographic Bibliography*. New Haven: HRAF Press, 1969. 544 pp.
2. *International Dictionary of Regional European Ethnology and Folklore*. Copenhagen: Rosenkilde and Bagger, 1960–.
3. Graves, Robert. *The Greek Myths*. 2 vols. New York: Braziller, 1959.
4. *Archaeological Bibliography for Great Britain and Ireland*. London: Council for British Archaeology, 1949–.

L.2.b

1. Blake, Judith. *Western European Censuses: 1960*. Population Monograph series, no. 8. Berkeley: University of California, Institute of International Studies, 1971. 421 pp.

L.2.c

1. Walsh, A. E., and Paxton, J. *Trade and Industrial Resources of the Common Market and EFTA Countries: A Comparative Statistical Analysis*. London: Garnstone Press, 1970. 158 pp.
2. Hamilton, F. E. Ian. *Regional Economic Analysis in Great Britain and the Commonwealth: A Bibliographical Guide*. New York: Schocken Books, 1969. 410 pp.
3. *The Cambridge Economic History of Europe*. Cambridge: Cambridge University Press, 1941–.
4. *Economic History Review*. Utrecht, 1927–.
5. Mitchell, Brian R., and Deane, Phyllis. *Abstract of British Historical Statistics*. Rev. ed. Cambridge: Cambridge University Press, 1970. 513 pp.
6. Schumpeter, Elizabeth B. *English Overseas Trade Statistics, 1697–1808*. Oxford: Clarendon, 1960. 72 pp.
7. Beveridge, William. *Prices and Wages in England from the Twelfth to the Nineteenth Century*. Vol. 1. *Price Tables: Mercantile Era*. London: Longmans, 1939–.
8. Rogers, J. E. Thorald. *A History of Agriculture and Prices in England*. 7 vols. Oxford: Clarendon, 1886–1902.

L.2.d

1. Edelman, Cornelius, and Eeuwens, B. E. P. *Bibliography on Land and Water Utilization and Conservation in Europe*. Rome: FAO, 1955. 347 pp.
2. Plaisance, Georges. *Les Formations végétales et paysages ruraux: Lexique et guide bibliographique*. Paris: Gauthiers-Villars, 1959. 418 pp.
3. Houston, James M. *The Western Mediterranean World: An Introduction to Its Regional Landscapes*. London: Longmans, 1964. 800 pp.

4. Watson, James Wreford, and Sissons, J. B., eds. *The British Isles: A Systematic Geography*. Edinburgh: Nelson, 1964. 452 pp.
5. Taylor, Eva G. R. *Tudor Geography, 1485–1583*. New York: Octagon Books, 1930. Reprinted, 1968. 290 pp.
6. ———. *Later Tudor and Early Stuart Geography, 1583–1650*. London: Methuen, 1934. 322 pp.
7. *Larousse Encyclopedia of Geography: Europe*. General editor, Pierre Deffontaines. New York: Prometheus Press, 1961.

L.2.e

1. Fox, Edward W., ed. *Atlas of European History*. Oxford: Oxford University Press, 1957. 64 pp.
2. Breasted, J. H. *European History Atlas*. Chicago: Dennoyer-Geppert, 1954. 62 pp.
3. Horrabin, J. F. *An Atlas of European History from the Second to the Twentieth Century*. London: Gollancz, 1935. 141 pp.
4. Verlag Enzyklopädie Leipzig. *Historisch-geographisches Kartenwerk*. Unter Leitung von Edgar Dahmann. Leipzig, 1958–.
5. Heyden, A. A. M. van der, ed. *Atlas of the Classical World*. New York: Nelson, 1960. 221 pp.
6. McEvedy, Colin. *Penguin Atlas of Ancient History*. Harmondsworth, England: Penguin, 1967. 96 pp.
7. ———. *Penguin Atlas of Medieval History*. Harmondsworth, England: Penguin, 1961. 96 pp.
8. Darby, H. C., ed. *New Cambridge Modern History Atlas*. Vol. 14 of *New Cambridge Modern History*. Cambridge: Cambridge University Press, 1970. 319 pp.
9. *New Cambridge Modern History*. 14 vols. Cambridge: Cambridge University Press, 1957–70.
10. Poole, R. L. *Oxford Historical Atlas of Modern Europe*. Oxford: Clarendon, 1902. 328 pp.
11. Freeman, E. A. *Historical Geography of Europe*. 3d ed. New York: Longmans, 1920. 611 pp.
12. Lobel, M. D., ed. *Historic Towns: Maps and Plans of Towns and Cities in the British Isles*. London: Lovell Johns-Cook, Hammond and Kell, 1969.
13. *International Bibliography of Urban History*. Stockholm: Swedish Institute for Urban History, 1960–.
14. *Cambridge Ancient History*. 12 vols. New York: Macmillan, 1923–39.
15. Davis, R. H. C. *Medieval European History: A Select Bibliography*. Helps for Students of History, no. 67. London: Historical Association, 1963. 47 pp.
16. Paetow, Louis John. *Guide to the Study of Medieval History*. Rev. ed., prepared under the auspices of the Medieval Academy of America. New York: Crofts, 1931. Reprinted, New York: Kraus, 1959. 643 pp.
17. Halphen, Louis. *Initiation aux études d'histoire du Moyen Age*. 3d ed. Paris: Presses universitaires de France, 1952. 205 pp.

18. Atiya, Aziz Suryal. *The Crusades: Historiography and Bibliography*. Bloomington: Indiana University Press, 1962. 170 pp.
19. *Cambridge Medieval History*. 2d ed. Cambridge: Cambridge University Press, 1966–.
20. *The Cambridge Modern History*. Edited by A. W. Ward, G. W. Prothero and Stanley Leathes. 13 vols. plus atlas. New York, London: Macmillan, 1907–24.
21. Roach, John. *Bibliography of Modern History*. London: Cambridge University Press, 1968. 388 pp.
22. Davies, A. *Modern European History, 1494–1788: A Select Bibliography*. Helps for Students of History, no. 68. London: Historical Association, 1966. 39 pp.
23. Medlicott, William N. *Modern European History, 1789–1945: A Select Bibliography*. London: Routledge & Kegan Paul for Historical Association, 1960. 38 pp.
24. Bromley, J. S. *A Select List of Works on Europe and Europe Overseas, 1715–1815*. Oxford: Clarendon, 1956. 79 pp.
25. Bullock Alan. *A Select List of Books on European History, 1815–1914*. 2d ed. Oxford: Clarendon, 1957. 79 pp.
26. Ragatz, Lowell J. *A Bibliography for the Study of European History, 1815–1939*. Supplements: 1943, 1945, 1956. Ann Arbor: Edwards, 1942.
27. *Writings on British History*. London: Cape, 1934–.
28. Royal Historical Society, London. *Writings on British History, 1901–1933*. London: Cape, 1968–.
29. Read, Conyers, ed. *Bibliography of British History: Tudor Period, 1485–1603*. 2d ed. London: Oxford University Press, 1959. 624 pp.
30. Davies, Godfrey, ed. *Bibliography of British History: Stuart Period, 1603–1714*. London: Oxford University Press for the Royal Historical Society and the American Historical Society, 1928. 459 pp.
31. Pargellis, S. M. *Bibliography of British History: The Eighteenth Century, 1714–1789*. London: Oxford University Press for the Royal Historical Society and the American Historical Society, 1951. 642 pp.
32. Altschul, Michael. *Anglo-Norman England, 1066–1154*. Cambridge and New York: Cambridge University Press for the Conference on British Studies, 1969. 83 pp.
33. Levine, Mortimer. *Tudor England, 1485–1603*. Cambridge: Cambridge University Press for the Conference on British Studies, 1968. 115 pp.
34. Sachse, William L. *Restoration England, 1660–1689*. Cambridge and New York: Cambridge University Press for the Conference on British Studies, 1971. 114 pp.
35. Altholz, Josef L. *Victorian England, 1837–1901*. Cambridge and New York: Cambridge University Press for the Conference on British Studies, 1971. 114 pp.
36. Miller, Helen, and Newman, Aubrey. *Early Modern British History, 1485–1760: A Select Bibliography*. London: Historical Association, 1970. 42 pp.

37. Christie, Ian R. *British History since 1760: A Select Bibliography*. London: Historical Association, 1970. 56 pp.

38. Bonser, Wilfred. *An Anglo-Saxon and Celtic Bibliography, 450–1087*. 2 vols. Berkeley: University of California, 1957.

39. Gross, Charles. *The Sources and Literature of English History from the Earliest Times to about 1485*. 2d ed. 1915. Reprinted, Gloucester, Mass.: Smith, 1951. 820 pp.

40. Grose, Clyde L. *A Select Bibliography of British History, 1660–1760*. 1939. Reprinted, New York: Octagon, 1967. 507 pp.

41. Williams, Judith B. *A Guide to the Printed Materials for English Social and Economic History, 1750–1850*. 2 vols. New York: Columbia University Press, 1926.

42. Galbraith, V. H. *Introduction to the Use of the Public Records*. 2d ed. London: Oxford University Press, 1952. 120 pp.

43. Giuseppi, M. S. *Guide to the Manuscripts Preserved in the Public Record Office*. 2 vols. London: H.M.S.O., 1923–24.

44. Great Britain. Record Office. *Guide to the Contents of the Public Record Office*. 2 vols. London: H.M.S.O., 1963.

45. Great Britain. Her Majesty's Stationery Office. *British National Archives*. Government Publications. Sectional List no. 24. London: H.M.S.O., 1968.

46. ———. *Publications of the Royal Commission on Historical Manuscripts*. Government Publications. Sectional List no. 17. London: H.M.S.O., 1967. 31 pp.

47. Great Britain. Historical Manuscripts Commission. *Record Repositories in Great Britain: A List*. . . . London: H.M.S.O., 1966. 49 pp.

48. Upton, Eleanor S. *Guide to Sources of English History from 1603 to 1660 in Early Reports of the Royal Commission on Historical Manuscripts*. 2d ed. Metuchen, N.J.: Scarecrow, 1964. 258 pp.

49. Great Britain. Historical Manuscripts Commission. *Guide to the Reports on the Collections of Manuscripts of Private Families*. 2 vols. London: H.M.S.O., 1914–38.

50. Tate, W. E. *The Parish Chest*. 2d ed. Cambridge: Cambridge University Press, 1951. 346 pp.

51. West, John. *Village Records*. New York: St. Martin, 1962. 208 pp.

52. Redstone, L. J., and Steers, F. W., eds. *Local Records: Their Nature and Care*. London: Bell, 1953. 246 pp.

53. Emmison, F. G., and Gray, Irvine. *County Records*. Historical Association, London Pamphlets H. 62. London: Historical Association, 1967. 31 pp.

54. Historical Association, London. *English Local History Handlist*. Rev. ed. London: Historical Association, 1952. 74 pp.

55. Steinberg, S. H., ed. *New Dictionary of British History*. New York: St. Martin, 1963. 407 pp.

56. *Dictionnaire historique et biographique de la Suisse* . . . sous la direction de Marcel Godeb. 7 vols. Neuchatel, 1931–34.

57. Powicke, Maurice. *Handbook of British Chronology*. Royal Historical Society Guides and Handbooks, no. 2. London: Royal Historical Society, 1961. 565 pp.

58. Elton, Geoffrey R. *Modern Historians on British History, 1485–1945*. Ithaca, N.Y.: Cornell University Press, 1970. 239 pp.
59. Fussner, F. Smith. *Tudor History and the Historians*. London: Basic Books, 1970. 312 pp.
60. "Writings on Irish History." In *Irish Historical Studies,* vol. 1. 1938–.
61. *A Bibliography of the History of Wales*. 2d ed. Cardiff: University of Wales Press, 1962. 330 pp.
62. *Bibliographie annuelle de l'histoire de France du cinquième siècle à 1939*. Paris: Editions du Centre national de la recherche scientifique, 1956–.
63. Caron, Pierre. *Répertoire bibliographique de l'histoire de France*. 6 vols. Paris: Picard, 1923–38.
64. Gandilhon, R., and Samaran, C. *Bibliographie générale des travaux et archéologiques*. Paris: Imprimerie nationale, 1944–.
65. Molinier, A. *Les Sources de l'histoire de France depuis les origines jusqu'au 1815*. 18 vols. Manuels de bibliographie historique, 2–5. Paris: Picard, 1901–35.
66. Mongland, Andre. *La France revolutionnaire et impériale*. Paris: Imprimerie nationale, 1930–.
67. Dahlmann, Friedrich C., and Waitz, Georg. *Quellenkunde der deutschen Geschichte*. 10th edition. Edited by H. Heimpel and H. Geuss. Stuttgart: Hiersemann, 1965–.
68. Thomas, Daniel H., and Case, Lynn M., eds. *Guide to the Diplomatic Archives of Western Europe*. Philadelphia: University of Pennsylvania Press, 1959. 389 pp.

L.2.f

1. *Penguin Companion to World Literature*. 4 vols. New York: McGraw-Hill, 1971.
2. Steinberg, S. H., ed. *Cassell's Encyclopedia of Literature*. 2 vols. New York: Funk & Wagnalls, 1953.

L.2.g

1. Holt, Stephen. *Six European States: The Countries of the European Community and Their Political Systems*. New York: Taplinger, 1970. 414 pp.
2. Henig, Stanley, ed. *European Political Parties: A Handbook*. New York: Praeger, 1970. 565 pp.
3. Palmer, John. *Government and Parliament in Britain: A Bibliography*. 2d ed. London: Hansard Society, 1964. 51 pp.
4. Wilding, Norman W. *An Encyclopedia of Parliament*. 3d ed. New York: Praeger, 1968. 912 pp.
5. Butler, David, and Freeman, Jennie. *British Political Facts, 1900–1968*. 3d ed. London: Macmillan, 1969. 314 pp.
6. Olle, James G. H. *An Introduction to British Government Publications*. London: Association of Assistant Librarians, 1965. 128 pp.
7. Morgan, Mary. *British Government Publications: An Index to*

Chairmen and Authors, 1941–1966. London: Library Association, 1969. 193 pp.

8. Cole, Arthur Harrison, ed. *A Finding-List of Royal Commission Reports on the British Dominions*. Cambridge: Harvard University Press, 1939. 134 pp.

9. Rodgers, Frank, and Phelp, Rose B. *A Guide to British Parliamentary Papers*. University of Illinois Graduate School of Library Science. Occasional Papers, 82. Urbana: University of Illinois Graduate School of Library Science, 1967. 37 pp.

10. Rodgers, Frank. *Serial Publications in the British Parliamentary Papers, 1900–1968: A Bibliography*. Chicago: American Library Association, 1971. 146 pp.

11. British Museum. State Paper Room. *Checklist of British Official Serial Publications to June 1968*. Second provisional issue. London: British Museum, 1968.

12. Ford, Percy, and Ford, Grace. *A Breviate of Parliamentary Papers, 1900–1916: The Foundation of the Welfare State*. Oxford: Blackwell, 1957. 470 pp.

13. ———. *A Breviate of Parliamentary Papers, 1917–1939*. 1951. Reprinted, Shannon: Irish Universities Press, 1969. 571 pp.

14. ———. *A Breviate of Parliamentary Papers, 1940–1954: War and Reconstruction*. Oxford: Blackwell, 1961. 515 pp.

15. ———. *Select List of Parliamentary Papers, 1833–1899*. Oxford: Blackwell, 1953. 165 pp.

16. ———. *A Guide to Parliamentary Papers*. 2d ed. Oxford: Blackwell, 1956. 79 pp.

17. Great Britain. House of Commons. *A Bibliography of Parliamentary Debates on Great Britain*. House of Commons Library document no. 2. London: H.M.S.O., 1959. 62 pp.

18. Craig, F.W.S. *British Parliamentary Election Statistics, 1918–1968*. Glasgow: Political Reference Publications, 1968. 110 pp.

19. Snape, Wilfrid H. *How to Find Out about Local Government*. Oxford: Pergamon, 1970. 173 pp.

20. *The British Commonwealth Yearbook*. London: MacGibbon and Kee, 1952–.

21. Flint, John E. *Books on the British Empire and Commonwealth: A Guide for Students*. London: Published on behalf of the Royal Commonwealth Society by Oxford University Press, 1968. 66 pp.

22. National Book League. *Commonwealth Reference Books: A Bibliographical Guide*. London: National Book League, 1965. 54 pp.

23. Horne, A. J. *The Commonwealth Today: A Select Bibliography on the Commonwealth and Its Constituent Countries*. Library Association Subject list no. 45. London: Library Association, 1965. 107 pp.

24. Royal Empire Society. *Subject Catalogue of the Library of the Royal Empire Society*. 4 vols. London: The Society, 1930–37.

25. Coston, Henry. *Dictionnaire de la politique française*. Paris: Publications H. Coston, 1967. 1,088 pp.

26. Meyriat, Jean. *Political Science, 1950–1958*. French Bibliographi-

cal Digest, series 2, no. 28. New York: French Government Cultural Center, 1960.

27. Gouray, Bernard, comp. *Public Administration*. New York: French Government Cultural Center, 1963. 207 pp.

28. Carlson, Andrew R. *German Foreign Policy, 1890–1914, and Colonial Policy to 1914: A Handbook and Annotated Bibliography*. Metuchen, N.J.: Scarecrow, 1970. 333 pp.

29. Wiener Library, London. *After Hitler: Germany, 1945–1963*. London: Vallentine, 1963. 261 pp.

30. Lane, John C., and Pollock, James K., comps. *Source Materials on the Government and Politics of Germany*. Ann Arbor, Mich.: Wahrs Publishing Co., 1964. 404 pp.

31. American Historical Association. Committee for the Study of War Documents. *A Catalogue of Files and Microfilms of the German Foreign Ministry Archive, 1867–1920*. New York: Oxford University Press, 1959. 1,290 cols.

32. U.S. Department of State. Historical Office. *A Catalogue of Files and Microfilm of the German Foreign Ministry Archive, 1920–1945*. Stanford: Hoover Institution, 1962–.

33. U.S. National Archives and Record Service. *A Guide to German Records Microfilmed at Alexandria, Virginia*. 47 parts. Washington: GPO, 1958–65.

34. Germany. Auswärtiges amt. *German Diplomatic Documents, 1871–1914*. 4 vols. Selected and translated by E. T. S. Dugdale. London: Methuen, 1928.

35. *Scandinavian Political Studies*. Helsinki, 1966–.

36. Julkunen, Martii, and Lehikoinen, Anja. *A Select List of Books and Articles in English, French, and German on Finnish Politics in the Nineteenth and Twentieth Century*. Turku, Finland: Institute of Political History, University of Turku, 1967. 125 pp.

37. *European and Atlantic Affairs*. 2d ed. London: National Book League, 1971. 29 pp.

Part M

M.1.b

1. Maichel, Karol. *Guide to Russian Reference Books*. Stanford, Calif.: Hoover Institution, 1962–.

2. Horecky, Paul Louis, ed. *Russia and the Soviet Union: A Bibliographic Guide to Western-Language Publications*. Chicago: University of Chicago Press, 1965. 473 pp.

3. Horecky, Paul Louis. *Basic Russian Publications*. Chicago: University of Chicago Press, 1962. 313 pp.

4. Horecky, Paul Louis, ed. *East Central Europe: A Guide to Basic Publications*. Chicago: University of Chicago Press, 1969. 956 pp.

5. ———. *Southeastern Europe: A Guide to Basic Publications*. Chicago and London: University of Chicago Press, 1969. 755 pp.

6. Byrnes, Robert F. *Bibliography of American Publications on East*

Central Europe, 1945–1957. Indiana University Publications. Slavic and East European Series, vol. 12. Bloomington: Indiana University, 1958. 213 pp.

7. *The American Bibliography of Russian and East European Studies.* Bloomington: Indiana University Press, 1956–.

8. Horak, Stephan M. *Junior Slavica.* Rochester, N.Y.: Libraries Unlimited, 1968. 244 pp.

9. Pidhainy, Oleh Sememovych. *The Ukrainian Republic in the Great East-European Revolution: A Bibliography.* Vols. 5–7. Toronto: New Review Books, 1971–.

10. U.S. Library of Congress. *Rumania: A Bibliographic Guide.* Washington: GPO, 1963. 75 pp.

11. ————. *Bulgaria: A Bibliographic Guide.* Washington: GPO, 1965. 98 pp.

12. ————. *Czechoslovakia: A Bibliographic Guide.* Washington: GPO, 1967. 157 pp.

13. ————. *East Germany: A Selected Bibliography.* Washington: GPO, 1967. 133 pp.

14. *ABSEES.* Soviet and East European Abstracts Series. Glasgow: National Association for Soviet and East European Studies, Institute of Soviet and East European Studies, University of Glasgow, 1970–.

15. U.S. Library of Congress. Slavic and Central European Division. *The USSR and Eastern Europe: Periodicals in Western Languages.* 3d ed. rev. and enl. Washington: GPO, 1967. 89 pp.

M.I.c

1. *Prominent Personalities in the USSR.* Metuchen, N.J.: Scarecrow, 1968–.

2. *Portraits of Prominent USSR Personalities.* Metuchen, N.J.: Scarecrow, 1968–.

3. Institut zur Erforschung der UdSSR. *Party and Government Officials of the Soviet Union, 1917–1967.* Edited by E. L. Crowley, A. I. Lebed and H. E. Schultz. Metuchen, N.J.: Scarecrow, 1969. 214 pp.

4. Institut zur Erforschung der UdSSR. *Biographic Directory of the USSR.* Metuchen, N.J.: Scarecrow, 1958. 782 pp.

5. *Who's Who in the USSR, 1965/66.* 2d ed. Metuchen, N.J.: Scarecrow, 1966. 1,189 pp.

6. Institut zur Erforschung der UdSSR. *Who Was Who in the USSR.* Metuchen, N.J.: Scarecrow, 1972. 687 pp.

M.I.d

1. *McGraw-Hill Encyclopedia of Russia and the Soviet Union.* Edited by Michael T. Florinsky. New York: McGraw-Hill, 1961. 624 pp.

2. *Slavonic Encyclopedia.* Edited by Joseph S. Roucek. New York: Philosophical Library, 1949. 1,445 pp.

3. Kernig, C. D., ed. *Marxism, Communism, and Western Society*. 8 vols. New York: Herder and Herder, 1972–.
4. Maxwell, Robert, ed. and comp. *Information USSR*. Oxford: Pergamon, 1962. 982 pp.
5. Kubijovyc, Volodymyr, ed. *Ukraine: A Concise Encyclopedia*. Toronto: University of Toronto Press, 1963–70.
6. *Encyclopedia Lituanica*. Edited by Simas Suziedelis. Toronto: Encyclopedia Lituanica, 1970.
7. Eterovich, Francis H., ed. and Christopher Spalatin Association, ed. *Croatia: Land, People, Culture*. 2 vols. Toronto: University of Toronto Press, 1970.

M.1.e

1. Strakhovsky. Leonid I., ed. *A Handbook of Slavic Studies*. Cambridge: Harvard Univ. Press, 1949. 753 pp.

M.1.f

1. *Current Digest of the Soviet Press*. New York: Joint Committee on Slavic Studies, 1949–.
2. *Reprints from the Soviet Press*. New York: Compass, 1966–.

M.2.a

1. Jakobson, Roman. *Paleosiberian Peoples and Languages: A Bibliographic Guide*. New Haven: HRAF Press, 1957. 222 pp.

M.2.c

1. Kish, George. *Economic Atlas of the Soviet Union*. 2d ed. Ann Arbor: University of Michigan Press, 1971. 90 pp.

M.2.d

1. U.S. Library of Congress. Reference Department. *Soviet Geography: A Bibliography*. 2 vols. Washington, 1951.

M.2.e

1. Crowther, Peter A., comp. *A Bibliography of Works in English on Early Russian History to 1800*. New York: Barnes & Noble, 1969. 236 pp.
2. Shapiro, David M., *A Select Bibliography of Works in English on Russian History, 1801–1917*. Oxford: Blackwell, 1962. 106 pp.
3. Pushkarev, Sergei G., comp. *Dictionary of Russian Historical Terms from the Eleventh Century to 1917*. George Vernadsky and Ralph T. Fisher, Jr., eds. New Haven: Yale University Press, 1970. 199 pp.
4. Adams, Arthur E. *An Atlas of Russian and East European History*. New York: Praeger, 1966. 204 pp.

5. Chew, Allen F. *An Atlas of Russian History*. Rev. ed. New Haven: Yale University Press, 1970. 114 pp.
6. Pundeff, Marin, ed. and comp. *History in the USSR*. San Francisco: Chandler, 1967. 313 pp.
7. *Language and Area Studies: East Central and Southeastern Europe: A Survey*. Edited by Charles Jelavich. Chicago: University of Chicago Press, 1969. 483 pp.
8. Problems in European Civilization (series). Ralph W. Greenlaw and Dwight E. Lee, general eds. Lexington, Mass.: Heath, 1958–.
9. European Problem Studies (series). New York: Holt, Rinehart & Winston, 1963–.

M.2.g

1. Staar, Richard F. *The Communist Regimes in Eastern Europe: An Introduction*. Stanford, Calif.: Hoover Institution, 1967. 387 pp.
2. Triska, Jan F., ed. *Constitutions of the Communist Party-States*. Stanford, Calif.: Hoover Institution, 1968. 541 pp.
3. Hammond, Thomas T., ed. *Soviet Foreign Relations and World Communism*. Princeton: Princeton University Press, 1965. 1,240 pp.
4. *Yearbook on International Communist Affairs*. Stanford, Calif.: Hoover Institution, 1966–.
5. Degras, Jane T., ed. *The Communist International, 1919–1943: Documents*. 2 vols. New York: Oxford University Press, 1956–60.
6. Degras, Jane T., ed. *Soviet Documents on Foreign Policy*. 3 vols. London: Oxford University Press, 1951–53.
7. Degras, Jane T. *Calendar of Soviet Documents on Foreign Policy*. London: Royal Institute of International Affairs, 1948. 248 pp.
8. *Current Soviet Policies: The Documentary Record of the Communist Party Congress*. New York: Columbia University Press, 1952–.
9. Eudin, Xenia Joukoff. *Soviet Russia and the East, 1920–1927*. Stanford: Stanford University Press, 1957.
10. ———. *Soviet Russia and the West, 1920–1927*. Stanford: Stanford University Press, 1957. 450 pp.
11. ———. *Soviet Foreign Policy, 1928–1934: Documents and Materials*. University Park: Pennsylvania State University Press, 1967.
12. Clemens, Walter C. *Soviet Disarmament Policy, 1917–1962*. Stanford, Calif.: Hoover Institution, 1965. 151 pp.
13. Gittings, John. *Survey of the Sino-Soviet Dispute*. London: Oxford University Press, 1968. 410 pp.

M.2.h

1. Halpern, Joel M., McKinstry, John A., and Saund, Dalip. *Bibliography of Anthropological and Sociological Publications on Eastern Europe and the USSR*. Russian and East European Studies Center Series, vol. 1, no. 2. Los Angeles: Russian and East European Studies Center, University of California, 1961. 142 pp.

Part N

N.I.a

1. Wilgus, A. Curtis. *Latin America in Maps*. New York: Barnes & Noble, 1951. 330 pp.
2. Ferriday, Alan. *A Map Book of Africa and South America*. London, Melbourne: Macmillan, 1967. 65 pp.
3. American Geographical Society. *Map of Hispanic America*. Washington: GPO, 1922–45. 923 pp.
4. Cayo, Roberto Manuel. *Compendio geográfico y atlas argentino*. Buenos Aires: Ediciones G.L.G., 1965. 70 pp.
5. Camacho Lara, Rene R. *Atlas de Bolivia*. La Paz, 1958. 18 pp.
6. Brazil. Conselho Nacional do Geografia. *Atlas nacional do Brasil*. Rio de Janeiro: Instituto Brasileiro de Geografia e Estadistica, Conselho Nacional do Geografia, 1966. no paging.
7. British Honduras. Lands and Survey Dept. *Atlas of British Honduras*. Belize?, 1939.
8. Chile. Instituto Geográfico Militar. *Atlas de la República de Chile*. Santiago, 1966. 120 pp.
9. Cortes, Vicenta. *La colección de mapas y planos del Archivo Nacional de Colombia*. Madrid?, 1959. 22–34 pp.
10. Costa Rica. Instituto Geográfico Nacional. *Costa Rica: 1:25,000*. San José, 1952–.
11. Canet, Alvarez, Gerardo A. *Atlas de Cuba*. Cambridge: Harvard University Press, 1949. 63 pp.
12. Salvador. Dirección General de Estadística y Censos. *Atlas censal de El Salvador*. San Salvador, 1955. 110 pp.
13. Tamayo, Jorge L. *Atlas geográfico general de México*. 1 vol. 2d ed. Mexico City: Instituto Mexicano de Investigaciones Económicas, 1962.
14. Venezuela. Dirección de Cartografia Nacional. *Atlas de Venezuela*. Caracas: Ministerio de Obras Públicas, Dirección de Cartografia Nacional, 1969. 216 pp.
15. American Geographical Society. *A Catalog of Maps of Hispanic America*. . . . 4 vols. New York: American Geographical Society, 1930–32.
16. Monteiro, Palmyra V. M. *A Catalog of Latin-American Flat Maps, 1926–1964*. 2 vols. Austin: University of Texas, Institute of Latin American Studies, 1967–69.
17. Pan American Union. Natural Resources Unit. *Annotated Index of Aerial Photography Coverage and Mapping of Topography and Natural Resources Undertaken in the Latin American Member Countries of the OAS*. 19 vols. Washington: Unión Panamericana, Departamento de Asuntos Económicos, 1964–1966.

N.I.b

1. Gropp, Arthur E., comp. *A Bibliography of Latin American Bibliographies*. 3d ed. Metuchen, N.J.: Scarecrow, 1968. 515 pp. (Supplement, 1971. 277 pp.)

2. Sable, Martin H. *A Guide to Latin American Studies.* 2 vols. Los Angeles: University of California Press, 1967.

3. Geohegan, Abel Rodolfo, comp. *Obras de referencia de América Latina.* Buenos Aires: Imp. Crisol, 1965. 280 pp.

4. *Handbook of Latin American Studies.* Gainesville: University of Florida Press, 1935–.

5. *British Bulletin of Publications on Latin America, The West Indies, Portugal, and Spain.* London: Hispanic and Luso-Brazilian Councils, Canning House Library, 1949–.

6. *Inter-American Review of Bibliography.* Washington: Pan American Union, 1951–.

7. *Current Caribbean Bibliography.* Port of Spain, Trinidad: Caribbean Commission, 1951–.

8. U.S. Library of Congress. Hispanic Foundation. *Latin America, Spain, and Portugal: An Annotated Bibliography.* Bibliographical Series no. 13. Compiled by Georgette M. Dorn. Washington: Library of Congress, 1971. 180 pp.

9. United Kingdom. Hispanic Council and Luzo-Brazilian Council. *Latin America: An Introduction to Modern Books in England Covering the Countries of Latin America.* 2d ed., rev. London: Library Association, 1966. 41 pp.

10. Bayitch, S. A. *Latin America: A Bibliographical Guide to Economy, History, Law, Politics, and Society.* Coral Gables, Fla.: University of Miami Press, 1961. 335 pp.

11. ———. *Latin America and the Caribbean: A Bibliographical Guide to Works in English.* Interamerican Legal Studies, vol. 10. Coral Gables, Fla.: University of Miami Press, 1967. 943 pp.

12. U.S. Library of Congress. Slavic and Central European Division and Hispanic Foundation. *Latin America in Soviet Writings, 1945–1958: A Bibliography.* Hispanic Foundation Bibliographical series no. 5. Washington, 1959. 275 pp.

13. Grieder, Terence. *Bibliography of Latin American Philosophy and Art since Independence.* Austin: University of Texas, Institute of Latin American Studies, 1964. 114 pp.

14. Rodríguez, Mario. *A Guide for the Study of Culture in Central America: Humanities and Social Sciences.* Washington: Pan American Union, 1968. 88 pp.

15. Rogers, Francis M. *Brazil, Portugal, and Other Portuguese-Speaking Lands: A List of Books Primarily in English.* Cambridge: Harvard University Press, 1968. 73 pp.

16. Comitas, Lambros. *Caribbeana, 1900–1965: A Topical Bibliography.* Seattle: Published for the Research Institute for the Study of Man by University of Washington Press, 1968. 909 pp.

17. Pan American Union. Columbus Memorial Library. *Indice general de publicaciones periódicas latinoamericanas: humanidades y ciencias sociales.* Washington: Pan American Union, 1961–.

18. ———. *Index to Latin American Periodical Literature, 1929–1960.* 8 vols. Boston: G. K. Hall, 1962.

19. Zimmerman, Irene. *A Guide to Current Latin American Periodi-*

cals: Humanities and Social Sciences. Gainesville, Fla.: Kallman Publishing Co., 1961. 357 pp.

20. Brunnschweiler, Tamara. *Current Periodicals: A Select Bibliography in the Area of Latin American Studies*. East Lansing: Michigan State University Press, 1968. 100 pp.

21. Committee on Latin America. *Latin American Economic and Social Serials*. Hamden, Conn.: Archon Books, 1969, 189 pp.

22. *Latin American Serial Documents*. Compiled by Ross Quintero Mesa. Ann Arbor, Mich.: Bowker, 1968–.

23. *Latin American Research Review*. Austin: University of Texas Press, 1966–.

24. Seminar on Latin American Studies in the United States, Stanford, California, 1963. *Social Science Research on Latin America: Report and Papers*. Edited by Charles Wagley. New York: Columbia University Press, 1964. 338 pp.

25. Esquenazi-Mayo, Roberto. *Latin American Scholarship since World War II: Trends in History, Political Science, Literature, Geography, Economics*. Lincoln: University of Nebraska Press, 1971. 335 pp.

26. *Latin American Urban Research*. Gainesville, Fla.: Center for Latin American Studies, 1970–.

N.I.c

1. Hilton, Ronald, ed. *Who's Who in Latin America: A Bibliographical Dictionary of Notable Living Men and Women of Latin America*. 7 vols. 3d ed. rev. Palo Alto: Stanford University Press, 1945–51.

2. Alisky, Marvin. *Who's Who in Mexican Government*. Tempe: Arizona State University, 1969. 64 pp.

3. U.S. Library of Congress. Hispanic Foundation. *National Directory of Latin Americanists*. Hispanic Foundation Bibliographical series no. 12. 2d ed. Washington, 1971. 684 pp.

4. Cline, Howard F., comp. *Historians of Latin America in the United States, 1965*. Durham, N.C.: Duke University Press for the Conference on Latin American History, 1966. 105 pp.

N.I.d

1. *Enciclopedia universal illustrada europea-americana*. 70 vols. in 71. Barcelona: J. Espasa, 1907–30. Appendix in 10 vols. 1930–33. Annual supplements, 1935–.

2. *Diccionario enciclopédico de las Americas*. Buenos Aires: Editiones Futuro, 1947. 711 pp.

3. *Gran enciclopedia argentina*. 9 vols. Buenos Aires: Ediar, 1956–64.

4. *Enciclopedia de México*. Mexico City: Instituto de la enciclopedia de México, 1966–.

5. Brazil. (Rio de Janeiro) Instituto Historico e Geografico Brasileiro. *Diccionario historico, geográphico e etnographico do Brasil*. 2 vols. Rio de Janeiro: Impresa Nacional, 1922.

N.I.e

1. *South American Handbook*. Chicago: Rand McNally, 1924–.
2. Hanson, Earl Parker, ed. *The New World Guides to the Latin American Republics*. 3 vols. 3d ed. New York: Duell, Sloan and Pearce, 1950.
3. *Yearbook of the West Indies and the Countries of the Caribbean*. London: Skinner, 1969–.
4. Fodor, Eugene, ed. *Fodor's Guide to the Caribbean, Bahamas, and Bermuda: A Comprehensive Handbook of the Islands and the Spanish Main*. New York: Fodor, 1960–.
5. *The Caribbean Who, What, Why*. Kingston, Jamaica: L. S. Smith, 1965. 844 pp.
6. Stoetzer, O. C. *The Organization of American States*. New York: Praeger, 1965. 213 pp.
7. Pan American Union. *Yearbook of Education, Scientific, and Cultural Development in Latin America*. Washington: Pan-American Union, 1966–.
8. Sable, Martin H., ed. *Master Directory for Latin America*. Los Angeles: Latin American Center, U.C.L.A., 1965. 438 pp.
9. Wrzoz, C. B. R., ed. *Brazilian Information Handbook*. Rio de Janeiro: C. B. R. Wrzoz, 1956–.
10. Colombian Institute of Public Opinion. *Quick Colombian Facts*. Bogota: Instituto Colombiano de Opinión Pública, 1955–.
11. *Handbook of Jamaica*. Kingston, Jamaica: Government Printing Office, 1881–.
12. México. Banco Nacional de Comercio Exterior. *Mexico: Facts, Figures, and Trends*. Mexico City, Banco Nacional de Comercio Exterior, 1960–.
13. *Trinidad and Tobago Yearbook*. Trinidad: Yuille, 1865–.

N.I.f

1. Charno, Steven M. *Latin American Newspapers in United States Libraries: A Union List Compiled in the Serial Division, Library of Congress*. Austin: University of Texas Press, 1969. 619 pp.
2. *Latin America*. London: Latin American Newsletters, 1967–.
3. *Airmail News from Latin America*. Madison: University of Wisconsin, Center for International Communication Studies, 1967–71.
4. *Latin American Digest*. Tempe: Center for Latin American Studies, Arizona State University, 1966–.

N.I.g

1. United Nations. Economic Commission for Latin America. *The Economic Survey of Latin America*. New York: United Nations, 1957–.
2. United Nations. Economic Commission for Latin America. *Boletín estadístico de América Latina* [Statistical bulletin for Latin America]. New York: United Nations, 1964–.

3. University of California at Los Angeles. Latin American Center. *Statistical Abstract of Latin America.* Los Angeles: University of California Press, 1955–.
4. Inter-American Development Bank. *Socioeconomic Progress in Latin America.* Washington: Inter-American Development Bank, 1961–.
5. Inter-American Development Bank. *The Process of Industrialization in Latin America.* Washington: Inter-American Development Bank, 1969. 308 pp.
6. Bank of London and South America. *BOLSA Review.* London, Bank of London & South America, Economic Intelligence Department, 1967–.

N.2.a

1. Gibson, Gordon D. "A Bibliography of Anthropological Bibliographies: The Americas." *Current Anthropology* 1, no. 1 (January 1960):61–73.
2. O'Leary, Timothy J. *Ethnographic Bibliography of South America.* New Haven, Conn.: Human Relations Area Files, 1963. 387 pp.
3. Steward, Julian H., ed. *Handbook of South American Indians.* U.S. Bureau of American Ethnology, Bulletin 143. 7 vols. Washington: GPO, 1946–59.
4. *Handbook of Middle American Indians.* Austin: University of Texas Press, 1964–.

N.2.b

1. Smith, Thomas Lynn. *Latin American Population Studies.* Gainesville: University of Florida Press, 1960. 83 pp.
2. Arriaga, Eduardo E. *New Life Tables for Latin American Populations in the Nineteenth and Twentieth Centuries.* Berkeley: University of California, Institute of International Studies, 1968. 324 pp.
3. Vaughan, Denton R. *Urbanization in Twentieth-Century Latin America: A Working Bibliography.* Austin: University of Texas Press, 1970. 122 pp.
4. Avila, Fernando Bastos do. *Immigration in Latin America: A Study Made with the Cooperation of the Intergovernmental Committee for European Migration.* Washington: Pan-American Union, 1964. 299 pp.
5. Solberg, Carl. *Immigration and Nationalism: Argentina and Chile, 1890–1914.* Austin: University of Texas Press, Institute of Latin American Studies, 1970. 222 pp.

N.2.c

1. Harvard University. Bureau for Economic Research in Latin America. *The Economic Literature of Latin America: A Tenta-*

tive Bibliography. 2 vols. Cambridge: Harvard University Press, 1935–36.
2. Weaver, Jerry L., ed. *Latin American Development: A Selected Bibliography, 1950–1967.* Santa Barbara, Calif.: American Bibliographical Center, Clio Press, 1969. 87 pp.
3. Wish, John R. *Economic Development in Latin America: An Annotated Bibliography.* New York: Praeger, 1965. 114 pp.
4. Jones, Tom Bard. *A Bibliography of South American Economic Affairs: Articles in Nineteenth Century Periodicals.* Minneapolis: University of Minnesota Press, 1955. 146 pp.
5. Banco de México. Departamento de Estudios Económicos. *Bibliografía económica de México.* Mexico City, 1955–.
6. Mings, Robert C. *A Bibliography of the Tourist Industry of Latin America.* Special Publication no. 3. Washington: U.S. National Section, Pan-American Institute of Geography and History, 1971. 25 pp.

N.2.d

1. Rubio y Munoz-Bocanegra, Angel. *Bibliografía de geografía urbana de America.* Coleção Geografía Urbana, publ. 1. Rio de Janeiro: Instituto Panamericano de Geografía e Historia Comissao de Geografía, 1961. 229 pp.
2. Harris, Chauncy D. *Annotated List of Selected Current Geographical Serials of the Americas and the Iberian Peninsula.* Chicago: Center for International Studies, University of Chicago, 1967. 16 pp.
3. Bartlett, Harley Harris. *Fire in Relation to Primitive Agriculture and Grazing in the Tropics: Annotated Bibliography.* 3 vols. Ann Arbor: University of Michigan Botanical Gardens, 1955–57.
4. Inter-American Committee for Agricultural Development. *Inventory of Information Basic to the Planning of Agricultural Development in Latin America: Selected Bibliography.* 7 vols. Washington: Pan-American Union, 1963–.
5. Rio de Janerio. Universidade do Brasil. Centro de pesquisas de Geografía do Brasil. *Bibliografia geográfica do Brasil, 1951–.* Bibliographical series 2, Geography, publication no. 1. Rio de Janeiro, 1956–.
6. Mexico. Dirección General de Geografía y Meteorología. *Bibliografía geográfica de Mexico.* Compiled by Angel Bassols Batalla. Mexico City, 1955. 652 pp.

N.2.e

1. Griffin, Charles G., ed. *Latin America: A Guide to the Historical Literature.* Conference on Latin American History Publications, no. 4. Austin: University of Texas Press, 1971. 700 pp.
2. Humphreys, Robin A. *Latin American History: A Guide to the Literature in English.* London: Oxford University Press/Royal Institute of International Affairs, 1958. 197 pp.

3. Cline, Howard F., comp. *Latin American History: Essays on the Study and Teaching, 1898–1965.* Conference on Latin American History, Publication no. 1. 2 vols. Austin: Published for the Conference on Latin American History by the University of Texas Press, 1967. 813 pp.
4. Wilgus, Alva Curtis. *Histories and Historians of Hispanic America.* New York: Cooper Square Publishers, 1965. (Reprint of 1942 ed.) 144 pp.
5. Trask, D. F., comp. and ed. *A Bibliography of United States–Latin American Relations since 1810.* Lincoln: University of Nebraska Press, 1968. 441 pp.
6. Martin, Michael Rheta. *Encyclopedia of Latin American History.* Rev. ed. New York: Bobbs-Merrill, 1968. 348 pp.

N.2.f

1. Newmark, Maxim. *Dictionary of Spanish Literature.* Paterson, N.J.: Littlefield, Adams, 1963. 352 pp.

N.2.g

1. Kantor, Harry. *Latin American Political Parties: A Bibliography.* Gainesville: University of Florida Press, 1968. 113 pp.
2. Rabinovitz, Francine F. *Latin American Political Systems in an Urban Setting: A Preliminary Bibliography.* Gainesville: Center for Latin-American Studies, University of Florida, 1967. 42 pp.
3. Weaver, Jerry L., ed. *The Political Dimensions of Rural Development in Latin America: A Selected Bibliography, 1950–1967.* Long Beach: California State College, 1968. 92 pp.
4. Chilcote, Ronald H. *Revolution and Structural Change in Latin America: A Bibliography on Ideology, Development, and the Radical Left (1930–1965).* 2 vols. Stanford, Calif.: Hoover Institution, 1971.
5. *Latin American Political Guide.* Boulder: University of Colorado, Department of Political Science, 1957–.
6. Ratliff, William E., ed. *The Yearbook on Latin American Communist Affairs.* Stanford, Calif.: Hoover Institution, 1971–.

N.2.h

1. *Anuario de sociología de los pueblos ibéricos.* Madrid: Instituto de Estudios Sindicales, Sociales y Cooperativos, 1966–.
2. Pan American Union. Division of Labor and Social Affairs. *Bibliography on Labor and Social Welfare in Latin America.* Compiled by Sylvia Pollack Bernstein. Washington: Pan American Union, 1944. 76 leaves.
3. Pierson, Donald. *Survey of the Literature in Brazil of Sociological Significance Published up to 1940.* Cambridge: Harvard University Press, 1945. 60 pp.

4. Remmling, Günter W. *South American Sociologists: A Directory.* Austin: University of Texas Press, 1970. 59 pp.

Part O

O.l.a

1. U.S. Department of the Interior. *The National Atlas of the United States of America.* Washington: U.S. Department of the Interior, 1970. 417 pp.
2. *Rand McNally Commercial Atlas and Marketing Guide.* Chicago: Rand McNally, 1869–.
3. Reader's Digest Association, Ltd. *These United States: Our Nation's Geography, History, and People.* Pleasantville, N.Y.: Reader's Digest Association, 1968. 236 pp.

O.l.b

1. Wynkoop, Sally, comp. *Government Reference Books.* Littleton, Colorado: Libraries Unlimited, 1970–.
2. U.S. Library of Congress. *A Guide to the Study of the United States of America.* Washington: GPO, 1960. 1,193 pp. (Supplement forthcoming.)
3. *American Quarterly.* Philadelphia, 1949–.
4. Winther, Oscar Osburn. *A Classified Bibliography of the Periodical Literature of the Trans-Mississippi West (1811–1967).* 2 vols. Bloomington: Indiana University Press, 1961–71.
5. *Alternative Press Index.* Northfield, Minn.: Radical Research Center, 1969–.
6. *Underground Newspaper Collection.* Wooster, Ohio: Bell and Howell, 1965–.

O.l.c

1. *Who's Who in America.* Chicago: Marquis, 1899–1900–.
2. *Who's Who in the East.* Chicago: Marquis, 1943–.
3. *Who's Who in the Midwest.* Chicago: Marquis, 1950–.
4. *Who's Who in the South and Southwest.* Chicago: Marquis, 1950–.
5. *Who's Who in the West.* Chicago: Marquis, 1949–.
6. *Who Was Who in America: Historical volume, 1607–1896.* Chicago: Marquis, 1963. 670 pp.
7. *Who Was Who in America.* Chicago: Marquis, 1942–.
8. *Dictionary of American Biography.* 22 vols. New York: Scribner, 1928–58.
9. *Concise Dictionary of American Biography.* New York: Scribner, 1964. 1,273 pp.
10. U.S. Congress. *Biographical Directory of the American Congress, 1774–1971.* Senate Document no. 92–8. 92d Cong., 1st Sess. Washington: GPO, 1971. 1,922 pp.

11. U.S. Congress. *Official Congressional Directory*. Washington: GPO, 1809–.
12. Kane, Joseph Nathan. *Facts about the Presidents*. 2d ed. New York: Wilson, 1968. 384 pp.
13. *Who's Who in American Politics*. New York: Bowker, 1967–68–.

O.I.d

1. Filler, Louis. *A Dictionary of American Social Reform*. New York: Philosophical Library, 1963. 854 pp.
2. Mathews, Mitford McLeod. *A Dictionary of Americanisms on Historical Principles*. 2 vols. Chicago: University of Chicago Press, 1951.
3. Wentworth, Harold, and Flexner, Stuart Berg. *Dictionary of American Slang*. New York: Crowell Collier Macmillan, 1960. 669 pp.

O.I.e

1. *Appleton's Annual Cyclopedia*. 16 vols. New York, 1861–1902.
2. *American Yearbook*. New York: Appleton, 1911–50.
3. Carruth, Gorton, ed. *The Encyclopedia of American Facts and Dates*. 4th ed. New York: Crowell Collier Macmillan, 1966. 821 pp.

O.I.f

1. *Newspapers on Microfilm*. 6th ed. Washington: GPO, 1967. 487 pp.
2. "Subject Index." *Christian Science Monitor*. Boston, 1960–.
3. *Wall Street Journal*. New York: Dow Jones, 1899–.
4. *Newsbank Urban Affairs Library*. Chicago, 1970–.

O.I.g

1. *American Statistics Index*. Washington: Congressional Information Service, 1973–.
2. U.S. Bureau of the Census. *Statistical Abstract of the United States*. Washington: GPO, 1878–.
3. ———. *Historical Statistics of the United States, Colonial Times to 1962*. Washington: GPO, 1965. 154 pp.
4. ———. *County and City Data Book*. Washington: GPO, 1949–.
5. U.S. Bureau of the Budget. Office of Statistical Standards. *Statistical Service of the United States Government*. Rev. ed. Washington: GPO, 1968. 156 pp.

O.2.a

1. Murdock, George Peter. *Ethnographic Bibliography of North America*. Behavior Science Bibliographies. 3d ed. New Haven: HRAF Press, 1960. 393 pp.

2. Hodge, Frederick Webb. *Handbook of American Indians North of Mexico*. U.S. Bureau of American Ethnology, Bulletin 30; Smithsonian Institution, Bureau of American Ethnology, Bulletin 30. 2 vols. Washington: GPO, 1907–10.
3. Swanton, John R. *The Indian Tribes of North America*. Smithsonian Institution, Bureau of American Ethnology, Bulletin 145. Washington: Smithsonian Institution Press, 1952. 726 pp.
4. Arctic Institute of North America. *Arctic Bibliography*. 14 vols. published. Washington: GPO, 1953–.
5. Haywood, Charles. *A Bibliography of North American Folklore and Folksong*. 2 vols. 2d rev. ed. New York: Dover, 1961. 1,301 pp.
6. U.S. Library of Congress. General Reference and Bibliography Division. *Folklore of the North American Indians: An Annotated Bibliography*. Compiled by Judith C. Ullom. Washington: GPO, 1969.
7. Wildhaber, Robert. "A Bibliographical Introduction to American Folklife." *New York Folklore Quarterly* 21, no. 4 (1965):285–89. (First published in *Schweizerischen Archiv fur Volkskunde* Basel, 1964.)
8. Tallman, Marjorie. *Dictionary of American Folklore*. New York: Philosophical Library, 1959. 320 pp.

O.2.c

1. *F and S Index to Corporations and Industries*. Cleveland: Predicasts, 1965–.
2. Brimmer, Andrew F., and Harper, Harriet. "Economists' Perception of Minority Economic Problems: A View of Emerging Literature." *Journal of Economic Literature* 8, no. 3 (September 1970):783–806.
3. Lovett, Robert W., ed. *American Economic and Business History Information Sources*. Detroit: Gale Research, 1971. 323 pp.
4. Harvard University. Graduate School of Business Administration. Baker Library. *Studies in Enterprise*. Compiled by Lorna M. Daniells. Boston, 1957. 169 pp.
5. Larson, Henrietta. *Guide to Business History*. Harvard Studies in Business History, 12. Boston: J. S. Canner, 1948. 1,181 pp.
6. Schlebecker, John T. *Bibliography of Books and Pamphlets on the History of Agriculture in the United States, 1607–1967*. Santa Barbara, Calif: Clio Press, 1969. 183 pp.
7. Pursell, Carroll W. *Preliminary List of References for the History of Agriculture, Science, and Technology in the U.S.* Davis, Calif: Agricultural History Branch, Department of Agriculture and Agricultural History Center, 1966–.
8. Taylor, George Rogers. *American Economic History before 1860*. New York: Appleton, 1969. 108 pp.
9. Kirkland, Edward Chase, comp. *American Economic History since 1860*. New York: Appleton, 1971. 78 pp.

O.2.d

1. Berry, Brian Joe Lobley. *A Bibliographic Guide to the Economic Regions of the U.S.* Research Paper no. 87. Chicago: University of Chicago, Department of Geography, 1963. 101 pp.
2. McManis, Douglas R. *Historical Geography of the United States: A Bibliography, Excluding Alaska and Hawaii.* Ypsilanti: Eastern Michigan University, 1965. 249 pp.

O.2.e

1. Paullin, Charles O., ed. *Atlas of the Historical Geography of the U.S.* Washington and New York: Carnegie Institution & American Geographical Society, 1932. 162 pp.
2. Lord, Clifford Lee. *Historical Atlas of the United States.* New York: Holt, Rinehart & Winston, 1953. 238 pp.
3. American Heritage. *American Heritage Pictorial Atlas of United States History.* New York: American Heritage Publishing, 1966. 424 pp.
4. Adams, James T., ed. *Atlas of American History.* New York: Scribner, 1943. 360 pp.
5. Handlin, Oscar., ed. *Harvard Guide to American History.* Cambridge, Mass.: Belknap Press, 1955. 689 pp.
6. *America: History and Life.* Santa Barbara, Calif.: Clio Press, 1954–.
7. *Writings on American History.* Washington: GPO, 1902–03, 1906–40, 1948–(59?).
8. Service Center for Teachers of History (series). Washington: American Historical Association, 1956–70.
9. American Problem Studies (series). New York: Holt, Rinehart & Winston, 1962–.
10. Problems in American Civilization (series). Edwin C. Roswenc, gen. ed. Lexington, Mass.: Heath, 1949–.
11. Adams, James T., ed. *Dictionary of American History.* 7 vols. New York: Scribner, 1940–63.
12. ———. *Concise Dictionary of American History.* New York: Scribner, 1962. 1,156 pp.
13. Adams, James T., ed. *Album of American History.* 6 vols. New York: Scribner, 1960.
14. Morris, Richard, ed. *Encyclopedia of American History.* 2d ed. New York: Harper & Row, 1970. 840 pp.
15. *Webster's Guide to American History.* Springfield, Mass.: Merriam, 1971, 1,428 pp.
16. Johnson, Thomas H. *The Oxford Companion to American History.* New York: Oxford University Press, 1966. 906 pp.
17. Kull, Irving S. *A Chronological Encyclopedia of American History.* New York: Popular Library, 1969. 640 pp.
18. Boatner, Mark Mayo. *Encyclopedia of the American Revolution.* New York: D. McKay Co., 1966, 1,287 pp.

19. Boatner, Mark Mayo. *The Civil War Dictionary.* New York: McKay, 1966. 974 pp.

20. *The Annals of America.* Edited by Mortimer J. Adler, Charles Van Doren, and others. 20 vols. Chicago: Encyclopaedia Britannica, 1969.

21. Commager, Henry Steele. *Documents of American History.* 7th ed. New York: Appleton, 1963. 739 pp.

22. Berkeley Series in American History. Skokie, Ill.: Rand McNally, 1963–.

23. Bremner, Robert H. *American Social History since 1860.* New York: Appleton, 1969. 132 pp.

24. Greene, Jack P. *The American Colonies in the Eighteenth Century, 1689–1783.* New York: Appleton, 1969. 132 pp.

25. Grob, Gerald N., ed. *American Social History before 1860.* New York: Appleton, 1970. 137 pp.

26. Donald, David, comp. *The Nation in Crisis, 1861—1877.* New York: Appleton, 1969.

27. Link, Arthur S. *The Progressive Era and the Great War, 1896–1920.* New York: Appleton, 1969. 85 pp.

28. Burr, Nelson, ed. *Religion in American Life.* New York: Appleton, 1971. 171 pp.

29. Canada. Department of Mines and Technical Surveys. Geography Branch. *Colonization and Settlement in the Americas: A Selected Bibliography.* Bibliographical series, no. 25. Ottawa, 1960.

30. Bemis, Samuel Flagg. *Guide to the Diplomatic History of the United States, 1775–1921.* Washington: Carnegie Institution, 1935.

31. Smith, James Ward, ed. *Religion in American Life.* 4 vols. Princeton University Press, 1961–.

32. Egbert, Donald Drew. *Socialism and American Life.* 2 vols. Princeton, N.J.: Princeton University Press, 1952.

33. Adams, Ramon F. *The Rampaging Herd: A Bibliography of Books and Pamphlets of Men and Events in the Cattle Industry.* Norman: University of Oklahoma Press, 1959. 610 pp.

34. Adams, Ramon F. *Burs under the Saddle: A Second Look at Books and Histories of the West.* Norman: University of Oklahoma Press, 1964. 610 pp.

35. Localized History Series. New York: Teachers College, 1965–.

O.2.f

1. *Literary History of the U.S.* Edited by Robert E. Spiller et al. 2 vols. 3d ed., rev. New York: Macmillan, 1963. (Supplement, 1972.)

2. Altick, Richard. *Selective Bibliography for the Study of English and American Literature.* 4th ed. New York: Macmillan, 1971. 164 pp.

O.2.g

1. Plano, Jack C. *American Political Dictionary.* Rev. ed., New York: Holt, Rinehart & Winston, 1967. 401 pp.

2. *Congressional Quarterly Almanac*. Washington: Congressional Quarterly, 1943–.
3. *Congressional Quarterly Weekly Report*. Washington: Congressional Quarterly 1943–.
4. Congressional Quarterly Service. *Congress and the Nation*. Washington, 1965–.
5. Congressional Quarterly Service. *Guide to the Congress of the U.S.* Washington, 1972.
6. *Congressional Index*. Chicago: Commerce Clearing House, 1937–.
7. Barone, Michael. *Almanac of American Politics*. Boston: Gambit, 1972–.
8. *U.S. Federal Register*. Washington: GPO, 1936–.
9. U.S. National Archives and Records Service. *Weekly Compilation of Presidential Documents*. Washington: GPO, 1965–.
10. U.S. National Archives and Records Service. *Code of Federal Regulations*. Washington: GPO, 1938–.
11. *U.S. Government Organization Manual*. Washington: Office of the Federal Register, National Archives and Record Service, GPO, 1937–.
12. U.S. Congress. *Congressional Record*. 1789–.
13. *U.S. Statutes at Large*. Washington: GPO, 1789–.
14. U.S. Library of Congress. Legislative Reference Service. *Digest of Public General Bills and Selected Resolutions with Index*. Washington: GPO, 1936–.
15. *United States Code*. Washington: GPO, 1926–.
16. U.S. Supreme Court. *United States Reports*. Washington: GPO, 1875–.
17. *The Constitution of the United States of America. . . .* Washington: GPO, 1964. 1,693 pp.
18. *United States Supreme Court Digest, 1754 to Date. . . .* St. Paul: West, 1943–.
19. Price, Miles Oscar. *Effective Legal Research*. 3d ed. Boston: Little, Brown, 1969. 501 pp.
20. *United States Law Week*. Washington: Bureau of National Affairs, 1933–.
21. *America Votes: A Handbook of Contemporary American Elections Statistics*. New York: Macmillan, 1956–.
23. Jones, B. Crichton. *State Government: A Selected Bibliography*. Center for Government Studies, 1970. 29 pp.
24. *The Book of the States*. Chicago: Council of State Governments and the American Legislators' Association, 1935–.
25. *The Municipal Yearbook*. Washington: International City Management Association, 1934–.
26. *Index to Current Urban Documents*. Westport, Conn.: Greenwood Press, 1972–.
27. Bollens, John C. *American County Government, with an Annotated Bibliography*. Beverly Hills, Calif.: Sage Publications, 1969. 433 pp.
28. Government Affairs Foundation, Inc. *Metropolitan Communities*. 4 vols. Chicago: Public Administration Service, 1956–.

29. Wynar, Lubomyr R. *American Political Parties*. Littleton, Colo.: Libraries Unlimited, 1969. 427 pp.
30. Muller, Robert. *From Radical Left to Extreme Right*. 2 vols. 2d ed. Ann Arbor, Mich.: Campus Publishers, 1970–72.
31. Wilcox, Laird M., comp. *Guide to the American Left*. 5th ed. Kansas City: United States Directory, 1970.
32. ————. *Guide to the American Right*. 2d ed. Kansas City: United States Directory, 1970.
33. Seidman, Joel Isaac. *Communism in the United States: A Bibliography*. Ithaca, N.Y.: Cornell University Press, 1969. 526 pp.
34. *Digest of the Public Record of Communism in the United States*. New York: Fund for the Republic, 1955. 753 pp.
35. U.S. Department of State. *Foreign Relations of the United States: Diplomatic Papers*. Washington: GPO, 1861–.
36. *The United States in World Affairs*. New York: Harper & Row for the Council on Foreign Relations, 1931–.
37. *Documents on American Foreign Relations*. New York: Harper & Row, 1953–.
38. *Law and Society Review*. Beverly Hills, Calif.: Sage Publications, 1966–.

O.2.h

1. Gaustad, Edwin Scott. *Historical Atlas of Religion in America*. New York: Harper & Row, 1962. 179 pp.
2. Tompkins, Dorothy Campbell, comp. *Poverty in the United States during the Sixties: A Bibliography*. Berkeley: Institute of Governmental Studies, University of California, 1970. 542 pp.
3. Encyclopaedia Britannica Educational Corporation. *Makers of America*. 10 vols. Chicago, 1971.
4. Coan, Otis Welton. *America in Fiction*. 5th ed. Palo Alto, Calif.: Pacific Books, 1967. 232 pp.
5. Adams, A. John, and Burke, Joan Martin. *Civil Rights: A Current Guide to the People, Organizations, and Events*. New York: Bowker, 1970.
6. Davis, John P., ed. *The American Negro Reference Book*. Englewood Cliffs, N.J.: Prentice-Hall, 1966. 969 pp.
7. Ebony Magazine. *Negro Handbook*. Chicago: Johnson Publishing Co., 1966. 535 pp.
8. Ploski, Harry A., ed. *The Negro Almanac*. Rev. ed. New York: Bellwether, 1971. 1,110 pp.
9. Pettigrew, Thomas. *A Profile of the Negro American*. Princeton, N.J.: Van Nostrand Reinhold, 1964. 250 pp.
10. Major, Clarence. *A Short Dictionary of Afro-American Slang*. New York: International Publishers, 1970. 127 pp.
11. McPherson, James. *Blacks in America: Bibliographical Essays*. New York: Doubleday, 1971. 430 pp.
12. Miller, Elizabeth W. *The Negro in America: A Bibliography*. 2d ed. Cambridge: Harvard University Press, 1970. 351 pp.
13. U.S. Library of Congress. *The Negro in the United States*. Com-

piled by Dorothy B. Porter. Washington, D.C., Library of Congress, 1970. 313 pp.

14. *Negro in Print*. Washington: Negro Bibliographic and Research Center, 1965–.

15. Ohio. Central State University, Wilberforce. Library. *Index to Periodical Articles by and about Negroes*. Vols. 1–10, 1950–59; vol. 11–. Boston: G. K. Hall, 1962–.

16. Clark y Moreno, Joseph A., comp. "A Bibliography of Bibliographies Relating to Mexican-American Studies." *El Grito*, 5, no. 2 (Winter 1971–2):47–79.

17. U.S. Inter-Agency Committee on Mexican American Affairs. *The Mexican American: A New Focus on Opportunity: A Guide to Materials Relating to Persons of Mexican American Heritage in the United States*. Washington: Inter-Agency Commitee on Mexican American Affairs, 1969. 186 pp.

18. Grebler, Leo. *The Mexican-American People: The World's Second Largest Minority*. New York: Free Press, 1970. 777 pp.

19. Fontana, Bernard L. *The Indians of North America: Bibliographical Sources*. Tucson: Arizona State Museum, Univ. of Arizona, 1972. 22 l.

20. *Index to Literature on the Native Americans*. San Francisco: American Indian Historical Society, 1971–.

21. Vogel, V. J., *The Indian in American History*. Chicago: Integrated Educational Associates, 1968. 27 pp.

22. U.S. Department of the Interior. *Biographical and Historical Index of American Indians and Persons Involved in Indian Affairs*. 8 vols. Boston: G. K. Hall, 1966.

23. Hirschfelder, Arlene B., comp. *American Indian Authors: A Representative Bibliography*. Rev. ed. New York: Association on American Indian Affairs, 1973. 102 pp.

24. Klein, Bernard, and Icolori, Daniel, eds. *Reference Encyclopedia of the American Indian*. New York: B. Klein, 1967. 536 pp.

25. U.S. Congress. House Committee on Interior and Insular Affairs. *Report with Respect to the House Resolution Authorizing the Committee on Interior and Insular Affairs to Conduct an Investigation of the Bureau of Indian Affairs*. Pursuant to House Resolution 698 (82d Congress). Washington: GPO, 1953–.

26. U.S. Solicitor for the Department of the Interior. Office of the Solicitor. *Handbook of Federal Indian Law*. By Felix S. Cohen. Washington, GPO, 1942. 455 pp.

27. U.S. Solicitor for the Department of the Interior. *Federal Indian Law*. Washington: GPO, 1958. 1,106 pp.

28. *Indian Affairs, Laws, and Treaties*. . . . Compiled and collected by Charles J. Kappler. 5 vols. Washington: Superintendent of Documents, 1903–1941.

29. *American Indian Law Newsletter*. Albuquerque: University of New Mexico School of Law, 1969–.

30. Fujimoto, Isao. *Asians in America: A Selected Annotated Bibliography*. Working Publication no. 5. Davis, Calif.: Asian American

Research Project, Department of Applied Behavioral Sciences,
1971. 295 pp.

O.3.

1. Schmeckebier, Laurence F., *Government Publications and Their
   Use*. 2d rev. ed. Washington: Brookings Institution, 1969. 502 pp.
2. Jackson, Ellen. *Subject Guide to Major United States Government
   Publications*. Chicago: American Library Association, 1968. 175
   pp.
3. Andriot, John L. *Guide to U.S. Government Serials and Periodicals*. McLean, Va.: Documents Index, 1962–.
4. Body, Alexander C. *Annotated Bibliography of Bibliographies on
   Selected Government Publications and Supplementary Guides to
   the Superintendent of Documents Classification System*. Kalama-
   zoo: Western Michigan University, 1967–.
5. *CIS Index to Publications of the United States Congress*. Washington: Congressional Information Service, 1970–.
6. U.S. Library of Congress. Serial Division. *Popular Names of U.S.
   Government Reports: A Catalog*. Washington: GPO, 1971. 43 pp.

Part P

P.I.a

1. Canada. Department of Mines and Technical Surveys. Geographical Branch. *Atlas of Canada*. Ottawa, 1957–.
2. Canada. Department of Energy, Mines, and Resources. Surveys
   and Mapping Branch. *The National Atlas of Canada*. 4th ed.
   1970–.
3. Kerr, D. G. G. *Historical Atlas of Canada*. Don Mills, Ontario:
   Nelson, 1966. 120 pp.

P.I.b

1. Lochead, Douglas. *Bibliography of Canadian Bibliographies*. Toronto: University of Toronto Press, 1972.
2. *Canadiana*. Ottawa: National Library of Canada, 1951–.
3. Campbell, H. C., ed. *How to Find Out about Canada*. Oxford:
   Pergamon, 1967. 248 pp.
4. *Canadian Periodical Index*. Ottawa: Canadian Library Association,
   1928–.

P.I.c

1. *Dictionary of Canadian Biography*. Toronto: University of Toronto
   Press, 1966–.
2. Wallace, W. S. *The Macmillan Dictionary of Canadian Biography*. London: Macmillan, 1963. 822 pp.
3. *Canadian Who's Who*. Toronto. Trans-Canada Press, 1910–.
4. *Who's Who in Canada*. Toronto: International Press, 1914–.

P.l.d

1. *Encyclopedia Canadiana*. John E. Robins, ed. in chief. 10 vols. Ottawa: Canadiana Co., 1966–68.
2. Avis, Walter S., ed. *A Dictionary of Canadianisms on Historical Principles*. Toronto: Gage, 1967. 926 pp.

P.l.e

1. *Canadian Annual Review*. Toronto: University of Toronto Press, 1960–.
2. *Canadian Almanac and Dictionary*. Toronto: University of Toronto Press, 1960–.
3. *McGraw-Hill Directory and Almanac of Canada*. 6 vols. Toronto: McGraw-Hill, 1966. (Later volumes under title: *Corpus Directory and Almanac of Canada*.)
4. Taplin, Glen W. *Canadian Chronology*. Metuchen, N.J.: Scarecrow, 1970. 174 pp.

P.l.f

1. *Canadian News Facts*. Toronto, 1967–.
2. *Canadian News Index*. Regina, Canada: University of Saskatchewan, Regina Campus, 1967–.

P.l.g

1. Canada. Bureau of Statistics. *Canada Year Book*. Ottawa, 1905–.
2. Urquhart, M. C., ed. *Historical Statistics of Canada*. Cambridge: Cambridge University Press, 1965. 672 pp.

P.2.a

1. Canada. Museum of Man. *Annual Report*. Ottawa, 1928–.
2. *Canadian Historical Review*. Toronto, 1921–.

P.2.d

1. Canada. Department of Mines and Technical Surveys. Geographical Branch. "Bibliography of Periodical Literature on Canadian Geography, 1930 to 1955." Bibliographical Series, no. 22, parts 1–6. Ottawa, 1960.
2. Canada. Department of Mines and Technical Surveys. Geographical Branch. *Bibliographical Series*. Ottawa, 1950–.
3. Canada. Department of Mines and Technical Surveys. Geographical Branch. *Canadian Urban Geography*. Bibliographical series, no. 13. Rev. ed. Ottawa, 1957.

P.2.e

1. Story, Norah. *The Oxford Companion to Canadian History and Literature*. Toronto: Oxford University Press, 1967. 935 pp. Supplement, 1973. 318 pp.

2. Beaulieu, André. *Guide d'histoire du Canada*. Quebec: Presses de l'Université Laval, 1969. 540 pp.
3. Canadian Historical Association Historical Booklets (series). Ottawa: Canadian Historical Association, n.d.
4. Problems in Canadian History (series). Toronto: Copp Clark, 1966–1968.
5. Issues in Canadian History (series). Toronto: Copp Clark, 1969–1970.

P.2.g

1. Carrigan, D. Owen, comp. *Canadian Party Platforms, 1867–1968*. Urbana: University of Illinois Press, 1969. 363 pp.

P.2.h

1. Hodge, F. W. *Handbook of Indians of Canada*. Ottawa: Parmelee, 1913. 632 pp.

Part Q

Q.I.a

1. Kennedy, T. F. *A Descriptive Atlas of the Pacific Islands, New Zealand, Australia, Melanesia, Micronesia, Philippines*. New York: Praeger, 1966. 65 pp.
2. Australia. Department of National Development. Regional Development Division. *Atlas of Australian Resources*. Canberra: First Series, 1953–1960; Second Series, 1962–.
3. Ferriday, Alan. *A Map Book of Australasia*. 3d ed. London and Melbourne: Macmillan, 1966. 52 pp.
4. New South Wales. Department of National Development. *A Regional Atlas of New South Wales*. Sydney: Government of New South Wales, 1966–.
5. Holmes, James Macdonald. *An Atlas of Population and Production for New South Wales*. Sydney: Angus & Robertson, 1932. 70 pp.
6. Tasmania. Department of Lands and Surveys. Mapping Branch. *Regional Planning Atlas of Tasmania*. Edited by J. L. Dorris. 4th ed. Hobart: Tasmanian Government, 1965.
7. Rural Bank of South Wales, Sydney. *Australian Rural Industries: A Graphic Representation*. Sydney, 1948. 144 pp.
8. McLintock, Alexander H., ed. *A Descriptive Atlas of New Zealand*. Wellington: R. E. Owen, Government Printer, 1959. 109 pp.
9. Linge, G. J. R. *Atlas of New Zealand Geography*. Rev. ed. Wellington: A. H. and A. W. Reed, 1968. 64 pp.
10. *The Oxford Atlas of New Zealand*. Edited by R. G. Lister. 2d ed. London: Oxford University Press, 1966. 75 pp.
11. *Oxford Australian Atlas*. 2d ed. Melbourne: Oxford University Press, 1966. 75 pp.

12. USSR. Soviet Academy of Sciences. *Atlas Antarktiki*. Moscow: GUGK, 1966–67.
13. American Geographic Society. *Antarctic Map Folio Series*. New York: American Geographical Society, 1964–.
14. U.S. Hydrographic Office, United States Navy. *The Oceanographic Areas of the Polar Seas*. Washington: GPO, 1957–.

Q.I.b

1. Leeson, Ida. *A Bibliography of Bibliographies of the South Pacific*. London: Oxford University Press, 1954. 61 pp.
2. New Zealand Library Association. *A Bibliography of New Zealand Bibliographies*. Preliminary ed. Wellington: Library Association, 1967. 58 pp.
3. ———. *Guide to New Zealand Reference Materials*. Compiled by J. Harris. 2d ed. Wellington: Library Association, 1950. 114 pp. (Supplements no. 1, 1951, and no. 2, 1957.)
4. Borchardt, Dietrick Hans. *Australian Bibliography: A Guide to Printed Sources of Information*. Melbourne: F. W. Cheshire, 1963. 72 pp.
5. *Australian National Bibliography*. Canberra: National Library of Australia, 1961–.
6. U.S. Library of Congress. *Antarctic Bibliography*. Washington: GPO, 1965–.
7. Southwest Pacific Area. General Headquarters. Allied Geographical Section. *An Annotated Bibliography of the Southwest Pacific and Adjacent Areas*. 4 vols. 1944.
8. Sachet, Marie H. *Island Bibliographies: Micronesian Botany; Land Environment and Ecology of Coral Atolls; Vegetation of Tropical Islands*. National Research Council Technical Series no. 335. Washington: National Academy of Sciences, National Research Council, 1965. 577 pp.
9. Day, A. C. *Pacific Island Literature: One Hundred Basic Books*. Honolulu: University of Hawaii Press, 1971.
10. Ferguson, John Alexander. *Bibliography of Australia, 1784–1900*. Sydney and London: Angus & Robertson, 1941–.
11. Australia. Department of Territories. *Annotated Bibliography of Select Government Publications on Australian Territories, 1951–1964*. Canberra: Government Printing Office, 1965. 55 pp.
12. Politzer, Ludwig L. *Bibliography of Dutch Literature on Australia*. Melbourne: privately printed, 1953. 13 pp.
13. ———. *Bibliography of French Literature on Australia, 1595–1946*. Melbourne: privately printed, 1952. 44 pp.
14. ———. *Bibliography of German Literature on Australia, 1770–1947*. Melbourne: Pan Press, 1952. 47 pp.
15. Hocken, Thomas Morland. *Bibliography to the Literature Relating to New Zealand*. Wellington: Mackay, 1909. 619 pp.
16. Chapple, Leonard James Bancroft. *Biblio-brochure Containing Addenda and Corrigenda to Extant Bibliographies of New Zealand*. Dunedin, New Zealand: Reed, 1938. 47 pp.

17. Snow, Philip A. *A Bibliography of Fiji, Tonga, and Rotuma*. Coral Gables, Fla.: University of Miami Press, 1969. 418 pp.
18. Spence, S. A. *Antarctica: Its Books and Papers from the Earliest to the Present Time*. Mitcham, England: S. A. Spence, 1966. 82 pp.
19. U.S. Antarctic Projects Officer. *National Interests in Antarctica: An Annotated Bibliography*. Compiled by Robert D. Hayton. Washington: GPO, 1960. 137 pp.
20. *Australian Public Affairs Information Service: Subject Index to Current Literature*. Canberra, 1945–.
21. Keesing, Felix M. *Social Anthropology in Polynesia: A Review of Research*. London: Oxford University Press, 1953. 126 pp.
22. Priestley, Sir Raymond. *Antarctic Research: A Review of British Scientific Achievement in Antarctica*. London: Butterworth, 1964. 360 pp.

Q.l.c

1. *Pacific Islands Yearbook and Who's Who*. Sydney: Pacific Publications, 1932–.
2. Serle, Percival. *Dictionary of Australian Biography*. 2 vols. Sydney: Angus & Robertson, 1949.
3. *Australian Dictionary of Biography*. Carleton: Melbourne University Press; Canberra: Australian National University Press, 1966–.
4. *Who's Who in Australia*. Melbourne: Colorgravure Publications, 1906–.
5. *Who's Who in New Zealand*. Wellington: A. H. & A. W. Reed, 1908–.

Q.l.d

1. *Modern Encyclopedia of Australia and New Zealand*. Sydney and Melbourne: Horwitz-Grahame, 1964. 1,199 pp.
2. *The Australian Encyclopedia*. Editor-in-chief, Alec H. Chisholm. 10 vols. 2d ed. Sydney and London: Angus & Robertson; East Lansing: Michigan State University Press, 1958.
3. Learmouth, Andrew T. A. *Encyclopedia of Australia*. London: Frederick Warne, 1968. 606 pp.
4. McLintock, Alexander H., ed. *An Encyclopedia of New Zealand*. 3 vols. Wellington: R. E. Owen, Government Printer, 1966.
5. *Oxford New Zealand Encyclopedia*. London: Oxford University Press, 1965. 376 pp.
6. *Encyclopedia of Papua and New Guinea*. 3 vols. Melbourne: Melbourne University Press; Port Moresby: University of Papua and New Guinea Press, 1972.
7. Massola, Aldo. *Aboriginal Place Names of Southeast Australia and Their Meanings*. Melbourne: Lansdowne Press, 1968. 62 pp.

Q.l.e

1. U.S. Office of the Chief of Naval Operations. *Handbook of the*

Trust Territories of the Pacific Islands. Washington: GPO, 1948. 311 pp.

2. Daniel, Hawthorne. *Islands of the Pacific.* New York: Putnam, 1943. 228 pp.

3. Coulter, John Wesley. *The Pacific Dependencies of the United States.* New York: Macmillan, 1957. 388 pp.

4. Kluge, P. F., and Boeberitz, Bob. *Micronesian Guide Book: Official Visitor's Guide Book to the Trust Territories of the Pacific Islands.* Guam: NPPBO, 1968. 49 pp.

5. Kane, Robert S. *South Pacific A to Z: Australia, New Zealand, the Tropic Isle of Fiji, New Caledonia, the Samoas, Tahiti, Tonga, and Hawaii.* Garden City, N.Y.: Doubleday, 1966. 320 pp.

6. Tudor, Judy. *Handbook of Fiji.* 3d ed. Sydney: Pacific Publications, 1968. 262 pp.

7. *Handbook of Papua and New Guinea.* 5th ed. Sydney: Pacific Publications, 1966.

8. Australia. Bureau of Census and Statistics. *Official Year Book of the Commonwealth of Australia.* Canberra: Government Printing Office, 1908–.

9. White, Osmar. *Guide to Australia.* Melbourne: Heinemann, 1968. 387 pp.

10. New Zealand. Department of Census and Statistics. *New Zealand Official Yearbook.* Wellington: Department of Census and Statistics, 1892–.

11. *Wise's New Zealand Guide.* 4th ed. Dunedin: Wise, 1969. 420 pp.

12. Hatherton, Trevor, ed. *Antarctica.* New York: Praeger, 1965. 511 pp.

13. Mieghem, Jacques van, ed. *Biogeography and Ecology in Antarctica.* Monographiae Biologicae, vol. 15. The Hague: W. Junk, 1965. 762 pp.

Q.1.f

1. *Polar Record.* Cambridge: Scott Polar Research Institute, 1931–.
2. *Antarctic Journal of the United States.* Washington: National Science Foundation, 1966–.
3. USSR. Arctic and Antarctic Scientific Research Institute. *Information Bulletins.* Issued by M. M. Somov and sponsored by the Geophysical and Polar Research Center, University of Wisconsin, 1964–.

Q.1.g

1. Australia. News and Information Bureau. *Australia in Facts and Figures.* Canberra, n.d.

Q.2.a

1. Taylor, Clyde R. H. *A Pacific Bibliography: Printed Matter Re-*

lating to the Native Peoples of Polynesia, Melanesia, and Micronesia. 2d ed. New York: Oxford University Press, 1965. 692 pp.

2. Cammack, Floyd M. *Pacific Island Bibliography.* Metuchen, N.J.: Scarecrow, 1962. 421 pp.

3. Vayda, Andrew P., ed. *People and Cultures of the Pacific: An Anthropological Reader.* New York: The American Museum of Natural History, 1968. 557 pp.

4. Greenway, John. *Bibliography of the Australian Aborigines and the Native Peoples of Torres Strait to 1959.* Sydney: Angus & Robertson, 1963. 420 pp.

5. Australian Institute of Aboriginal Studies. *Arnhem Land Peninsula Region (Including Bathurst and Melville Islands).* Compiled by Beryl F. Craig. Australian Aboriginal Studies, no. 8; Bibliographical Series, no. 1. Canberra: Australian Institute of Aboriginal Studies, 1966.

6. ————. *Cape York.* Compiled by Beryl F. Craig. Australian Aboriginal Studies, no. 9; Bibliographical Series, no. 2. Canberra: Australian Institute of Aboriginal Studies, 1967.

7. ————. *Kimberley Region: An Annotated Bibliography.* Compiled by Beryl F. Craig. Australian Aboriginal Studies no. 13, Bibliographical Series no. 3. Canberra: Australian Institute of Aboriginal Studies, 1968. 209 pp.

8. ————. *Central Australia and Western Desert Region: An Annotated Bibliography.* Compiled by Beryl F. Craig. Australian Aboriginal Studies, no. 31; Bibliographical Series, no. 5. Canberra: Australian Institute of Aboriginal Studies, 1969. 351 pp.

9. Australian National University. Department of Anthropology and Sociology. *Ethnographic Bibliography of New Guinea.* 3 vols. Canberra: Australian National University Press, 1968.

10. Kliencberger, H. L. *Bibliography of Oceanic Linguistics.* London Oriental Bibliographies, vol. 1. London: Oxford University Press, 1957. 143 pp.

11. Fraser, Douglas. *Bibliography of Torres Straits Art.* Primitive Art Bibliographies, no. 1. New York: The Library, Museum of Primitive Art, 1963. 6 pp.

12. Reed, Alexander Wycliffe, ed. *An Illustrated Encyclopedia of Aboriginal Life.* Sydney: A. H. & A. W. Reed, 1969. 175 pp.

13. McCulloch, Alan. *Encyclopedia of Australian Art.* London: Hutchinson, 1968. 668 pp.

Q.2.b

1. McArthur, Norma. *Island Populations of the Pacific.* Canberra: Australian National University Press, 1967; Honolulu: University of Hawaii Press, 1968. 381 pp.

2. Schmitt, Robert C. *Demographic Statistics of Hawaii, 1779–1965.* Honolulu: University of Hawaii Press, 1968. 271 pp.

Q.2.c

1. Palmer, George R. *A Guide to Australian Economic Statistics.* Melbourne: Macmillan, 1966. 324 pp.

2. Australia. Commonwealth Bureau of Census and Statistics. *Publications of the Commonwealth Bureau of Census and Statistics.* Canberra: Government Printing Office.
3. Finlayson, Jennifer. *Historical Statistics of Australia: A Select List of Official Sources.* Canberra: Department of Economic History, Research School of Social Sciences, Australian National University, 1970.

Q.2.e

1. *Historical Studies: Australia and New Zealand.* Melbourne: Melbourne University Press, 1940–.

Q.2.g

1. Whittington, Don. *Inside Canberra: A Guide to Australian Federal Politics.* Adelaide: Rigby, 1971. 296 pp.